THE MIND OF THE CRIMINAL

In American criminal law, if a defendant demonstrates that they lack certain psychological capabilities, they may be excused of blame and punishment for wrongdoing. However, criminal defense law often fails to consider the developmental science of individual differences in ability and functioning that may inform jurisprudential issues of rational capacity and criminal responsibility. This book discusses the excusing nature of a range of both traditional and nontraditional criminal law defenses and questions the structure of these defenses based on scientific findings from social and developmental psychology. This book explores how research on individual differences in the development of social perception, judgment, and decision making explains why some youths and adults develop psychological tendencies that favor criminal behavior, and considers how developmental science can guide the understanding of criminal excuses and affirmative defense law.

Reid Griffith Fontaine is assistant professor at the Florida State University College of Law. Professor Fontaine has published numerous peer-reviewed scholarly and scientific articles on the development of social-cognitive processing and antisocial conduct, which have appeared in many of the top behavioral science journals, including *Aggressive Behavior, Child Development, Development and Psychopathology, Developmental Psychology, Journal of Abnormal Psychology,* and *Journal of Abnormal Child Psychology.* His scholarly writings on intersections of developmental and social-cognitive psychology and public policy, jurisprudence, and law have been published in leading refereed interdisciplinary journals, such as *New Criminal Law Review*; the *International Journal of Law and Psychiatry*; and *Psychology, Public Policy, and Law.* In addition, two symposia on his scholarly writings on affirmative defense law have been published in the *University of Michigan Journal of Law Reform* and the *American Criminal Law Review.* Professor Fontaine received a Fulbright Senior Scholar award for the 2009–2010 academic year, which funded his visiting appointment at the University of Rome.

The Mind of the Criminal

THE ROLE OF DEVELOPMENTAL SOCIAL COGNITION IN CRIMINAL DEFENSE LAW

REID GRIFFITH FONTAINE
Florida State University
College of Law

To my friends, Heather & Alan,
with respect & affection.
My best always,
Reid

CAMBRIDGE
UNIVERSITY PRESS

CAMBRIDGE UNIVERSITY PRESS
Cambridge, New York, Melbourne, Madrid, Cape Town,
Singapore, São Paulo, Delhi, Mexico City

Cambridge University Press
32 Avenue of the Americas, New York, NY 10013-2473, USA

www.cambridge.org
Information on this title: www.cambridge.org/9780521513760

First published 2012

Printed in the United States of America

A catalog record for this publication is available from the British Library.

Library of Congress Cataloging in Publication data
Fontaine, Reid Griffith, 1971–
The mind of the criminal : the role of developmental social cognition in criminal defense law / Reid Griffith Fontaine.
p. cm.
Includes index.
ISBN 978-0-521-51376-0 (hardback)
1. Defense (Criminal procedure) – United States. 2. Insanity (Law) – United States. 3. Criminal psychology – United States. I. Title.
KF9242.F64 2012
345.73′05044–dc23 2011041597

ISBN 978-0-521-51376-0 Hardback

For my grandmother, Memé, who, through her unwavering wisdom, love, and dedication to her family, has brought immeasurable richness to our lives – my own, as a result, has been transformed in ways in which words could do little justice.

Contents

Preface

The influence of empirical science data on Anglo-American lawmaking and judicial decision making has grown considerably during the last fifty years.[1] Increasingly, scholars and legal professionals have emphasized the importance of the social and behavioral sciences in policy and lawmaking, as well as how criminal jurisprudence and law may be informed by scientific psychology.[2] Although relatively underappreciated, recent scholarship has pointed to the potential value in the drawing from social-cognitive psychology (i.e., the science of how social factors influence human information processing, and how, in turn, cognitive processing mediates relations between environmental factors and human interpersonal behavior), particularly when studied from a developmental perspective, to answer critical empirical questions that are central to criminal jurisprudence and law.[3]

1 Harold I. Schwartz & Robert Boland, *Using Science to Influence the Supreme Court on the Right to Refuse Treatment: Amicus Curiae Briefs in* Washington v. Harper, 23 BULL. AM. ACAD. PSYCHIATRY & L. 135 (1995); see Mark A. Small, *Advancing Psychological Jurisprudence*, 11 BEHAV. SCI. & L. 3 (1993).

2 Reid G. Fontaine, *Disentangling the Psychology and Law of Instrumental and Reactive Subtypes of Aggression*, 13 PSYCHOL. PUB. POL'Y & L. 143 (2007) [hereinafter Fontaine, *Disentangling*]; Reid G. Fontaine, *Social Information Processing, Subtypes of Violence, and a Progressive Construction of Culpability and Punishment in Juvenile Justice*, 31 INT'L J.L. & PSYCHIATRY 136 (2008) [hereinafter Fontaine, *Social Information*]; Robert F. Schopp & Marc W. Patry, *The Guilty Mind and Criminal Sentencing: Integrating Legal and Empirical Inquiry as Illustrated by Capital Sentencing*, 21 BEHAV. SCI. & L. 631 (2003); Small, *supra* note 1, at 3; Laurence Steinberg & Elizabeth Cauffman, *Maturity of Judgment in Adolescence: Psychosocial Factors in Adolescent Decision Making*, 20 LAW & HUM. BEHAV. 249 (1996); Laurence Steinberg & Elizabeth S. Scott, *Less Guilty by Reason of Adolescence: Developmental Immaturity, Diminished Responsibility, and the Juvenile Death Penalty*, 58 AM. PSYCHOLOGIST 1009 (2003).

3 *See, e.g.*, Fontaine, *Disentangling*, *supra* note 2; Fontaine, *Social Information*, *supra* note 2; Reid G. Fontaine, *The Wrongfulness of Wrongly Interpreting Wrongfulness: Provocation, Interpretational Bias, and Heat of Passion Homicide*, 12 NEW CRIM. L. REV. 69 (2009);

The utility of social-cognitive developmental research (or, simply, developmental social cognition) in criminal jurisprudence and law does not lie in providing answers to questions of morality. For instance, science cannot answer the question of whether it is morally right or wrong to strike someone who has provoked you. However, science may generate important data that apply to empirical issues that are typically considered when the moral nature of an act, series of acts, or actor is judged. For example, science may be used to assess issues of perception and interpretation,[4] judgment and decision making,[5] emotional and psychophysiological arousal,[6] rational capacity,[7] intentionality and willfulness,[8] instrumentality versus reactivity,[9] motives and goals,[10] and self-control.[11] These forms of functioning may bear considerable relevance for

Richard L. Wiener, Barbara A. Watts, & Dennis P. Stolle, *Psychological Jurisprudence and the Information Processing Paradigm*, 11 BEHAV. SCI. & L. 79 (1993).

4 *E.g.*, Kenneth A. Dodge, Joseph M. Price, Jo-Anne Bachoroski, & Joseph P. Newman, *Hostile Attributional Biases in Severely Aggressive Adolescents*, 99 J. ABNORMAL PSYCHOL. 385 (1990); Jennifer E. Vitale, Joseph P. Newman, Ralph C. Serin, & Daniel M. Bolt, *Hostile Attributions in Incarcerated Adult Male Offenders: An Exploration of Diverse Pathways*, 31 AGGRESSIVE BEHAV. 99 (2005).

5 *E.g.*, Kenneth A. Dodge & Joseph P. Newman, *Biased Decision-Making Processes in Aggressive Boys*, 90 J. ABNORMAL PSYCHOL. 375 (1981); Reid G. Fontaine, Virginia S. Burks, & Kenneth A. Dodge, *Response Decision Processes and Externalizing Behavior Problems in Adolescents*, 14 DEV. & PSYCHOPATHOLOGY 107 (2002); Reid G. Fontaine, Chongming Yang, Kenneth A. Dodge, John E. Bates, & Gregory S. Pettit, *Testing an Individual Systems Model of Response Evaluation and Decision (RED) and Antisocial Behavior Across Adolescence*, 79 CHILD DEV. 462, 462–63 (2008).

6 Craig R. Colder & Eric Stice, *Longitudinal Study of the Interactive Effects of Impulsivity and Anger on Adolescent Problem Behavior*, 27 J. YOUTH & ADOLESCENCE 255 (1998) (examining the effect of impulsivity on the relation between anger and problem behavior); Craig A. Smith & Richard S. Lazarus, *Appraisal Components, Core Relational Themes, and the Emotions*, 7 COGNITION & EMOTION 233 (1993); Jack V. Honk, Adriaan Tuiten, Edward D. Haan, Marcel V. Hout, & Henderickus Stam, *Attentional Biases for Angry Faces: Relationships to Trait Anger and Anxiety*, 15 COGNITION & EMOTION 279 (2001).

7 Stephen J. Morse, *Diminished Rationality, Diminished Responsibility*, 1 OHIO ST. J. CRIM. LAW 289 (2003); *see also* Valerie F. Reyna & Susan E. Rivers, *Current Theories of Risk and Rational Decision Making*, 28 DEVELOPMENTAL REV. 1 (2008).

8 *E.g.*, RATIONAL CHOICE AND CRIMINAL BEHAVIOR: RECENT RESEARCH AND FUTURE CHALLENGES (Alex R. Piquero & Stephen G. Tibbetts eds., 2002).

9 *E.g.*, Nicki R. Crick & Kenneth A. Dodge, *A Review and Reformulation of Social Information-Processing Mechanisms in Children's Social Adjustment*, 115 PSYCHOL. BULL. 74, 84, 92 (1994); Fontaine, *Disentangling*, *supra* note 2.

10 *E.g.*, Annemaree Carroll, Stephen Houghton, John Hattie, & Kevin Durkin, *Reputation Enhancing Goals: Integrating Reputation Enhancement and Goal Setting Theory as an Explanation of Delinquent Involvement*, *in* 4 ADVANCES IN PSYCHOLOGY RESEARCH 101 (Frank Columbus ed., 2001); Ulrich Orth, Leo Montada & Andreas Maercker, *Feelings of Revenge, Retaliation Motive, and Posttraumatic Stress Reactions in Crime Victims*, 21 J. INTERPERSONAL VIOLENCE 229 (2006).

11 *E.g.*, Charles R. Tittle, David A. Ward, & Harold G. Grasmick, *Self-Control and Crime/Deviance: Cognitive vs. Behavioral Measures*, 19 J. QUANTITATIVE CRIMINOLOGY 333 (2003).

the case of assessing the morality – or, in legal terms, criminal culpability – of an alleged act.

Consider the killer who has been accused of first-degree murder. Did she kill her victim for personal gain or because she believed she had been significantly provoked? If she believed she was provoked, was her assessment of the nature and severity of the situation valid? Did she become so emotionally aroused that she was not fully rational when she committed the killing? Was she in control of her actions? Answers to these questions may be needed before a determination of the degree of criminal culpability can be realized. Developmental and social-cognitive research may be used to inform these and numerous related issues and, in this way, challenge and potentially reform theory and practice in criminal law.

Some of these issues of mental capacity and functioning have been examined in research programs in developmental social cognition (e.g., is reactive violence associated with a tendency to interpret certain types of social stimuli as hostile and intentionally harmful?). Others, although equally empirical by their nature, have either not yet been scientifically examined or require far more scientific substantiation before sound recommendations can be made (e.g., to what degree does moral disengagement follow a predatory versus reactive developmental path?). As such, scientific data may be used to guide certain scholarly discussions whereas hypotheses must be drawn to ignite the necessary science to guide others.

Historically, questions of empirical science such as these and numerous others, although of direct relevance to legal decision making and, more specifically, determinations of criminal culpability, have been addressed by philosophy. There is a plethora of questions that are, by their nature, philosophical and, as such, should be handled by moral and legal philosophers. However, questions that are naturally empirical should be examined and answered by empirical science. Although this may sound obvious, the practice of informing empirical questions of self-control, affect, rationality, and like topics central to criminal law doctrine with actual empirical science is only relatively recent. Increasingly, research on social-cognitive development has much to say about issues and debates in criminal law and may be used so that empirical matters of criminal capacity and functioning correctly rely more on the empirical science of developmental psychology.

This volume recognizes developmental social cognition and criminal law as an emerging interdisciplinary area of study that combines empirical psychological science with criminal law theory (and criminal justice policy) and explores the intersection of these historically separate scholarly traditions in a way that reveals some noteworthy implications for criminal jurisprudence and law. In its treatment of different ways in which social-cognitive research may have implications for criminal excuses in criminal law theory, this volume identifies and distinguishes between empirical possibility and substantiation. In this volume, not only is the state of social-cognitive inquiry clarified with respect to different issues, but guidelines for future research are introduced and examined.

The first two chapters of this volume present the principles and structural bases of criminal law and developmental psychology, respectively, on which subsequent chapters rest. Chapter 1 clarifies the jurisprudential foundations of American criminal law and emphasizes the goal of retribution to its function. Chapter 2 reviews several major research programs in developmental and social psychology and highlights several of their key contributions. These introductory chapters are referred to repeatedly throughout the volume as necessary, in reference to specific intersections between developmental social cognition and affirmative defense law.

In Chapter 3, I provide a discussion of the justification/excuse distinction in affirmative defense law. Whereas an objectively criminal act may be deemed *justified* when it is committed under conditions that provide the actor the right to perform it (such as in the case of one who defends herself with violence against a threatening attacker), it may, at best, only be *excused* when it is wrongful (i.e., not within one's rights to perform) and causes social harm. In such cases, the defendant may be excused of blame and punishment for her wrongful, harmful act if her capacity to act otherwise was compromised through no doing or allowance of her own (such as in the case of psychological dysfunction), or there is a basis on which to understand why she acted as she did (such as in the case of a reasonable mistake). In this chapter, rationality is identified as the key capacity on which social agents' personal responsibility and culpability for wrongdoing rest. I present the argument that criminal misconduct that results from nonculpable cognitive dysfunction may not serve as justification for blaming or punishing the defendant. Rather, a defendant should be excused of said (admittedly wrongful and harmful) conduct on this ground. Although there are legal conditions by which some criminal excuses function (e.g., insanity), I argue that affirmative defense law would be more consistently framed if it were to draw from scientific research in developmental social cognition.

Chapters 4 and 5 speak specifically to developmental conditions. In Chapter 4, the "developmental immaturity argument" is reviewed, by which it is asserted that, because juveniles have not developed psychologically and socially to the extent that adults have, they should not be held responsible to the same degree; as such, they should receive less severe punishments than adults who commit the same or like crimes. Maturity arguments on behalf of juvenile offenders (including those tried as adults) have drawn heavily from developmental science, although Chapter 4 points to areas of research in developmental social cognition, specifically, that have been neglected, and how more focused attention to this science may inform the moral debate about youth responsibility and juvenile justice policy.

Chapter 5 builds on this discussion of developmental immaturity and focuses on developmental *moral* cognition in the context of assigning blame and punishment to adult offenders who, for a variety of reasons, may not have developed the same capacities for moral understanding, reasoning, judgment, and decision making that other adults have. It is stressed that alternative developmental trajectories of moral cognitive deficits should be considered in legal determinations of wrongdoing. This perspective is considered in light of current debate about the role of psychopathy in determinations of criminal culpability, and is distinguished from, and places in question, the widely recognized defense of insanity.

Chapters 6 through 8 analyze defenses to reactive crime, with a focus on reactive homicide scenarios. In the behavioral sciences and, less formally, in the criminal law, recognition is given to a dichotomy of subtypes of violence and antisocial behavior. Whereas *instrumental* violence is carried out with a cool head for the purpose of personal gain (e.g., acquisition of money or power), *reactive* violence is enacted in response to an aversive stimulus, such as a provocation or a threat. Reactive violence (and crime) is typically more impulsive and emotional and is guided by one's interests of harming a provocateur or defending oneself or others against a threat.

Some scholars have drawn a parallel of the instrumental and reactive violence dichotomy in psychology and the murder-manslaughter distinction in criminal law. In fact, developmental social cognition has proven useful to understanding this area of homicide law and has received notable attention as of late.[12] Chapter 6 explores the defense of provocation/heat of passion, which functions to mitigate murder to manslaughter in the case of a defendant who is provoked and reacts by killing the provocateur in an emotionally disturbed and compromising state. This chapter pushes the debate to question how the defense may be reframed based on the considerable scientific evidence that reactive aggressive individuals typically have perceptual and judgment biases that hinder them from properly assessing social stimuli that are open or ambiguous as to their provocative content.

Chapter 7 builds from this discussion and considers the question: If research on judgment biases is relevant to possible law reform of the provocation/

[12] *See, e.g.*, Fontaine, *Disentangling, supra* note 2.

heat-of-passion defense, does it also have something important to say about other defenses of reactive crime? In particular, this chapter addresses how research on developmental social cognition may inform (1) cases of self-defense and defense of others that are based on mistaken threats and (2) the defense of duress. Traditionally, reactive killings in self-defense and defense of others have been treated as cases of *justifiable* homicide, even when the defendant was *reasonably* mistaken about the threat at hand. In this chapter, I discuss the value of developmental social cognition – in particular, the well-established finding that certain developmental conditions promote interpretational biases and deficits in some individuals – in considering cases of nonreasonable mistakes about threatening stimuli that result from nonculpable cognitive dysfunction.

In addition, Chapter 7 addresses a number of decision-making problems that may contribute to one's behavioral decisions and enactments in coercive or duress-promoting scenarios. Does research on developmental social cognition tell us something important about how meaningful the "reasonable firmness" requirement of the duress defense is to overwhelmingly threatening, coercive conditions? I explore this question, pointing to the critical role played by anxiety in such situations, and how social-cognitive mechanisms of anxiety may help scholars understand why some individuals are more likely to submit to a coercer's demands than are others.

In Chapter 8, I address perhaps the trickiest, most convoluted, and most controversial affirmative defense to "reactive" homicide – *battered-woman defense* (or, perhaps more appropriately, battered-*person* defense) – which, despite it having gained some acceptance in recent years, remains unrecognized in most jurisdictions. Here, I have "reactive" in quotes because some killings by chronically abused individuals are planned and committed in between battering incidents. In this chapter, I distinguish between killings by battered persons that should be deemed justifiable (such as in the case where there exists a constant "state of imminence") and those that may only be excusable, at least in part because of the pervasive impairing psychological effects that often result from being repeatedly victimized in an escalating pattern of physical and emotional abuse. It is argued that an excuse-based defense to this latter category of killings by battered persons may be better understood in light of substantial developmental research on the processing effects of recurrent abuse and trauma. While historically proponents of battered-woman defense have discussed research on posttraumatic stress disorder, research on the development of abuse and social cognition has far more to offer.

Finally, some concluding thoughts are offered in Chapter 9. The importance of examining structural, functional, and phenomenological differences in instrumental and reactive violence subtypes in contexts that are specifically applicable to ongoing inquiry and debate in criminal law and jurisprudence is emphasized. Future directions for research are offered with an eye toward further intersection of social-cognitive research and criminal law and criminal justice policy.

I am grateful to numerous friends and colleagues who helped make this volume possible via their challenging discourse and critical commentary, as well as general support. Although not an exhaustive list by any means, I thank Professors Steve Asher, Marcia Baron, Vera Bergelson, Gian Vittorio Caprara, Dante Cicchetti, Michael Corrado, Phil Costanzo, Joe Hoffman, Kyron Huigens, Heidi Hurd, Len Kaplan, Leo Katz, John Lochman, Dan Markel, Michael Moore, Ron Roesch, Bruce Sales, Jim Sherman, Manuel Utset, and Bruce Winick. I am further grateful to Dean Don Weidner and the entire faculty at the Florida State University College of Law for their continued support of this project. Special thanks are in order for the following scholars who offered detailed commentary on sections and/or complete drafts of this manuscript as the project developed: Professors Gabriel "Jack" Chin, Ken Dodge, Joshua Dressler, Mark Fondacaro, Wayne Logan, Marc Miller, Stephen Morse, Chris Slobogin, Neil Vidmar, Bob Weisberg, and David Wexler. Also quite deserving of recognition are my three Florida State Law research assistants: Patrick Flemming – who took on a highly valued leadership role – Dominique Elden, and Michael Titus. Furthermore, I extend my sincere appreciation to my esteemed editor at Cambridge University Press, John Berger, who was nothing but patient and supportive from beginning to end. Finally, I am endlessly grateful to my family for their tremendous love and support. In particular, my wife, Andrea Julian Fontaine, a brilliant lawyer in her own right, quite selflessly edited significant portions of this volume, all while juggling her own work, creative projects, and, last but so very far from least, our newborn baby girl, Avery.

1

A Meeting of Developmental Social Cognition and Criminal Jurisprudence and Law

Actual and potential intersections of psychology and criminal law exist at many levels and, within a particular level, may take different forms. For example, lessons from psychological science may be used to inform legal judgment and decision making; alternatively, legal judgment and decision making may serve to guide empirical research in psychology. Furthermore, within either of these broad levels, the principal psycholegal issue may vary according to substantive topic (e.g., how emotion is conceptualized or what, if any, effect race has on behavioral judgment) or analytic perspective (e.g., how and to what degree empirical science should affect legal processes). As such, any discussion at the interface of psychology and law has the inherent potential of quickly becoming quite complicated.

The degree of complication may be managed by clarifying the respective goals of psychology and law, identifying the preferred analytic approach toward understanding how these fields may interrelate, and clearly stating the specific substantive intersection of interest. First, although the respective goals of psychology and law are distinct, it should be understood that they are not entirely unrelated; in some important ways, they are, or at least have the potential to be, mutually complementary. In psychology, the goal is to discern, understand, predict, and explain individual differences in behavior and related forms of functioning (e.g., attention, perception, cognition, and emotion). Although psychologists utilize various tools and employ alternative methodologies in the systematic investigation of hypotheses or empirical questions of interest, psychological studies, whether of a correlational or experimental/causal nature, typically examine mean differences between alternative groups of participants or subjects. For example, a study designed to examine differences in reactivity between aggressive and nonaggressive individuals may explore whether there is a statistically significant (and meaningful) difference between the two groups' average heart rates when exposed to a mild provocation. In contrast, the goal of the criminal law is to negatively prescribe behavior, judge the wrongfulness and harmfulness of specified forms of conduct, and determine what, if anything, should be the response on the part of the government when it has been determined that criminal wrongdoing has occurred. Whereas psychology is interested in empirical issues (e.g., does *x* cause *y*?), the criminal law is primarily concerned with normative ones (e.g., is *x* wrong and, if so, what needs to happen to eliminate the moral imbalance caused by *x*?).

This is not to say, however, that the law is unconcerned with empirical matters, as much as it is to observe that such matters are often subsidiary. The law has a responsibility to concern itself with empirical matters when determinations of such matters are necessary to make proper judgments about core normative legal issues. For example, in the case of the crime of passion, the law may consider how wrongful the act is compared to the commission of the same act in cold blood with premeditation. However, the question of what effects high arousal and strong emotion have on individual mental functioning (e.g., control and rationality) is, by its nature, an empirical one. Therefore, the law has a responsibility to draw from scientific research that examines this cause (emotional arousal) and effect (undermined functioning) relation so that it may more properly assess the moral issue of how wrongful the act in question is, as well as the normative question as to what the response on the part of the justice system should be.

The idea that the law should draw from psychological science where and when it is faced with an empirical question of a psychological nature reflects a preferable analytic approach in psychology and law and the analytic approach that guides lessons and discussions that we are herewith concerned. Just as it is unwise to attempt to answer questions of morality with science, it is equally wrongheaded to attend to empirical questions with nonscientific methodologies that are traditional to philosophy and the humanities. Rather, a combination of methodologies is required in the case of the normative issue of morality to which empirical matters are of clear relevance. Such cases are not at all uncommon, and the law has, in recent years, become increasingly aware of and attentive to this reality. Questions that are, by their nature, empirical can only be answered via empirical investigation. It is just this simple. As such, when moral questions (e.g., how culpable is *x* actor for the commission of *y* act?) are directly related to empirical ones (e.g., to what degree are actors in *x*'s condition capable of controlling their behavior?), drawing from relevant findings in psychology becomes an absolutely critical step in the legal process.

I am reminded of the words of political scientist and Professor James Q. Wilson: "Social science seeks to explain behavior, criminal law to judge it."[1] Surely, the distinction Wilson clarifies is correct. Nevertheless, it should be asked how the criminal law may properly judge behavior unless it has been explained. That is, the criminal law has a responsibility to understand that which it is designed to judge. Without recognizing and being informed by the developmental science of antisocial conduct, I must insist that such a responsibility cannot be fulfilled.

Having discerned the respective goals of psychology and law and identified the preferred analytic approach, we turn to the specific substantive focus with which this volume is concerned. In doing so, the focus and reach of this volume should be clarified according to topics and issues that, although they could be misunderstood to be central to present interests, are purposefully excluded. This is not to disparage other schools of thought or the foci of other scholars or scientific programs of research, but rather to make clear at the outset what is, as well as what is not, the contribution of the present work.

Any introduction to the field of psychology and law (or psycholegal studies) may immediately give rise to certain well-established and important areas of scholarly research. Some of the more popular or commonly studied areas in psychology and law are these: eyewitness testimony,[2] expert witness testimony[3] and reliability,[4] jury selection,[5] jury decision making,[6] eyewitness line-ups,[7] and psychopathy.[8] Undoubtedly, contributions of enormous import from each of these areas have been made to the advancement of psychology and law as a

[1] James Q. Wilson, *Moral Judgment: Does the Abuse Excuse Threaten Our Legal System?* 7 (1997).

[2] *E.g.*, Elizabeth F. Loftus, *Eyewitness Testimony* (1979).

[3] *E.g.*, Blake M. McKimmie, Cameron J. Newton, Deborah J. Terry & Regina A. Schuller, *Jurors' Responses to Expert Witness Testimony: The Effects of Gender Stereotypes*, 7 Group Processes & Intergroup Rel. 131 (2004).

[4] *E.g.*, Steven Penrod & Brian H. Bornstein, *Generalizing Eyewitness Reliability Research, in* 2 Handbook of Eyewitness Psychology: Memory for People 529 (Rod C. L. Lindsay, David F. Ross, J. Don Read & Michael P. Toglia eds., 2007).

[5] *E.g.*, Joel D. Lieberman & Bruce D. Sales, *Scientific Jury Selection* (2007).

[6] *E.g.*, Christina A. Studebaker & Steven D. Penrod, *Pretrial Publicity and Its Influence on Juror Decision Making, in* Psychology and Law: An Empirical Perspective 254 (Neil Brewer & Kipling D. Williams eds., 2005).

[7] *E.g.*, Gary L. Wells, *Police Lineups: Data, Theory, and Policy*, 7 Psychol. Pub. Pol'y & L. 791, 791 (2001).

[8] *E.g.*, Jennifer Skeem, Peter Johansson, Henrik Andershed, Margaret Kerr & Jennifer E. Louden, *Two Subtypes of Psychopathic Violent Offenders That Parallel Primary and Secondary Variants*, 116 J. Abnormal Psychol. 395, 395 (2007).

scholarly field of study. However, these are not topics with which this volume is substantially concerned.[9]

The contents of this volume may suggest that a new subfield of interdisciplinary jurisprudence be recognized, one that is perhaps aptly named *social-cognitive jurisprudence*. Social-cognitive jurisprudence may be broadly defined as "the application of social cognitive psychology to issues that are, by their nature, empirical and germane to legal philosophy and doctrinal law."[10] Through a criminal-jurisprudence lens, social-cognitive psychology may be viewed as a vehicle by which empirical matters related to core moral philosophical issues (e.g., questions of functional capacity that are inherent to a retributive theory of criminal responsibility) may be addressed. Although this volume focuses on the intersection of developmental social cognition and criminal law, there is no reason, of course, to exclusively bridge developmental social-cognitive research with jurisprudential and legal issues located in this corner of the law.[11] That is, although the definition of social-cognitive jurisprudence that is here introduced accurately reflects the intersection that is focal throughout this volume, social-cognitive jurisprudence is no less applicable to other intersections between this area of scientific psychology and jurisprudence as an intellectual or scholarly pursuit and legal domain.

This term is introduced more out of an interest in exactness than for the purpose of terming a new subfield of study. As such, social-cognitive jurisprudence should be distinguished from other subfields of study that may otherwise be confused to share significant overlap. Perhaps the most popular and well-known of these has become "[t]herapeutic jurisprudence,"[12] which focuses on ways in which substantive law, legal procedures, and legal actors (e.g., judges and lawyers) may have a therapeutic (or healing, as opposed to antitherapeutic or harming) impact on individuals who have entered and are subject to the legal system. Unlike therapeutic jurisprudence, which is focused on mechanisms of therapeutic effect, social-cognitive jurisprudence is concerned with conducting and drawing from empirical research in order to illuminate jurisprudence, legal theory, and legal doctrine.

9 Some of these areas of study will be addressed, however secondarily, in the context of larger discussions throughout this volume. For example, psychopathy is discussed in the context of moral development, biases, and deficits. *See infra* Chapter 5.

10 Reid G. Fontaine, *On Passion's Potential to Undermine Rationality: A Reply*, 43 U. Mich. J.L. Reform 207, 242 n.159 (2009).

11 One can easily imagine applications to areas in civil law such as torts (e.g., intentional torts and negligence), property (e.g., property disputes), and contracts (e.g., issues of misrepresentation versus mistake), as well as numerous others.

12 *E.g.*, David B. Wexler, *Therapeutic Jurisprudence: An Overview*, 17 T. M. Cooley L. Rev. 125 (2000).

Second is *psychological jurisprudence*, which focuses on how the law is perceived by citizens and how it impacts their lives on a day-to-day basis within the society it governs. Although multiple versions of, or perspectives on, psychological jurisprudence have been offered,[13] none reflect the science-to-law (and back again[14]) intersection intended by social-cognitive jurisprudence. A special note should be made to clarify that the information-processing perspective on psychological jurisprudence that has been offered in previous scholarship[15] is largely unrelated to how a paradigm of social-information processing – an inherently developmental model of social-cognitive functioning – is utilized in social-cognitive jurisprudence. Whereas the former is concerned with how the law may be designed and reframed so that it minimizes shortcomings in naturally problematic human processing of social information (i.e., how citizens understand the laws by which they are governed), the latter has to do with how the systematic study of how individual social-information processing in humans may inform our understanding of human functioning and capacities within contexts that have legal implications (e.g., how the science of cognitive capacity and dysfunction may inform a theory of excuses in criminal law). In these ways, the former reflects an interest in the path from law to psychology and the latter, at least with respect to the primary purposes underlying this current volume, is more focused on how psychological science may influence jurisprudential issues in legal doctrine.[16]

Social-cognitive jurisprudence, as it is here conceptualized, may be better said to have been derived, at least to some meaningful degree, from "social analytic jurisprudence," a perspective that is typically credited to Professor Richard Wiener.[17] However, social-cognitive jurisprudence is more sibling (or perhaps cousin) than offspring in some ways. Wiener differentiated social-analytic jurisprudence from therapeutic jurisprudence and psychological jurisprudence on epistemological grounds. Wiener stressed that the study of law and psychology is an empirical science and, as such, social-analytic jurisprudence is unique in that it dictates that legal issues be analyzed from a

[13] *See* Mark A. Small, *Advancing Psychological Jurisprudence*, 11 BEHAV. SCI. & L. 3, 3–4 (1993).

[14] A broader explanation of social-cognitive jurisprudence articulates not only the need for psychological science to inform empirical issues in law, but the need for empirical issues that are posed by the law to guide scientific inquiry in social-cognitive psychology.

[15] *See* Richard L. Wiener, Barbara A. Watts & Dennis P. Stolle, *Psychological Jurisprudence and the Information Processing Paradigm*, 11 BEHAV. SCI. & L. 79, 80 (1993).

[16] Of course, social-cognitive jurisprudence is far from unilateral. Naturally, in reciprocal turn, legal doctrine should play a strong role in shaping theoretical and empirical inquiry in psychology.

[17] *See* Richard L. Wiener, *Social Analytic Jurisprudence and Tort Law: Social Cognition Goes to Court*, 37 ST. LOUIS U. L.J. 503, 505 (1993).

"disconfirming epistemology."[18] Social-cognitive jurisprudence should be distinguished from social-analytic jurisprudence, however, with respect to some critical points of interest. Social-analytic jurisprudence was advanced more with civil law than criminal law in mind.[19] This is not to say that its principles cannot be applied to empirical matters in criminal law, but that the perspective was developed outside of a general theory of punishment (as punishment largely pertains to criminal matters). In his 1993 foundational article, Wiener advanced his social-analytic jurisprudence in the context of negligent torts. Wiener specified that "[t]ort laws are not operational definitions of wrongdoings. They usually do not articulate, in concrete terms, specific actions or behaviors that are prohibited by law."[20] This, of course, is quite different than in criminal law, where specific acts of wrongdoing are formally stated as legal prohibitions.

Social-cognitive jurisprudence considers the study of psychology and criminal law within a larger theory of wrongdoing and, as such, articulates that this area of inquiry is broader than empirical science allows. It is recognized that, although empirical matters may only be resolved via empirical science, criminal law reflects judgments about morality that cannot be addressed through scientific inquiry. Empirical science becomes relevant in criminal law only when and where answers to empirical questions are needed to better achieve, or at least approach, resolution to the larger moral issues in which criminal law is squarely grounded.

There are a number of reasons why the importance of social cognition, as an area of scientific study, needs to be recognized and rigorously explored in the advancement of interdisciplinary psychology and criminal law. Social cognition may be defined as the science of how social variables affect an individual's mental functioning, and how cognitive processing mediates relations between environmental factors and human social behavior. Crime is, by its nature, a social condition. A crime does not need to be committed directly

[18] *Id.* at 511.

[19] In Wiener's seminal article on social analytic jurisprudence, he articulated his perspective in the context of tort law. *See id.* at 515. For an application of social-analytic jurisprudence to other areas of civil law such as bankruptcy law, see Richard L. Wiener, Susan Block-Lieb, Karen Gross & Corinne Baron-Donovan, *Unwrapping Assumptions: Applying Social Analytic Jurisprudence to Consumer Bankruptcy Education Requirements and Policy*, 79 AM. BANKR. L.J. 453, 454 (2005). For an excepted case in which social-analytic jurisprudence is identified as the guiding perspective in criminal law analysis, see Steven J. Sherman & Joseph L. Hoffman, *The Psychology and Law of Voluntary Manslaughter: What Can Psychology Research Teach Us About the "Heat of Passion" Defense?*, 20 J. BEHAV. DECISION MAKING 499, 500 (2007).

[20] Weiner, *supra* note 17, at 515.

against another individual for it to be social because any crime is a violation of the law that governs the society in which it is recognized, and in this way, any crime is naturally an antisocial act (or an act against society). Like all behavior from a psychological or cognitive-science perspective,[21] crime is viewed to be social-cognitively mediated – that is, antisocial behavior is the product of how one has processed (either consciously or nonconsciously) internal (individual) and external (environmental) information as it becomes available, or made meaning of various cues as they are presented within one's perceptual sphere.[22] As such, it is not surprising that independent research programs that assess social-cognitive functioning have shared notable success in accounting for individual differences in antisocial behavior across developmental periods and qualitatively distinct populations.[23]

Social cognition, as a psychological realm of functioning, broadly represents all mental processes that are either directly interpersonal (i.e., mechanisms underlying behavior at the level of personal exchange, such as conversation or fighting) or otherwise socially implicative (i.e., mechanisms underlying behavior at the level of society, such as voting or destruction of public property) by nature. Embodied within this volume is a statement of various mental capacities to which individual responsibility may be argued (and indeed has been argued!) [24] to be a correlative. These capacities include, but are far from limited to, social interpretation, controlled cognitive processing (or, more simply, psychological control), evaluative judgment, and rational decision making. Because the criminal's behavior is social-cognitively mediated, and because the criminal's underlying mental capabilities and state are central to determinations of personal responsibility and criminal culpability, social cognition may be identified as the nexus of psychological science and criminal law. As such, the term *social-cognitive jurisprudence* best reflects the utility of drawing

[21] The idea that only via cognition can environment be related to individual behavior is one that emerged in the 1950s and is the centerpiece of the cognitive revolution. Since this time, it has become a universally accepted perspective throughout the psychological and behavioral sciences. *See generally* George A. Miller, *The Cognitive Revolution: A Historical Perspective*, 7 TRENDS COGNITIVE SCI. 141 (2003) (outlining the evolution of cognitive science).

[22] *See* Emma J. Palmer, *Criminal Thinking*, *in* APPLYING PSYCHOLOGY TO CRIMINAL JUSTICE 147, 149, 151 (David Carson, Rebecca Milne, Francis Pakes, Karen Shalev & Andrea Shawyer eds., 2007); *see also infra* Chapter 2.

[23] *See* Kenneth A. Dodge, *Do Social Information-Processing Patterns Mediate Aggressive Behavior?*, *in* CAUSES OF CONDUCT DISORDER AND JUVENILE DELINQUENCY 254 (Benjamin B. Lahey, Terrie E. Moffitt & Avshalom Caspi eds., 2003); *see also infra* Chapter 2.

[24] *See, e.g.*, Stephen J. Morse, *Rationality and Responsibility*, 74 S. CAL. L. REV. 251, 253 (2000) [hereinafter Morse, *Rationality and Responsibility*]; Stephen J. Morse, *Diminished Rationality, Diminished Responsibility*, 1 OHIO ST. J. CRIM. LAW 289, 301–02 (2003) [hereinafter Morse, *Diminished Rationality*].

from psychology where determinations of empirical matters are needed to properly frame criminal-law doctrine so that it may systematically advance and apply a proper theory of wrongdoing and criminal justice.

Theories of criminal justice may be distinguished by their respective justifications of punishment. Numerous justifications of punishment have been advanced. Retributive justice dictates that punishment needs to be directly proportional to the degree of wrongdoing to which an identified harm was caused. Any causation of a social harm for which the actor is responsible should be punished in proportion not only to the degree of harm caused (e.g., nongrievous injury versus death), but also to the level of reprehensibility with which it was performed (e.g., unintentional versus purposeful). In retributive terms, the commission of a criminal act is defined in terms of conduct that unjustifiably causes a moral imbalance between the actor and society; as a result, the actor is punished in exact accordance (no less, no more) with the degrees of blameworthiness with which he acted and the amount of social harm that he caused. Retributive justice is concerned with the moral properties of the criminal action as well as the identifiable social harm that results.

Deterrence, or crime prevention, is often touted as a justification of punishment. Specific deterrence refers to the ability of a punishment to reduce the likelihood the individual who is the recipient of the punishment will reoffend. In contrast, general deterrence refers to the ability of a punishment to reduce the likelihood of similar offenses by citizens at large. Of course, whether any individual punishment specifically or generally deters crime is necessarily uncertain at the time that it is rendered. Sentences based on a deterrence justification are predictive statements about hypothesized causal relations between punishment and future outcomes. In this way, the deterrence argument is future-focused or forward-looking and, as such, based on notions that are, in any individual case, unknowable. The justification of punishment via deterrence in any individual case, then, is more a justification via hope or expectation of deterrence than via actual deterrence.

Rehabilitation is another justification of punishment that is commonly espoused. Rehabilitation of criminals may be defined as the process or set of processes by which offenders are restored or improved so that they may be more functionally capable and thus more able and inclined to lawfully act in their pursuit of desired outcomes. Rehabilitation, however, is a specific statement about how specific deterrence may be accomplished. That is, by rehabilitating offenders, it may be expected that the offenders in question will be less likely to reoffend. As in the case of deterrence, any rehabilitation rationale is forward-looking and equally uncertain in that it is unknown in any individual case as to whether an offender is even amenable to rehabilitation, never mind whether she will in fact be rehabilitated such that she will be less likely to reoffend.

Other justifications of punishment that have been advanced include incapacitation (or incarceration), education, and denunciation. Incapacitation prevents criminals from reoffending by removing them from society and restricting their freedom. The education rationale rests on the mechanism of learning either by the punished individual specifically or citizens at large generally, or both. There are two ideas here. First, individuals who learn and understand that specified acts are prohibited will be better able to avoid enacting them. Second, education leads to social advancement and provides more opportunities to succeed and reducing the perceived need to reoffend to realize one's goals. Both ideas point to the fact that education is really a component of rehabilitation. Denunciation has been offered as a justification of punishment as either a means to deter reoffending via official recognition of wrongdoing and correlative experiences of guilt and shame or a way to maintain a sense of social cohesion and understanding that the social contract by which citizens are bound is legitimate. With the exception of the latter of the two rationales underlying denunciation, all of these justifications of punishment are specific statements of deterrence in that they all derive from a general interest in crime prevention.

Many of these proposed justifications of punishment are empirical statements, of course, or, at least, presume answers to empirical questions. For instance, the statement that punishment is justified when it deters future crime is, in effect, a statement that punishment can have the effect of crime prevention. This is, by its nature, an empirical statement. Likewise, implicit in the statement that punishment is justified in that it serves the purpose of denunciation via experiences of guilt and/or shame on the part of its recipient is a presumption of an empirical issue: that punishment causes in its recipient the type of emotion that is so meaningful that it significantly reduces his likelihood of reoffending. Similarly, justifying punishment via rehabilitation and education begs numerous empirical questions: (1) What kinds of criminals are amenable to rehabilitation? (2) What psychological mechanisms need be targeted such that legitimate rehabilitation may be realized? (3) Does punishment actually educate individuals, whether the individuals of interest are criminals or the noncriminal public, about the boundaries of lawful conduct? (4) If punishment does serve to educate, what are the psychological mechanisms by which individuals learn from their own or others' punishment? These questions can only be answered by empirical science. This practice of translating ideological statements of what justifies punishment into empirical statements of cause and effect should immediately make evident the range and importance of drawing from developmental social cognition in forming a proper theory of criminal justice and punishment.

Before exploring specific intersections of developmental social cognition and criminal jurisprudence and law, however, it is critical that a proper taxonomy of purposes of punishment be explicated, even if only in summary form.[25] All of the justifications of punishment introduced earlier may be categorized into two pure theories of punishment. The first justification, retribution, stands alone as its own theory. Retributive theory states that punishment is justified when it is proportional to the wrongdoing committed, where wrongdoing functions as a multiplicative term of degree of social harm by reprehensibility or moral wrongfulness of the act, or failure to act where there was a duty, that caused said social harm. Retributive theory views punishment as the mechanism by which moral balance may be restored after a responsible wrongdoer has upset it. Retributive justice dictates that the person who deserves punishment needs to be punished. The intrinsic wrongfulness of the actor's conduct alone justifies his punishment. This, in short, articulates the retributive concept of *just deserts*.

The rest of the asserted justifications of punishment (deterrence, rehabilitation, incapacitation, education, and denunciation) are utilitarian. Utilitarian theory views punishment in and of itself as inherently wrong. As such, utilitarianism does not share the retributive notion that punishment serves to restore moral balance in response to one's wrongdoing, but rather that punishment augments moral imbalance. Instead, utilitarian theory is concerned with social net gain. As such, infliction of punishment is only justified from a utilitarian perspective in the case that the future good that it causes (or, in practicality, is hoped or expected to cause) outweighs the bad that it naturally produces. For example, although punishment in and of itself is viewed to be naturally wrong, it is justified from a utilitarian perspective where it deters (or is expected to deter) an amount of future crime that outweighs its inherent wrongfulness. Strict utilitarianism dictates that innocent individuals should be punished and guilty individuals should go unpunished when such an action (or nonaction) will produce a social net gain or, in other words, an improvement in societal welfare. Because these scenarios – punishing the innocent and nonpunishing the guilty – upset the sensibilities of some individuals who are otherwise inclined to adopt utilitarian theory, utilitarianism

[25] For a clear and accessible discussion of specific justifications of punishment, pure theories of punishment, and mixed theories of punishment, see Michael S. Moore, *A Taxonomy of Purposes of Punishment*, *in* FOUNDATIONS OF CRIMINAL LAW 60 (Leo Katz, Michael S. Moore & Stephen J. Morse eds., 1999).

in this pure sense does not carry any meaningful weight in Anglo-American criminal law.

From these two pure theories of punishment, two possible mixed theories may be derived. The first mixed theory proposes that punishment is justified in the case in which it is *both* deserved (meeting the retributive purpose of just deserts) *and* when it leads to a net social gain (meeting one or more utilitarian values, such as deterrence). This mixed theory dictates that in a case in which the wrongdoer deserves punishment but the punishment would not lead to some future social good, the wrongdoer goes unpunished. Alternatively, even in a case in which punishment of an individual would produce a considerable social gain (e.g., the individual is famous and therefore society would pay close attention to his punishment), he is not punished if he does not deserve to be. Via this mixed theory, utilitarian interests may be viewed as a limitation on retribution (i.e., those who deserve to be punished should be punished only if the punishment will produce some net social gain), or retributive desert may be viewed as a limitation on utilitarian theory (i.e., punishment should be inflicted when it leads to a social net gain, but only when the recipient deserves it). However, the former of these views is far more sensible as the question of whether to punish an individual does not arise unless there already exists the idea that she is indeed deserving of punishment. In contrast, a second mixed theory may be derived in which punishment is justified in the case that *either* the wrongdoer deserves it *or* the punishment would produce a significant social benefit. According to this second mixed theory, any one of the purposes of punishment discussed previously would be sufficient to justify punishment.

Of the four theories – two pure and two mixed – two dominate jurisprudential debate: retributivism and the first of the two mixed theories. Although the second of the two mixed theories is a logical possibility, it exists only as a logical possibility and absent of any support. Also, nowhere is strict utilitarianism reflected in Anglo-American criminal law, theory, or practice. That is, nowhere is it the case that the criminal law applies a standard by which an undeserving individual may be punished based solely on the expectation that the punishment will produce a social net gain. Rather, the criminal law is inclined to lean in the opposite direction in that an individual accused of a crime must be found guilty of the charge beyond a reasonable doubt for the conviction and punishment to be deemed justified. This high standard reflects the criminal law's insistence that an individual's guilt must be proven before he can be justly punished. This reflects the criminal law's unwavering dedication to the retributive principle of desert.

Note, then, that the retributive principle of just deserts is a necessary condition for both pure retributivism (sometimes called *deontological retributivism* to reflect the intrinsic good of punishing one who deserves to be punished), for which it is the sole requirement, and the first of the two mixed theories (sometimes called *consequential retributivism* to reflect the necessarily limiting condition of just deserts and net social gain that each poses for the other).[26] This points to the substantial agreement among criminal-law theorists, judges, legislators, and related authoritative entities that desert is essential.[27] However, the prominence of the retributive principle of just deserts in justice systems throughout Anglo-America is perhaps even more immediately evident from an examination of the basic structure of criminal laws themselves.

Anglo-American criminal law recognizes two basic elements of any crime:[28] *actus reus* (guilty act) and *mens rea* (guilty mind). In addition, the act and mental state typically need to co-occur; that is, the mental state needs to be concurrent with the prohibited act. The mens rea requirement is crucial in that the law's "evaluation of both the morality and prudence of conduct is based largely on the mental states that accompany the conduct."[29] Degrees

[26] The term *consequential retributivism*, rather than some alternative possible label such as *retributive utilitarianism*, is surely preferred to clarify that, according to this hybrid theory, it is the expectation of some social net gain that poses a limitation on desert, and not vice versa. As discussed earlier, the issue of desert (i.e., that the defendant may have engaged in wrongdoing) must necessarily exist before any discussion of punishing for the purpose of realizing a social net gain may be justifiably introduced. *See* Michael S. Moore, *The Argument for Retributivism, in* FOUNDATIONS OF CRIMINAL LAW 68, 68–69 (Leo Katz, Michael S. Moore & Stephen J. Morse eds., 1999); Michael S. Moore, *Justifying Retributivism*, 27 ISR. L. REV. 15, 16 (1993); David Dolinko, *Retributivism, Consequentialism, and the Intrinsic Goodness of Punishment*, 16 LAW & PHIL. 507, 508 (1997); MICHAEL MOORE, PLACING BLAME: A GENERAL THEORY OF THE CRIMINAL LAW 92–93 (1997); *cf.* Michael T. Cahill, *Retributive Justice in the Real World*, 85 WASH. U. L. REV. 815, 861–69 (2007).

[27] As an aside, I believe that there is a place for what I call *progressive retributivism*, by which I mean very simply that where utilitarian values such as deterrence, rehabilitation, and public safety can be achieved without interfering with the *necessary and sufficient* condition of desert, they should be pursued. For example, if there is a feasible (i.e., not financially prohibitive) carceral option for the perpetrator of a sexual offense, which is equipped with rehabilitative mechanisms designed to attend to his specific psychopathological profile, then it would make good sense for him to be punished in this venue. This topic requires a separate, lengthy discussion, of course. Progressive retributivism should not be confused with other terms such as *liberal retributivism, constrained retributivism*, or other terms that may be likened to consequential retributivism as herein described. *See* David Gurnham, *The Moral Narrative of Criminal Responsibility and the Principled Justification of Tariffs for Murder: Myra Hindley and Thompson and Venables*, 23 LEGAL STUD. 605, 609–11 (2003) (examining classical liberal retributivism); Thaddeus Metz, *How to Reconcile Liberal Politics with Retributive Punishment*, 27 O.J.L.S. 683, 701 (2007); LEO ZAIBERT, PUNISHMENT AND RETRIBUTION 155 (2006) (defining constrained retributivism as a version of modest retributivism).

[28] A minority of crimes known as strict-liability crimes, such as statutory rape and some traffic violations (e.g., speeding), do not have as a requirement any mental state. The act alone is sufficient. This volume is not concerned with strict-liability crimes.

[29] FOUNDATIONS OF CRIMINAL LAW 203 (Leo Katz, Michael S. Moore & Stephen J. Morse eds., 1999).

(or levels or states) of guilty mind (*mentes reae*) vary from common law to statutory law and by jurisdiction. In general, there are four basic mentes reae.[30] From most to least culpable, they are the following: (1) *purposely,* where the actor has as his conscious objective the harm associated with the act; (2) *knowingly,* where the actor, although he does not have as his conscious objective the harm caused, acts with conscious awareness that his conduct is practically certain to cause such a result; (3) *recklessly,* where the actor acts with conscious awareness that there exists the substantial risk that his act will cause the harm realized; and (4) *negligently,* where, although a reasonable person would have been aware of the substantial risk posed by the act in question, the actor acted without said awareness. That is, in that it is understood that the actor should have been aware of the risk, his lack of awareness, which on its face appears to be in the absence of a guilty mind, is itself a culpable mental state.

A word should be said about the "reasonable person" standard on which criminal negligence rests (i.e., criminal acts for which the mens rea of negligence is sufficient). In law, the reasonable person is not the average person but rather a fictional character whom the fact finder (e.g., juror) is asked to consider in (and, in essence, project into) the fact pattern of the case at hand. The reasonable person, although fictional, is the "person" whom the defendant is compared to in order to discern whether the defendant's lack of conscious awareness of risk is acceptable or, alternatively, reflects a failure to meet a responsibility to know better. The reasonable person is conceptualized to have the typical abilities and information of a prudent individual.[31] The reasonable person standard is considered to be an objective standard in that the specific characteristics and qualities of the defendant are not transferred to the fictional character of the reasonable person. The degree of objectivity of the reasonable person standard, including how it is defined, varies across jurisdiction. Note that the standard is naturally subjective in its application in that each individual fact finder must create for himself the reasonable person in the given fact pattern, although this is irrelevant to how "objectivity" is defined with respect to the standard itself.

Note that, as one compares mentes reae from most to least culpable, one finds that what distinguishes each pair of adjacent levels is different. Knowingly differs from purposely in that the actor who only knowingly

[30] This taxonomy of mental states is advanced by the Model Penal Code (MPC), which is a proposed code of criminal law that has been highly influential in the United States, although this hierarchy is by no means limited to MPC jurisdictions. Model Penal Code § 2.02(2) (Official Draft and Revised Comments 1985).

[31] Of course, as with the question of how to define the reasonable person, one may ask how to define the "prudent individual." The reasonable person is often defined by language that leaves much open to the mind of the fact finder.

commits the wrongful act does not have as his conscious objective the harm caused. Recklessly differs from knowingly by the degree of likelihood that the actor's act will cause the harm realized. Whereas the act committed must be practically certain to occur in the case of crimes that are committed knowingly, all that is required for a crime to be committed recklessly is a substantial risk that harm will result. Here the difference is not in the actor's motive, but in the probability that *x* act will cause *y* harm. Finally, negligently differs from recklessly with respect to conscious awareness of the risk.

These "levels" of guilty mind, as well as the factors that distinguish adjacent levels of mens rea, are, in essence, social-cognitive statements. They are statements of social goals (intentions and objectives), recognition and understanding of one's social world and the rules of cause and effect by which it is bound (acting with, and sometimes despite, the belief that one's behavior will lead to an identified outcome), outcomes expectations (estimating probabilities of specific behavior outcome sequences), and processing social information conceptually versus automatically (having to do with the degree of "mindfulness" with which one acts). In this way, the broad construct of criminal mind may be considered and directly investigated via a social-cognitive lens. I will leave a more illustrative discussion of this translation to Chapters 2 and 3, but the critical idea here is that by understanding social cognitive processes and conditions, we may consider and better understand how criminals function and, central to the issue of criminal responsibility, how alternative social-cognitive capacities may vary according to individual differences as well as differential development among humans.

To properly discuss criminal responsibility, however, we must return our attention to a retributive theory of punishment and the notion that retribution is the primary goal of criminal law.[32] Criminal law is designed to match crimes (or official statements of criminal culpability) and their corresponding punishments with acts of wrongdoing. That is, it is for criminal law to exact just deserts by punishing wrongdoers to the precise degree that they are responsible for the harm they cause. This principle, called penal proportionality, dictates

[32] Even by a mixed theory of consequential retribution that dictates that both desert on the part of the offender and net social gain must be present (again, by net social gain, utilitarian theorists really mean the expectation of net social gain, as there is no way to know in advance if X punishment will cause Y net social gain), it must be recognized that retribution, at the very least, is *a* function of criminal law. Thus, whether one adheres to a pure deontological retributive or mixed consequential retributive theory of punishment, retribution is recognized at least as a critical function of criminal law. In contrast, I will discuss the increased importance of utilitarian values such as rehabilitation that arise with respect to juvenile offenders. See *infra* Chapter 4.

that punishment is just only if it is balanced with the wrongdoing committed. Whereas it is unjust to punish a wrongdoer too severely for a given crime, it is equally unjust to punish him too lightly. Only the ratio of 1:1 – degree of punishment to degree of moral reprehensibility – is just in retributive terms. Via the consistent application of penal proportionality, criminal law may balance the moral scales after they have been upset by the commission of wrongdoing.

An even more precise statement of penal proportionality is that punishment must equal the degree to which one is *responsible* for his criminal wrongdoing. That is, punishment can only serve the retributive goal of the criminal law when its recipient is responsible, and thus may be held accountable, for the wrong he committed and the social harm he caused. We cannot speak of just deserts, as either a retributive concept or the goal of Anglo-American criminal law, without speaking of personal responsibility. A person cannot be said to deserve punishment for that which he is not responsible; this is no less true for the most horrendous of criminal acts (e.g., murder). Likewise, many scholars insist that personal or moral responsibility presumes free will. That is, a person cannot be said to be responsible for any act that did not occur of his own free choice and willful action.[33]

There is enormous debate in the academia, primarily among scholars in psychology,[34] neuroscience,[35] philosophy,[36] and law,[37] as to the existence and

[33] *See* JOHN M. FISCHER & MARK RAVIZZA, *RESPONSIBILITY AND CONTROL: A THEORY OF MORAL RESPONSIBILITY* (1998); John M. Fischer, *Recent Work on Moral Responsibility*, 110 ETHICS 93 (1999); FREE WILL (Robert Kane ed. 2002). Alternatively, Professor Stephen J. Morse has argued that it is the general capacity for rationality on which criminal responsibility rests. A discussion of Morse's theory, what he calls the "non-problem of free will in law," is addressed in Chapter 3. *See* Stephen J. Morse, *Determinism and the Death of Folk Psychology: Two Challenges to Responsibility from Neuroscience*, 9 MINN. J.L. SCI. & TECH. 1, 3–13 (2008).

[34] *E.g.*, Albert Bandura, *Reconstrual of "Free Will" from the Agentic Perspective of Social Cognitive Theory*, *in* ARE WE FREE? PSYCHOLOGY AND FREE WILL 86 (John Baer, James C. Kaufman & Roy F. Baumeister eds., 2008); Sherman & Hoffman, *supra* note 19, at 515.

[35] *E.g.*, R. J. R. Blair, *Aggression, Psychopathy and Free Will from a Cognitive Neuroscience Perspective*, 25 BEHAV. SCI. & L. 321 (2007); Joshua Greene, *From Neural "Is" to Moral "Ought": What are the Moral Implications of Neuroscientific Moral Psychology?*, 4 NATURE REVIEWS NEUROSCIENCE 847 (2003) [hereinafter Greene, *From Neural*]; Joshua Greene & Jonathan Cohen, *For the Law, Neuroscience Changes Nothing and Everything*, 359 PHIL. TRANSACTIONS ROYAL SOC'Y LONDON B 1775, 1777–78 (2004).

[36] *E.g.*, TED HONDERICH, *HOW FREE ARE YOU?: THE DETERMINISM PROBLEM* (1993); Shaun Nichols, *How Can Psychology Contribute to the Free Will Debate?*, *in* ARE WE FREE? PSYCHOLOGY AND FREE WILL 10 (John Baer, James C. Kaufman & Roy F. Baumeister eds., 2008); Galen Strawson, *Consciousness, Free Will, and the Unimportance of Determinism*, 32 INQUIRY 3 (1989).

[37] *See, e.g.*, James Grant, *Determinism, Neuroscience and Responsibility*, 2 INT'L J.L. CONTEXT 221, 221–22 & n. 4 (2006); Morse, *Diminished* Rationality, *supra* note 24.

nature of free will. In fact, it is perhaps safe to say that debate has never been more furious. Such fury has evolved out of a combination of three primary factors: (1) advances in psychology and neuroscience have produced scientific findings that have been interpreted to mean that we live in a purely physical world in which everything – even the most seemingly self-controlled processes of the human mind – is subject to the all-governing physical laws of nature;[38] (2) based in part on (1), some scholars have advanced the hard deterministic view that free will and determinism are necessarily mutually exclusive and entirely incompatible[39] – that is, free will and determinism cannot coexist as they are structurally unable to accommodate each other on any level; and (3) based on (1) and (2), one may conclude that legal doctrines of responsibility, as well as those that presume responsibility (e.g., criminal intent), are meaningless if the metaphysical problem of free will is resolved by hard determinism – that is, if we live in a purely physical world, then there is no free will, rendering it unjust to find and hold a wrongdoer responsible for his action no matter how egregious it may be.[40]

Free will may be defined as an individual's capacity to use reason to direct his thought processes and make decisions (and, in turn, direct his actions).[41] In that free will has traditionally been conceptualized as a metaphysical entity, it is unclear by which specific mental mechanism or faculty (or set of mechanisms or faculties) free will functions. If free will is metaphysical, then resolution of this issue is not, of course, physically discoverable. However, we can liken various mental processes – perception, attribution, interpretation, goal clarification, evaluative judgment, behavioral selection, and the like – to the notion of free will as these cognitive mechanisms, individually and collectively, clearly play a considerable role in individual decision making and behavior.

[38] *See, e.g.*, Greene, *From Neural*, *supra* note 35, at 849 (noting that neuroscientific evidence has the ability to influence the way we understand morality).

[39] *See, e.g.*, Derk Pereboom, *Living Without Free Will* 127 (2001). Professor Pereboom's perspective is one of incompatibilism or hard determinism. According to hard determinism, a person's belief in or sense of free will is nothing more than that – a belief or sense. Whereas one may believe that he is in control of his thoughts and that he has free choice, such a belief is nothing more than an illusion determined by the physical properties and laws of nature. *Id.* at 127–28; Daniel M. Wegner, *Self is Magic*, *in* Are We Free? Psychology and Free Will 226, 236–37 (John Baer, James C. Kaufman & Roy F. Baumeister eds., 2008).

[40] *See* Stephen J. Morse, *The Non-Problem of Free Will in Forensic Psychiatry and Psychology*, 25 Behav. Sci. & L. 203, 213–14 (2007).

[41] Some may more simply state that free will is one's ability to control his actions; however, a sharpened understanding focuses on thought, or the cognitive underpinnings that mediate relations between stimuli and behavioral responses. This distinction should become clear in Chapter 2 where I discuss cognitive models of social behavior and empirical support for such theories.

Free will is to be distinguished from free action, the latter of which refers to conduct enacted as a function of exercising one's free will, unobstructed by external constraints.[42] Similarly, free will should be distinguished from moral responsibility, the latter of which has to do with an individual's responsibility to act in accordance with an established, principled code of conduct. Whereas it is important to distinguish free will from free action and moral responsibility, it is equally important to recognize that all of these concepts are related, and, typically, free action and moral responsibility are conceptualized such that they presume free will.[43]

There is no question that the law views actors as reason-based and actions as "reason-governed."[44] Criminal laws are designed to protect standards and define serious violations of moral responsibility. Some scholars have argued that recent behavioral science findings have moved intellectual thought toward a deterministic view and that, as a result, it is becoming more difficult for the law to assign criminal culpability and punish individuals for their criminal acts.[45] This conclusion may necessarily follow from a theory of criminal law that is bound by hard determinism; however, criminal law throughout Anglo-American history has neither given any indication of adopting such a perspective nor demonstrated even an inkling of a shift away from its focus on moral responsibility and retributive desert. The case is quite the opposite, in fact, as the very nature of law has always been, and continues to be, based on an understanding that law affects citizen action via the citizen's ability to make meaning out of the law and internalize it as a personal rule that guides his own action. This understanding is, by its nature, a psychological one that articulates the law's recognition of basic mental functioning shared by humans. Additionally, it represents an association between law and citizen that can only be understood in terms of a cognitive mediational sequence that may simply be called *learning*. As Professor Stephen Morse artfully stated, "Unless human beings are rational creatures who can understand the applicable rules and standards, and can conform to those legal requirements through intentional action, the law would be powerless to affect human behavior."[46] Morse's observation reflects not only the law's view of humans as rational

[42] Of course, in this broad sense, no action is truly free. If I decide to fly and attempt to jump up a large flight of stairs, gravity will prevent me from successfully doing so.

[43] *Cf.* John M. Fischer, The Metaphysics of Free Will: An Essay on Control (1994) (arguing that although humans do not have free will, they are morally responsible for their choices and actions).

[44] Morse, *Rationality and Responsibility*, *supra* note 24, at 252–53.

[45] Sherman & Hoffman, *supra* note 19, at 515.

[46] Morse, *Rationality and Responsibility*, *supra* note 24, at 253.

beings, but that it is this ability – rationality – that is most critical in the law's functionality.[47]

Anglo-American criminal law rests on retribution-based legal doctrines of criminal responsibility and just deserts. Such doctrines presume free will in that it may not be said that one is responsible for wrongdoing, and therefore deserves to be punished for it, if he did not act freely in his commission of it. If free will, as I have here defined it, is an individual's ability to use reason to direct his thought processes and make behavioral decisions, then it follows that the absence of rationality precludes a determination that one has acted out of his own free will, is responsible for his conduct, and deserves to be punished in the case that his action is objectively criminal. This definition, of course, identifies rationality as *the* critical mechanism of free will and, in like kind, individual (or personal) responsibility.

Rationality should be distinguished from a general concept of self-control. Whereas self-control may broadly encompass basic physical (e.g., digestion, reflex actions) and psychological (e.g., perception or self-cognizance) qualities and operations, rationality has to do with one's capacity to understand and apply rules and balance values (even when such values are in competition with each other) in the course of evaluative judgment and decision making that guide behavior toward desired outcomes. In this way, rationality reflects higher-ordered mental functioning, the likes of which is considered to be uniquely human.[48]

The law presumes that adult agents are equipped with the mental faculties and psychological capacities by which they may sufficiently reason and, in doing so, make meaning of laws. The law presumes that these faculties and capacities may serve to guide individual conduct. Thus, in the context of law, rationality is central to our understanding of responsibility. The individual who is of rational capacity that is consistent with that presumed by law is held fully accountable for his criminal conduct. Alternatively, one who is insufficiently rational (or "subrational") *may* not justly be held fully responsible.[49] Such an

47 Of course, Morse's assertion is more a recognition of the role of rationality than free will, and it is not clear that the former depends on the existence of the latter. That is, in a purely physical, naturally determined world, an individual may engage in rational thought and, in turn, enact reason-based behavior. The difference is that said thought and behavior may only be explained as outcomes of physical properties that are not his own.

48 Rationality is often attributed to a level of mental functioning unique to humans or, alternatively, conceptualized as an ideal that only humans approach. The law's presumption of rational capacity in humans is specific to adults. In Chapter 4, I will turn to the subject of rational capacity in the context of development and discuss the concept of "developmental immaturity" in the interdisciplinary context of psychological science and juvenile justice.

49 In Chapter 3, I discuss and clarify this point. Specifically, I define nonculpable cognitive dysfunction with respect to diminished capacity and demonstrate how this term

insufficient state of rationality has been referred to as "diminished capacity,"[50] "diminished responsibility,"[51] and "diminished rationality."[52] Technically, however, diminished rationality may be realized in two forms: that which never sufficiently developed and that which is lessened by some means subsequent to its sufficient development. The former may be illustrated by the individual who has not reached developmental maturity (i.e., a juvenile) or an individual who entered adulthood with mental retardation. The latter of these forms may be realized via either of two alternative courses: a nonculpable path, such as mental illness, or a culpable path, such as the willful ingestion of a mind-altering substance (e.g., alcohol).[53]

In psychological terms, rationality is a broad construct that involves numerous mental capacities, including – but not limited to – perception, interpretation, formation and realization of goals, consideration of alternative behavioral routes or strategies toward some desired end, and evaluative judgment and decision making. Seriously insufficient (or severely diminished) functioning in any one of these areas may serve to undermine or impede rationality such that a person may not act in accordance with what would typically be expected of a reasonable person in the given circumstances. The translation of diminished rationality into psychological terms allows us to consider empirical findings from behavioral science in the process of making informed determinations of what the term in a legal context may rightly entail. That is, scientific research that demonstrates that a failure of one psychological process to operate sufficiently is associated with a socially problematic behavior may inform our understanding of the development, function, structure, and phenomenology of diminished rationality in criminal law theory and practice.

Criminal defenses may be classified as either negative or affirmative. A negative criminal defense is a declaration of actual innocence. In this case, the defendant pleads "not guilty" and asserts that he did not commit the criminal act that is charged. Alternatively, an affirmative criminal defense admits

is useful in distinguishing states of diminished capacity that correspond with diminished responsibility.

50 *See, e.g.*, Barry W. Wall, *Criminal Responsibility, Diminished Capacity, and the Gay Panic Defense*, 28 J. AM. ACAD. PSYCHIATRY & L. 454, 454 (2000).

51 Muench v. Israel, 715 F.2d 1124, 1142–43 (7th Cir. 1983); *see also* J. E. Hall Williams, *The Homicide Act, 1957, and Diminished Responsibility – An Abdication of Responsibility?*, 21 MOD. L. REV. 318 (1958).

52 *E.g.*, Morse, *Diminished Rationality*, *supra* note 24. Of these three alternative labels, diminished rationality seems to most closely approach a description of the type of mental condition that may negate mens rea. However, in Chapter 3, I question this term and offer the broader – and I believe fairer – term *insufficient rationality*.

53 Nonculpable versus culpable etiological courses of diminished rationality are distinguished and discussed in detail in Chapter 3.

that the defendant did indeed commit the criminal act charged, but that he should not be found guilty or punished because of specific circumstances of the act that are related to its moral content. That is, affirmative defenses do not dispute that the defendant acted as alleged, but rather refute that either the act was wrong or that the defendant should be held responsible, blamed, and punished for having committed the admittedly wrongful act. In either case, the core assertion of an affirmative defense is that the defendant cannot be justly blamed or punished because he is not deserving of blame or punishment. This assertion reflects the purely retributive nature of affirmative defenses as recognized by Anglo-American criminal law. That is, according to the retributive principle of just deserts, one who has either engaged in no criminal wrongdoing or is not responsible for his criminal action is neither blameworthy nor punishable. The long-standing, pervasive recognition of numerous affirmative defenses throughout Anglo-America is further evidence of the retributive foundation and goal of criminal law.

There are two types of affirmative defenses. Justification defenses are affirmative statements that the defendant committed the act that is charged but that he was not wrong for doing so. For example, one who kills another in response to an imminent, wrongful, mortal threat is said to have acted in self-defense, or to have committed justifiable homicide. Although she did kill another person, her action was not wrong because it prevented the other person from wrongfully taking her life. In contrast, excuse defenses admit not only that the defendant committed the alleged act, but also that the act was criminally wrong. However, excuse defenses assert that although the defendant acted wrongfully, he should not be deemed culpable or punished for his act because either his commission of the act was understandable, such as in the case of reasonable mistake, or he was not responsible for its commission, such as in the case of acting out of psychiatric disorder (e.g., psychosis).

With respect to findings of culpability and rulings of punishment, justification and excuse defenses, when successful, both produce the same end result: The defendant is exonerated of at least some blame and punishment. Both types of affirmative defense may be further subclassified as either complete or partial. Complete defenses fully relieve the defendant of criminal responsibility of punishment, whereas partial defenses only reduce the degrees of blameworthiness assigned and punishment sentenced (e.g., a successful heat-of-passion defense generally reduces murder to manslaughter). Although outcomes of blame and punishment are identical, the distinction between justification and excuse is critical, for numerous reasons. Comprehensive discussions of such reasons have been provided elsewhere, most notably by

Professor Joshua Dressler;[54] perhaps the most critical reason, having to do with the moral relevance of the distinction, should be made clear, if it is not already. That is, whereas the defendant who acted justifiably is legally determined to have not engaged in an unlawful act (and may even be praised for having acted in a meritorious fashion) or caused a substantial social harm, the excused defendant, although not held criminally responsible for his act, is said to have acted wrongfully, and often egregiously so, and caused a significant social harm. Succinctly stated, the difference between justification and excuse reflects the basic moral distinction between right and wrong on which the criminal law stands.[55]

At the root of the excuse defense is the assertion that there are circumstances by which the defendant's wrongful act may be explained or understood such that he is not morally accountable for its commission. It may be that the sufficiently rational defendant acted reasonably but mistakenly – a case that may be excused via the rationale that a reasonable person would have acted in a similarly mistaken fashion. It may also be that the defendant acted with insufficient capacity such that the presumption of self-control and rationality that the law makes of humans may not be fairly attributed. In this case, it may be said that although the defendant's act is criminally wrongful, he is not to be held criminally responsible because, through no fault of his own, he did not commit the act with the level of functioning that is presumed of him by the law. The defendant's insufficient capacity may be deemed to challenge the requisite mens rea of the crime charged. In this way, issues of functional capacity, central to which is rationality, play a varied role in the determination of criminal responsibility. As I discuss in Chapter 3, the spirit or nature of diminished (or insufficient) rationality touches on numerous affirmative defenses of the excuse variety.

As such, an understanding of the types of mental processes that may contribute to rationality seems critical. Rationality, of course, may be conceptualized in a number of ways. Basic to such conceptualizations, however, is a definition that emphasizes an individual's ability to properly understand his social world and activate (or carry out) evaluative judgment and decision making

[54] *E.g.*, Joshua Dressler, *Justifications and Excuses: A Brief Review of the Concepts and the Literature*, 33 Wayne L. Rev. 1155 (1987); Joshua Dressler, *Provocation: Partial Justification or Partial Excuse?*, 51 Mod. L. Rev. 467 (1988).

[55] Elsewhere, I have argued this point with respect to the affirmative defenses of provocation/heat of passion. Fontaine, *supra* note 10, at 228. I have also argued this point with respect to mistaken self-defense. Reid G. Fontaine, *An Attack on Self-Defense*, 47 Am. Crim. L. Rev. 57, 83 (2010).

to properly navigate his way through said social world given his subjective understanding of it. The operative word here is *properly*. Properly may mean that one's subjective understanding is reflective of objective reality; alternatively, it may be defined according to the degree of success one achieves in realizing desired outcomes. Another conceptualization articulates that one's mental functioning is proper if it lends itself to adaptation. For the purpose of identifying the meaning of rationality in the relation between law and the citizens it governs, all three of these definitions apply. For the law to work, its citizens need to understand it, as well as that to which it corresponds (e.g., context, conduct) in a fashion that sufficiently reflects objective reality. In addition, citizens need to have internalized the values represented by law such that their judgment and decision making are geared to promote actions that are consistent with these values. Finally, abiding by the law is an important part of social acceptance, which is central to adaptation.[56]

Models of human perception, judgment, and decision making, and how these processes are related to other aspects and systems of individual functioning (e.g., emotion, behavior), have drawn from scientific research in biological, clinical, cognitive, developmental, and social psychology, as well as other areas of behavioral science (e.g., economics and experimental philosophy), to make sense of how humans transact with their social environments. Such social-cognitive frameworks and theories are designed to represent and account for individual differences in human functioning – that is, ways in which humans are similar and different at an individual (as opposed to group or institutional) level – and are studied systematically such that greater insight and more comprehensive understanding may develop as to how alternative cause-and-effect sequences (e.g., provocation-to-retaliation versus provocation-to-withdrawal) may emerge and transpire. Some of these theories have been particularly effective in accounting for and explaining individual differences in styles and patterns of thinking that are uniquely associated with socially competent versus antisocial conduct (and, more specifically, subtypes of antisocial conduct). In this way, psychology may be used to understand and describe how and why some individuals engage in

[56] It reasons that, on average, and all other factors being equal, one who is socially accepted is more likely than one who is socially unaccepted to successfully reproduce. This is a well-accepted premise in both social and evolutionary psychology as well as sociobiology. *See, e.g.*, Dianne M. Tice, Jean M. Twenge & Brandon J. Schmeichel, *Threatened Selves: The Effects of Social Exclusion on Prosocial and Antisocial Behavior, in* THE SOCIAL SELF: COGNITIVE, INTERPERSONAL, AND INTERGROUP PERSPECTIVES 175 (Joseph P. Forgas & Kipling D. Williams eds., 2002); CHRISTOPHER BADCOCK, *EVOLUTION AND INDIVIDUAL BEHAVIOR: AN INTRODUCTION TO HUMAN SOCIOBIOLOGY* 267 (1991).

antisocial behavior that qualifies as crime and others do not. This is the psychology of wrongdoing. It may be used to investigate a range of behavior that stems from clinical (e.g., psychosis) to normal (e.g., neighborly conversation), low functioning (e.g., retarded processing) to high functioning (e.g., cunningness), antisocial (e.g., fighting) to prosocial (e.g., sharing), and egregiously reprehensible (e.g., murder) to remarkably honorable (e.g., sacrificing oneself to save another). Just as there are mechanisms in criminal law to account for individual differences in mental capacity and functioning (e.g., criminal excuses) so that judgments of wrongdoing may be properly made, psychology has systematic approaches by which individual differences in cognitive ability and processing may be identified, understood, and explained. In essence, this is the intersection of social cognition and criminal law, and the premise of this volume.

To further illuminate the essence of this volume, it is important to clearly state what this volume does *not* set out to (and, at times, simply could not) accomplish. That is, the focus and reach of this volume may be better calculated by distinguishing its goals via its negative space, the topics it purposefully excludes (e.g., noncriminal moral matters) and the confounding or otherwise problematic issues it is designed to avoid (e.g., an overapplication of science to law). Not only is the substantive scope of this volume defined such that it conservatively explores basic intersections of developmental social cognition and criminal law in the context of potentially excusing conditions, but it is cognizant of and abides by natural limitations of bridging psychological science and jurisprudential matters.

First, social science and behavioral science should be distinguished as often related but separate areas of scientific study, particularly because they are typically – and erroneously – used interchangeably. Social science, including disciplines such as anthropology, economics, political science, and sociology, studies the structure and process of social systems and how such systems are organized and interrelated. For example, the political scientist may study the attitudes and behaviors of political parties and how attitudes and behaviors of one party may affect those of another. Here, the level of analysis is typically at the group or institution. Alternatively, behavioral science, which encompasses disciplines such as psychology and social neuroscience, examines processes (e.g., decision making) of individuals within a social system, how such processes develop and change across time, and what this means for understanding how individuals relate to each other within a larger system. For example, a developmental psychologist may examine how early experiences affect the onset, maintenance, and convergence versus divergence of developmental courses of social conduct (e.g., socially competent as compared to antisocial behavioral trajectories) among youths. Here, the analysis is at the individual level. Although this volume draws from both social and behavioral science research, lessons from social science are indirectly related. It is the study of individual differences in capacity and functioning embodied by behavioral science that is most pressing for current concerns and goals.

The separate goals of criminal law and behavioral science should also be made clear such that there is a reasonable expectation as to what the former may gain from findings generated by the latter. Whereas criminal law seeks to make determinations of culpability and distinguish criminally guilty acts from those that are not, behavioral science sets out to systematically investigate and explain such acts. These goals are so sufficiently different that it would be more than unreasonable – indeed, it would be impossible – to expect that empirical behavioral science can answer normative legal questions. There are, of course, important empirical questions that arise in the process of resolving normative ones, and in this way, science is critical as empirical questions may only be answered via empirical avenues of investigation. For example, the law is charged with articulating a taxonomy of violent crimes. In retributive terms, violent crimes may be hierarchically organized according to their respective degrees of reprehensibility. However, if reprehensibility is dependent on empirical issues such as the type of mental processing associated with the crime (such as in the case of premeditated murder versus heat-of-passion manslaughter), the degree of victim suffering typically caused by the crime, and the general dangerousness and risk of harm presented by the type of conduct that is defined by the crime, then the empirical nature of this set of questions would naturally (or, at least, ideally) call on empirical science for answers, or at least useful information. Although behavioral science is unable to dictate the law, it can and should inform it in numerous, important ways. Drawing from social-cognitive science, this volume intends to illustrate exactly this point.

Further, it is important to recognize that much – that is, the vast majority – of the science that would test hypotheses related to pressing normative issues in law has yet to be conducted. This is not to say that there is not considerable science that has already been carried out from which to draw. If there were not, there would be insufficient reason and foundation for this volume. Present purposes are thus twofold: (1) to illustrate linkages between social cognitive science and criminal jurisprudence and law; and (2) to explore, at a theoretical level, additional possible connections that may be informed if the proper scientific work were to be executed. In other words, this volume is intended to explore ways in which science can both now and in the future inform criminal law theory.

It may be easy to mistake the proposed connections as ones characterized by psychiatry and criminal law. However, whereas scientific research in psychiatry most assuredly proves useful to current goals, psychiatric models and perspectives are of only peripheral interest. Psychiatry has long preferred a taxonomy of mental illness that is organized according to categorical groupings of mental disease (or disorder or illness). Diagnostic criteria of such mental disorders are delineated and, to some limited degree, discussed in a manual published by the American Psychiatric Association, *Diagnostic and Statistical Manual of Mental Disorders* (DSM).[57] The DSM has been revised several times over the years in repeated attempts to respond not only to scientific updates and changes in sociocultural norms but to numerous criticisms of its contents and organization. Although a thorough analysis of these criticisms is outside the scope of this discussion, there are three criticisms that deserve mention.

First, the DSM does not sufficiently recognize or reflect the importance of individual differences. For example, because the disorder as it is psychiatrically recognized and defined involves only a behavioral checklist that includes a broad array of antisocial behaviors, it is not at all difficult for adolescents to be similarly diagnosed with *conduct disorder* despite the obvious differences in the antisocial behavioral patterns they demonstrate. Along this line, the DSM does not adequately account for empirically substantiated subtypes of functioning. Continuing with the example of conduct disorder, whereas one adolescent may exhibit a pattern of instrumental aggression, by which he bullies others, steals, and picks fights, another adolescent may demonstrate a reactive antisocial style, impulsively retaliating to modestly aversive stimuli in his environment.[58] Because the DSM does not recognize the considerable empirical research that has validated these alternative forms and patterns of antisocial behavior, such adolescents would be classified identically despite the clear differences in the structure, function, and phenomenology of their behavioral patterns.

The degree to which the DSM is informed by science is a matter of general question and certainly not limited to the issue of subtypes of functioning. Behavioral scientists have long been baffled by the recognition of some disorders and the failure to recognize others, as well as how the disorders are organized and differentiated from each other.[59] For example, there is little

57 American Psychiatric Association, *Diagnostic and Statistical Manual of Mental Disorders* (4th ed. Text rev. 2000).

58 For a recent review, see Reid G. Fontaine, *Disentangling the Psychology and Law of Instrumental and Reactive Subtypes of Aggression*, 13 Psychol. Pub. Pol'y & L. 143 (2007).

59 *See, e.g.*, John Z. Sadler, *Values and Psychiatric Diagnosis* (2005).

empirical substantiation for the differential diagnosis of impulse control disorder and intermittent explosive disorder in the DSM, although these disorders are explicitly treated as separate disruptive behavioral disorders.

Perhaps two of the most striking limitations of the DSM are its inattention to development and environmental (or social) context. Intuitively, it is hard to even imagine how a phenomenon as complex as psychiatric disorder could be understood outside of development and environmental context. It is particularly remarkable that child and adolescent psychiatric disorders fail to account for basic developmental principles and processes. This list of criticisms represents just a small sample. However, these particular criticisms have been carefully chosen as they represent basic premises of developmental psychopathology, a scientific approach that poses a strong challenge to the traditional medical/psychiatric model.[60]

Developmental psychopathology is an area of study that derives most directly from clinical and developmental psychology but draws from numerous fields including various subfields in psychology (including social and cognitive psychology), developmental biology, neuroscience, and behavioral genetics. Developmental psychopathologists study individual differences in development and change in trajectory across time. Developmental trajectories are understood according to their contextual significance and meaning. Central to this approach is that functioning that may be adaptive (and typical) in one social context may be maladaptive (and atypical) in another context, and vice versa. Adaptive (or normal) and maladaptive (or abnormal) patterns of functioning cannot be comprehensively understood when studied exclusively – that is, each must be studied in the context of the other. Human functioning is conceptualized as constantly changing and dependent on numerous factors of various types (biological, psychological, social, etc.). As a result, developmental trajectories may converge with or diverge from each other as individuals develop and time passes. Thus, different individuals may develop in such a way that they achieve similar outcomes (equifinality); alternatively, similar individuals may grow and continue along paths that diverge, leading to differential outcomes (multifinality). Developmental psychopathology thus views individual differences as not only prominent in understanding of human behavior and functioning, but also that they may only be understood according to alternative developmental (adjusted versus maladjusted) contexts and trajectories. For these critical reasons, developmental psychopathology may serve as a clearer lens to explore how the psychological, developmental

[60] *See* Developmental Psychopathology (Dante Cicchetti & Donald J. Cohen eds., 2d ed. 2006).

science of individual differences in ability and functioning may inform jurisprudential issues of capacity and rationality in criminal law.

A note should be made about criminal law in the United States as compared to elsewhere in Anglo-America. Certainly, there remains much that is consistent in doctrinal criminal law across Anglo-American jurisdictions. Just as certain, however, is that important differences have evolved and that there continues to be aggressive divergence with respect to particular doctrines. For example, provocation/heat-of-passion doctrine remains a topic that is heavily debated with respect to several substantive issues, including whether it is a partial justification or excuse.[61] Although there is by no means consensus, most American criminal-law theorists understand provocation/heat of passion as an excuse.[62] In England, however, The Law Commission has delineated guidelines by which the provocation defense would more clearly focus on the criterion of provocation and more closely approximate justification.[63] Furthermore, The Law Commission specifically distinguishes the proposed reframing from Scottish provocation law.[64] This volume is focused on U.S. criminal law, although references to other Anglo-American jurisdictions, made where comparing and contrasting doctrinal principle, interpretation, and efforts of legal reform, may be helpful illustrating points of interest.

With respect to U.S. criminal law, this volume is concerned both with legal doctrine as it has evolved and continues to actively guide common law, as well as with the Model Penal Code (MPC). The MPC has been highly influential since its introduction in 1962, and numerous states have adopted parts and principles of it. No state, however, has adopted the MPC in its entirety, and the degree to which MPC principles guide state criminal law varies considerably from jurisdiction to jurisdiction, not only in amount but also class of crime. As a result, it is important to distinguish whether the criminal law in question is based in common law or the MPC. Of particular interest to

[61] *E.g.*, Joshua Dressler, *Why Keep the Provocation Defense?: Some Reflections on a Difficult Subject*, 86 MINN. L. REV. 959, 959–60 n.5 (2002).

[62] *E.g.*, Reid G. Fontaine, *Adequate (Non)Provocation and Heat of Passion as Excuse Not Justification*, 43 U. MICH. J.L. REFORM 27 (2009).

[63] In the guidelines advanced by England's Law Commission, the provocation defense was framed to require that the defendant charged with murder needed to have had "a justifiable sense of being seriously wronged," the specification of which may be interpreted as an effort to limit the defense to scenarios that may be explained as partial justifications. THE LAW COMMISSION, LAW COM NO 304, MURDER, MANSLAUGHTER AND INFANTICIDE, 2006, H.C. 30, at 78 (U.K.) [hereinafter THE REPORT]. For reasons that are too involved to discuss here, it may be argued that the addition of this language alone does not suffice in the recreation of heat-of-passion doctrine as justification. For my analysis of this matter, see Fontaine, *supra* note 62.

[64] THE REPORT, *supra* note 63, at 88 & n. 43.

present purposes is the MPC's shift toward accounting for individual differences in subjective functioning and the greater weight the MPC has given to the individual's frame of mind.[65]

A brief discussion of caveats and limitations of behavioral science research, as well as interpretations and written reports of behavioral science, is in order as well. Whereas advances in knowledge base and methodology in behavioral science continue to travel at an accelerated rate, there remain important issues that deserve some attention because of their relevance to proper treatment of bridging social cognition with criminal jurisprudence and law. As such, let us address a few important observations and principles of which one should be cognizant as she considers and reflects on ideas and lessons that are herein provided.

Two principles are critical to the building of a scientific theory. First, Professor Karl Popper is credited for having advanced the principle of falsifiability,[66] which is "the idea that a theory should be not only testable but also falsifiable."[67] A theory should be stated such that, upon a test of it, it may be determined that the theory is false. Second is the principle of parsimony, which states that the simplest theory, or the simplest interpretation of data, is the best.[68] A theory should not be made more complex than it needs to be, and data should not be interpreted to have a more complex meaning than they naturally require.

A perhaps more obvious value in building a scientific theory – one that is related to but separate from parsimony – is exercising a degree of conservatism in the interpretation of empirical findings. That is, just as the principle of parsimony states that one should not interpret the meaning of findings to be more complex than they naturally suggest, it is equally important to not attribute other kinds of undeserved meaning. A common point of confusion (although, at times, the error is not merely based on confusion) is that a correlation implies causality. A correlation of two or more variables means that values of the variables change (decrease and increase) according to similar patterns. Two or more variables that are causally related must necessarily be correlated in that one cannot be said to cause another if their patterns of change sufficiently vary, but one may not interpret a causal relation among variables based solely on the finding of a statistically significant correlation. It is not at all uncommon for correlated variables to not be causally related but rather

[65] Sherman & Hoffman, *supra* note 19, at 509, 514.

[66] Karl R. Popper, *The Logic of Scientific Discovery* 78–92 (1968).

[67] Pamela J. Shoemaker, James William Tankard, & Dominic L. Lasorsa, *How to Build Social Science Theories* 172 (2004).

[68] *Id.*

correlated because they are causally related to a third variable. A common illustration is that of ice cream sales and shark attacks, both of which increase from spring to summer and decrease from summer to fall. Ice cream sales do not cause shark attacks, nor do shark attacks cause ice cream sales, of course. However, the summer heat (third variable) does cause people to desire to cool off, an interest that may be realized both by swimming in cool waters, some of which are inhabited by sharks, and eating cool and refreshing treats such as ice cream.

A conservative scientific approach states that causality may only be concluded from a true experiment; that is, a systematic study in which groups are randomly assigned to experimental and control conditions to examine the causal effect of the manipulated independent variable. However, numerous hypothesized causal relations among variables may not be testable via random assignment experiments. It may be that it is impossible (or at least impractical) to manipulate the independent variable of interest, such as in the case of a hypothesized relation between experiencing a natural disaster (e.g., earthquake) and suffering psychological trauma. Natural disasters are not controllable such that they may be manipulated in an experimental paradigm. It may also be that, although it is possible, it is definitively unethical to manipulate the independent variable of interest such that individuals would be randomly assigned to an experimental group, such as in the case of a hypothesized relation between depression and divorce. Whereas it may be possible to randomly assign individuals to a group that is subject to depressing conditions or stimuli, it would be unethical to do so. Therefore, the causal relation between depression and divorce is untestable via this conservative scientific approach.

There are conditions, however, that, when met, allow a researcher to *approach* (albeit not definitively conclude) an inference that two or more variables are causally related. First, as stated, the variables must be correlated. Second, there must exist temporal antecedence that is consistent with the hypothesized relation. That is, the independent variable must occur prior to the dependent variable. Third, tests of alternative explanations of how the variables are related must have been conducted and failed. Contrary to popular misconception, the objective in science is to refute one's own hypotheses. Only when one has rigorously tested hypotheses that are alternative (or in opposition) to one's principal hypothesis and such testing has failed to refute the principal hypothesis may the principal hypothesis be advanced. The import of clarifying that correlation does not imply causality is indisputable – particularly in behavioral science where, because it is impossible, impractical, or unethical, true experiments that test the relatedness of the variables of interest cannot be conducted.

Finally, a word about the translation of behavioral science findings and data to principles and doctrines in criminal law should be offered. It is important to remember that there are a number of levels of translation involved in the intellectual pursuit of science-to-law scholarship. Scientific studies in psychology typically examine the degree to which mean scores or values with respect to the independent variable of interest differs between alternative groups. Inferences from these group-difference findings are often made and applied at an individual level. However, it is important to remember that within any one of the alternative groups (e.g., within the experimental or control group) there is often considerable individual variation. As a result, it is dangerous to definitively conclude that the relation between two or more variables that has been discovered at the group level (i.e., from a comparison of group means) applies to a specific individual. Of course, in criminal law, the unit of analysis is entirely different. Criminal law seeks to make determinations about single acts by specific individuals. As such, great care must be taken so that the applicable meaning of lessons in psychology to criminal law, at the level of the individual case, is not overstated. Of course, this is not the type of translation that this volume sets out to make. Rather, the primary goal is to draw from theory and science in social-cognitive psychology so that empirical issues related to long-standing doctrinal debates in criminal law may be better informed.

Before we explore more fully how psychological science may be used to inform doctrines of rationality and capacity in criminal law, a discussion of social-cognitive theory along with an introduction of key process models is in order. Just as an articulation of punishment theory and, more generally, criminal-law theory is essential to making the intersection of developmental social cognition and excusing conditions in criminal law accessible, so is a chapter that reviews, compares, and contrasts scientific theories of the development of social cognition and antisocial conduct. As such, we now turn our attention to critical movements in psychology and highlight areas of empirical research that have informed scientific understanding of the development of mental capacity and functioning in humans.

2

Developmental Social Cognition and Antisocial Behavior

Theory and Science

Justifications of punishment have acknowledged scholarly theory and research in many areas. Whereas some criminal justice policy and law challenges have been attended to by criminology and economics (e.g., how law may be framed so that it provides a cost-efficient way to meet utilitarian values such as deterrence and public safety) and moral philosophy (e.g., how the law should be framed so that wrongdoers get their just deserts per the retributive mandate), behavioral science, broadly, has offered responses to questions related to psychological functioning and the workings of the human mind, particularly with respect to wrongdoing and antisocial conduct. The primary goal at hand is to explore the degree to which examining criminal jurisprudence and law through a developmental social-cognitive lens is useful.

Certainly, several disciplines within the social and behavioral sciences have investigated factors related to the onset and maintenance of antisocial and criminal behavior. For example, sociologists and criminologists have examined the influences of social structures, networks, and norms, such as how family composition is related to youth delinquent behavior.[1] Social anthropologists have focused on cultural context and cross-cultural relativity, such as how particular groups and activities become criminalized by social entities (e.g., government, media, and citizenry).[2] Economists study determinants of crime and crime rates as a function of individuals' behavioral choices aimed at meeting self-interests. For example, economists may investigate how the

[1] *E.g.*, Robert Apel & Catherine Kaukinen, *On the Relationship Between Family Structure and Antisocial Behavior: Parental Cohabitation and Blended Households*, 46 Criminology 35 (2008).

[2] *E.g.*, Jane Schneider & Peter Schneider, *The Anthropology of Crime and Criminalization*, 37 Ann. Rev. Anthropology 351 (2008).

rate (or supply) of crime is related to public interest in (or demand for) crime prevention.[3] Neuroscientists and genetic psychologists employ brain imaging and genetic analysis to examine criminogenic variables such as brain-level mechanisms that may be unique to criminals.[4] In addition, developmental psychologists and psychopathologists have studied clinical (e.g., psychiatric disorder[5]), familial (e.g., parenting style[6]), and social (e.g., effects of video games[7]) factors in the study of individual differences in violent and criminal behavior across time.

Also to be credited to psychology are social-cognitive models of emotional and behavioral development and competence, which have been advanced as both heuristics of individual differences in human operating and scientific theories of how humans learn as a function of their information processing and decision making. In particular, social-information processing (SIP) theories, including those of Professors Kenneth Dodge[8] and Rowell Huesmann,[9] have been designed to test hypotheses about "online" and latent social-cognitive mechanisms of aggression and violence. With respect to emotional functioning, appraisal theories have evolved out of repeated empirical investigations of social-cognitive foundations of discrete emotions such as anger, fear, and guilt.[10] Furthermore, research on implicit social cognition has examined nonconscious biases in humans and how such biases contribute to social action of legal relevance. Out of these scientific theories and research programs have developed further advances, such as theoretical statements of evaluative

[3] *See, e.g.*, Isaac Ehrlich, *On the Usefulness of Controlling Individuals: An Economic Analysis of Rehabilitation, Incapacitation, and Deterrence*, 71 AM. ECON. REV. 307 (1981).

[4] *E.g.*, Adrian Raine, *Psychopathy, Violence, and Brain Imaging*, *in* VIOLENCE AND PSYCHOPATHY 35 (Adrian Raine & José Sanmartín eds., 2001).

[5] *E.g.*, William E. Copeland, Shari Miller-Johnson, Gordon Keeler, Adrian Angold & E. Jane Costello, *Childhood Psychiatric Disorders and Young Adult Crime: A Prospective, Population-Based Study*, 164 AM. J. PSYCHIATRY 1668 (2007).

[6] *E.g.*, Machteld Hoeve, Arjan Blokland, Judith S. Dubas, Rolf Loeber, Jan R.M. Gerris & Peter H. van der Laan, *Trajectories of Delinquency and Parenting Styles*, 36 J. ABNORMAL CHILD PSYCHOL. 223 (2008).

[7] Craig A. Anderson & Karen E. Dill, *Video Games and Aggressive Thoughts, Feelings, and Behavior in the Laboratory and in Life*, 78 J. PERSONALITY & SOC. PSYCHOL. 772 (2000).

[8] *E.g.*, Nicki R. Crick & Kenneth A. Dodge, *A Review and Reformulation of Social Information-Processing Mechanisms in Children's Social Adjustment*, 115 PSYCHOL. BULL. 74 (1994).

[9] *E.g.*, L. Rowell Huesmann, *The Role of Social Information Processing and Cognitive Schema in the Acquisition and Maintenance of Habitual Aggressive Behavior*, *in* HUMAN AGGRESSION: THEORIES, RESEARCH, AND IMPLICATIONS FOR SOCIAL POLICY 73 (Russell G. Geen & Edward Donnerstein eds., 1998).

[10] *E.g.*, Craig A. Smith & Richard S. Lazarus, *Appraisal Components, Core Relational Themes, and the Emotions*, 7 COGNITION & EMOTION 233 (1993).

judgment and decision making[11] in the development of antisocial behavior and violence subtypes models that delineate alternative forms of antisocial conduct according to etiology, structure, function, phenomenology, and developmental course.[12]

Dodge's SIP model is highlighted here for four reasons:

1. Compared to other psychological models, SIP has received considerable empirical support and has been demonstrated with a broad variety of populations to account for individual differences in various components of antisocial functioning.
2. SIP is configured such that it may explain both emotional and behavioral outcomes – as a result, it can account for processes that have been the focus of alternative models such as appraisal theories of emotion.
3. SIP recognizes a broad range of social-cognitive research, including that which has nonconscious operating as its focus (e.g., research on implicit social cognition) in its explanation of both latent (or offline) mental structures and real-time (or online) cognitive processing.
4. SIP is uniquely formulated such that it may be used as a heuristic for understanding mens rea as well as framings of rationality in affirmative defenses in criminal law.

In this vein, a critical analysis of models of primary (online) versus secondary (latent) social cognition is presented to demonstrate how functionally distinct components of mental operating may play different roles in understanding and assessing the mental states of criminal wrongdoing. The progress of the social-cognitive models presented herein in identifying (and capturing the extent of) the role of social cognition in antisocial development is demonstrated, and directions in which such research is going (and needs to go) are identified. The role of social cognition in a larger, more interdisciplinary framework of the development of antisocial behavior is also considered.[13] This chapter provides the foundation on which discussion of specific intersections between developmental social cognition and criminal law in subsequent chapters rests.

[11] Reid G. Fontaine, *Toward a Conceptual Framework of Instrumental Antisocial Decision-Making and Behavior in Youth*, 27 CLINICAL PSYCHOL. REV. 655 (2007).

[12] Kenneth A. Dodge, *The Structure and Function of Reactive and Proactive Aggression, in* THE DEVELOPMENT AND TREATMENT OF CHILDHOOD AGGRESSION 201 (Debra J. Pepler & Kenneth H. Rubin eds., 1991).

[13] Kenneth A. Dodge, Gregory S. Pettit, Cynthia L. McClaskey & Melissa M. Brown, *Social Competence in Children*, 51 MONOGRAPHS SOC'Y RES. CHILD DEV. i (1986); Isabela Granic & Gerald R. Patterson, *Toward a Comprehensive Model of Antisocial Development: A Dynamic Systems Approach*, 113 PSYCHOL. REV. 101 (2006).

EARLY SOCIAL-COGNITIVE MODELS OF AGGRESSIVE BEHAVIOR

In the early to mid-twentieth century, two social-cognitive models of aggressive behavior in humans prevailed: Professor Len Berkowitz's frustration-aggression hypothesis and Professor Al Bandura's social learning theory. Both models represented significant advances from earlier theories. The emphasis that each placed on social-cognitive processes was undeniably critical to their empirical successes and contributed significantly to their improvement from theories that characterized aggression as instinct.[14] As is later evidenced, however, more recent social-cognitive models, highlighted by research on subtypes of antisocial behavior, have suggested that these early theories were each geared toward explaining individual subtypes of antisocial behavior. Regardless, the influence of these early models has been long-standing, and some of their principle lessons remain at the forefront of contemporary research on the psychology of aggression and violence.

Berkowitz's Frustration-Aggression Hypothesis

The idea that aggression stems from frustration was first posited by a group of behavioral scientists led by Professor John Dollard in 1939.[15] In this work, Dollard and his colleagues made sweeping, definitive assertions about the relation of frustration and aggressive behavior, including that "the occurrence of aggressive behavior always presupposes the existence of frustration" and "that the existence of frustration always leads to some form of aggression."[16] Although there was early empirical support for the frustration-aggression link,[17] the breadth of its validity was soon challenged by research that suggested that frustration may not *always* produce aggression, and in addition, aggression may not *always* be preceded by frustration.[18]

14 Although lacking empirical support in human studies, the aggression-as-instinct perspectives persisted into the second half of the twentieth century. Perhaps most popular among them was that of Professor Konrad Lorenz. *See* KONRAD LORENZ, *ON AGGRESSION* (Marjorie K. Wilson trans., 1966).

15 JOHN DOLLARD, LEONARD W. DOOB, NEAL E. MILLER, O.H. MOWRER & ROBERT R. SEARS, *FRUSTRATION AND AGGRESSION* (1939).

16 *Id.* at 1.

17 Leonard W. Doob & Robert R. Sears, *Factors Determining Substitute Behavior and the Overt Expression of Aggression*, 34 J. ABNORMAL & SOCIAL PSYCHOL. 293 (1939).

18 Scientists who disseminated this body of research included some of Dollard's coauthors on the original 1939 paper that advanced the frustration-aggression relation. *Id.*; O. HOBART MOWRER, *LEARNING THEORY AND BEHAVIOR* (1960); Robert R. Sears, *Non-Aggressive Reactions to Frustration*, 48 PSYCHOL. REV. 343 (1941); Neal E. Miller, *The Frustration-Aggression Hypothesis*, 48 PSYCHOL. REV. 337 (1941). As will soon be evident, however, the

Berkowitz subsequently contributed a remarkable body of theoretical and scientific work to the topic and, as a result, is credited for having refined the frustration-aggression hypothesis in important ways.[19] Critical to the advances made by Berkowitz was his persistence in questioning the breadth of the causal statement of frustration and aggression and identifying key social-cognitive and emotional mechanisms (or "instigators") in the enactment of aggressive conduct. Berkowitz characterized aggression as an angry, hostile response to cues that are perceived in ways that cause a person to experience frustration. This articulation of the phenomenology of aggression was far more complex than that of Dollard and his colleagues in that it recognized the importance of anger and hostility as aggressogenic agents in the stimulus-response sequence, as well as social-cognitive mechanisms such as interpretation, goal clarification, outcome expectation, and emotion regulation. Stimuli that are frustrating for various reasons may promote aggressive reactivity. However, frustrating stimuli that are interpreted as unjustifiably hostile or threatening, or are deemed to unfairly undermine one's goals and desired outcomes, are more likely to cause the individual anger in response, an emotional instigator that operates to release an aggressive response to the aversive cue. In this way, Berkowitz described social cognition as a mediator of the stimulus-emotional response course and, more completely, explained its importance to our understanding of antisocial behavior, social cognition, and emotion as unique mediators (or instigators) of aggressive reactivity in the larger stimulus-behavioral response sequence.

Berkowitz's model acknowledges the basic sequence of stimulus-to-frustration experience to aggressive response first submitted by Dollard and his colleagues, although it emphasizes the importance of these additional components and purports that a more valid explanation of aggression must recognize a greater range of complexities in human processing and functioning. By structuring his model this way, Berkowitz not only advanced the idea

language "some form of aggression" later took on new meaning after research on antisocial subtypes uniquely characterized frustrated aggression as *reactive* as opposed to *instrumental*. For a review, see Reid G. Fontaine, *Disentangling the Psychology and Law of Instrumental and Reactive Subtypes of Aggression*, 13 PSYCHOL. PUB. POL'Y & L. 143 (2007).

19 LEONARD BERKOWITZ, *AGGRESSION: A SOCIAL PSYCHOLOGICAL ANALYSIS* (1962) [hereinafter BERKOWITZ, *AGGRESSION*]; Leonard Berkowitz, *Situational and Personal Conditions Governing Reactions to Aggressive Cues*, *in* PERSONALITY AT THE CROSSROADS: CURRENT ISSUES IN INTERACTIONAL PSYCHOLOGY 165 (David Magnusson & Norman S. Endler eds., 1977); Leonard Berkowitz, *Whatever Happened to the Frustration-Aggression Hypothesis?*, 21 AM. BEHAV. SCIENTIST 691 (1978); Leonard Berkowtiz, *The Experience of Anger as a Parallel Process in the Display of Impulsive, "Angry" Aggression*, *in* 1 AGGRESSION: THEORETICAL AND EMPIRICAL REVIEWS, THEORETICAL AND METHODOLOGICAL ISSUES 103 (Russell G. Geen & Edward I. Donnerstein eds., 1983).

that the relation between frustration and aggression may be limited by circumstance and context, but, via his emphasis on the role of social cognition, also set the stage for aggression to be understood and studied as a product of human learning and development. However refined, the frustration-aggression hypothesis has continued to have as its focus the negative, potentially dysregulating emotions of frustration, anger, and hostility. From this perspective, aggression is a function of unpleasant emotional arousal experienced in response to the perception of an aversive stimulus. As is discussed later in this chapter, this characterization may be more uniquely tied to a subtype of externalizing conduct called reactive aggression, a point that is central to scientific criticism of the frustration-aggression hypothesis.[20]

Bandura's Social Learning Theory

In contrast to the frustration-aggression hypothesis that placed aggression squarely in the camp of emotion dysregulation, Bandura theorized that aggression is learned by observing its enactment in one's social environment.[21] Observational learning dictates that children learn how to act by watching how others – most importantly, adults – behave and associating these behaviors with the results to which they lead, or alternatively, the absence of particular results. Children who are exposed to aggressive exchanges by which the aggressor is rewarded or, at least, avoids punishment are more likely to internalize aggressive behaviors as their own. In contrast, children who are exposed to aggressive exchanges in which the aggressor is punished are less likely to internalize and imitate aggressive behavior. Likewise, children for whom aggressive behavior is not modeled by adults are less likely than those who observe aggressive behavior to lead to nonnegative (neutral and positive) outcomes to demonstrate an aggressive social style for the simple reason that they cannot observationally learn a behavior to which they have no exposure.

As children who have learned aggressive behavior grow and develop cognitively, they may become more skilled at defining aggressive strategies for approaching and realizing their goals. This is particularly likely if their initial, less developed aggressive strategies were met with success, serving to reinforce their association between aggression and positive results. This reflects

[20] *See, e.g.*, Dodge, *supra* note 12.

[21] Albert Bandura & Richard H. Walters, *Social Learning and Personality Development* (1963); Albert Bandura, *Aggression: A Social Learning Analysis* (1973) [hereinafter Bandura, *Aggression*]; Albert Bandura, *Social Learning Theory* (1977) [hereinafter Bandura, *Social Learning Theory*]; Albert Bandura, *Social Foundations of Thought and Action: A Social Cognitive Theory* (1986).

the importance of both observational and enactive learning in the development of antisocial behavior.[22] In addition, implicit in this developmental statement is (1) the interaction of individual systems[23] (cognition and behavior), by which one's thoughts and behaviors influence each other in a reciprocal fashion across time, as well as (2) transactions between the individual and environment,[24] by which one's exchanges with his environment shape both his own functioning and external factors in his social world, in a dynamic, reciprocal fashion, in the course of aggressive social development. These principles

[22] As opposed to observational learning that occurs as a function of watching the attitudes (e.g., hostility) and behaviors (e.g., aggression) of others and associating these forms of functioning with specific outcomes (e.g., rewards), "enactive" learning occurs as a function of one engaging in behavior himself and developing his social attitude and behavioral approach by associating environmental responses with his enacted behaviors. Professor Rowell Huesmann has discussed the distinction between observational and enactive learning. *See* Huesmann, *supra* note 9, at 73; L. Rowell Huesmann & Jessica F. Moise, *Stability and Continuity of Aggression from Early Childhood to Young Adulthood, in* YOUTH VIOLENCE: PREVENTION, INTERVENTION, AND SOCIAL POLICY 73 (Daniel J. Flannery & C. Ronald Huff eds., 1999); *see also* Reid G. Fontaine, *Online Social Decision Making and Antisocial Behavior: Some Essential but Neglected Issues*, 28 CLINICAL PSYCHOL. REV. 17 (2008) (discussing the distinction as it relates to the development of social-information-processing models of aggression). In addition, the role of enactive learning in the development of children's aggressive behavior has been explored and supported in independent empirical investigations. *See* Reid G. Fontaine, Chongming Yang, Kenneth A. Dodge, John E. Bates & Gregory S. Pettit, *Testing an Individual Systems Model of Response Evaluation and Decision (RED) and Antisocial Behavior Across Adolescence*, 79 CHILD DEV. 462 (2008) [hereinafter Fontaine et al., *Testing*]; L. Rowell Huesmann & Nancy G. Guerra, *Children's Normative Beliefs About Aggression and Aggressive Behavior*, 72 J. PERSONALITY & SOC. PSYCHOL. 408 (1997).

[23] Individual systems models have been advanced theoretically and supported empirically in recent scientific studies. Reid G. Fontaine, *Applying Systems Principles to Models of Social Information Processing and Aggressive Behavior in Youth*, 11 AGGRESSION & VIOLENT BEHAV. 64 (2006) (discussing theoretical advancement of individual systems models); Fontaine et al., *Testing*, *supra* note 22 (providing empirical support); Gian V. Caprara, Reid G. Fontaine, Roberta Fida, Marinella Paciello, Marie S. Tisak & Kenneth A. Dodge, *The Contributions and Reciprocal Influences of Irritability, Hostile Rumination, and Moral Disengagement to Aggression and Violence in Adolescence* (Nov. 5, 2010) (unpublished manuscript, on file with lead author).

[24] Transactional systems theory has received considerable theoretical and scientific attention, perhaps most notably by Professor Arnold Sameroff. *See, e.g.*, Arnold J. Sameroff, *Transactional Risk Factors and Prevention, in* PREVENTING MENTAL DISORDERS: A RESEARCH PERSPECTIVE 74 (Jane A. Steinberg & Morton M. Silverman eds., 1987); Arnold J. Sameroff & Michael J. MacKenzie, *Research Strategies for Capturing Transactional Models of Development: The Limits of the Possible*, 15 DEV. & PSYCHOPATHOLOGY 613 (2003); *see also* Reid G. Fontaine & Kenneth A. Dodge, *Social Information Processing and Aggressive Behavior: A Transactional Perspective, in* THE TRANSACTIONAL MODEL OF DEVELOPMENT: HOW CHILDREN AND CONTEXTS SHAPE EACH OTHER 117 (Arnold Sameroff ed., 2009) (demonstrating a conceptual application of transactional systems theory to the development of social-information processing and aggression).

have remained important in social-cognitive theories of aggression and have been refined considerably in contemporary models of the development of social-cognitive processing and antisocial conduct.

More than any theory of aggression before it, Bandura's social learning theory emphasized the role of social cognition in the development of antisocial behavior. It continues to be a highly influential model and has impacted contemporary behavioral science in numerous ways. In addition to the broad impact of social learning theory, Bandura's research on two specific areas of social-cognitive functioning – that of self-efficacy and moral disengagement – deserve special note.

Research on self-efficacy beliefs, or one's confidence in carrying out a particular behavior, is critical to understanding differences in individuals' behavioral proclivities and styles.[25] Self-efficacy is positively related to preference for the behavior over alternative behaviors, frequency of engaging in the behavior, and the success with which the behavior is performed (i.e., the likelihood that enactment of the behavior serves to realize the desired goal). Of course, the degree to which self-efficacy with respect to a specified behavior is related to the behavior's enactment may vary by context.[26] Still, the correlation is undeniable, and this psychological construct has played an important role in contemporary models of aggressogenic decision making.[27]

More recently, Bandura, along with Professor Gian Vittorio Caprara and other Roman colleagues, has investigated a complex social-cognitive construct called moral disengagement.[28] Moral disengagement is the process by which the moral content or qualities of an antisocial behavior are detached from it, whereby a person may then be more likely and able to enact the antisocial behavior as a means by which to achieve an instrumental goal. The disengagement of the moral aspects of the behavior relieves the ethical conflict that a potential actor may otherwise have in the course of considering performing a

[25] *See* Albert Bandura, *Self-Efficacy: Toward a Unifying Theory of Behavioral Change*, 84 PSYCHOL. REV. 191 (1977); ALBERT BANDURA, *SELF-EFFICACY: THE EXERCISE OF CONTROL* (1997); *see also* Cynthia A. Erdley & Steven R. Asher, *Children's Social Goals and Self-Efficacy Perceptions as Influences on Their Responses to Ambiguous Provocation*, 67 CHILD DEV. 1329 (1996).

[26] Norman T. Feather, *Expectancy-Value Approaches: Present Status and Future Directions*, *in* EXPECTATIONS AND ACTIONS: EXPECTANCY-VALUE MODELS IN PSYCHOLOGY 395 (Norman T. Feather ed., 1982).

[27] *See, e.g.*, Fontaine, *supra* note 11; Reid G. Fontaine & Kenneth A. Dodge, *Real-Time Decision Making and Aggressive Behavior in Youth: A Heuristic Model of Response Evaluation and Decision (RED)*, 32 AGGRESSIVE BEHAV. 604 (2006).

[28] Albert Bandura, Claudio Barbaranelli, Gian V. Caprara & Concetta Pastorelli, *Mechanisms of Moral Disengagement in the Exercise of Moral Agency*, 71 J. OF PERSONALITY & SOC. PSYCHOL. 364 (1996); Caprara et al., *supra* note 23.

behavior that would naturally be understood as morally wrong. For example, if an individual identifies an opportunity to easily steal a purse from a woman who has it hanging on the back of her chair in a restaurant, the potential actor may nullify the wrongfulness of stealing the purse by telling himself that anyone stupid enough to leave her purse out in the open deserves to have it stolen. Of course, if the woman *deserves* to have her purse stolen, then the immoral content of stealing the purse has been removed. There are numerous mechanisms by which moral disengagement may be realized. Likewise, there may be alternative developmental courses by which one arrives at the practice of moral disengagement and by which it becomes a persistent characteristic of a person's antisocial lifestyle. A fuller discussion and analysis of these and other issues with respect to what this psychological phenomenon may mean for legal wrongdoing and culpability is provided in Chapter 5.

SOCIAL-INFORMATION PROCESSING

Beginning in the 1980s, the focus of social-cognitive models of aggression shifted from global psychological constructs (e.g., emotion regulation) to online (or "in the moment") processing of social and environmental cues in real time.[29] The impetus for this shift was twofold. First, psychologists appreciated the merits of the theories advanced by Berkowitz and Bandura but considered that a more comprehensive model might have accounted for the key sets of mechanisms that these theories articulated.[30] Second, the latter half of the twentieth century saw a considerable increase in scientific attention to information-processing theories in traditional cognitive psychology, computer science, and artificial intelligence.[31] With this new theoretical focus came a

[29] Kenneth A. Dodge, *A Social Information Processing Model of Social Competence in Children*, *in* 18 COGNITIVE PERSPECTIVES ON CHILDREN'S SOCIAL AND BEHAVIORAL DEVELOPMENT: THE MINNESOTA SYMPOSIA ON CHILD PSYCHOLOGY 77–125 (Marion Perlmutter ed., 1986); L. Rowell Huesmann, *An Information Processing Model for the Development of Aggression*, 14 AGGRESSIVE BEHAV. 13 (1988); Richard M. McFall, *A Review and Reformulation of the Concept of Social Skills*, 4 BEHAV. ASSESSMENT 1 (1982).

[30] Dodge, *supra* note 12; Kenneth A. Dodge & David Schwartz, *Social Information Processing Mechanisms in Aggressive Behavior*, *in* HANDBOOK OF ANTISOCIAL BEHAVIOR 171 (David M. Stoff, James Breiling & Jack D. Maser eds., 1997).

[31] JOHN MCSHANE, *COGNITIVE DEVELOPMENT: AN INFORMATION PROCESSING APPROACH* (1991); Allen Newell, *The Knowledge Level*, 18 ARTIFICIAL INTELLIGENCE 87 (1982); ALLEN NEWELL & HERBERT A. SIMON, *HUMAN PROBLEM SOLVING* (1972); Stephen E. Palmer & Ruth Kimchi, *The Information Processing Approach to Cognition*, *in* APPROACHES TO COGNITION: CONTRASTS AND CONTROVERSIES 37 (Terry J. Knapp & Lynn C. Robertson eds., 1986); La Pearl L. Winfrey & Marvin R. Goldfried, *Information Processing and the Human Change Process*, *in* INFORMATION PROCESSING APPROACHES TO CLINICAL PSYCHOLOGY 241 (Rick E. Ingram ed., 1986).

shift in methodology and empirical approach. It was asserted that the development of social cognition and aggression may be better studied and understood according to a perspective that framed social learning in the transactional context of ongoing social interaction.

During this period, SIP models were designed to depict various mental processes that might be activated in the course of making meaning of continual changes in one's social environment and determining how to behaviorally respond when cued by it. Introductory models from the 1980s served as a theoretical platform for immediate empirical investigation, and the results from early studies fed directly back into the evolution of SIP theory. Reformulated models of SIP were primarily advanced by two independent research programs, those of Professors Kenneth Dodge[32] and Rowell Huesmann.[33] Although both programs of investigating SIP have shared a theoretical focus, they are conceptually distinct in important ways, and, as a result, have contributed uniquely to the science and knowledge base of social cognition and aggressive behavior.

Dodge's Social-Information Processing Model

Of the two models, Dodge's has received the most empirical support. For that matter, there is no social-cognitive model of aggressive behavior – SIP or otherwise – that is more empirically substantiated. Dodge formulated SIP as a developmental model of social learning and behavioral competence in children. According to Dodge's framework, children who develop and maintain greater SIP skills are more likely to demonstrate an interpersonal behavioral pattern that is socially adjusted, adaptive, and normal. Those who lack SIP skills and demonstrate social-cognitive problems of various sorts (e.g., decision-making biases) are less likely to be socially competent, and in the extreme, SIP problems may play a critical pathogenic role in the development of mental illness and chronic antisocial conduct problems.

Although there have since been numerous, significant advancements and refinements in the evolution of SIP theory, the reformulated statement of SIP, offered in 1994 by Dodge and his colleague, Professor Nicki Crick, posits a series of five steps (or sets) of social-cognitive operations that are potentially activated in response to being presented with a social cue.[34] Upon the introduction of a social stimulus, the responding individual (1) perceives, transforms,

[32] Crick & Dodge, *supra* note 8; Dodge & Schwartz, *supra* note 30.

[33] Craig A. Anderson & L. Rowell Huesmann, *Human Aggression: A Social-Cognitive View, in* THE SAGE HANDBOOK OF SOCIAL PSYCHOLOGY 296 (Michael A. Hogg & Joel Cooper eds., 2003); Huesmann, *supra* note 9, at 73.

[34] Crick & Dodge, *supra* note 8.

and organizes incoming information related to the stimulus (*encoding of cues*); (2) makes meaning of the stimulus via causality, affect, and intent attributions, and discerns its personal significance (*interpretation of cues*); (3) identifies and prioritizes goals that may bear relevance to how to respond to the stimulus (*clarification of goals*); (4) formulates alternative responses to the stimulus either by generating them anew or retrieving them from memory (*response access or construction*); and (5) assesses said alternative responses across different evaluative domains in the process of selecting one (*response decision*) for behavioral enactment. The product of this sequence – a behavioral response to the social stimulus – may serve as a stimulus itself, calling for a response from the initial stimulus actor or others in the responding individual's social sphere. In this reciprocal fashion, an individual continues to transact with her environment in the context of ongoing social interaction. Of course, the individual's processing changes as a function of her interactions with her environment and, in this way, illustrates that concept of enactive learning (or learning by doing). Thus the model, by its nature, reflects transactional development at the level of the individual human. Although fuller discussions of certain components of SIP are provided in subsequent chapters that address specific links between social-cognitive functioning and issues of rational capacity and criminal responsibility in law, a brief review of the current state of research across SIP steps is in order.

Step One: Encoding of Cues

The first step of SIP, *encoding of cues*, has remained understudied, as compared to some other social-cognitive operations posited by SIP. At times, it has been studied in conjunction with step two, *interpretation of cues*,[35] and has been treated, at least at a conceptual level, as the necessary underpinning of subsequent attributional and interpretational operations.[36] Encoding of cues

[35] *E.g.*, Kenneth A. Dodge & Cynthia L. Frame, *Social Cognitive Biases and Deficits in Aggressive Boys*, 53 Child Dev. 620 (1982).

[36] In their 1994 reformulation of SIP, Crick and Dodge discussed the encoding of cues and interpretation of cues steps in combination. *See* Crick & Dodge, *supra* note 8, at 83–87. In addition, in the psycholegal and criminal-law theory literatures, I have emphasized the importance of considering both steps together in an attempt to better explain the psychological factors involved in cognitive biases by which individuals tend to interpret ambiguous social cues as wrongful and intentionally hostile. *See* Reid G. Fontaine, *Reactive Cognition, Reactive Emotion: Toward a More Psychologically-Informed Understanding of Reactive Homicide*, 14 Psychol. Pub. Pol'y & L. 243 (2008) [hereinafter Fontaine, *Reactive Cognition*]; Reid G. Fontaine, *The Wrongfulness of Wrongly Interpreting Wrongfulness: Provocation, Interpretational Bias, and Heat of Passion Homicide*, 12 New Crim. L. Rev. 69 (2009) [hereinafter Fontaine, *Wrongfulness*].

involves, at a basic processing level, identification or acknowledgment of the stimulus, as well as transformation of information about the stimulus and its various features so that it may be represented in a fashion that the responding individual can recognize and interpret. Encoding is at the foundation of perception, by which an individual makes meaning of sensory information by transforming and arranging it into a pattern that can be related to internalized (or stored) information that is organized schematically in one's memory. The responding individual develops a representation of the situation at hand and matches it – or at least attempts to match it – to representations of past similar situations that are internally stored. The encoding-of-cues step of SIP is hypothesized to embody not only the transformation and organization of external cues, such as structural features of the social stimulus, but internal cues, such as physiological functions that are activated or experienced at the time the social stimulus is presented.

Early SIP research examined encoding-of-cues processes in aggressive and otherwise socially maladjusted youths as compared to their nonaggressive, socially adjusted peers. A set of studies from the 1980s demonstrated that, compared to their socially competent peers, aggressive youths are more likely to encode a smaller number of cues,[37] are less likely to seek additional information in situations that are unclear as to their meaning,[38] selectively attend to and focus on hostile[39] and threatening[40] cues, and recall threatening cues from memory when perceiving social stimuli.[41] Empirical research that has employed direct observation of children in natural play suggests that these cognitive tendencies are related to being the subject of not only negative social treatment, but also the infliction of negative social treatment on others.[42] Subsequent research uniquely linked encoding errors to *reactive* aggressive youths (or youths who have a tendency to react aggressively in situations that leave open the question as to whether they are being adversely treated by others).[43]

37 *See, e.g.*, Kenneth A. Dodge & Joseph P. Newman, *Biased Decision-Making Processes in Aggressive Boys*, 90 J. ABNORMAL PSYCHOL. 375 (1981); Kenneth A. Dodge & A. M. Tomlin, *Utilization of Self-Schemas as a Mechanism of Interpretational Bias in Aggressive Children*, 5 SOC. COGNITION 280 (1987).

38 *See, e.g.*, Ronald G. Slaby & Nancy G. Guerra, *Cognitive Mediators of Aggression in Adolescent Offenders: 1. Assessment*, 24 DEVELOPMENTAL PSYCHOL. 580 (1988).

39 Karen R. Gouze, *Attention and Social Problem Solving as Correlates of Aggression in Preschool Males*, 15 J. ABNORMAL CHILD PSYCHOL. 181 (1987).

40 Dodge & Frame, *supra* note 35.

41 *Id.*

42 *Id.*

43 *See* Kenneth A. Dodge, John E. Lochman, Jennifer D. Harnish, John E. Bates & Gregory S. Pettit, *Reactive and Proactive Aggression in School Children and Psychiatrically Impaired*

Research on social-cognitive processing and trait anger has also made a substantial contribution toward understanding relations between lower-ordered processing mechanisms and antisocial inclination.[44] Numerous studies have found that angry individuals selectively attend to hostile cues.[45] This finding has been replicated across independent laboratories using various methodologies.[46] Angry individuals tend to focus their attention on stimuli, and aspects of stimuli, that lend themselves to hostile interpretations and, in turn, angry responses. In this way, angry individuals exhibit social-cognitive biases that reinforce a stable pattern of anger experiences.

There remains some question, however, as to whether such an encoding problem precedes or follows a related bias toward interpreting ambiguously provocative or otherwise negative cues as hostile (represented by step two of SIP).[47] SIP asserts encoding-of-cues as the first step of social-cognitive processing, suggesting that *encoding* precedes *interpretation*, an idea that is consistent with some scholars' view that the type of conscious, conceptual processing that may be characteristic of attributional and interpretational operations necessitates some prior degree of attention, encoding, and perception.[48] However, SIP also accommodates social-cognitive pathways that are alternative to those depicted linearly, including that by which encoding is informed by interpretational processes via a feedback loop.[49] This is a critical point because it is

Chronically Assaultive Youth, 106 J. ABNORMAL PSYCHOL. 37 (1997). A discussion of instrumental (or proactive) and reactive subtypes of aggression is provided later in this chapter.

44 For a small sample of this research, see Paul Smith & Mitch Waterman, *Processing Bias for Aggression Words in Forensic and Nonforensic Samples*, 17 COGNITION & EMOTION 681 (2003); Paula Smith & Mitch Waterman, *Role of Experience in Processing Bias for Aggressive Words in Forensic and Non-Forensic Populations*, 30 AGGRESSIVE BEHAV. 105 (2004); Jack van Honk, Adriaan Tuiten, Edward de Haan, Marcel van den Hout & Henderickus Stam, *Attention Biases for Angry Faces: Relationships to Trait Anger and Anxiety*, 15 COGNITION & EMOTION 279 (2001).

45 For a brief overview, see Benjamin M. Wilkowski, Michael D. Robinson, Robert D. Gordon & Wendy Troop-Gordon, *Tracking the Evil Eye: Trait Anger and Selective Attention within Ambiguously Hostile Scenes*, 41 J. RES. PERSONALITY 650, 651 (2007).

46 *Id.*

47 *Id.*

48 Stanislas Dehaene, *Imaging Conscious and Subliminal Word Processing*, *in* DEVELOPING INDIVIDUALITY IN THE HUMAN BRAIN: A TRIBUTE TO MICHAEL I. POSNER 65 (Ulrich Mayr, Edward Awh & Stephen W. Keele eds., 2005); Pierre Philippot, Céline Baeyens, Céline Douilliez & Benjamin Francart, *Cognitive Regulation of Emotion: Application to Clinical Disorders*, *in* THE REGULATION OF EMOTION 71, 82 (Pierre Philippot & Robert S. Feldman eds., 2004). For a recent empirical examination that supports the relation between encoding and interpretation, as related to anger, in the opposite direction, see Wilkowski et al., *supra* note 45, at 651.

49 Crick & Dodge, *supra* note 8, at 76 (schematically illustrating in figure 2 the specific feedback loop by which encoding may be informed by interpretation).

likely the case that most processing of social cues is nonlinear and that the order of SIP operations across humans takes on infinite patterns or sequences. Furthermore, it may well be that encoding often precedes interpretation *and* interpretation often precedes encoding. If so, this may explain, at least in part, why scientists disagree as to the order of these social-cognitive processes with respect to trait anger – that is, both paths may be valid, dependent on the specific social-cognitive context. Also, this may explain – again, at least in part – why some scholars have continued to discuss the first two SIP steps in conjunction with each other.[50] Discussion of the interpretation-of-cues step may bring further clarity to this latter point.

Step Two: Interpretation of Cues

Elsewhere, I have repeatedly stressed the need to recognize research on the encoding-of-cues step of SIP in discussions of attributional and interpretational processes related to aggression and anger.[51] During the second step of SIP, *interpretation of cues*, the responder attempts to understand the degree to which the social stimulus has personal meaning. SIP asserts that this "meaning making" and understanding of personal relevance is conducted via multiple attributions of causality, intent, and affect, as well as other evaluative processes such as the history or nature of the relationship between the stimulus actor and the responding individual.

Causal attributions are subjective determinations that an individual, or collection of individuals, caused a particular outcome. If the responding individual believes that he has suffered some form of harm, he may naturally be interested in determining the source of the harm. This process, of course, is easier to complete with confidence in some scenarios and harder in others. If the responding individual is hit by an object and there is only one other person in the vicinity, a causal attribution is more likely to be quickly and definitively made.

Research on the relation between causal attributions and aggression in youths has been mixed.[52] Some recent research, however, has supported the hypothesis that aggression is founded, in part, on causal attributions in adult males. Professor Todd Moore and his colleagues found that abusive males are more likely than their nonabusive male peers to attribute responsibility to female romantic partners in provocative situations. Perhaps most critical,

[50] *Id.* at 83–87.

[51] Fontaine, *supra* note 18, at 145–46; Fontaine, *Reactive Cognition*, *supra* note 36; Fontaine, *Wrongfulness*, *supra* note 36, at 79–85.

[52] Crick & Dodge, *supra* note 8.

however, is that the greatest difference was found with respect to female partners' behaviors that were only moderately (as opposed to highly) provocative. That is, in situations that were more definitively provocative, there was less of a difference between abusive and nonabusive males, suggesting that abusive males may be more likely to attribute responsibility to female partners in situations in which the cause of negative outcomes is unclear.[53]

Having made a causal attribution, the responding individual may be further interested in making an inference as to what was the motivation or interest on the part of the causal agent. This is an intent attribution. If the responding individual determines that another person has caused him harm, he may think it important to assess what the person's intent was in doing so. That is, did this person intentionally cause the harm? If so, was the intention positive, such as in the case that the responding individual was forcefully pushed in order to clear him from a larger harm's way (e.g., an uncontrolled automobile), or negative, such as in the case that the stimulus actor simply wanted to cause him pain? Perhaps the stimulus actor caused the harm but did so entirely by accident (benign intent). Judgments as to the nature of the stimulus actor's prebehavioral mental state all fall under the umbrella of intent attributions.

Another type of attribution that may be useful in determining the stimulus actor's intent – and, for this reason, may be necessary to make prior to drawing an inferential conclusion as to the intent of the stimulus – has to do with the stimulus actor's affect. Does the stimulus actor appear to be angry? If so, it may be more likely that his intent was to cause harm. Perhaps the stimulus actor is in a jovial mood, in which case it may be more likely that the harm was caused accidentally or, alternatively, intentionally but with the (perhaps distorted) understanding that his actions were nothing more than friendly horseplay.

In this way, attributions of intent and affect tend to go hand in hand. Unlike the modest link between causal attributional style and aggressive behavior patterns, there has been considerable empirical support for the hypothesis that aggressive behavior emerges out of an individual's judgment that another has caused, or at least attempted to cause, him harm out of negative (or culpable) intent. Called "hostile attributional bias,"[54] the tendency

[53] Todd M. Moore, Richard M. Eisler & Joseph J. Franchina, *Causal Attributions and Affective Responses to Provocative Female Partner Behavior by Abusive and Nonabusive Males*, 15 J. FAM. VIOLENCE 69 (2000).

[54] William Nasby, Brian Hayden & Bella M. DePaulo, *Attributional Bias Among Aggressive Boys to Interpret Unambiguous Social Stimuli as Displays of Hostility*, 89 J. ABNORMAL PSYCHOL. 459 (1980) (coining the term "hostile attributional bias"). This term has remained most popular. *See, e.g.*, James Epps & Philip C. Kendall, *Hostile Attributional Bias in Adults*,

among aggressive individuals to attribute negative intent in ambiguous provocation situations has been found across independent laboratories, participant populations, geographic locations (e.g., different nations), and age groups.[55] In adverse situations in which the stimulus actor's intentions are unclear, antisocial individuals tend to believe that they are being unfairly treated, the stimulus actor's intentions are wrongful, and that the provocateur has acted out of meanness or nastiness. The relation between this set of social-cognitive processes and antisocial behavior has been widely studied.[56] In addition, recent research has linked intent attributional style with a pattern of favorably evaluating aggressive response behaviors. This suggests that the responding individual's judgment that another person is acting with wrongful intent may be followed by the former's determination that aggression is a socially appropriate response.[57]

Finally, as mentioned in the discussion of the encoding-of-cues step, a relation between trait anger and hostile attributional style has been found.[58] Just as antisocial behavior cannot be explained by a single cognitive process, cognitive processes may contribute to multiple outcomes with respect to individual functioning. Individuals who tend to focus on aggressive cues and interpret ambiguous stimuli as definitively hostile and provocative also tend to be angry. Whereas such encoding and interpretation processes likely contribute to anger maintenance, trait anger, in reciprocal turn, likely reinforces one's negative emotogenic processing.[59]

19 COGNITIVE THERAPY & RES. 159 (1995). However, the term "hostile attributional style" has been used increasingly in recent years, in part to highlight the phenomenon as a processing tendency rather than error pattern. *See, e.g.*, Kenneth A. Dodge, *Translational Science in Action: Hostile Attributional Style and the Development of Aggressive Behavior Problems*, 18 DEV. & PSYCHOPATHOLOGY 791 (2006). I prefer the broader term, "provocation interpretational bias," again to emphasize the need to recognize the important role that encoding plays in a bias toward interpreting ambiguous provocations as definitively intentionally harmful. *See, e.g.*, Fontaine, *Reactive Cognition*, note 36.

55 For a qualitative review, see generally Crick & Dodge, *supra* note 8.

56 Bram Orobio de Castro, Jan W. Veerman, Willem Koops, Joop D. Bosch & Heidi J. Monshouwer, *Hostile Attribution of Intent and Aggressive Behavior: A Meta-Analysis*, 73 CHILD DEV. 916 (2002).

57 Reid G. Fontaine, Marieh Tanha, Chongming Yang, Kenneth A. Dodge, John E. Bates & Gregory S. Pettit, *Does Response Evaluation and Decision (RED) Mediate the Relation Between Hostile Attributional Style and Antisocial Behavior in Adolescence?*, 38 J. ABNORMAL CHILD PSYCHOL. 615 (2010).

58 *See, e.g.*, Wilkowski et al., *supra* note 45, at 651.

59 Elsewhere, I have discussed this reciprocal relation among an individual's internal (or intrapersonal) systems (e.g., cognition and emotion) in the development of aggressive behavior. *See* Fontaine, *supra* note 23.

Step Three: Clarification of Goals

According to SIP, an individual identifies and prioritizes his goals in the course of responding to the stimulus actor. This set of processes is hypothesized as step three, clarification of goals. In SIP terms, goals are defined as "focused arousal states that function as orientations toward producing (or wanting to produce) particular outcomes."[60] Goals may be internal (e.g., emotional states) or external (e.g., acquisition of desired goods), and they may be short-term (e.g., outcomes that provide immediate gratification) or long-term (e.g., outcomes that lend themselves to personal reputation or interpersonal relationship development). Certain social cues may be closely tied with specific goals, such as in the case of the provoked individual who wants to avoid appearing weak to others and losing their respect. Other social cues may trigger multiple goals, which at times compete with each other, such as in the case of the provoked individual who wants to both save face in front of his peers and avoid social punishment (such as school detention or police intervention).

Support for this SIP step has largely been drawn from research on the relation between social goals and behavioral adjustment in youths. The basic hypothesis is that youths' behavioral patterns are guided by the types of goals they form and desire to pursue.[61] Restated in terms of antisocial development, youths who generate, maintain, and have interest in pursuing antisocial goals (e.g., wrongfully taking others' belongings) are more likely to demonstrate aggressive and delinquent behavioral patterns.[62] Recent research has shown that both physically (e.g., hitting) and relationally (e.g., social exclusion) aggressive behavioral strategies are related to self-interest, control, and revenge goals in elementary- and middle-school-aged youths.[63] Further understanding may be drawn from research on the kinds of situational outcomes favored by antisocial youths. Outcomes of aggressive strategies that are of especially high value to aggressive youths include gaining control over[64] and

[60] Crick & Dodge, *supra* note 8, at 87.

[61] Kenneth A. Dodge, Steven R. Asher & Jennifer T. Parkhurst, *Social Life as a Goal Coordination Task*, *in* 3 RESEARCH ON MOTIVATION IN EDUCATION 107 (Carole Ames & Russell Ames eds., 1989).

[62] Cynthia A. Erdley & Steven R. Asher, *A Social Goals Perspective on Children's Social Competence*, 7 J. EMOTIONAL & BEHAV. DISORDERS 156 (1999).

[63] Kendra D. Delveaux & Tina Daniels, *Children's Social Cognitions: Physically and Relationally Aggressive Strategies and Children's Goals in Peer Conflict Situations*, 46 MERRILL-PALMER Q. 672 (2000).

[64] Janet P. Boldizar, David G. Perry & Louise C. Perry, *Outcome Values and Aggression*, 60 CHILD DEV. 571 (1989).

causing injury to[65] the target (or victim). In addition, the subtype of proactive aggression (self-initiated aggression enacted in the interest of personal gain) has been uniquely linked with instrumental goals (e.g., acquisition of desired material items) in youth populations.[66]

Another area of scholarly inquiry that is conceptually related to the link between goals and antisocial behavior in social development research is represented in the sociological and criminological literatures. Rational-choice theory[67] states that actors commit crime after estimating the risk involved and comparing the probability of such risk with the desire to achieve the anticipated outcomes of the criminal act in question. Rational-choice theory is not particular to a specific goal or type of goal. The criminal may act out of a variety of interests including thrill seeking, acquisition of money and material belongings, reduction of unpleasant states (e.g., hunger), and exacting revenge or control. Research on rational-choice theory and crime has been met with mixed results. Although there are likely several explanations as to why research findings have not been more consistent, one obvious limitation is that the types of cognitive biases and deficits that have been empirically linked to antisocial individuals are not recognized as playing a role in the enactment of crime. That is, the theory presumes that the criminal is a rational actor, an assumption that is often false.[68] Furthermore, rational-choice theory does not take development (or individual differences in developmental course) of mental processes, goals, and behavioral strategies into account, thus limiting the degree to which it can explain how and why decision-making processes – such as cost-benefit analysis – and crime are related across varied individuals.

The relation between goals and antisocial behavior is reflected throughout criminal law. Demonstrating motive is often a crucial task in criminal procedure, playing an important role in multiple phases of prosecution and sentencing.[69] For example, at trial, demonstration of motive can go directly to the fact finder's determination as to a defendant's mens rea (e.g., whether there

[65] David G. Perry & Kay Bussey, *Self-Reinforcement in High- and Low-Aggressive Boys Following Acts of Aggression*, 48 CHILD DEV. 653 (1977).

[66] *See, e.g.*, Nicki R. Crick & Kenneth A. Dodge, *Social Information-Processing Mechanisms in Reactive and Proactive Aggression*, 67 CHILD DEV. 993 (1996).

[67] *E.g.*, THE REASONING CRIMINAL: RATIONAL CHOICE PERSPECTIVES ON OFFENDING (Derek B. Cornish & Ronald V. Clarke eds., 1986).

[68] *See Are Offenders' Choices Rational?, in* CRIMINOLOGICAL THEORY: CONTEXT AND CONSEQUENCES 278, 278–79 (J. Robert Lilly, Francis T. Cullen & Richard A. Ball eds., 4th ed. 2007).

[69] *See* Douglas N. Husak, *Motive and Criminal Liability*, 8 CRIM. JUST. ETHICS 3 (1989); Carissa B. Hessick, *Motive's Role in Criminal Punishment*, 80 S. CAL. L. REV. 89 (2007); *cf.* Whitley R.P. Kaufman, *Motive, Intention, and Morality in the Criminal Law*, 28 CRIM. JUST. REV. 317 (2003).

existed intent or purpose). At sentencing, motive can be very meaningful with respect to whether the convicted defendant receives a lighter or heavier punishment (functioning as a mitigating or aggravating factor). Furthermore, in homicide law, although statutes are generally not framed according to motive, motives can be related to the type or level of homicide charged and found. For example, homicides that are committed out of monetary and material greed may be more likely framed as first-degree murder, whereas homicides that are committed out of the (at least perceived) retributive goal of exacting justice on a wrongdoer are often treated as the lesser homicides such as second-degree murder or heat-of-passion manslaughter.[70]

Step Four: Response Access or Construction

After the responding individual has some understanding (or mental representation) of the situation at hand and has formed one or more goals, he may begin to consider how to respond. Of course, to do this, one needs to identify at least one possible response to consider. SIP theory posits that during step four, response access or construction (hereafter response access/construction), response options may be (1) recalled from memories of past similar (or at least related) scenarios or, in the case in which the situation at hand is novel in important ways, (2) generated anew. Memories of one's own past behaviors or observations of others' behaviors may be stored in one's associative cognitive network in relation to social schemata (called "behavioral scripts"). Generally stated, a social schema is a mental representation of an interpersonal situation or exchange. Based on personal experiences and observations, a person may develop mental connections between specific social schemata and behavioral scripts. When a social stimulus or situation is presented and (via SIP steps one and two, encoding and interpretation of cues) it is "matched" with a stored schema, the associated behavioral scripts may be accessed (via SIP step four, response access/construction) and used to guide the responding individual's behavior.

In the 1980s, a large number of studies examined the relation between this step of SIP and aggressive behavior in youths. As compared to their nonaggressive peers, aggressive youths generate few response options in social situations and are biased toward generating more aggressive, less prosocial responses across a variety of types of social situations.[71] Collectively, this body of research suggests that, at least in youths, aggressive individuals are limited, in both number and variety, in the degree to which they generate alternative ways of responding in social situations, and that their accessed responses typically

70 Fontaine, *supra* note 18.

71 Crick & Dodge, *supra* note 8, at 88 (providing a review of these studies).

share an antisocial theme. A more recent study found that, at least with respect to a subgroup of aggressive youths who were identified as peer-rejected and reactive in aggressive style, a bias in selecting aggressive responses in social situations may be reduced or eliminated when nonaggressive response options are introduced.[72] This suggests that although some aggressive individuals may be limited in self-generating nonaggressive responses, they are not necessarily prone to disfavoring them when their attention is actively drawn to them.

This body of evidence highlights the likelihood that aggressive individuals vary according to their response access/construction. Whereas some aggressive individuals may be less able to generate nonaggressive response options, others may be quite capable of generating nonaggressive responses but typically do not because they are quicker to access and find acceptable aggressive ones (eliminating the need to consider alternative response routes). Others still may actively consider alternative responses but, after more thoughtful consideration, favor aggressive courses of action. The cognitive issue(s) may vary within individual across time and context, as well.

Step Five: Response Decision

It is difficult to properly discuss processes of response access/construction without contemplating highly related operations by which generated responses are evaluated, compared, and considered for selection and enactment. The fifth and final step of SIP, response decision, posits that, after generating one or more possible responses to the presented stimulus, the responding individual assesses the responses across various domains to select a response for behavioral enactment. Just as SIP presumes the presentation of a social stimulus, the response decision step presumes the identification of at least one possible response. As such, response decision may be immediately limited if an individual's response-access/construction capacity is restricted – that is, one can only evaluate response options to the degree that response options are identified in the first place.

The response decision step has been the focus of numerous empirical studies[73] since it was reformulated by Crick and Dodge in 1994.[74] Response

[72] C. Nannette Wood & Alan M. Gross, *Behavioral Response Generation and Selection of Rejected-Reactive Aggressive, Rejected-Nonagressive, and Average Status Children*, 24 CHILD & FAM. BEHAV. THERAPY 1 (2002).

[73] Reid G. Fontaine, Chongming Yang, Kenneth A. Dodge, Gregory S. Pettit & John E. Bates, *Development of Response Evaluation and Decision (RED) and Antisocial Behavior in Childhood and Adolescence*, 45 DEVELOPMENTAL PSYCHOL. 447 (2009) [hereinafter Fontaine et al., *Development*]; Fontaine et al., *Testing*, *supra* note 22; Reid G. Fontaine, Virginia S. Burks & Kenneth A. Dodge, *Response Decision Processes and Externalizing Behavior Problems in Adolescents*, 14 DEV. & PSYCHOPATHOLOGY 107 (2002) [hereinafter Fontaine et al., *Response*]; Fontaine et al., *supra* note 57.

[74] Crick & Dodge, *supra* note 8.

decision making as a realm of processing has also undergone considerable conceptual development. Recently, my coauthor, Kenneth Dodge, and I advanced an elaborate process model of the response decision step, renamed *response evaluation and decision* (RED).[75] RED proposes a series of online cognitive operations that occur in real time as an individual considers alternative responses to a perceived stimulus situation. For example, when deciding how to respond to a perceived provocation, a person may consider aggressive retaliation. Does he believe that he can successfully retaliate against the perceived provocateur (response efficacy)?[76] Is this a sociomorally acceptable way to behave (response valuation)?[77] What is likely to happen if he retaliates (outcome expectancy)?[78] Is the likely outcome valued favorably, or is it a consequence that should be avoided (outcome valuation)?[79] These questions represent some of the evaluative domains that are hypothesized to be active during response decision making.

RED also incorporates rational thought and impulsivity into the response decision-making framework. For example, the concept of evaluative thresholds is introduced by which mental representations of possible responses may be quickly discarded (if they are obviously infeasible or inadequate in some way) or impulsively selected for immediate behavioral enactment. As discussed in the previous subsection on response-access/construction, some aggressive individuals – most likely those who are prone to impulsive or reactive aggressive behavior – may quickly generate, approve, and select an aggressive behavioral response in the course of processing and determining how to react to a social stimulus that is experienced as unpleasant or aversive.

Recent studies have provided support for a number of critical hypotheses about the role of response decision making in the processing of aggressogenic social cues. RED has been shown to become a reliable, multidimensional psychological construct by the time children enter adolescence.[80] Across adolescence, RED appears to interact with aggressive behavioral patterns in a way that impacts behavioral change across this developmental period.[81] Furthermore, support for the hypothesis that RED mediates the relation between hostile attributional style and antisocial behavior in adolescence has been demonstrated.[82] These and related studies[83] have pointed to the critical

75 Fontaine & Dodge, *supra* note 27.

76 *Id.* at 610.

77 *Id.* at 611.

78 *Id.* at 613.

79 *Id.*

80 Fontaine et al., *Development*, *supra* note 73.

81 Fontaine et al., *Testing*, *supra* note 22.

82 Fontaine et al., *supra* note 57.

83 *E.g.*, Fontaine et al., *Response*, *supra* note 73.

role that evaluative judgment and decision making plays in youth development as children enter adolescence and approach adulthood.

Social-Information Processing and Subtypes of Antisocial Behavior

Research on social information processing and aggressive behavior has also pointed to a distinction between instrumental (or proactive or offensive) and reactive (or hostile or defensive) subtypes of antisocial conduct.[84] Instrumental aggression is characterized as self-initiated, driven by goals of personal gain (e.g., acquisition of money or desired material goods), planned, and executed in a calm, relatively unemotional manner. In contrast, reactive aggression is enacted in emotional response to a stimulus that is perceived to be provocative (evoking anger) or threatening (evoking fear). As such, the goal of reactive aggression is to harm the perceived provocateur or defend oneself. Of course, not all instances of aggressive acts are neatly categorized as instrumental or reactive, and it is not unusual for chronically aggressive individuals to demonstrate patterns of both subtypes of behavior.

Several bodies of scientific research on human and nonhuman animals have contributed to scholarly understanding of the instrumental/reactive aggression dichotomy.[85] One of the most (if not *the* most) substantial contributions is credited to SIP research. Two main SIP hypotheses about subtypes of violence have been advanced.[86] The first uniquely links early processes associated with the first two steps of SIP (encoding and interpretation of cues) with reactive aggression.[87] Reactive aggressive individuals have been found to be particularly biased, even compared to their nonreactive, instrumental aggressive peers, in

84 *See* Dodge, *supra* note 12, at 201–18; Fontaine, *supra* note 18.

85 Dodge, *supra* note 12, at 201–18; Fontaine, *supra* note 18; *see also* Maaike Kempes, Walter Matthys, Han de Vries & Herman van Engeland, *Reactive and Proactive Aggression in Children: A Review of Theory, Findings and the Relevance for Child and Adolescent Psychiatry*, 14 Eur. Child & Adolescent Psychiatry 11 (2005); Benedetto Vitiello & David M. Stoff, *Subtypes of Aggression and Their Relevance to Child Psychiatry*, 36 J. Am. Acad. Child & Adolescent Psychiatry 307 (1997); *cf.* Brad J. Bushman & Craig A. Anderson, *Is It Time to Pull the Plug on the Hostile Versus Instrumental Aggression Dichotomy?*, 108 Psychol. Rev. 273 (2001).

86 For a specific discussion and review of these hypotheses, see Fontaine, *supra* note 18, at 145–46.

87 Crick & Dodge, *supra* note 66; Kenneth A. Dodge & John D. Coie, *Social-Information-Processing Factors in Reactive and Proactive Aggression in Children's Peer Groups*, 53 J. Personality & Soc. Psychol. 1146 (1987); Dodge et al., *supra* note 43; Kenneth A. Dodge, Joseph M. Price, Jo-Anne Bachorowski & Joseph P. Newman, *Hostile Attributional Biases in Severely Aggressive Adolescents*, 99 J. Abnormal Psychol. 385 (1990); David Schwartz, Kenneth A. Dodge, John D. Coie, Julie A. Hubbard, Antonius H.N. Cillessen, Elizabeth A. Lemerise & Helen Bateman, *Social-Cognitive and Behavioral Correlates of Aggression and Victimization in Boys' Play Groups*, 26 J. Abnormal Child Psychol. 431 (1998).

their processing of ambiguous provocation cues. That is, reactive aggressive individuals are especially likely to quickly and definitively interpret ambiguous provocation situations as ones in which the provocateur is acting with hostile intent for the purpose of causing harm to the responding individual.

The second set of findings points to a unique relation between RED biases and instrumental aggressive behavior.[88] As compared to their reactive aggressive and nonaggressive peers, instrumental aggressive youths have been found to favor aggressive behavioral strategies and expect such strategies to lead to positive outcomes. In addition, instrumental aggressive youths prefer goals that are oriented toward personal gain (e.g., acquisition of desired materials objects) as opposed to relational goals that focus on interpersonal values (e.g., friendship development).

RED may provide further utility in the scientific pursuit of defining the distinction between instrumental and reactive violence. One RED hypothesis asserts that whereas instrumental violence is associated with RED mechanisms that are focused on personal gain (such as an expectation that responding aggressively will lead to personal interests such as gaining power and desired material items), reactive violence is uniquely associated with RED mechanisms that lend themselves to retribution, revenge, and self-defense (such as an appraisal that responding aggressively will lead to moral balance because the provocateur's behavior was unwarranted).[89] Although this hypothesis has yet to be rigorously tested, its conceptual basis stems directly from the distinction between goals (or motives) commonly attributed to the instrumental and reactive subtypes of aggression.

Huesmann's Social-Cognitive Information Processing

Another important model of SIP and aggressive behavior has been advanced by Professor Rowell Huesmann.[90] Although Dodge's and Huesmann's models have different foci, they are largely consistent with each other. Whereas Dodge's model has emphasized the importance of conceptual processes of interpretation of cues and evaluation of response options, Huesmann's model has focused on cognitive schemata, behavioral scripts, and normative

[88] Crick & Dodge, *supra* note 66; Schwartz et al., *supra* note 87; Catherine M. Smithmyer, Julie A. Hubbard & Robert F. Simons, *Proactive and Reactive Aggression in Delinquent Adolescents: Relations to Aggression Outcomes Expectancies*, 29 J. CLINICAL CHILD PSYCHOL. 86 (2000).

[89] *See* Fontaine & Dodge, *supra* note 27, at 619–20.

[90] Anderson & Huesmann, *supra* note 33; Huesmann, *supra* note 29; Huesmann, *supra* note 9, at 73–109.

beliefs – processes that are considered to typically activate and operate automatically. In further contrast, Dodge and his colleagues have stressed models of enactive learning via recurrent interpersonal exchange,[91] whereas Huesmann's model has evolved largely as a function of empirical studies of observational learning of aggression.[92]

Still, the models reflect a similar basic framework that has drawn heavily from information-processing models in cognitive psychology,[93] as well as the research programs of Bandura[94] and Berkowitz.[95] Cognitive schemata are the mental representations of social stimuli and situations that are hypothesized to take form as individuals transform incoming information during encoding of cues. Mental representations of social stimuli may then activate behavioral scripts, a process that may be likened to response access. Finally, normative beliefs are internal standards that individuals apply when assessing the acceptability of behaviors. Normative beliefs are consistent with response evaluation processes articulated by RED[96] and representative of the final step of Dodge's SIP model.[97]

Huesmann offers SIP as a mental heuristic by which an individual engages in social responsivity by encoding social stimuli and accessing and enacting their corresponding behavioral scripts. A script represents how to behave in the situation to which it is matched by the responder and functions to guide his behavioral response. Aggressive individuals are expected to have had more opportunity to observe others behaving aggressively – a notion that is consistent with Bandura's social learning theory[98] – and to have developed a greater number of aggressive behavioral scripts that may be triggered by a wider array of interpersonal exchanges.[99] Based on observational learning, which gives rise to one's understanding of functions and outcomes of aggressive behavior by watching the social actions and interactions of others, the individual's associative network may develop such that he may quickly (or even automatically) access and carry out aggressive responses across a variety of social contexts. In this way, Huesmann's model differs from that of Dodge's, the latter of which

91 Fontaine et al., *Testing*, *supra* note 22.

92 L. Rowell Huesmann, *Observational Learning of Violent Behavior: Social and Biological Processes*, *in* THE BIOSOCIAL BASES OF VIOLENCE 69 (Adrain Raine, David P. Farrington, Patricia Brennan & Sarnoff A. Mednick eds., 1997).

93 *E.g.*, Palmer & Kimchi, *supra* note 31; Winfrey & Goldfried, *supra* note 31.

94 *E.g.*, BANDURA, AGGRESSION, *supra* note 21.

95 *E.g.*, BERKOWITZ, AGGRESSION, *supra* note 19.

96 *See* Fontaine & Dodge, *supra* note 27.

97 *See* Crick & Dodge, *supra* note 8, at 88–91.

98 BANDURA, *SOCIAL LEARNING THEORY*, *supra* note 21.

99 Huesmann, *supra* note 9.

places greater emphasis on processes of social evaluation and decision making that are associated with executive function.[100]

Social-Information Processing: Contributions and Caveats

Indeed, SIP has been found to predict alternative patterns of emotional functioning and social conduct within a variety of populations in a variety of settings, from social competence[101] to depression and internalizing problems[102] and antisocial behavior (aggression[103] and delinquency[104]). Relations between SIP operations and antisocial behavior have been found within populations that range by developmental period (childhood,[105] adolescence,[106] and adulthood[107]) and emotional and behavioral distribution (normative,[108] clinical,[109] and incarcerated[110]). This is important to note, because the breadth with which science has demonstrated that SIP is linked with maladjusted, conduct-problem behaviors suggests that the role of SIP in behavioral development and functioning is pervasive across social context, type of individual, and life-course development.

100 *See* Fontaine & Dodge, *supra* note 24; Fontaine et al., *Development*, *supra* note 73.

101 *E.g.*, David J. McDowell, Ross D. Parke & Sue Spitzer, *Parent and Child Cognitive Representations of Social Situations and Children's Social Competence*, 11 Soc. Dev. 469 (2002).

102 *E.g.*, Nancy L. Quiggle, Judy Garber, William F. Panak & Kenneth A. Dodge, *Social Information Processing in Aggressive and Depressed Children*, 63 Child Dev. 1305 (1992).

103 *E.g.*, M. Elizabeth Cuddy & Cynthia Frame, *Comparison of Aggressive and Nonaggressive Boys' Self-Efficacy and Outcome Expectancy Beliefs*, 21 Child Study J. 135 (1991); Amori Y. Mikami, Steve S. Lee, Stephen P. Hinshaw & Benjamin C. Mullin, *Relationships Between Social Information Processing and Aggression Among Adolescent Girls with and without ADHD*, 37 J. Youth & Adolescence 761 (2008).

104 *E.g.*, Coralijn N. Nas, Daniel Brugman & Willem Koops, *Effects of the EQUIP Programme on the Moral Judgement, Cognitive Distortions, and Social Skills of Juvenile Delinquents*, 11 Psychol. Crime & L. 421 (2005).

105 *E.g.*, Robert H. Deluty, *Cognitive Mediation of Aggressive, Assertive, and Submissive Behavior in Children*, 8 Int'l J. Behav. Dev. 355 (1985); Kenneth A. Dodge, *Social Cognition and Children's Aggressive Behavior*, 51 Child Dev. 162 (1980).

106 *E.g.*, Fontaine, *Development*, *supra* note 73; Fontaine et al., *Testing*, *supra* note 22.

107 *E.g.*, Jennifer E. Vitale, Joseph P. Newman, Ralph C. Serin & Daniel M. Bolt, *Hostile Attributions in Incarcerated Adult Male Offenders: An Exploration of Diverse Pathways*, 31 Aggressive Behav. 99 (2005); Epps & Kendall, *supra* note 54.

108 *E.g.*, Kenneth A. Dodge & Joseph M. Price, *On the Relation Between Social Information Processing and Socially Competent Behavior in Early School-Aged Children*, 65 Child Dev. 1385 (1994); Fontaine et al., *Development*, *supra* note 73.

109 *E.g.*, Dodge et al., *supra* note 43; Richard Milich & Kenneth A. Dodge, *Social Information Processing in Child Psychiatric Populations*, 12 J. Abnormal Child Psychol. 471 (1984).

110 *E.g.*, Nancy G. Guerra & Ronald G. Slaby, *Cognitive Mediators of Aggression in Adolescent Offenders: 2. Intervention*, 26 Developmental Psychol. 269 (1990); Vitale et al., *supra* note 107.

It is important to note that, although there is an important and growing body of exceptions,[111] research on SIP and antisocial behavior has largely been conducted using youth populations. There are a number of reasons that explain this developmental focus. First, researchers are often interested not only in the development of phenomena, but also in their emergence. Emergence of major SIP operations is concentrated in childhood and adolescence. Second, because development is rapider earlier in life, and thus easier to observe, developmental change may be assessed across a shorter period of time. Third, it is often easier to access individuals when they are contained in a single location. Schools provide this convenience and allow researchers to more successfully track and assess study participants. Fourth, whereas parent-, peer-, teacher-, and youths' own self-reports are often attainable with respect to youth samples, it is usually the case that only self-report measures are practically administrable with adults (an obvious exception is institutionalized – e.g., hospitalized or incarcerated – adults; of course, studies that utilize such adult samples are substantially limited in terms of the degree to which findings thereof can be generalized).

This is not an exhaustive list, as there are surely additional reasons why research on SIP and aggression has focused on youth populations. It should be stressed, however, that the heavy attention to children and adolescents is not at all because it is understood or even considered that relations between SIP and antisocial behavior are contained to preadult development or are any more typical of youths than they are of adults. There is no good reason whatsoever to expect that aggressive adults do not operate according to the same basic processing patterns and biases that youths (especially adolescents) do. Of course, with maturity, some adults become better able to resist processing tendencies that may otherwise lead to aggressive outputs, but this is an entirely separate issue that goes to basic adolescence-to-adulthood development and not to hypothesized or realized differences in fundamental processing between aggressive youths and adults.

A word should be said about the methodology employed in developmental research on SIP and aggression. In studies of younger children, participants are typically shown cartoon or pictures of ambiguous social scenarios. The children are asked questions designed to represent SIP steps about the characters and happenings depicted in the visuals. Often, participants are asked to imagine themselves as specific characters in the visuals so that the SIP questions may be directly related to their thoughts about the situation as if they were experiencing it themselves. Some studies of children, and almost

[111] *See, e.g.*, Epps & Kendall, *supra* note 54; Vitale et al., *supra* note 107.

all studies of adolescents, have used videotaped vignettes of social scenarios that focus groups have determined are typical of daily youth life. As with the cartoons and pictures used with younger children, the video vignettes depict ambiguous social situations by which it is unclear as to why the social stimulus caused a harmful outcome to the protagonist (or responding individual). Participants are asked to imagine themselves as the responding individual and asked questions that reflect SIP operations that have been hypothesized to be associated with antisocial behavioral responses.

Although this methodology has been used successfully in numerous independent research programs that study social-cognitive underpinnings of antisocial behavior, there are some limitations that should be recognized. First, participants may or may not identify with the social scenarios presented to them. Second, participants are not experiencing the interpersonal exchanges in real life, but rather are asked to imagine themselves in the depicted scenarios. Third, it is likely that some participants are more "cognitively involved" than others in the task of imagining themselves in the scenarios. Fourth, even among the more cognitively involved participants, the degree to which a youth participant can imagine herself in a social scenario that actually matches how she would mentally operate if she were actually in the scenario likely varies. Whereas this may not be a complete list of caveats, it quickly points to obstacles presented by this methodology in the pursuit of valid assessment of social-cognitive processing of antisocial behavior.

Certainly, improvements in methodology are needed. However, it is equally important to recognize that this methodology has allowed behavioral scientists to assess links between social cognition and antisocial behavior in youths that other methodologies could not. For example, it may be unethical to place youth participants in real scenarios in which they are (even ambiguously) provoked. In addition, even if the provocation were designed to be so mild that ethical issues did not present an irresolvable obstacle, the use of a confederate brings its own problems, not least of which is that a confederate's performance varies across trials, thus potentially confounding the interpretation of results of individual differences among study participants. Finally, it should be noted that much non-SIP social-cognitive research on antisocial behavior does not employ this methodology (i.e., the presentation of visual stimuli such as pictures and video vignettes). Of course, other methodological approaches, such as self-report instruments that are designed to assess latent cognitions, have their own limitations.

Finally, a warning against definitively concluding a false negative from the absence of scientific data is warranted. It cannot be reasonably concluded that an *individual* does not have a particular cognitive difficulty (e.g., bias or deficit) simply because the difficulty has not been scientifically substantiated. Most social-cognitive research produces findings of differences between group means. Considerable variability among individuals within a group may exist that is often lost in such data analysis. This is an important point, because the unit of analysis in law is typically the single act by the single person, not patterns of functioning investigated among discernible groups of persons. Also, it may be that a person's cognitive difficulty operates only within a certain context and that related research has not been designed such that it has sufficiently explored individual differences across contexts.

MORAL DISENGAGEMENT

Social-cognitive theories of interpersonal behavior have also been applied to moral agency,[112] which is a person's capacity to engage in moral judgment and decision making and behave in accordance with accepted moral norms and standards. As an individual develops, he learns and internalizes moral rules based on his observations and interactions with others. These internalized moral rules function to regulate one's social behavior. As one might suspect, moral development is a complicated process, and its understanding requires theoretical formulation and empirical investigation of numerous social-cognitive mechanisms.

Several psychologists have offered theories of moral development, reasoning, and agency.[113] Few, however, have examined the mechanisms by which a normal or acceptable course of moral thought and action may break down or be altered such that one's functioning lends itself to antisocial or immoral conduct. Bandura[114] and his colleagues[115] have advanced a model of *moral disengagement* by which an individual detaches the moral qualities of a considered behavior or moral components of a social context (e.g., the behavioral target) in which the behavior is to be enacted. The individual's action serves to eliminate, or at least significantly discount, the regulatory effect of the actor's internalized rules of moral conduct. In other words, via moral disengagement,

[112] Lawrence Kohlberg, *The Psychology of Moral Development: The Nature and Validity of Moral Stages* (1984).

[113] For a review, see Handbook of Moral Development (Melanie Killen & Judith G. Smetana eds., 2006).

[114] *E.g.*, Albert Bandura et al., *supra* note 28; Albert Bandura, *Moral Disengagement in the Perpetration of Inhumanities*, 3 Personality & Soc. Psychol. Rev. 193 (1999) [hereinafter Bandura, *Disengagement*].

[115] Caprara et al., *supra* note 23; Marinella Paciello, Roberta Fida, Carlo Tramontano, Catia Lupinetti & Gian V. Caprara, *Stability and Change of Moral Disengagement and Its Impact on Aggression and Violence in Late Adolescence*, 79 Child Dev. 1288 (2008).

a person reconstrues the nature of a considered behavior or its associated context so that carrying out the behavior no longer violates regulatory moral rules that would otherwise obstruct or completely prevent performance. Moral disengagement allows one to avoid the experience of psychological states, such as self-condemnation and cognitive dissonance, which may serve to impede the behavior or cause the actor mental discomfort following behavioral enactment.

According to Bandura's model of moral disengagement,[116] self-sanctioning regulatory mechanisms become disconnected from antisocial, harmful conduct by converting morally bad acts into morally good (or at least acceptable) ones. Bandura and his colleagues have hypothesized eight separate processes of moral disengagement, which are classified into four sets of disengagement practices. These four areas of disengagement play a role at different points in the process of acting in an antisocial manner in the execution of a detrimental outcome.

The first set of disengagement practices is directed toward reconstruing the moral nature of the reprehensible conduct. Harmful behavior may be justified by convincing oneself that it is conducted for a larger, moral or socially valuable purpose ("moral justification"), such as in the case of a person who justified hurting another person because the latter has acted dishonorably. "Euphemistic language" may be used to mask the reprehensible nature of the behavior, such as when a harmful act is described as playful or a joke. Finally, the immoral nature of the behavior may be discounted by comparing to conduct that is more reprehensible ("advantageous comparison"), such as in the case that someone excuses property destruction because it is not as bad a physically harming a person.

The second set of disengagement practices serves to excuse one's personal agency from having caused harm to another as a result of acting in a reprehensible manner. Via "displacement of responsibility," the actor attributes responsibility for the harmful conduct to another individual (or set of individuals) or larger social system, as in the case of one who excuses his stealing because he is a victim of an unfair society that gave him no choice but to act in such a way. Alternatively, a person may minimize his responsibility by viewing his behavior as meaningless because it was only a nominal part of a larger social behavior committed by many. "Diffusion of responsibility" is typical of the rioter who destroys and steals property but excuses himself because, given that so many others participated in the riot, his contribution was nothing more than nominal.

[116] Bandura et al., *supra* note 28.

Moral disengagement may also be realized by reconstruing the detrimental effects themselves. The third set of detachment (or rationalization) practices involves "disregarding or distorting the consequences" of the conduct. For example, one may convince himself that lying is okay because the recipient remains unaware of his dishonest practice and is thus not harmed.

The final set of practices by which the antisocial actor may disconnect the immoral properties of the conduct is by reconstruing the victim. Via "dehumanization," the victim is viewed to be subhuman (devoid of human qualities such as intelligence and feelings), perhaps by likening the victim to an animal so that the aggravator discerns his behavior as acceptable. Alternatively, the aggravator may reconstrue the moral status of the victim so that the victim *deserves* the harm he suffers. "Attribution of blame" to the victim relieves the aggravator of sanctioning himself from committing a wrongful act against an innocent other. For example, the aggravator may convince himself that anyone who is stupid enough to walk through the city at night alone deserves to be mugged.

Moral disengagement has been conceptually tied to numerous types of violent and otherwise antisocial forms of behavior,[117] including terrorism,[118] executions,[119] delinquency,[120] and white-collar crime,[121] and has been demonstrated in multiple studies to play a critical role in the development of antisocial behavior. Furthermore, it is worth noting that moral disengagement may be reframed in SIP terms. Specifically, mechanisms of moral disengagement may be conceptualized as domains of *response evaluation and decision*. Reconstrual of reprehensible behavior may be likened to response valuation, by which the antisocial actor may be biased in favor of positively evaluating antisocial forms of conduct. Similarly, reconstrual of detrimental effects and victims may be explained according to biased outcome expectancy and

[117] *See* Bandura, *Disengagement, supra* note 114.

[118] Albert Bandura, *The Role of Selective Moral Disengagement in Terrorism and Counterterrorism*, *in* UNDERSTANDING TERRORISM: PSYCHOLOGICAL ROOTS, CONSEQUENCES, AND INTERVENTIONS 121 (Fathali M. Moghaddam & Anthony J. Marsella eds., 2003); Albert Bandura, *Training in Terrorism Through Selective Moral Disengagement*, *in* 2 THE MAKING OF A TERRORIST: RECRUITMENT, TRAINING AND ROOT CAUSES 34 (James J.F. Forest ed., 2006).

[119] Michael J. Osofsky, Albert Bandura & Philip G. Zimbardo, *The Role of Moral Disengagement in the Execution Process*, 29 LAW & HUM. BEHAV. 371 (2005).

[120] Stavros P. Kiriakidis, *Moral Disengagement: Relation to Delinquency and Independence from Indices of Social Dysfunction*, 52 INT'L J. OFFENDER THERAPY & COMP. CRIMINOLOGY 571 (2008).

[121] Albert Bandura, Gian V. Caprara & Laszlo Zsolnai, *Corporate Transgressions*, *in* ETHICS IN THE ECONOMY: HANDBOOK OF BUSINESS ETHICS 151 (Laszlo Zsolnai ed., 2002).

valuation. As discussed earlier, as compared to their nonaggressive peers, antisocial youths tend to expect aggressive behaviors to lead to less aversive treatment by others[122] (moral justification) and believe that aggression will not lead to suffering in their victims (distorting the consequences).[123] Moral disengagement is explored in greater detail in Chapter 5.

APPRAISAL THEORY

Social-information processing (SIP) theories have focused on explaining the development of behavior. They have been criticized for neglecting emotion,[124] although models of SIP have been advanced with an eye toward accounting for emotional outputs.[125] Another literature, however, has presented cognitive theories that are specifically designed to account for emotional functioning. Several cognitive theories of emotion have been advanced in recent decades,[126] although perhaps none has received more theoretical and scientific attention, as well as empirical support, than Professor Richard Lazarus's *appraisal theory*.[127] Similar to SIP, appraisal theory links cognitive processes with functioning outputs – whereas SIP focuses on behavior, appraisal theory is designed to account for emotional outputs.

[122] David G. Perry, Louise C. Perry & Paul Rasmussen, *Cognitive Social Learning Mediators of Aggression*, 57 CHILD DEV. 700 (1986).

[123] Slaby & Guerra, *supra* note 38.

[124] *E.g.*, Elizabeth A. Lemerise & William F. Arsenio, *An Integrated Model of Emotion Processes and Cognition in Social Information Processing*, 71 CHILD DEV. 107 (2000).

[125] *Id.*; Elizabeth A. Lemerise & Kenneth A. Dodge, *The Development of Anger and Hostile Interactions*, *in* HANDBOOK OF EMOTIONS 537 (Michael Lewis & Jeannette M. Haviland eds., 1993).

[126] *E.g.*, Howard Leventhal, *A Perceptual Motor Theory of Emotion*, *in* APPROACHES TO EMOTION 271 (Klaus R. Scherer & Paul Ekman eds., 1984); Ira J. Roseman, *Cognitive Determinants of Emotion: A Structural Theory*, *in* 5 REVIEW OF PERSONALITY AND SOCIAL PSYCHOLOGY, EMOTIONS, RELATIONSHIPS, AND HEALTH 11 (P. Shaver ed., 1984); Klaus R. Scherer, *On the Nature and Function of Emotion: A Component Process Approach*, *in* APPROACHES TO EMOTION 293 (Klaus R. Scherer & Paul Ekman eds., 1984).

[127] Richard S. Lazarus, James R. Averill & Edward M. Opton, Jr., *Towards a Cognitive Theory of Emotion*, *in* FEELINGS AND EMOTIONS: THE LOYOLA SYMPOSIUM 207 (Magda B. Arnold ed., 1970); RICHARD S. LAZARUS & SUSAN FOLKMAN, STRESS, APPRAISAL, AND COPING (1984); Richard S. Lazarus & Craig A. Smith, *Knowledge and Appraisal in the Cognition-Emotion Relationship*, 2 COGNITION & EMOTION 281 (1988); Richard S. Lazarus, *On the Primacy of Cognition*, 39 AM. PSYCHOLOGIST 124 (1984); RICHARD S. LAZARUS, EMOTION AND ADAPTATION (1991); Richard S. Lazarus, *Vexing Research Problems Inherent in Cognitive-Mediational Theories of Emotion – and Some Solutions*, 6 PSYCHOL. INQUIRY 183 (1995); Craig A. Smith & Richard S. Lazarus, *Appraisal Components, Core Relational Themes, and the Emotions*, 7 COGNITION & EMOTION 233 (1993) [hereinafter Smith & Lazarus, *Appraisal Components*].

An appraisal is the process, or set of processes, by which an individual evaluates his situation by assessing how his environment relates to him and what this relation means with respect to his personal well-being, which is an understanding founded on the individual's belief system and personal values and goals. Positive emotions (e.g., happiness, pride) result when the person-environment relation is determined to be beneficial to one's well-being; in contrast, negative emotions (e.g., anger, fear) are produced when the relation is evaluated to be detrimental or in opposition to one's beliefs, values, and goals. According to appraisal theory, emotions play an adaptive role in that they serve to orient and prepare a person to respond to alternative situations as a direct result of how the individual assesses the situations. Emotions, then, can be explained according to the cognitive processing of one's social world. Theoretically, emotions change in real time according to ongoing evaluations of one's relation to his environment.

Of course, it follows that the degree to which one's emotional functioning can act to prepare her to respond to her social world is directly dependent on – and thus limited by – her ability to accurately appraise. That is, if a person is less skilled at evaluating her social world and how her environment relates to her, then her emotional outputs are more likely to be mismatched with the demands of social stimuli. For example, as discussed earlier, scientists have found that trait anger is associated with selective attention to hostile cues.[128] It is likely that anger is not helpful (but is perhaps hurtful) in situations that are nonhostile and nonprovocative in that it is an emotional output that is incongruent with the benign environment-person relation. This may be further problematic if the experience of anger primes the individual to respond to benign social cues in an aggressive or otherwise antisocial manner. This is a critical idea with respect to understanding how social-cognitive theory and science may be useful in understanding the mindsets of individuals who are charged with violent crimes.

Appraisal theory, and cognitive theories of emotion in general, would of course seem to be most relevant to affirmative defenses that consider the role of emotion in one's objectively criminal conduct. For example, the clear role of anger in heat-of-passion homicide and the less clear but important role of fear in duress crimes[129] may be more comprehensively understood via appraisal theory. For example, the hypothesis advanced by appraisal theory that the

[128] *See, e.g.*, Wilkowski et al., *supra* note 45, at 651.

[129] Specifically, duress per minas by which the defendant feared for his life or of mayhem or loss of limb (as distinguished from duress of imprisonment). Additional discussion is provided in Chapter 8.

anger is associated with the core relational theme of "other blame" has been supported.[130] There are three required appraisals to satisfy this core relational theme: (1) the primary appraisals of *motivational relevance* (the situation is personally relevant), (2) *motivational incongruence* (the situation opposes personal goals or values), and (3) the secondary appraisal of *other-accountability* (another person is responsible for making the situation motivationally incongruent). This detailed, empirically substantiated account of the cognitive mechanisms of anger may be useful in terms of evaluating provocation situations and anger responses in heat-of-passion cases. Cognitive models of other emotions, such as guilt, fear/anxiety, and sadness, have also found empirical support.[131]

AUTOMATIC PROCESSING AND IMPLICIT SOCIAL COGNITION

Although SIP theories have drawn a distinction between mechanisms that are conceptually or actively processed and those that are automatically or schematically processed,[132] greater empirical attention has been paid to the role of conceptual processing.[133] The majority of scientific research on automatic cognitive processing and social behavior has not focused specifically on antisocial conduct. Still, there is no reason to believe that automaticity plays a less prominent role in antisocial behavior as compared to socially adjusted types of conduct, and it is widely accepted that automatic processes account for a broad range of behaviors and interpersonal functions.[134]

In particular, Professor John Bargh is perhaps best known among researchers who study automaticity in cognitive processing and goal-directed social

[130] Smith & Lazarus, *Appraisal Components*, *supra* note 127.

[131] *Id.*

[132] Crick & Dodge, *supra* note 8; Huesmann, *supra* note 9.

[133] Of the two, Huesmann has placed greater emphasis on automatic processing. Some empirical studies have distinguished between latent constructs and "online" social-cognitive processing in their examination of the relation between social cognition and antisocial behavior. *See, e.g.*, Kenneth A. Dodge, Robert Laird, John E. Lochman, Arnaldo Zelli & Conduct Problems Prevention Research Group, *Multidimensional Latent-Construct Analysis of Children's Social Information Processing Patterns: Correlations with Aggressive Behavior Problems*, 14 PSYCHOL. ASSESSMENT 60 (2002); Arnaldo Zelli, Kenneth A. Dodge, John E. Lochman, Robert D. Laird & Conduct Problems Prevention Research Group, *The Distinction Between Beliefs Legitimizing Aggression and Deviant Processing of Social Cues: Testing Measurement Validity and the Hypothesis that Biased Processing Mediates the Effects of Beliefs on Aggression*, 77 J. PERSONALITY & SOC. PSYCHOL. 150 (1999).

[134] *See* 10 THE AUTOMATICITY OF EVERYDAY LIFE: ADVANCES IN SOCIAL COGNITION (Robert S. Wyer Jr., ed., 1997).

behavior.[135] Automaticity refers to unconscious mechanisms that have become habitualized or crystallized via learning and persistent practice and repetition. Processing information in one's social sphere may be adaptive to the degree that it allows an individual a mentally efficient way to maneuver through his environment without requiring large amounts of incoming social information to be conceptually (and more effortfully) processed. Alternatively, automatic processing of information can be problematic when cues are misread such that they are erroneously deemed to not require one's conscious attention and active consideration.

A major question raised by Bargh's research is, if much of human mental operating occurs outside of conscious awareness and intent, how may this reality be balanced with doctrines of free will in philosophy and personal responsibility in law. Psycholegal study of the relation between unconscious cognitive mechanisms associated with automaticity and law has grown considerably in recent years.[136] Research on *implicit social cognition* and, more specifically, implicit bias has been applied to numerous discussions in law. If implicit social cognition is mental operation that functions at a nonconscious level, then implicit bias may be understood as nonconscious information-processing mechanisms that favor specific functioning styles or outcomes. For example, an implicit racial bias may lead to feelings and behaviors that accommodate said bias, such as in the case of voting for a candidate based, even if just in part, on his ethnic background.

For the most part, the science of implicit social cognition has been applied to areas and issues of civil law, such as equal protection and employment discrimination.[137] However, it is not difficult to imagine how research on implicit social cognition and antisocial behavior may be similarly useful. For example, individuals who have learned that the world is a hostile, unsafe place, and have repeatedly interacted with others who have acted in personally harmful manners, may come to automatically process cues that are ambiguous as to provocation as definitively hostile and dangerous. If so, such research may be relevant to legal understanding of the nature of violent crimes committed by such individuals, including issues of criminal responsibility and punishment.

[135] *E.g.*, John A. Bargh & Tanya L. Chartrand, *The Unbearable Automaticity of Being*, 54 AM. PSYCHOLOGIST 462 (1999); John A. Bargh, *What Have We Been Priming All These Years? On the Development, Mechanisms, and Ecology of Nonconscious Social Behavior*, 36 EUR. J. SOC. PSYCHOL. 147 (2006); John A. Bargh & Melissa J. Ferguson, *Beyond Behaviorism: On the Automaticity of Higher Mental Processes*, 126 PSYCHOL. BULL. 925 (2000).

[136] For recent reviews, see Anthony G. Greenwald & Linda H. Krieger, *Implicit Bias: Scientific Foundations*, 94 CALIF. L. REV. 945 (2006); Kristin A. Lane, Jerry Kang & Mahzarin R. Banaji, *Implicit Social Cognition and Law*, 3 ANN. REV. L. & SOC. SCI. 427 (2007).

[137] Greenwald & Krieger, *supra* note 136; Lane et al., *supra* note 136.

FURTHER CONSIDERATIONS

All of the social-cognitive models and areas of research discussed in this chapter have a critical structural commonality: cognitive mediation. That is, each model represents a hypothesized causal chain by which a social event or stimulus (cause) leads to an individual's social-cognitive processing of the event (mediator), which, in mediational turn, leads to the individual's functional output or response (effect), whether it be cognitive (e.g., judgment that the stimulus actor is a dangerous person), emotional (e.g., anger), or behavioral (e.g., aggressive retaliation). This sequence may be simply illustrated as follows:

> Social stimulus (Cause) → Processing of stimulus (Mediator) → Response (Effect)

It is via social-cognitive processing – or "meaning making" – of the stimulus that an individual becomes able, whether appropriately or inappropriately, to respond to the stimulus. This is how one makes meaning of his social world as it unfolds. If a person has a problem in his meaning making, he may have less control, less rationality, and thus, at least potentially, less responsibility. He may not experience reality as does the "reasonable person" – that is, the person whose rationality meets the threshold assumed of adult actors by the law – whatsoever. Arguably, it is this point in the mediational sequence that is most important to resolving issues of criminal responsibility. As a result, social-cognitive (or "meaning making") models of interpersonal behavior and, more specifically, antisocial conduct are indispensible in the pursuit of properly framing criminal-law doctrine.

Throughout this volume, SIP is used to illustrate and highlight how social-cognitive science may be useful to better understanding issues of criminal responsibility and punishment. As previously discussed, there are multiple reasons why SIP is used in this fashion. One reason is that SIP may be neatly reframed to account for other social-cognitive models of human functioning. Some ways in which SIP may account for processes articulated by other models have already been mentioned. For example, moral disengagement may be represented by the *response evaluation and decision* step of SIP. At this step, antisocial behaviors may be evaluated and even reconceptualized such that their moral qualities are detached and the responding individual is able to avoid self-sanctioning. Appraisal theory is reflected by the *interpretation-of-cues* step of SIP. At this step, attributions of cause and responsibility are made, much in the same way as primary and secondary appraisals are articulated in appraisal theory. Finally, implicit social cognition is captured by the *data base of cognition* discussed by Crick and Dodge in their 1994 reformulated model, as well as Fontaine and Dodge in their 2006 proposed model of social-response decision making.[138] Furthermore, Huesmann has emphasized schematic processing in his model of SIP,[139] stressing the importance of normative beliefs and behavioral scripts that may be automatically accessed and put to work in the mental operating of everyday life and enactment of everyday behavior. As a result, SIP proves a useful heuristic by which all developmental social cognition may be investigated, understood, and related to issues of antisocial mentality, conduct, and, with respect to the relation between social-cognitive science and law, criminal responsibility (i.e., diminished capacity/rationality).

138 Crick & Dodge, *supra* note 8; Fontaine & Dodge, *supra* note 27.
139 Huesmann, *supra* note 29.

3

Substandard Rational Capacity and Criminal Responsibility

In Chapter 1, the jurisprudential foundation of criminal law was introduced and our interdisciplinary focus – that of developmental social cognition and criminal law – was identified. Chapter 2 reviewed major social cognitive models and highlighted social-information processing (SIP) theory as a heuristic by which contributions from social cognitive science to criminal jurisprudence and law may be explained and understood. This brings us to Chapter 3, which bridges Chapters 1 and 2 and provides the conceptual framework for the rest of this volume. Specifically, this chapter explores the nexus of developmental social cognition and criminal responsibility in the context of the uniquely human capacity for rationality.

In American criminal law, the doctrine of diminished capacity states that an actor's criminal culpability is mitigated in the case that her functional ability is restricted due to unforeseeable and uncontrollable impairment. The actor who commits a crime with diminished capacity either does not adequately understand the nature of his crime or is unable to prevent herself from committing it. This chapter discusses the nature of diminished capacity, identifies rationality as its core component, and highlights SIP as a developmental model of rationality in the social domain. This will prove useful as components of rationality or SIP – social understanding, judgment, and decision making – are discussed in relation to a range of (at least potentially) excusing conditions in the chapters that follow, to illustrate the differential applicability of the "spirit" of diminished capacity across excuse-based affirmative defenses in the criminal law. The retributive principle of penal proportionality is thematic throughout this discussion, consistent with Morse's argument that diminished rationality necessitates diminished responsibility (which in turn dictates lesser punishment),[1] and is specifically contextualized in SIP theory and research.

I say the "spirit" of diminished capacity to distinguish the key capacity of rationality from the formal defense of diminished capacity. Two decades ago, Professor Ralph Slovenko asked, "Is diminished capacity really dead?"[2] Slovenko, of course, was discussing the formal defense of diminished capacity in light of California's highly publicized abolition of the defense in 1981. The question bears the obvious implication that at least some recognizable legal body does indeed consider the defense to be dead. I would argue, however, that the defense is very much alive and well in its spirit but not as a widely accepted formal defense. That is, if we accept that the key capacity for criminal responsibility is rationality – as this chapter explores – then we may consider the degree to which rationality (or the undermining, underdevelopment, or dysfunction of rationality) is the mechanism by which excuse-based defenses in American criminal law function. In this way, I introduce the idea of rationality as a common theme across criminal excuses and set the foundation for the chapters that follow, each of which links aspects of rationality (or social-cognitive functioning) with the operative mechanisms in specific excuse-based defenses (e.g., immaturity, insanity, heat of passion/provocation, duress, etc.).

At the outset, it should be recognized that a crucial question in legal theory and practice has persisted: In structural and functional terms, what is diminished capacity? That is, what end does diminished capacity serve, and what are its boundaries? Whereas it may not be possible to definitively answer this question, as it is naturally normative at its foundation, exploration of the matter is prudent. Whereas some scholarship has placed rationality at center stage, arguing that "the general capacity for rationality is the fundamental criterion of responsibility,"[3] elsewhere the matter remains foggy, intrinsically inconsistent, or decidedly undecided. Some diligent attempts to clarify matters of capacity and responsibility have raised equally difficult questions of their own.[4] Much to the frustration of some scholars, Morse's 1984 article

1 Stephen J. Morse, *Rationality and Responsibility*, 74 S. CAL. L. REV. 251, 262–68 (2000) [hereinafter Morse, *Rationality*]; Stephen J. Morse, *Diminished Rationality, Diminished Responsibility*, 1 OHIO ST. J. CRIM. L. 289 (2003) [hereinafter Morse, *Diminished Rationality*].

2 Ralph Slovenko, Commentary, *Is Diminished Capacity Really Dead?*, 20 J. PSYCHIATRY & L. 123, 123 (1992).

3 Morse, *Rationality*, *supra* note 1, at 252.

4 *See, e.g.*, Robert F. Schopp & Marc W. Patry, *The Guilty Mind and Criminal Sentencing: Integrating Legal and Empirical Inquiry as Illustrated by Capital Sentencing*, 21 BEHAV. SCI. & L. 631, 646–47 (2003).

on the topic, *Undiminished Confusion in Diminished Capacity*, continues to accurately characterize the majority of literature on the topic.[5]

One question that *is* clear about the nature of diminished capacity is that it functions to *excuse* a defendant of his admitted wrongdoing.[6] To conduct a proper exploration of diminished capacity in developmental social-cognitive terms, attention must be paid to both the normative question of when a wrongdoer should be excused because of capacity problems and the empirical question of what psychological processes may be involved (or fail to be involved) in mental states that satisfy accepted diminished-capacity framings. Of course, before one can answer the question of when one should be excused specifically via diminished capacity, the larger normative issue as to when a criminal actor should be excused as a general matter needs to be addressed. As such, some elucidation of the nature and boundaries of excuse, as distinguished from justification, is in order.

EXCUSE

It is via excuse, rather than justification, that developmental social cognition is relevant to criminal culpability and punishment. Action that is justified is permissible and acceptable, whereas action that is excused is impermissible and decidedly wrong. The defendant who is successful in his claim of a justification-based affirmative defense (e.g., self-defense) is found not guilty. He is attributed no culpability and is not punished as he acted properly and within his legal rights. Likewise, the defendant whose action is excused is not assigned culpability or punished. However, in the case of the excused defendant, it is not that he is found blameless or unpunishable because his action was not wrongful. Rather, his indisputably wrong and socially harmful action is excused because either one of these conditions have been met: (1) the context in which the action was performed were such that the actor's reasons for acting wrongly are understandable, or (2) the act was performed as a function of a substandard functional capacity on the part of the defendant. In the first scenario, there may be features of the context in which the action was performed that are material to understanding the actor's reasons for having acted wrongfully. Perhaps the context was coercive; or perhaps the defendant

5 Stephen J. Morse, *Undiminished Confusion in Diminished Capacity*, 75 J. CRIM. L. & CRIMINOLOGY 1 (1984). It should be noted that Morse himself has diligently and distinctly brought great clarity to the topic during the past quarter-century.

6 *See* Henry F. Fradella, *From Insanity to Beyond Diminished Capacity: Mental Illness and Criminal Excuse in the Post-*Clark *Era*, 18 U. FLA. J.L. & PUB. POL'Y 7, 47–49 (2007) (addressing the debated issue whether diminished capacity even constitutes a defense).

acted based on a mistaken understanding that a reasonable person would have similarly held (although acts based on reasonable mistakes of facts are often treated as justifications in American criminal law, this position remains a topic of lively debate[7]). In the second scenario, an individual may not function or be rational to the level presumed by law of adult actors. This basis for excuse is perhaps most clearly exemplified by insanity, diminished capacity, and infancy/immaturity defenses in criminal law. The common element is that the defendant's rationality (or rational capacity) was insufficient to meet a presumption of responsibility. In sum, a justified act is not punished because it is right or at least acceptable; an excused act is not punished because, despite the fact that it is wrong and socially harmful, its committer is not responsible for having performed it.

As Professor Joshua Dressler has articulated, "Whereas a justification negates the social harm of an offense, an excuse negates the moral blameworthiness of the actor for causing the harm."[8] Of course, justification and excuse-based defenses, when successful, produce the same outcome in that in either case the defendant is not held culpable or punished. Just as one who has acted rightfully should not be punished, neither should one who is not responsible for having acted wrongfully. For this and other reasons, some scholars have questioned the importance of the distinction between justification and excuse.[9]

7 *See* Marcia Baron, *The Provocation Defense and the Nature of Justification*, 43 U. MICH. J.L. REFORM 117 (2009); Michael L. Corrado, *Self-Defense, Moral Acceptability, and Compensation: A Response to Professor Fontaine*, 47 AM. CRIM. L. REV. 91 (2010); Reid G. Fontaine, *Adequate (Non)Provocation and Heat of Passion as Excuse Not Justification*, 43 U. MICH. J.L. REFORM 27 (2009); Reid G. Fontaine, *On Passion's Potential to Undermine Rationality: A Reply*, 43 U. MICH. J.L. REFORM 207 (2009) [hereinafter Fontaine, *On Passion's Potential*]; Reid G. Fontaine, *An Attack on Self-Defense*, 47 AM. CRIM. L. REV. 57 (2010) [hereinafter Fontaine, *Attack*]; Stephen J. Morse, *The Irreducibly Normative Nature of Provocation/Passion*, 43 U. MICH. J.L. REFORM 193 (2009).

8 Joshua Dressler, *Justifications and Excuses: A Brief Review of the Concepts and the Literature*, 33 WAYNE L. REV. 1155, 1163 (1987) (explaining the importance of maintaining a clear theoretical distinction between justification and excuse-based defenses) [hereinafter Dressler, *Justifications*]; *accord* Joshua Dressler, *Exegesis of the Law of Duress: Justifying the Excuse and Searching for its Proper Limits*, 62 S. CAL. L. REV. 1331, 1349 n.124 (1989); (explaining the importance of maintaining a clear theoretical distinction between justification and excuse-based defenses); Joshua Dressler, *Provocation: Partial Justification or Partial Excuse?*, 51 MOD. L. REV. 467, 476–80 (1988) (discussing the justification versus excuse distinction in terms of provocation crimes only) [hereinafter Dressler, *Provocation*]; PAUL H. ROBINSON, *CRIMINAL LAW DEFENSES* 100–01 (1984); Fontaine, *On Passion's Potential*, *supra* note 7.

9 Most famous for arguing against importance of the distinction is Professor Kent Greenawalt. Kent Greenawalt, *The Perplexing Borders of Justification and Excuse*, 84 COLUM. L. REV. 1897 (1984); *see also* Gabriel J. Chin, *Unjustified: The Practical Irrelevance of the Justification/Excuse Distinction*, 43 U. MICH. J.L. REFORM 79 (2009) (questioning the importance of the

On its face, the distinction between justification and excuse may appear to be one of solely theoretical relevance. Certainly, defining the distinction should promote understanding and consistency in the development of criminal rules of responsibility. Undoubtedly, the criminal law has as one of its purposes the duty to send clear moral messages. Several scholars argue, however, that the distinction between justification and excuse is both theoretically *and* practically important.[10] For example, the lawyer who has a grasp on the distinction as it applies to a specific case may be more likely to emerge victorious. The defense attorney may be able to better identify what defenses apply and how alternative defenses may be organized, whereas the prosecutor may be better able to combat the defense's measures and strategies. Additional benefits may be realized with respect to issues of burden of proof, accomplice liability, and rules of evidence.[11]

Elsewhere, I have written that perhaps the most important purpose of recognizing and clarifying the distinction between justification and excuse is to accurately and consistently discern the boundaries of right and wrong.[12] Indeed, is this not the most crucial issue in criminal law – to identify that which is so wrongful and socially harmful that it needs to be legally prohibited? With the considerable value that society attributes to protecting negative liberty, should we not be acutely concerned with issues on which restriction of said liberty rests? It seems odd that we would be more interested in the distinction between right and wrong with respect to devising and applying criminal laws than we would in devising and applying defenses to violations of said laws. To treat justification and excuse defenses equally would be to say that it is wrong to act in ways in which the actor is legally entitled to act (treating justification as excuse) or that it is acceptable to commit wrongful, socially harmful acts for which one is not responsible (treating excuse as justification). The absurdity of either statement lies not only in both its moral and logical self-contradictions, but in the observation that making such

distinction outside the realm of legal philosophy). *But see, e.g.*, Dressler, *Justifications*, *supra* note 8, at 1167–74) (explaining the importance of maintaining a clear theoretical distinction between justification and excuse-based defenses); Dressler, *Provocation*, *supra* note 8, at 468.

10 Of course, if we agree that the legitimacy of the criminal law depends, in part, on it being theoretically consistent (I do not know of a scholar who argues otherwise), then, indirectly, the justification/excuse distinction is practically important to the criminal law *because* it is theoretically important to the criminal law. *See* Fontaine, *On Passion's Potential*, *supra* note 7, at 237.

11 Dressler, *Justifications*, *supra* note 8, at 1172–74; *see also* Fontaine, *On Passion's Potential*, *supra* note 7, at 213.

12 Fontaine, *Attack*, *supra* note 7; Fontaine, *On Passion's Potential*, *supra* note 7.

a statement would take place in a context in which the distinction between right and wrong is otherwise paramount (as in the case of developing, formally stating, and applying crime legislation).

Thus, if it is agreed that the distinction between justification and excuse is a critical one, and that it is via excuse, and excuse only, that social-cognitive processing, as well as the science thereof, is relevant to criminal defenses, it necessarily follows that questions of under what circumstances and in what ways (or forms) social-cognitive processing may justly serve as excuse should be addressed and explored. The law presumes a minimum level of rational capacity of humans, and it is this capacity that lies at the heart of responsibility.[13] Rationality encompasses a vast array of social-cognitive abilities and tools, such as judging personal relevance of one's social surroundings, estimating cause-and-effect relations, and differentially assessing behavioral options as a function of the alternative outcomes expected of them. As such, it seems sensible to conclude that social-cognitive processing, or lack thereof, may justly serve as an excuse for wrongdoing when it fails to meet the level and set of skills presumed of the adult actor by law. That is, a criminal defendant may be excused for wrongdoing when he does not have the capacity to *not* commit wrongful action that one who functions at or above the level of mental capacity presumed by the law would have been (at least significantly better) able to avoid performing.

DIMINISHED CAPACITY

Throughout Anglo-American criminal law, there have been many different conceptualizations, formal statements, and applications of the doctrine of *diminished capacity*. In general terms, the doctrine states that in the case of the defendant who, although not insane at the time of the alleged crime, due to factors outside of his control was less than fully able to understand the moral nature of his action or adequately function to prevent his wrongful action, may not be held entirely responsible for his bad act. Although it is not widely recognized as a formal defense across U.S. jurisdictions, the doctrine has most commonly applied to intent crimes to show that the defendant was not capable of forming the requisite mens rea of intent or purpose. Diminished capacity can and has taken many forms, however, and, in fact, its relation to (and distinction from) the defense of insanity has itself been a matter of great confusion and debate.[14] The spirit of the defense, however, which rests on

[13] Morse, *Rationality*, *supra* note 1, at 253.

[14] *See* Fradella, *supra* note 6 (reviewing and discussing the recent history of diminished capacity and insanity).

the presumed general capacity of rationality, is arguably central to multiple excuse-based defenses that remain firmly grounded in modern criminal jurisprudence and active criminal law.

Legal insanity is an excuse-based affirmative defense that states that where, due to (nonculpably formed) mental disease or defect, one who is unable to understand or appreciate the wrongful nature of her act at the time it is committed, that person will not be held responsible or punishable for said act. Statements of the defense have varied by jurisdiction and the scope of the defense's application has fluctuated considerably across history. Nevertheless, even in its most general form, and according to its broadest set of guidelines, the underlying notion that the defendant needed to have been unable to comprehend that her act was naturally unjust at the time of its commission has remained evident.

There is an obvious conceptual overlap between the doctrines of diminished capacity and insanity. Perhaps one simple and fair distinction between the two may be drawn from the specificity of their statements. That is, insanity may be viewed as a specific and more severe form of the more general condition of diminished capacity.[15] Where there is serious cognitive dysfunction or impairment that, although it may be relevant to the degree to which the actor understood the nature of her action or was able to prevent herself from performing it, does not satisfy the specific mental scenario reflected by the insanity defense, diminished capacity may apply. Similar to insanity, the effect of diminished capacity is the reduction of criminal responsibility and punishment. However, whereas insanity may fully excuse a defendant charged with murder, diminished capacity typically only results in a lesser penalty, either via negation of the requisite mens rea of the crime charged or by partially excusing the defendant's criminal conduct because she may not be said to be fully responsible for having formed the requisite mens rea. For example, the defendant charged with murder may be convicted of only the lesser crime of manslaughter after invoking diminished capacity.

Although insanity and diminished capacity may be distinguished by degree of severity and specificity of mental impairment, these distinctions themselves raise questions, some of which may contribute to confusion of either defense

[15] *See* Note, Johnson v. State – *Diminished Capacity Rejected as a Criminal Defense*, 42 Md. L. Rev. 522, 527–28, 535 (1983); Slovenko, *supra* note 2; Fradella, *supra* note 6, at 47; *see also* Morse, *supra* note 5, at 44. Note that Morse may argue that a more definitive distinction is that diminished capacity functions to negate mens rea and allow evidence of mental functioning before the prosecution has made its prima facie case, whereas insanity is an excuse-based affirmative defense.

or the relation of the two. For example, if insanity is nothing more than a specific case of diminished capacity, why is formal recognition of the former necessary? Are there other specific forms of diminished capacity, and, if there are, what forms do they take? What explains why these other specific forms of diminished capacity may not be officially recognized in the same capacity as insanity? If they serve the same kind of outcome, why is diminished capacity often conceptualized as a negation of mens rea, whereas insanity is strictly treated as an excuse-based affirmative defense? This is far from an exhaustive list, and comprehensive answers to these and related questions will surely require further investigation. For present purposes, two issues are most pressing. First, what are the nature, structure, and function of diminished capacity? Second, how may a social-cognitive framing of diminished capacity help us understand other scenarios in criminal law in which the issue of the defendant's criminal responsibility is at stake (in particular, alternative excuse-based defenses)?

Understanding the nature of diminished capacity rests on several critical issues, not least of which is whether diminished capacity is indeed a defense. Although diminished capacity is largely treated as a defense, scholars have disputed this issue.[16] For example, as introduced earlier, Morse has discussed two conceptualizations of, or approaches to, diminished capacity: the *mens rea* variant and the *partial-responsibility* variant. Some attention to this dichotomy is in order.

The mens rea variant views diminished capacity as an evidentiary issue and not a defense. In any criminal case, it is the prosecution's burden to prove beyond a reasonable doubt its prima facie case in order for the fact finder to convict the defendant of the crime(s) charged. More specifically, the prosecution is required to prove each definitional element of each crime of which the defendant is accused. As discussed in Chapter 1, there are generally two elements of a crime, that of the actus reus (guilty act) and mens rea (guilty mind). The mens rea variant of diminished capacity states that the defendant should be able to present evidence (e.g., expert witness testimony, psychological assessment) to dispute the mens rea element of the charged crime in order to prevent the prosecution from successfully proving its prima facie case. According to the mens rea variant, the defendant's position states, "I committed the act, but I was not of sufficient mental capacity to form the mens rea that is elemental to the act as a crime." In this way, diminished capacity serves as an allowance of evidence that goes to the question of whether the defendant's mental functioning at the time of the act's commission

[16] Morse, *supra* note 5, at 47–48.

meets the mens rea element. It is not an affirmative defense to a proven prima facie case.

With respect to the partial-responsibility variant, diminished capacity is treated as an excuse-based, partial, affirmative defense. Here, diminished capacity is not simply a negation of the elemental mens rea of the crime charged, but rather a formal defense invoked in response to the prosecution's prima facie case such that evidence as to the defendant's mental state at the time of the alleged criminal act may be presented. That is, the partial-responsibility variant states that the defendant should not be held entirely culpable for the charged crime because it was committed with a degree of mental capacity that does not meet the minimum threshold presumed by the law of human actors. The defendant's mental functioning at the time of the act, it is argued, was compromised by some form of impairment, such as a distorted understanding of his social reality. This variant is treated as a lesser degree of insanity (typically a complete excuse-based defense) and is not restricted to the narrow form of cognitive impairment (inability to appreciate the wrongfulness of the act) specified by the insanity defense.

At the time that Morse introduced this discussion, he argued that the mens rea variant is proper, although it is typically misunderstood and conflated with the partial-responsibility variant and, as such, treated as an affirmative, partial defense.[17] He asserted that the partial-responsibility variant has taken on different forms in American criminal law and that each of them is either illogical or arbitrarily applied.[18] Indeed, it matters for multiple reasons whether diminished capacity is a denial of mens rea or a defense. First, the likelihood or even possibility that a defendant will be completely – as opposed to only partially – exonerated may depend in part on whether the mens rea or partial-responsibility variant is adopted by the court. This is doubly important, as the difference between complete and partial exoneration is one of both stigma and punishment. Second, the criteria that must be met to determine a mental state (e.g., intent in the case of murder) in the prima facie phase of the case are different from the criteria that must be met for the invocation and success of an affirmative defense (e.g., insanity). As Morse stressed, the distinction may decide for the court whether the defendant has the right to present evidence of his mental condition at the time of the act.[19] In the case of the mens

[17] *Id.* at 44. Note that later Morse proposed a partial-excuse defense called "Guilty But Partially Responsible," which seems to act as what he described in his 1984 paper: the partial responsibility variant of diminished capacity. *See* Morse, *Diminished Rationality*, *supra* note 1, at 299–308.

[18] Morse, *supra* note 5, at 20–28.

[19] *Id.* at 5–7.

rea variant, the defendant is provided with constitutional protections that the partial-responsibility variant does not afford.[20]

According to Morse's early account, there is a logical inconsistency that poses a problem for the partial-responsibility variant. How can it be that both the prima facie case is satisfactorily made by the prosecution, and all of the elements of the crime charged are proven beyond a reasonable doubt, and yet the defendant's mental capacity at the time of the act was diminished in a way that meaningfully undermines a finding that he is completely responsible for its commission? Advocates of the partial-responsibility variant may argue that the defense of diminished capacity serves to undermine the prosecution's prima facie case. That is, the defense of diminished capacity acts to at least create a reasonable doubt as to the defendant's ability to form the requisite mens rea and, in this way, undermines or otherwise combats the prima facie case presented by the prosecution.

The mens rea variant would appear to avoid the possibility of such a logical inconsistency in that this framing of diminished capacity is not a defense at all, but rather a doctrine of law that specifically acknowledges the defendant's constitutional right to present legitimate, exculpatory evidence to defeat the prosecution's case. However, it is not difficult to see how and why courts have continued to treat diminished capacity as an affirmative defense (consistent with the partial-responsibility variant). Even in the case of the mens rea variant, the defendant concedes that he committed a wrongful, harmful act, just as he does in the case of the partial-responsibility variant. Certainly, this is not the same as conceding that he met all elements (including the requisite mens rea) of the charged crime, but it is an admission of considerable import nonetheless. In this way, it is true in the case of either variant that the doctrine has a strong flavor of excuse in that the defendant may concede that he committed an act that is seriously wrongful and harmful – so seriously wrongful and harmful that its commission is prohibited by law and punishable by loss of negative liberty – but that he is not responsible for having done so.

Surely, the concepts of capacity and responsibility are inherently interwoven. Indeed, Morse's more recent writings have called for a defense based on diminished rationality, which can be likened to the partial-responsibility variant of diminished capacity.[21] This would appear to be an adjustment of

[20] *Id.* at 7 (arguing that any limitation placed on the mens rea variant is a violation of the defendant's Sixth and Fourteenth Amendment rights).

[21] Stephen J. Morse, *Excusing and the New Excuse Defenses: A Legal and Conceptual Review*, 23 CRIME & JUST. 329 (1998); Morse, *Rationality, supra* note 1; Morse, *Diminished Rationality, supra* note 1.

understanding and philosophy of criminal responsibility on Morse's part, and one with which I concur. Morse's diminished rationality defense, called "Guilty But Partially Responsible," essentially states that in the case of the criminal defendant who has acted out of a nonculpable form of cognitive dysfunction but was not so severely impaired that he meets the criteria for insanity or other recognized excuse defense, he should not be found completely responsible for his bad act.[22]

Here, "rationality" represents a specific and uniquely important capacity (i.e., social-cognitive-operating),[23] as it is only via rationality that a person's functional capacity can be related to the criminal law. That is, a person can only understand the criminal law, as well as whether and how to abide by it, through his rational capacity and functioning. Rational capacity, then, lies at the foundation of culpability, which is a specific designation of responsibility. One can be responsible, of course, for acts that range broadly from morally good to bad (i.e., the most virtuous to the most evil). Culpability, however, specifically refers to responsibility for functioning that is necessarily bad and deserving of blame.[24] Whereas culpability may be conceptualized broadly as responsibility for that which is morally wrong, criminal culpability refers strictly to responsibility for conduct that violates the criminal law. Determinations of criminal culpability thus presume sufficient rational capacity on the part of the wrongdoer.

There are two further clarifications that should be made before moving forward with a specific discussion of rationality and its role in the intersection of social cognition and criminal law. The first has to do with the distinction between diminished capacity and *diminished actuality*. Diminished actuality is associated with a shift in California state law and refers not to the capacity to form the requisite mens rea of the crime charged, but rather whether the defendant *actually* formed the mens rea in question.[25] Note that the concept of diminished actuality is independent of social-cognitive impairment. That is, a fully rational, mentally sound person may demonstrate that she did not, in actuality, form the mens rea required by the crime charged.[26]

[22] Morse, *Diminished Rationality*, *supra* note 1. The concepts of *diminished rationality* (Morse's term) and *non-culpable cognitive dysfunction* (Fontaine's term) are important and discussion of each is provided in the following two subsections, respectively.

[23] A social-cognitive framing of rationality is presented and discussed later in this chapter.

[24] Typically, culpability is discussed with respect to conduct. However, one can be culpable for his bad thoughts and emotions, as well.

[25] *See* Robert Weinstock, Gregory B. Leong, & J. Arturo Silva, *California's Diminished Capacity Defense: Evolution and Transformation*, 24 Bull. Am. Acad. Psychiatry & L. 347, 350 (1996).

[26] *Id.*

Second, legitimate diminished capacity should be distinguished from "wayward desire" or "weak will."[27] In a pair of recent articles published in *Criminal Law and Philosophy*, Professors Stephen Garvey and Vera Bergelson debated whether a partial-excuse defense should be recognized for individuals who have the capacity to refrain from the criminality with which they are charged but ultimately give in to desires, urges, or pressures because continued resistance to such forces becomes "too hard."[28] Individual differences among humans are virtually limitless in number. In addition, individual differences in human character, personality, and social-cognitive functioning often range considerably. Certainly, it is easier for some to maintain a lawful pattern of conduct than it is for others (e.g., human variability in managing angry impulses). Nevertheless, all citizens are equally required to abide by the law. As citizens under the law, we accept that this requirement often means that more effort and diligence is demanded from certain individuals in certain contexts because of differences in skill sets (e.g., social perception, decision making). Diminished capacity, in contrast, regards the scenario in which the individual is not capable of *freely* forming the culpable mental state elemental to the crime charged or is otherwise *unable* to prevent himself from committing the wrongful, harmful act that is criminally prohibited. Diminished capacity does not apply to scenarios in which the defendant could have acted in accordance with the law but ultimately did not because it became difficult to do otherwise.

THE NATURE AND LEGAL FUNCTION OF RATIONALITY

Recent scholarship by Professors Robert Schopp and Marc Patry has pointed to the difficulty in neatly defining capacity in determinations of individual criminal culpability.[29] Based on their review of judicial findings in capital sentencing cases (and other legal sources that provide statements of culpability), they discerned two principal components of capacity such that an individual may be found to be sufficiently functional and held criminally responsible. First, he needs to have comprehended the harmful nature of his conduct and

[27] *See, e.g.*, Stephen P. Garvey, *Dealing with Wayward Desire*, 3 CRIM. L. & PHIL. 1 (2009); Vera Bergelson, *The Case of Weak Will and Wayward Desire*, 3 CRIM. L. AND PHIL. 19 (2009); *see also* RICHARD HOLTON, *WILLING, WANTING, WAITING* (2009).

[28] Garvey, *supra* note 27, at 10; Bergelson, supra note 27, at 21. Note that the language "too hard" may be interpreted to mean that the defendant reached a point at which he no longer had the capacity to control himself and refrain from criminal action. However, "too hard" in this context must be interpreted to mean "very hard" because the type of individual discussed by Garvey and Bergelson does indeed continue to have the capacity to act lawfully.

[29] Schopp & Patry, *supra* note 4, at 646–47.

its likely consequences.[30] Second, the defendant must be able to "direct one's conduct through a minimally adequate process of practical reasoning that incorporates this comprehension in the process of decision making."[31] As is often evident in discussions of individual capacity and responsibility, attempts to clarify and define these terms have the potential to lead to further perplexing issues. For example, with respect to the language "a minimally adequate process of practical reasoning," questions are begged as to what mechanisms and processes practical reasoning entails, as well as where legally and psychologically meaningful cutoffs should be set. What is clear here is that two basic mental abilities that are basic to rational judgment and decision making have been discerned, and these point to rationality as the centerpiece of functional capacity, personal responsibility, and criminal culpability.

The nature and scope of human rationality have been matters of great interest in philosophy, law, and the social and behavioral sciences since the earliest days of each of these fields. As with several of the terms and concepts already discussed, rationality has been defined in numerous fashions. Rationality involves many thought processes, including – but certainly not limited to – perception, interpretation, goal identification and assessment, estimation of cause-effect relations, and comparative selection. The rational actor is one who acts based on these items: (1) his identification and prioritization of his interests, (2) his association of causes and effects, and (3) his determination as to the relative likelihoods that certain actions will lead to desired outcomes and other actions will avoid or prevent aversive consequences. The assumption, held at times by disciplines within the social (economics) and behavioral (psychology) sciences, that humans are naturally rational actors, has been radically challenged. In psychology, for instance, it is now well accepted that much human action is more appropriately characterized as being automatically processed and enacted than operating by conscious, rational thought.

Just as clear, however, is that certain human actions are indeed guided by rational thought. There are at least three types of scenarios in which an individual is relatively likely to use rational decision making in the process of selecting a behavioral option for enactment.[32] First, novel situations may necessitate one to process information conceptually and engage in rational decision making to interpret the nature of the situation and its personal

30 *Id.* at 647.

31 *Id.*

32 *See* Reid G. Fontaine & Kenneth A. Dodge, *Real-Time Decision Making and Aggressive Behavior in Youth: A Heuristic Model of Response Evaluation and Decision (RED)*, 32 Aggressive Behav. 604 (2006) (discussing rational versus impulsive decision making in the development of aggressive behavior) [hereinafter Fontaine, *Real-Time Decision*].

relevance. For example, one who is new to a job is less likely to automatically or impulsively go about his day because he is presented with tasks for which he is not completely familiar. Second, situations that present a challenge to the responder are more likely to require rational thought. Typically, challenge situations are ones in which the responder has identified multiple, competing (or even diametrically opposing) goals. For example, one who is unsure as to how to respond to a coworker who has asked a personal question of him may need to estimate how he can tactfully avoid divulging information that should be kept private. Whereas he does not want to reveal the personal information requested, he also wants to avoid offending his coworker in order to maintain a good working relationship. Third are situations that are so highly valued by the actor that their outcomes are identified as being of crucial importance. Here, it is not that the scenario is new or that the actor must balance competing goals; rather, the actor so strongly desires that the scenario result in a certain outcome that she considers the features of the situation with great care and applies rational thought to estimate (and perhaps double-check) her expectation that her chosen course of conduct is indeed highly likely to lead to success.

Just as there are certain types of contexts that may be more likely to call for rational thought and conceptual processing of information, so is it probable that there exist instances or periods within other contexts that call for conceptual processing and rational thought. For example, affective states may impact the degree to which a person is contemplative, rational, or otherwise thoughtful. Whereas a person who is experiencing intense emotional arousal (e.g., fury or extreme fear) may be less likely to fully process incoming information and engage in rational decision making, other emotional conditions, such as strong interest,[33] may be more likely to promote reason-based outcomes.[34]

Rationality has been defined in many different ways, by various academic disciplines and intellectual entities. Even within psychological science it has been framed in several alternative lights. Whereas there is agreement among scholars that rationality involves mental processes that promote goal-directed

[33] Professor Carroll Izard was among the first to explore interest as a discrete emotion. Izard described interest (or, in its extreme form, excitement) as "the most frequently experienced positive emotion, [which] provides much of the motivation for learning, the development of skills and competencies, and ... creative endeavor." CARROLL E. IZARD, *HUMAN EMOTIONS* 85 (1977). A more recent exploration by Professor Paul Silvia demonstrates that interest plays a critical role in scientific understanding of why humans behave as they do. PAUL J. SILVIA, *EXPLORING THE PSYCHOLOGY OF INTEREST* (C. R. Snyder ed., 2006).

[34] *See* John A. Lambie, *On the Irrationality of Emotion and the Rationality of Awareness*, 17 CONSCIOUSNESS & COGNITION 946 (2007) (discussing the relationship between emotion and rationality).

behavioral decision making, consensus has yet to be reached as to more specific issues, such as how broad the scope of mental processes encompassed by rationality is (e.g., is cognitive functioning at a basic perceptual level a rational process?) and to what degree rationality is limited to conscious performance (e.g., can a person rationally pursue a goal of which he is not consciously aware?). Disagreement stems from differences in scholarly concentration (e.g., philosophy versus psychology), perspective (e.g., consequentialist versus deontological), scientific limitation (e.g., consciousness itself continues to be a matter of considerable scientific inquiry), and, of course, semantics.

The law is guided by an understanding or model of adult human behavior. Implicit in this model is the law's presumption that humans share some basic functional capacities. The general ability of humans to act in accordance with the law, of course, embodies multiple structurally and functionally discernible capacities, such as motor functioning and voluntary action. Among these capacities, it would seem that most critical is the general capacity of rationality. Without rational thought, one would not be able to understand the law such that it could influence, much less guide, one's conduct. Thus it is only via its presumption of rational capacity that the law could reasonably expect that it could bear meaning for human action such that one's assessment of her action may be determined to be either lawful or unlawful.

So there is a legal presumption that humans have the capacity to act for reasons and indeed do act for reasons. Consistent with this presumption is that citizens under the law maintain the capacity to understand, internalize, and act in abidance with the law such that they may navigate their lives in ways that meet their interests and desires (i.e., reason-directed action). Cooperation with the law on the part of its citizenry may be presumed to the degrees that citizens (1) share interests and values that the law is designed to reflect and protect, (2) can understand expressions and statements of the law, and (3) can act in accordance with said interests, values, and understanding.[35] In the absence of one or more of these three components of mental functioning, the expectation on the part of the law that citizens act in accordance with it may itself – at least from an empirical perspective – be deemed unreasonable.[36]

[35] I do not intend to communicate here that this is the only legal conceptualization of rationality, but rather that it is a framing that sensibly ties together the law and the conduct of its citizenry. *See, e.g.*, Morse, *Rationality*, *supra* note 1 at 254.

[36] Of course, this expectation is a normative one. Citizens are expected to abide by the law, in part, because they *should* abide by the law – that is, because lawful conduct is proper conduct. This overarching value trumps individual differences among citizens with respect to issue-specific values. For example, a citizen *x* may believe that it is morally acceptable, or even necessary, to use physical violence against citizen *y*, the latter of whom has made public statements that insult his children. X may believe that *y* deserves to be the recipient of his

When we discuss the role and importance of functional capacity in criminal law, we are, at some level, discussing a set of abilities that philosophers have long attributed to free will, which is the broad capacity by which rational actors may choose among alternative courses of conduct in order to pursue an identified goal or set of goals. Rationality lies at the heart of this premise. In fact, it is the key capacity on which personal responsibility rests. Whereas it is not necessary for an individual to have used rational judgment and decision making at the time that he acted in order for him to be responsible for his act, it is necessary that he had the general capacity of rationality at the time that he acted.[37] In the case of the defendant who acted in an unlawful manner, he is criminally responsible for his act if he had the general capacity of rationality at the time of the act, regardless of whether he indeed acted rationally.

If the general capacity of rationality is the critical criterion of criminal responsibility, then the absence of rationality must also be a condition by which one may be excused of criminal responsibility and, in turn, punishment. Of course, there are limitations.[38] Immanuel Kant stressed rationality as the principal element of human agency.[39] It is via an agent's rationality that he may be said to have moral worth or bear moral responsibility. Indeed numerous other philosophers, such as John Locke and Thomas Hobbes, have maintained rationality as a fundamental requirement of moral agency.[40] The citizen who lacks sufficient rationality to abide by the law cannot be said to be responsible for violating the law.

It should not be surprising, then, that the issue of rationality, either implicitly or explicitly, arises in consideration of excuse-based defenses in criminal law.

aggression and that *y* will continue to make similar derogatory statements unless he is subject to *x*'s retaliation. Nevertheless, the law expects *x* to abstain from enacting violence against *y* and refrain from all acts that, although potentially morally and consequentially compelling (depending on the citizen's personal values and cause-effect estimations), are unlawful. That is, the duty to abide by the law trumps the individual's "personal morality." In this way, the expectation on the part of the law that citizens abide by the law is not unreasonable even in the case of the citizen who holds values that are dramatically opposed to those on which the law stands. With this said, from an empirical perspective, it may be that x is far less likely to act in a lawful manner, at least with respect to criminal battery, than are citizens whose respective values are consistent with those reflected by the law. In other words, it may be *empirically* unreasonable to expect *x* to abide by the law.

37 Morse, *Rationality, supra* note 1, at 252–53.

38 See the discussion of nonculpable cognitive dysfunction later in the chapter.

39 *See, e.g.*, Andrews Reath, *The Categorical Imperative and Kant's Conception of Practical Rationality, in* AGENCY AND AUTONOMY IN KANT'S MORAL THEORY: SELECTED ESSAYS 67 (2006).

40 *See, e.g.*, Carol Rovane, *Rationality and Persons, in* THE OXFORD HANDBOOK OF RATIONALITY 320, 327 (Alfred R. Mele & Piers Rawling eds., 2004).

Its relevance to a general diminished capacity (or diminished responsibility) defense, as well as legal insanity, should already be abundantly clear. The capacity of rationality, however, is at least implicit in other excuse defenses as well. For example, the heat-of-passion (or provocation) defense partially excuses the murder defendant via an undermining of rationality that occurs as a result of extreme emotional arousal.[41] Juvenile violent offenders are said to be "less guilty" by reason that they have not yet fully developed the ability to engage in rational decision making as compared to adults.[42] Rationality may go to the defense of duress in that the defendant's wrongful conduct may have been at least partially realized out of extreme fear of harm, a condition that may limit evaluative decision-making processes central to rational thought and conduct.[43] Killings by battered individuals are sometimes (at least partially) excused on the grounds that chronic victimization caused them psychological dysfunction and a distorted sense of material issues of their objective realities (such as whether leaving the abuser is a course of action that is a legitimate alternative to reactive homicide).[44] These are but a few examples of excuse-based defenses for which the issue of rationality – or, rather, lack or impairment thereof – may be material. It is in this way that the spirit of the diminished capacity defense remains alive and well.

[41] *See* Reid G. Fontaine, *Reactive Cognition, Reactive Emotion: Toward a More Psychologically-Informed Understanding of Reactive Homicide*, 14 PSYCHOL. PUB. POL'Y & L. 243 (2008); Reid G. Fontaine, *The Wrongfulness of Wrongly Interpreting Wrongfulness: Provocation, Interpretational Bias, and Heat of Passion Homicide*, 12 NEW CRIM. L. REV. 69 (2009). This understanding of heat of passion/provocation is not without its opposition, however. *See* Symposium, *The Nature, Structure, and Function of Heat of Passion/Provocation as a Criminal Defense*, 43 U. MICH. J.L. REFORM 1 (2009).

[42] *E.g.*, Laurence Steinberg & Elizabeth S. Scott, *Less Guilty by Reason of Adolescence: Developmental Immaturity, Diminished Responsibility, and the Juvenile Death Penalty*, 58 AM. PSYCHOLOGIST 1009 (2003).

[43] *See e.g.*, Jason S. Moser, Greg Hajcak & Robert F. Simons, *The Effects of Fear on Performance Monitoring and Attentional Allocation*, 42 PSYCHOPHYSIOLOGY 261 (2005); James H. Geer, *Effect of Fear Arousal upon Task Performance and Verbal Behavior*, 71 J. ABNORMAL PSYCHOL. 119 (1966); Anna Pissiota, Örjan Frans, Åsa Michelgård, Lieuwe Appel, Bengt Långström, Magne A. Flaten & Mats Fredrikson, *Amygdala and Anterior Cingulate Cortex Activation During Affective Startle Modulation: A PET Study of Fear*, 18 EUROPEAN J. NEUROSCIENCE 1325 (2003); Gerald L. Clore, Norbert Schwarz & Michael Conway, *Affective Causes and Consequences of Social Information Processing*, *in* 1 HANDBOOK OF SOCIAL COGNITION, BASIC PROCESSES 323 (Robert S. Wyer, Jr. & Thomas K. Srull eds., 2d ed. 1994).

[44] Alternatively, feminist theorists argue that battered women who have committed homicides may be exonerated on the ground of *justification* because they killed in self-defense. *See* Robert T. Sigler & Chadwick L. Shook, *Judicial Acceptance of the Battered Woman Syndrome*, 8 CRIM. JUST. POL'Y REV. 365, 368–69 (1997).

"SUBRATIONALITY": UNDERDEVELOPED RATIONALITY AND NONCULPABLE COGNITIVE DYSFUNCTION

Morse has used the term "diminished rationality" to emphasize that it is the capacity for rationality that serves as the key mechanism (or set of mechanisms) or domain of human functioning by which personal responsibility arises and, likewise, a partial-responsibility defense is morally valid.[45] In particular, he proposes that it is the absence of the capacity for rationality, as opposed to some other capacity, or the prevalence of a syndrome such as a mental illness or disorder, that is grounds for a formal partial-responsibility defense. Although I agree with the premise, the term itself carries with it certain implications that require some inquiry.

My interest in the accuracy of the term lies in the word *diminished*. That which is diminished is decreased or lessened; it is less than it once was. The term diminished rationality thus depicts a condition of mental functioning that is lesser than it was at an earlier time. However, there are two alternatives to this depiction that are worth considering.

First is the case of juvenile offenders. Professors Larry Steinberg and Elizabeth Scott have argued that adolescents should be found "less guilty" and therefore punished less because, as compared to adults, they are significantly less developed in critical ways that are material to criminal responsibility.[46] This "developmental immaturity," as Steinberg and Scott have termed it, reflects more of an "underdeveloped rationality"[47] than a diminished rationality. That is, it is not that the adolescent wrongdoer's rationality is diminished, but rather that it has not sufficiently developed to the degree to which it may be said to meet the threshold of rationality that is presumed of adult agents by the law.

A related case is that of the adult actor with mental retardation, which is a developmental disability for which onset is prior to age eighteen. Mental retardation consists of subaverage intellectual and adaptive functioning by which one's cognitive abilities and functional skills in his environment are limited. One with mental retardation typically has difficulty in basic mental operations that are central to rationality, such as social learning, problem solving,

[45] Morse, *Diminished Rationality, supra* note 1.

[46] Steinberg, *Less Guilty, supra* note 42; *see also*, Elizabeth Cauffman & Laurence Steinberg, *(Im)maturity of Judgment in Adolescence: Why Adolescents May Be Less Culpable than Adults*, 18 BEHAV. SCI. & L.741 (2000); Laurence Steinberg & Elizabeth Cauffman, *Maturity of Judgment in Adolescence: Psychosocial Factors in Adolescent Decision Making*, 20 L. & HUM. BEHAV. 249 (1996).

[47] The concept of underdeveloped rationality is explored in Chapter 4.

and evaluative judgment and decision making. Because onset must be prior to age eighteen for mental retardation to be diagnosed, the adult with mental retardation may not be said to have ever reached the level of cognitive functioning sufficient to meet the presumption of rationality that the law makes of adult agents. That is, his rationality is "substandard" in that it is not sufficiently developed to meet the standard or threshold of rationality presumed of human actors by the law. As it is not that the adult with mental retardation lost sufficient rationality, but rather that he never developed it, the term "diminished rationality" seems odd if not outright inaccurate.

I believe that an alternative term may more fairly and comprehensively account for these alternative scenarios. I propose that either the term *insufficient rationality* or, more simply, *subrationality* would better reflect states in which one's rationality has been substantially lessened (as in the case of Morse's proposed partial-responsibility defense) or is, quite simply, underdeveloped (as in the case of Steinberg and Scott's developmental immaturity argument or the adult with mental retardation). Subrationality may be used to broadly account for any case in which, due to nonculpable causes or reasons, the actor's mental capacity does not meet the minimum standard of rationality necessary for the legal presumption of adult agents such that full responsibility for wrongdoing may be rightly attributed.

Subrationality, then, exists as a function of either underdevelopment or diminishment of rationality. The latter case may be most accurately and fully described by the term *nonculpable cognitive dysfunction* (NCCD). NCCD should be understood as a psycholegal term. It reflects the essence of Morse's concept of diminished rationality but it also emphasizes that any impairment in the defendant's functioning must have resulted from nonculpable causes for it to be material to his criminal responsibility and transfers the focus on mental functioning from philosophical terminology (rationality) to terminology that is founded in psychological science (cognitive operating or executive function).

The defendant who suffers from or exhibits legitimate cognitive dysfunction to the degree that it is substandard to that which is presumed by law of adult agents may have a rationality-based claim that is material to excusing her criminal responsibility. However, it is also the case that she may not. Not only must the defendant's rationality limitation be of a serious nature, but also the cognitive dysfunction in question must have been nonculpably formed. That is, the defendant could not have caused her own cognitive dysfunction by knowingly or willingly engaging in a form of conduct that the defendant either knew or should have known would likely cause impairment to her mental faculties.

If one's cognitive dysfunction is nonculpable, it may serve as a condition for which the sufferer is not responsible. However, there are two ways in which one's cognitive dysfunction may fail this requirement. First is the case of the individual who engaged in an act that he knew (or should have known) would cause cognitive impairment. A typical example is the person who drinks alcohol or uses illicit drugs.[48] The vast majority of individuals who drink and use drugs know that a likely, if not certain, causal chain will transpire by which the administered substance will dull and otherwise lessen one's cognitive capacity and functioning. Even in the unusual case that one does not understand or know of this causal relation, the sufficiently developed and cognitively intact adult *should* know of it. In such a case, the substance user's resultant cognitive dysfunction does not serve to excuse any wrongdoing committed while under the influence. In the case of the individual who is involuntarily subjected to the administration of alcohol or illicit drugs, however, it may be said that his resultant cognitive dysfunction is nonculpable as long as he acted reasonably, given the circumstances, to prevent its administration.

Second, we might also consider the case of one who has developed a cognitive bias such that his rationality is limited. Take, for example, the phenomenon of moral disengagement.[49] Moral disengagement is the process (or, more accurately, set of processes) by which a person disconnects the moral content of an antisocial act so that the act's moral qualities may not serve to inhibit him from carrying out the act. For example, a thief may consider that a woman who walks through the city streets late at night is so foolish that she deserves to be robbed. By conceptualizing the woman as someone who has acted so unwisely that she deserves the harm caused by robbery, the thief alleviates himself of moral inhibition and potential postbehavioral cognitive dissonance, thereby freeing himself to successfully carry out the criminal act.

It is likely, however, that moral disengagement can develop out of multiple alternative etiologies. For example, one may develop a processing style by which moral disengagement plays an active role in his behavioral decision making because he grew up in a coercive environment and learned that this thinking style is conducive to survival and adaptation. Alternatively, one may

[48] Michael L. Corrado, *Addiction and the Theory of Action*, 25 Quinnipiac L. Rev. 117 (2006) (arguing that addicts may suffer from a defect of will relevant to ascribing criminal responsibility to their addiction-related acts).

[49] Albert Bandura, Claudio Barbaranelli, Gian V. Caprara & Concetta Pastorelli, *Mechanisms of Moral Disengagement in the Exercise of Moral Agency*, 71 J. Personality & Soc. Psychol. 364 (1996). Gian V. Caprara, Reid G. Fontaine, Roberta Fida, Marinella Paciello, Marie S. Tisak & Kenneth A. Dodge, *The Contributions and Reciprocal Influences of Irritability, Hostile Rumination, and Moral Disengagement to Aggression and Violence in Adolescence* (unpublished manuscript, on file with lead author).

develop active and even automatic moral disengagement by repeated rationalization of antisocial behavioral options associated with desired outcomes. That is, one may rehearse antisocial behavioral scripts such that the moral content of the behavior under consideration is quickly and effectively discounted or reformulated such that it no longer serves to inhibit the actor. One who has developed an automatic or crystallized moral disengagement as part of his prebehavioral evaluative decision making may be cognitively and rationally limited in a way relevant to criminal responsibility. However, in the case of the first etiology (the person who has grown up in a coercive environment), the resultant cognitive dysfunction may be said to have been nonculpably formed. In contrast, in the case of the second etiology (the person who purposefully cerebrates moral disengagement as part of his rehearsal of antisocial behavioral scripts), the actor's cognitive limitation, although perhaps crystallized and even irreversible, must be discerned to have been formed in a culpable fashion.

Nonculpability also requires nonforeseeability (or, more exactly, nonreasonable foreseeability). In the case of an individual who is cognitively dysfunctional, and said dysfunction was initially nonculpably formed, she may be aware of her psychological condition. She may also be aware of how her psychological condition may be related to certain problem behaviors, such as antisocial and criminal conduct. In such a case, the individual is, or at least should be, able to foresee how her condition may contribute to or largely cause her criminal action. Where a person is able to foresee this causal chain, and she does not act reasonably to prevent the causal chain from being realized, her condition of cognitive dysfunction may not serve to excuse her criminal conduct.

For example, a person may be aware that he has a severe provocation interpretational bias. His bias may be sufficiently pervasive across varied social contexts such that it has caused him and those around him problems in the past. Perhaps he has suffered severe consequences as a result, such as losing his job due to his reactive hostility in the workplace. Or perhaps he has received angry feedback from family, friends, and acquaintances who have been subjected to his confrontational responses after he has misinterpreted social events. In such a case, the individual at least should be able to foresee how his processing style may contribute to his future criminal conduct, and so he has a responsibility to pursue an intervening course of action through which his bias may be corrected, or at least lessened or managed. This course of action may entail a variety of components, including both the removal of certain behaviors suspected to be conducive to and to reinforce the biased processing style (e.g., violent video games, hard pornography) as well as the addition of a variety of components, which may include therapy and/or medication. If he does not meet this responsibility, his cognitive limitation (or subrationality) may not be said to be nonculpable and so it would not suffice as an excusing condition if he were to find himself a criminal defendant.

Of course, there may be instances in which the causal association between one's cognitive dysfunction and criminal conduct is foreseeable, but the individual is unable to take a course of action by which the likelihood of the causal chain being realized may not be eliminated. Consider the case of the impoverished individual with no health insurance. Here, the person may not be able to secure professional help by which her psychological condition may be adequately treated. In the case of an individual who foresees (or should be able to foresee) that her rational limitation may lead to her criminal conduct but is not able to pursue a corrective course of action, foreseeability does not serve as an exception to the excusability of her otherwise nonculpable cognitive dysfunction.

It may be, however, that one's cognitive dysfunction is precisely related to her own subjective foreseeability. That is, one may have developed a processing limitation by which she is unable, or at least significantly less able, to associate cause-and-effect sequences. For example, in the case of the person who exhibits a severe provocation interpretational bias, she may have received considerable feedback over time and across contexts from others about her distorted interpretations of social events. Such feedback, however, may be viewed as hostile or provocative in and of itself, and so it may not be at all effective in promoting a better understanding of the individual's condition or what problem behaviors it may cause. Paradoxically, in this way the feedback may reinforce and even exacerbate the person's cognitive bias. In this case, the individual may be more likely to associate the cause of (perceived) provocation by others with the effect of her antisocial reactivity.

An individual may also be limited such that he has a difficult time associating causes with effects. During the response-evaluation-and-decision step of SIP, it is hypothesized that an individual computes relative likelihoods of alternative outcomes being realized when comparing different behavioral response options.[50] If a person's goal is to be socially respected, he may calculate a different likelihood for acting in a socially competent versus aggressive fashion. However, individual differences in this type of processing are likely wide-ranging, and some individuals may not be able to associate causal cognitions and behaviors with outcomes. This limitation, broadly conceived, may

[50] *See* Fontaine, *Real-Time Decision*, *supra* note 32.

be likened to an inability to foresee one's future criminal conduct even when he is largely aware of his problematic cognitive dysfunction.

This issue goes to the reasonable-person standard in that foreseeability rests on the objective test of whether a reasonable person would have foreseen that the subject's cognitive difficulty had the potential to lead to the defendant's subsequent criminal conduct. Reasonableness is a strange concept to introduce to this discussion because we are speaking of individuals who are necessarily "unreasonable" in that they have a cognitive dysfunction sufficiently severe that it may serve to excuse criminally wrongful conduct. Nevertheless, because foreseeability rests on reasonableness, the paradoxical question of whether a necessarily unreasonable person is sufficiently reasonable to recognize the foreseeability of his cognitive dysfunction leading to his criminal conduct may need to be ascertained. Of course, if the defendant is deemed so rationally limited that the reasonable-person standard does or should not apply, such as in the case of psychiatric illness, then the issue of foreseeability is moot with respect to the nature of the developmental course of the defendant's subrationality.

SOCIAL-INFORMATION PROCESSING AS A SOCIAL-COGNITIVE FRAMEWORK OF SUBRATIONALITY

Within psychology, alternative models of rationality have been offered. In social development, SIP theory has been empirically supported across several research paradigms and human populations. SIP has been characterized in a number of different ways. Early models framed SIP as a model of social competence. After several studies presented the predictive utility of SIP in relation to the development of aggression in youth, it became more common for SIP to be viewed as a model of aggressive social behavior. More in-depth theoretical accounts framed SIP as a learning model. However, SIP is also properly understood as a model of the development of rational thought and decision making. In fact, the model has been criticized for focusing too much on rational mental processes. Recent reformulations of SIP have directly responded to this criticism and have placed more emphasis on the roles of impulsivity and automatic processing.[51] In particular, the response decision step was expanded to reflect the development of evaluative behavioral judgment and rational decision making in balance with the role of impulsivity. Nevertheless, the model presents

[51] *See e.g.*, *Real-Time Decision*, *supra* note 32; Reid G. Fontaine, *Online Social Decision Making and Antisocial Behavior: Some Essential but Neglected Issues*, 28 CLINICAL PSYCHOL. REV. 17 (2008).

a comprehensive organization of the various perceptual and information-processing operations that are comprised by rationality in humans.

In recent years, SIP has been increasingly viewed as a model of criminogenic cognitive processing, or processing that contributes to the enactment of antisocial conduct. In particular, Professor Emma Palmer has written about thinking and reasoning styles associated with criminals and has focused on SIP as well as moral reasoning.[52] Research has shown that criminals tend to demonstrate these characteristics: (1) undercontrolled processing (or impulsive processing), (2) a reliance on an external locus of control, (3) concrete as opposed to abstract thinking, and (4) poor social perspective taking, social problem solving, and moral reasoning.[53] However, as Palmer points out, initial research tended to consist of studies that focused on only one or two variables and, as a result, early theoretical models of criminogenic cognitive processing were troubled by conceptual gaps, or critical questions as to the nature of criminal thinking that had been neglected and unanswered. Palmer correctly views contemporary models of social-information processing as a considerable improvement, demonstrating a more comprehensive organization of cognitive processing problems associated with offending behavior.[54]

Palmer also cites moral reasoning as an important area of empirical research for understanding group differences between criminal and noncriminal adults, as well as individual differences among adult offenders. Models of moral reasoning typically focus on social-cognitive domains such as moral judgment (e.g., assigning moral weights to individual behaviors based on their social meaning and what outcomes they are likely to produce) and perspective taking (or considering situations and events from the perspective of another). Here, I agree with Palmer, although I do not at all consider moral reasoning to be an entity separate from SIP, but rather a specific set of processes encompassed by SIP. For example, at step 2 of SIP, interpretation of cues, an individual may engage in perspective taking to consider alternative meanings

[52] Emma J. Palmer, *Criminal Thinking, in* APPLYING PSYCHOLOGY TO CRIMINAL JUSTICE 147 (David Carson, Rebecca Milne, Francis Pakes, Karen Shalev & Andrea Shawyer eds., 2007) [hereinafter Palmer, *Criminal Thinking*]; Emma J. Palmer, *An Overview of the Relationship Between Moral Reasoning and Offending*, 38 AUSTRALIAN PSYCHOLOGIST 165 (2003); EMMA J. PALMER, OFFENDING BEHAVIOUR: MORAL REASONING, CRIMINAL CONDUCT AND THE REHABILITATION OF OFFENDERS (2003).

[53] Palmer, *Criminal Thinking, supra* note 52; Daniel H. Antonowicz, *The Reasoning and Rehabilitation Program: Outcome Evaluations with Offenders*, in SOCIAL PROBLEM SOLVING AND OFFENDING: EVIDENCE, EVALUATION AND EVOLUTION 163 (Mary McMurran & James McGuire eds., 2005).

[54] Palmer, *Criminal Thinking, supra* note 52, at 148.

of a social cue and determine the most likely intent of the social stimulus.[55] At step 5 of SIP, response evaluation and decision, one may make a sociomoral valuation of a behavioral option based on the behavior's moral content and whether she identifies with the behavior as a civic agent.[56] Because SIP is a comprehensive model of evaluative and rational decision making, it naturally recognizes the processes that are potentially active in moral reasoning.

SIP accounts for the two sets of processes outlined by Schopp and Patry discussed earlier (comprehension of the nature of one's behavior and evaluative decision making based on said comprehension), and these processes are fundamental to rationality. Likewise, SIP encompasses the various psychological processes that may, when biased, distorted, or otherwise limited or dysfunctional, contribute to *subrationality* as a criminal law construct. For example, one may not be able to understand the wrongfulness of her criminal conduct, which would be material to a claim of legal insanity. This cognitive deficit is recognized by the response-evaluation-and-decision domain of SIP, as it is at this step of processing that the sociomoral meaning of behavioral options is assessed. Or perhaps an individual is biased in her interpretation of ambiguous provocations such that she quickly and rigidly determines that certain subjectively ambiguous but objectively benign social events are hostile, provocative, and potentially harmful. This deficit in rationality may be relevant to a determination of adequate provocation under the American criminal law doctrine of heat of passion/provocation. These and other psycholegal linkages are explored with respect to individual affirmative defenses in the chapters that follow.

55 Nicki R. Crick & Kenneth A. Dodge, *A Review and Reformulation of Social Information-Processing Mechanisms in Children's Social Adjustment*, 115 Psychological Bull. 74 (1994).

56 Fontaine, *Real-Time Decision*, *supra* note 32.

4

Underdeveloped Rationality and Wrongdoing in Youth

INTRODUCTION

In recent years, scientific focus on psychological differences between adolescents and adults has shifted from a basic research interest in developmental science to an interdisciplinary interest in how research on adolescent/adult differences may inform public policy and law. Psychologists and psycholegal scholars have integrated scientific research findings with critical issues in both civil (e.g., informed medical consent[1]) and criminal (e.g., juvenile death penalty[2]) law for the purpose of influencing lawmakers' and the courts' understanding and recognition of youths' rights and how minors are treated in juvenile justice.[3] Central to these interests and efforts has been social-cognitive and social-developmental research in psychology and behavioral science.[4] Although part of this scholarly shift may be explained by a general movement

[1] *E.g.*, Elizabeth S. Scott, *Judgment and Reasoning in Adolescent Decision Making*, 37 VILL. L. REV. 1607 (1992).

[2] *E.g.*, Laurence Steinberg & Elizabeth S. Scott, *Less Guilty by Reason of Adolescence: Developmental Immaturity, Diminished Responsibility, and the Juvenile Death Penalty*, 58 AM. PSYCHOLOGIST 1009 (2003) [hereinafter Steinburg & Scott, *Less Guilty by Reason of Adolescence*].

[3] *See* LAWRENCE S. WRIGHTSMAN, 11 *JUDICIAL DECISION MAKING: IS PSYCHOLOGY RELEVANT?* (1999).

[4] *See* Stephen J. Morse, *Brain Overclaim Syndrome and Criminal Responsibility: A Diagnostic Note*, 3 OHIO ST. J. CRIM. L. 397, 410 (2006). Here, Morse commented on *Roper v. Simmons*, 543 U.S. 551 (2005), in which the U.S. Supreme Court decided that the juvenile death penalty violates the Eighth Amendment and is thus unconstitutional. Although both behavioral science and neuroscience findings were presented to the Court, Morse pointed out that "[T]he Court did not cite *any* of the neuroscience evidence concerning myelination and pruning that the *amici* and others had urged them to rely on. It did cite six behavioral sources, five of which were high quality behavioral science. Perhaps the neuroscience evidence actually played a role in the decision, as many advocates for the use of neuroscience would like to believe, but there is no evidence in the opinion to support this speculation."

in the academy toward interdisciplinary and translational research,[5] much of it was a response to changes in juvenile justice policy that favored treatment of juvenile offenders as adult criminals. As Professor Laurence Steinberg recognized:

> During the last two decades of the twentieth century, there was a dramatic shift in the way juvenile crime was viewed by policy makers and the public. Rather than choosing to define offenses committed by youth as delinquent, society increasingly opted to deal with young offenders more punitively in the juvenile justice system or to redefine them as adults and try them in adult criminal court. This trend was reflected in the growing number of juvenile offenses adjudicated in adult criminal court, where adolescents are exposed to a far more adversarial proceeding than in juvenile court; in the increasingly punitive response of the criminal justice system to juvenile offenders who are found guilty; and in what some observers have referred to as the "criminalization" of the juvenile justice system itself through increased use of punishment, rather than rehabilitation, as a legitimate juvenile justice goal.[6]

Psychological and behavioral science research on juvenile justice issues has focused on a specific set of psychological differences between adults and juveniles, including susceptibility to coercive influence, decision-making capacity, and character development. The social-cognitive operation of adolescents, of course, lies at the heart of these differences. For example, how capable are adolescents of estimating the likely outcomes of their social behaviors (decision-making capacity)? How accurate are they in their interpretations of others' intentions (susceptibility to coercive influence)? Thus some scholars have specifically addressed social-cognitive issues that may be relevant to juvenile culpability.[7] The primary issue is whether adolescents, who have not reached complete psychological maturation, should be assigned the same degrees of culpability and punishment as adults for the same crimes.

5 *See, e.g.*, Dante Cicchetti & Sheree L. Toth, *Building Bridges and Crossing Them: Translational Research in Developmental Psychopathology*, 18(3) DEV. & PSYCHOPATHOLOGY 619 (2006).

6 Laurence Steinberg, *Adolescent Development and Juvenile Justice*, 5 ANN. REV. CLINICAL PSYCHOL. 47, 48 (2009) [hereinafter Steinberg, *Development*] (footnote omitted).

7 *See, e.g.*, Reid G. Fontaine, *Social Information Processing, Subtypes of Violence, and a Progressive Construction of Culpability and Punishment in Juvenile Justice*, 31 INT'L J.L. & PSYCHIATRY 136 (2008) [hereinafter Fontaine, *Social Information*]; Sandra Graham & Colleen Halliday, *The Social Cognitive (Attributional) Perspective on Culpability in Adolescent Offenders*, *in* YOUTH ON TRIAL: A DEVELOPMENTAL PERSPECTIVE ON JUVENILE JUSTICE 345 (1st. ed., Thomas Grisso & Robert G. Schwartz eds., 2000) (The second author now goes by Halliday-Boykins.).

The idea that adolescents do not yet function at the psychological level of adults is basic to the American justice system. The criminal law presumes a standard of rationality of adult actors that is not presumed of juveniles. In addition, the law's interest in juvenile offenders is more geared toward rehabilitation than it is with retribution, the latter of which is fundamental to the adult criminal justice system. This multifaceted approach toward juvenile offenders is consistent with the spirit of *parens patriae*, a public policy principle that places the best of interests of the child paramount to other interests and values and allows the government to intervene in cases in which the child's best interests have been undermined or discounted. Because youths are in a stage of development that is more rapid and potentially amenable to lasting change, designing a juvenile justice system that facilitates developmental assistance (e.g., rehabilitation) makes good sense. This is not to say, of course, that juvenile justice is not concerned with desert, as it surely is. Rather, juvenile justice attempts to balance retributive and utilitarian values so that social debts are paid for wrongdoing for which the juvenile offender is responsible and the juvenile's developmental trajectory may be "corrected" such that he is turned toward a future of lawful behavior and civic agency. Although much of the effort to tie psychological science findings to juvenile justice has focused on culpability, this research has clear implications for utilitarian values such as rehabilitation and deterrence (or recidivism prevention), as well, and so these issues are of considerable importance to the present discussion.[8]

The purpose of this chapter is to explore issues of adolescent psychological functioning and how social-cognitive research in this area may be useful to informing policy and law. In essence, Chapter 4 explores diminished capacity by examining how a social-developmental analysis may explain not only why adult offenders' moral cognitive functioning may vary, but how criminal law's differential treatment of these offenders may be justified. One issue central to this exploration is that of individual differences. Psychology may be understood as the study of individual differences in mental and behavioral capacities, functions, and processes. Within any group, no matter how similar members in the group may be, humans' individual differences in psychological and behavioral functioning abound. This is a critical issue for a discussion of adolescent/adult functioning differences for a number of reasons, not least of which is that within any developmental period or at any specified age, group members' psychological abilities vary. What this means is that although the law defines majority at the age of eighteen, there are *some* seventeen-year-olds who out-function eighteen-year-olds. Indeed the same may be said even when

[8] Fontaine, *supra* note 7.

comparing sixteen-year-olds with nineteen-year-olds, fifteen-year-olds with twenty-year-olds, and so on, although of course the likelihood that a member in the younger group out-functions a member in the older group quickly declines as the developmental range that separates the two groups increases.

Social-cognitive models may be used to explain how (alternative developmental trajectories) and in what fashion (differential cognitive patterns) some individuals have greater capacity and some are more highly psychologically functional. In this way, they may be highly useful to sharpening a juvenile justice system concerned with both issues of culpability and the betterment of youth and, more broadly, society. Surely, there is much research that is needed in this domain of interdisciplinary science, although a more comprehensive understanding of the most pressing issues is first required.

CONSIDERING DEVELOPMENTAL IMMATURITY AS UNDERDEVELOPED RATIONALITY

Over the last twenty years, considerable attention has been paid to criminal culpability in adolescence and how behavioral science can inform juvenile justice by assessing various aspects of adolescent mental capacity. The term *developmental immaturity* has been used by social scientists and legal scholars to characterize the "diminished capacity" that adolescents have as compared to adults. In particular, Professors Laurence Steinberg, Elizabeth Scott, and Elizabeth Cauffman[9] have argued that, due to adolescents' psychosocial immaturity, they should be assigned less culpability and punishment than adults who commit the same crimes.[10] Their primary argument is that, based on principles in criminal law that culpability is mitigated when the defendant's capacities to act rationally and control himself are diminished, adolescents, because they are necessarily limited in their decision making and other psychological capacities, as compared to adults, should be similarly considered.[11]

[9] Steinberg, Scott, and Cauffman represent an interdisciplinary psycholegal research group, bringing both psychology and law backgrounds to their interdisciplinary efforts (Steinberg and Cauffman are psychologists, whereas Scott is a legal scholar). This group reflects a growing trend in the legal academy to link empirical research with jurisprudence, law, and public policy. *See, e.g.*, PSYCHOLOGY AND LAW: AN EMPIRICAL PERSPECTIVE (Neil Brewer & Kipling D. Williams eds., 2005). As Steinberg is the most prolific and noted of this group with respect to linking adolescent psychological and behavioral development with public policy and juvenile law, I hereafter refer to this group succinctly as Steinberg et al.

[10] *E.g.*, Steinberg & Scott, *Less Guilty by Reason of Adolescence*, *supra* note 2; Elizabeth Cauffman & Laurence Steinberg, *(Im)maturity of Judgment in Adolescence: Why Adolescents May Be Less Culpable Than Adults*, 18 BEHAV. SCI. & L. 741 (2000).

[11] Indeed, Steinberg and Scott accurately point out that, given the clear differences in adolescent versus adult functional capacities, "the correct basis for evaluation [of adolescents] is not

Of course, a legal determination that adolescent capacity is significantly less than that of adults has implications for numerous juvenile justice issues (not just culpability), including how, where, and for how long juveniles are punished.[12] This is important to recognize because the law's responsibility to juvenile offenders is greater than it is to adult offenders because of the former's minority status.

Developmental immaturity as a psychological condition or state is consistent with the spirit of diminished capacity, with one notable qualifier. As articulated in Chapter 3, it is not that the offender's functional capacity has been diminished, but rather that it has not yet fully developed. If we accept that the general capacity of rationality is the key criterion by which responsibility – and with respect to wrongdoing, culpability – is defined, developmental immaturity, then, reflects an *underdeveloped rationality*, a framing that falls in line with the empirical literature on youth psychological functioning. In other words, youths' psychological functioning and capacities are, in general, not so sophisticated that they may be equated with those of adults.

Important to note is that underdeveloped rationality may serve as an excuse for wrongdoing but not as a justification of one's objectively criminal (or, in youths' case, delinquent) conduct. That is, an offender, because of age or developmental status, may be excused of wrongdoing because he does not have the rational capacity to justifiably find him fully responsible for his wrongdoing, but his underdeveloped psychological abilities are irrelevant to the wrongfulness of his unlawful act. It is because developmental immaturity (or underdeveloped rationality) *excuses* that a youth wrongdoer is relieved of culpability and punishment that social-cognitive science comes to bear on the concept's meaning and role in juvenile justice and criminal law.[13]

The developmental-immaturity position includes at least three arguments, defined by at least conceptually distinct areas of psychological and behavioral functioning differences that separate adolescents from adults: (1) decision-making capacity is still developing during adolescence; (2) adolescents are more easily coerced and susceptible to coercive influences than are adults; and (3) adolescents' character is not fully developed (i.e., their identity is not

comparison of the actor's behavior with that of an "ordinary" adult but rather with that of an "ordinary" adolescent." Steinberg & Scott, *Less Guilty by Reason of Adolescence*, *supra* note 2, at 1014. I agree with this conceptual distinction; however, I would argue that formal legal recognition of a reasonable (or ordinary) adolescent standard is *not* in order.

12 Jeffrey Fagan & Franklin E. Zimring, *The Changing Borders of Juvenile Justice: Transfer of Adolescents to the Criminal Court* (1st ed. 2000).

13 See Chapter 3 for a discussion of justification and excuse theories and how this distinction is critical to intersections of social cognitive psychology and criminal law.

fully formed). All three arguments have social-cognitive aspects to them, the most obvious of which is decision-making capacity. However, some research on adolescent decision making suggests that, at least with respect to certain social-cognitive processes, adolescents' psychological functioning does not significantly differ from that of adults.[14] Thus some important questions remain for empirical research. First, what aspects of decision-making and social-cognitive capacity are significantly different in adolescence compared to adulthood? Second, at what point do developmental differences sufficiently taper off such that they are no longer meaningful (in terms of effect size) to juvenile justice? Third, do differences in cognitive functioning between adolescents and adults vary as a function of type of violence (i.e., instrumental versus reactive)? Fourth, do published differences in adolescent and adult social-cognitive functioning emerge when comparison groups are close in age (i.e., comparing sixteen/seventeen-year olds with eighteen/nineteen-year olds versus comparing fourteen/fifteen-year olds with twenty/twenty-one-year olds)? Social-cognitive research in particular will continue to be crucial to progress in this area of interdisciplinary and translational study.

"Developmental Immaturity" Arguments

As described earlier, the developmental-immaturity position states that because functional capacities critical to determinations of culpability and punishment in the law are significantly lesser (or underdeveloped) in adolescence as compared to adulthood, adolescents should not be attributed the same degrees of culpability and punishment as are adults for the same crimes. There are three arguments on which this position is founded, all leading to the conclusion that adolescents' psychosocial status should serve to mitigate juveniles' culpability and punishment in criminal justice. First, it is argued that because adolescents' decision-making capacity is lesser, they do not function with the same level of rationality as is presumed by the law of adult agents. Second, because one aspect of adolescents' lesser decision-making capacity is susceptibility to the influence of others, adolescents should be viewed as less guilty than adults would be in situations in which they are subject to coercive social mechanisms. Third, the developmental-immaturity argument contends that because identity and character continue to undergo important developmental change in adolescence, bad acts that may otherwise be attributable to bad

[14] *See* Beth Beyth-Marom, Laurel Austin, Baruch Fischhoff, Claire Palmgren & Marilyn Jacobs-Quadrel, *Perceived Consequences of Risky Behaviors: Adults and Adolescents*, 29 Developmental Psychol. 549 (1993).

character would be better understood as a product of undermaturation in a developmental context. That is, adolescents' lack of good character should be attributed to the fact that they are still developing rather than that they are characterologically flawed people who are prone to chronic wrongthinking and wrongdoing. It is my contention that each of these tracks must "travel" through (or is contextualized by) social-cognitive development, and so this notion is discussed in the process of reviewing the three arguments.

Argument 1: Decision-Making Capacity

The first of the three developmental-immaturity arguments is that adolescent decision-making capacity is deficient, as compared to adults. There is some question as to what degree adolescent/adult differences in social decision making are a function of a disparity in decision-making capacity or psychosocial maturity, the latter of which may be important to accessing and utilizing the former in real-life social settings. This empirical question remains open. Whereas there is evidence that the decision-making capacity of older adolescents approaches that of young adults,[15] it is equally clear that further research is needed to specifically examine adolescents' decision making in everyday social dynamics and exchanges.

In their 2003 influential review[16] of the scientific research and policy argument against the juvenile death penalty,[17] Steinberg and Scott argued that the research on which it has been concluded by some that adolescent/adult differences in decision making have sufficiently tapered off by mid-adolescence for them to be no longer meaningful to juvenile justice is not conclusive.[18] They highlighted that such studies are typically conducted in a laboratory setting, not in a natural social dynamic, and in response to hypothetical scenarios. As adolescent decision making in the real world typically is not characterized by any of these features, Steinberg and Scott expressed skepticism about the idea that even older adolescents' decision making is equal to that of adults. In addition, they argued that, to the degree that adolescent decision making is close to that of adults by late adolescence, there remain critical

[15] *See* Steinberg, *Development*, *supra* note 6, at 56; ELIZABETH S. SCOTT & LAURENCE STEINBERG, *RETHINKING JUVENILE JUSTICE* 43–44 (2008); Baruch Fischhoff, *Risk Taking: A Developmental Perspective*, *in* RISK-TAKING BEHAVIOR (J. Frank Yates ed., 1st ed. 1992); Lita Furby & Ruth Beyth-Marom, *Risk Taking in Adolescence: A Decision-Making Perspective*, 12 DEVELOPMENTAL REV. 1 (1992).

[16] Steinberg & Scott, *Less Guilty by Reason of Adolescence*, *supra* note 2.

[17] The U.S. Supreme Court subsequently ruled that the juvenile death penalty is unconstitutional as it violates the "cruel and unusual punishment" clause of the Eighth Amendment. Roper v. Simmons, 543 U.S. 551 (2005).

[18] *See* Steinberg & Scott, *Less Guilty by Reason of Adolescence*, *supra* note 2, at 1011–12.

adolescent/adult differences in psychosocial maturity that are directly related to how adolescent decision making unfolds in the real (social) world. Indeed, this has been an area of increasing focus in both developmental and social-cognitive psychology[19] as well as developmental and social-cognitive neuroscience.[20] Four main components of underdeveloped psychosocial maturity have been identified as particularly important to understanding how adolescent decision making develops and how developmental differences between adolescent and adult decision making in everyday interpersonal exchanges – that is, in social-cognitive context – is relevant to juvenile justice.

The first of these is *susceptibility to peer influence*,[21] a quality that may be both directly (conforming in direct response to peer pressure) and indirectly (acting in accordance with expectations of peer interests) related to adolescent judgment and decision making. Early studies using hypothetical dilemmas showed that the power of peer influence on adolescent decision making peaks at approximately age fourteen, at which point it slowly declines across middle-to-late adolescence.[22] Whether there remain significant differences between older adolescents (e.g., sixteen/seventeen-year-olds) and younger adults (eighteen/nineteen-year-olds) is unclear. It should be pointed out, however, that these studies used hypothetical scenarios, as did the studies that showed that the decision making of older adolescents approximates that of adults. Remember that Steinberg and Scott asserted that this latter set of studies was inconclusive, in part because of the hypothetical-scenario methodology that was employed. Nevertheless, few scientists would argue that there are not meaningful differences in susceptibility to peer influence between adolescents and adults, or that such a difference is unrelated to social judgment and decision making.[23]

[19] *See, e.g.*, Thomas Grisso, *Adolescents' Decision Making: A developmental Perspective on Constitutional Provisions in Delinquency Cases*, 32 NEW. ENG. J. CRIM. & CIV. CONFINEMENT 3 (2006); Steinberg & Scott, *Less Guilty by Reason of Adolescence, supra* note 2.

[20] *See, e.g.*, B. J. Casey, Sarah Getz & Adriana Galvan, *The Adolescent Brain*, 28 DEVELOPMENTAL REV. 62 (2008); Laurence Steinberg, *A Social Neuroscience Perspective on Adolescent Risk-Taking*, 28 DEVELOPMENTAL REV. 78 (2008) [hereinafter Steinberg, *Adolescent Risk-Taking*].

[21] This component would seem to be highly related to the developmental-immaturity component of vulnerability to coercive influence (see discussion later in the chapter), although Steinberg and Scott treated it separately. An overall psychosocial maturity deficit may be more comprehensively described as susceptibility to social influence (influence by peers, coercers, and the like).

[22] Thomas J. Berndt, *Developmental Changes in Conformity to Peers and Parents*, 15 DEVELOPMENTAL PSYCHOL. 608 (1979); Laurence Steinberg & Susan B. Silverberg, *The Vicissitudes of Autonomy in Early Adolescence*, 57 CHILD DEV. 841 (1986).

[23] I would argue, however, that this difference is a disparity in decision-making capacity itself, and not merely a separate "psychosocial factor" that influences decision making capacity (see the Conclusions subsection in this chapter).

Second is *future orientation*. In decision-making scenarios, adults consider a much longer future time frame than do adolescents.[24] Also, in decision-making scenarios that involve risk, adolescents are much more likely to discount potential long-term consequences than are adults.[25] There are a number of reasons that may explain this difference. First, adolescents may be less concerned with the future because the present may play a disproportionately important role in their lives. Given the importance of the present, shorter-term consequences of decisions may be more salient and valued. Another possibility has to do with the differential amounts of responsibility that adolescents and adults typically have. Adolescents are less likely to have financial, familial, medical, and survival responsibilities normal to adult life because they are far more often being cared for by their parents and other adult authority figures. The difference in the natures of their respective existences means that adolescents do not have to consider longer-term consequences or be as oriented to the future as do typical adults.[26]

Third, adolescents appear to be less skilled at *risk assessment* and are more sensitive to rewards.[27] When calculating risks and rewards, adolescents tend to undervalue risks – or, as recent studies have suggested, attribute greater value to rewards associated with risky behaviors.[28] As a result, disproportionately risky social situations are assessed such that they are substantially more appealing than they would be to someone who has accurately evaluated the relative risks and rewards. It may be that because adolescents have less life

[24] A. L. Greene, *Future-Time Perspective in Adolescence: The Present of Things Future Revisited*, 15 J. Youth & Adolescence 99 (1986); Jari-Erik Nurmi, *How Do Adolescents See Their Future? A Review of the Development of Future Orientation and Planning*, 11 Developmental Rev. 1 (1991); Steinberg & Scott, *Less Guilty by Reason of Adolescence, supra* note 2.

[25] *See* William Gardner, *A Life-Span Rational-Choice Theory of Risk Taking, in* Adolescent Risk-Taking 66 (Nancy J. Bell & Robert W. Bell eds., 1993); Steinberg & Scott, *Less Guilty by Reason of Adolescence, supra* note 2.

[26] It is unclear whether this adolescent/adult difference is one of capacity deficit or decision-making bias. Regardless, I would argue again here that this is a difference in rational decision making as opposed to one of psychosocial maturity.

[27] Adriana Galvan, Todd Hare, Henning Voss, Gary Glover & B. J. Casey, *Risk-Taking and the Adolescent Brain: Who Is at Risk?* 10 Developmental Sci. F8 (2007); Laurence Steinberg, Dustin Albert, Elizabeth Cauffman, Marie T. Banich, Sandra Graham & Jennifer Woolard, *Age Differences in Sensation Seeking and Impulsivity As Indexed By Behavior and Self-Report: Evidence for a Dual Systems Model*, 44 Developmental Psychol. 1764 (2008) [hereinafter Steinberg et al, *Age*].

[28] Elizabeth Cauffman, Elizabeth P. Shulman, Laurence Steinberg, Eric Claus, Marie T. Banich, Sandra Graham & Jennifer Woolard, *Age Differences in Affective Decision Making As Indexed By Performance on the Iowa Gambling Task*, 46 Developmental Psychol. 193 (2010); Susan G. Millstein & Bonnie L. Halpern-Felsher, *Perceptions of Risk and Vulnerability* 31S J. Adolescent Health 10 (2002).

experience from which to build their decision, they are less able to accurately calculate risks and rewards. It may also be that because adolescents so highly value peer acceptance, they develop a biased sense of risk and reward because it more closely fits the behaviors they enact in accordance with perceived peer expectations. This psychological strategy, albeit likely largely nonconscious, would allow adolescents to avoid cognitive dissonance[29] that may result from a mismatch of one's thinking (or belief system) and one's behavior.

Fourth, Steinberg and Scott recognized a difference in self-control or *self-management* between adolescents and adults. In their 2003 review,[30] Steinberg and Scott clarified that, at the time, there existed insufficient empirical support to determine the validity of the stereotype that adolescents are impulsive. More recent studies, however, suggest that there is a real difference in the respective self-management capacities of adolescents and adults,[31] consistent with the position that impulse-control problems in adolescence may be due to an underdeveloped cognitive control system.[32]

Impulsivity, or the tendency to act on impulse, may be contrasted with controlled behaviors that balance impulses with rational thought.[33] Much of our daily thinking, emotion processing, and behavior are automatically impulsive. Processing incoming information and acting on it automatically can be highly efficient and adaptive. However, under certain circumstances, impulsive functioning can be quite problematic. Whereas understanding individual differences in automatic and conceptual processing mechanisms – the latter of which are typically associated with rational thought[34] – is critical to potential linkages between behavioral science and criminal law (e.g., understanding differential intentional action), so is the degree to which processing is impulsive or undercontrolled. Development of rational capacity would seem to be highly related to this line of inquiry. As youths mature, they develop both

29 Cognitive dissonance may be defined as the psychological distress that results from either simultaneously holding two opposing ideas or beliefs or acting in a manner that is in opposition to one's ideas and beliefs.

30 *E.g.*, Steinberg & Scott, *Less Guilty by Reason of Adolescence*, *supra* note 2.

31 *E.g.*, Galvan et al., *Risk-Taking & the Adolescent Brain*, *supra* note 27; Rotem Leshem & Joseph Glicksohn, *The Construct of Impulsivity Revisited*, 43 PERSONALITY & INDIVIDUAL DIFFERENCES 681 (2007); *see also* Steinberg et al., *Age*, *supra* note 27.

32 *See* Steinberg, *Development*, *supra* note 6.

33 *See, e.g.*, SCOTT & STEINBERG, *RETHINKING JUVENILE JUSTICE*, *supra* note 15; Elizabeth S. Scott & Laurence Steinberg, *Blaming Youth*, 81 TEX. L. REV. 799, 815 (2003); Steinberg, *Development*, *supra* note 6, at 58–59.

34 *See, e.g.*, Reid G. Fontaine & Kenneth A. Dodge, *Real-Time Decision Making and Aggressive Behavior in Youth: A Heuristic Model of Response Evaluation and Decision (RED)*, 32 AGGRESSIVE BEHAV. 604 (2006) [hereinafter Fontaine & Dodge, *Real-Time*].

greater rational capacity and skills in self-management.[35] It serves to reason that as adolescents approach status of rational adults, they gain control at least partly as a function of being better able to evaluate and make decisions about social cues and events as they occur and are identified.

Adolescents show improvement in two main areas related to impulsivity as they develop. First, there is a linear decrease of generalized or trait impulsivity across adolescence and into early adulthood.[36] Second, youths' inclination toward sensation-seeking behavior declines.[37] That is, as they mature, adolescents become less likely to pursue social events and situations that arouse their sensations (i.e., preimpulsive scenarios). This is related to impulsivity in that adolescents are less likely to act in an impulsive manner if they are in fewer situations that arouse their sensations such that impulsive functioning is activated and facilitated.

Not only is it the case that adolescents are relatively impulsive compared to adults, but there is empirical evidence that youths with undercontrolled personality traits such as impulsivity are more likely to develop aggressive behavioral patterns than are their nonaggressive peers. Although this would indicate an even greater difference when comparing the subset of adolescents whose conduct is more typical of youths who enter the juvenile justice system with adults, it is unclear as to whether impulsivity among aggressive adolescents is significantly greater than that which may be attributable to aggressive adults. I suspect, however, that the latter of the comparisons is marked by a significantly smaller difference. It may be that trait impulsivity ignores the typical developmental trend for a subset of individuals, for whom life-course persistent conduct problem behaviors are characteristic.[38]

It should be noted that the relation between control and rationality is not clear. Whereas some components of developmental immaturity are indisputably social-cognitive by nature, and central to rationality (e.g., decision-making

[35] *See* Steinberg et al., *Age*, *supra* note 27; Deanna Kuhn, *Adolescent Thinking*, *in* HANDBOOK OF ADOLESCENT PSYCHOLOGY (Richard M. Lerner & Laurence Steinberg eds., 3rd ed. 2009).

[36] Steinberg et al., *Age*, *supra* note 27.

[37] SCOTT & STEINBERG, *RETHINKING JUVENILE JUSTICE*, *supra* note 15, at 43; Laurence Steinberg & Elizabeth Cauffman, *Maturity of Judgment in Adolescence: Psychosocial Factors in Adolescent Decision Making*, 20 LAW & HUM. BEHAV. 249 (1996).

[38] *See* Terrie E. Moffitt, *Life-Course-Persistent and Adolescence-Limited Antisocial Behavior: A Developmental Taxonomy*, 100 PSYCHOL. REV. 764 (1993) [hereinafter Moffitt, *Life-Course-Persistent and Adolescence-Limited Antisocial Behavior*]; Terrie E. Moffitt, *Adolescence-Limited and Life-Course-Persistent Offending: A Complementary Pair of Developmental Theories*, *in* 7 DEVELOPMENTAL THEORIES OF CRIME AND DELINQUENCY 11 (Terence Thornberry ed., 1996) [hereinafter Moffitt, *Adolescence-Limited and Life-Course-Persistent Offending*].

capacity, risk assessment), the likeness may not as easily be made with respect to control. The distinction between control and rationality is muddy in the law, as well, although Morse has argued that "most 'control problems' are better conceptualized as rationality problems,"[39] an argument consistent with my position that developmental immaturity may be framed as underdeveloped rationality. Certainly, the capacities of control and rationality, even if qualitatively separate, are related in ways that are basic to human functioning as well as to the relation between behavioral science and the law.

The role of impulsivity in adolescent development and understanding issues of proportional culpability and punishment for juveniles is relevant to several other adolescent/adult psychological differences that are recognized by Steinberg et al.'s developmental-immaturity argument. For example, adolescents may be more willing to take risks because they are impulsive in their processing and do not take the sufficient time to consider the meaning of possible negative consequences. Similarly, they may be more susceptible to being influenced by coercive others because they impulsively interpret the meaning of such social cues and therefore misjudge others' intentions. It may be that, as impulsivity gradually lessens, adolescents become more able to access and utilize social-cognitive capacities already in place. This idea is consistent with the dual-systems model in developmental neuroscience by which one's cognitive capacities are moderated by one's abilities to process social and emotional information.[40] In this way, determinations of proportional culpability and punishment for juveniles may be influenced by the legal system's understanding of the interaction of cognitive and intellectual capacities and psychosocial and socioemotional maturity in developmental context.[41]

Argument 2: Vulnerability to Coercive Influence

In the case of decision-making capacity, the developmental-immaturity argument is one of mitigation by underdeveloped rationality, perhaps conceptually closest to the legal doctrine of diminished capacity. The argument is that because adolescents do not have the decision-making (or rational) capacity presumed by the law of adults, they should not be found guilty or punished to the degrees that adults are for the same criminal acts. One component of the decision-making capacity track is that of susceptibility to the influence of others. That is, adolescents are more easily guided in their thoughts and

39 Stephen J. Morse, *Diminished Rationality, Diminished Responsibility*, 1 Ohio St. J. Crim. L. 289, 300 n. 25 (2003).

40 Casey, Getz & Galvan, *supra* note 20; Steinberg, *Adolescent Risk-Taking*, *supra* note 20.

41 *See* Steinberg, *Development*, *supra* note 6.

behaviors by social influence than are adults. It follows that, as compared to adults, adolescents would be particularly vulnerable to the coercion – a particular kind of social influence – that is, the undue compelling or manipulation of another via the application of aversive treatments (e.g., threats, infliction of physical pain). It may be said that if adolescents are particularly susceptible to coercive influence due to psychological underdevelopment, bad acts they commit as a result of being coerced may not be fully of their own doing. That is, the bad act in question in this context, at least to some substantial degree, is performed involuntarily in that the actor, who by developmental definition is vulnerable to coercion, faces coercive pressure to act in the bad way that he cannot (at least sufficiently) resist or defend.

In the criminal law, the affirmative defense of duress states that a defendant is not criminally responsible for his admittedly bad act if he performed it under overwhelming coercive influence. For example, if a defendant who is charged with theft was reasonably convinced that another's threat that if he did not commit the burglary would lead to his wrongful death, he may raise the defense of duress in an attempt to be excused[42] for his wrongful act. As long as the defendant was of "reasonable firmness" – that is, a reasonable person (in this context, a person of normal resilience) would not have been able to resist the coercive pressure – then his crime may be mitigated or fully exonerated.

This concept may be likened to adolescent offenders. If adolescent offenders are significantly less able, because of psychosocial immaturity, to resist or withstand coercive influence than are adults, they may not be said – again, by developmental definition – to be of reasonable firmness attributable to adults. In this way, it may be argued that because of developmental differences, adolescents are less guilty than adults for the same crimes.

I agree with Steinberg et al.'s conclusion, but not with how they got there. That is, I agree that in cases in which an adolescent offender's bad act was the result in some significant part of being coerced, the offender's juvenile status is highly relevant to determinations of guilt and punishment. However,

[42] Duress is more commonly (and, in my view, accurately) treated as an excuse. In the example, I provided the thief's reasonable belief that another would carry out his wrongful, mortal threat does not make act of theft good or even okay. The theft is still wrong, but it may be understandable and thus excusable because of the special (coercive) circumstances by which the act was committed. Duress is discussed more comprehensively in Chapter 7 on insufficient rationality as a function of emotional arousal. The justification/excuse distinction as applied to duress was recently debated in a pair of scholarly articles: Peter Westen & James Mangiafico, *The Criminal Defense of Duress: A Justification, Not an Excuse – and Why it Matters*, 6 Buff. Crim. L. Rev. 833 (2003); Kyron Huigens, *Duress Is Not a Justification*, 2 Ohio St. J. Crim. L. 303 (2004).

I do not agree that this should be a separate argument from the decision-making capacity argument. Indeed, it should be emphasized that susceptibility to peer influence was recognized as a component of decision-making capacity by Steinberg and Scott.[43] It may be that a duress-like argument is different from a diminished capacity-like argument,[44] but both arguments rest on subrationality. In the same way that adolescents are not able to engage in adult-level assessments of risky choices and future consequences, they may be less able to assess coercive mechanisms in various social dynamics and, as a result, avoid, defend against, or overcome coercive pressures. This problematic reality is directly related to adolescents' social and moral judgment and decision making, domains that are central to rationality. As such, I agree that adolescents should be viewed differently and in the correct developmental context in cases in which they have acted wrongly at least in part due to significant coercive influence, but it should be because of the law's recognition and understanding that their rational capacity simply has not achieved the same level of maturation that may be fairly presumed of adults.

Argument 3: Unformed Character

Another adolescence/adulthood difference has to do with identity development. Adolescence is a developmental period marked by exploration of one's individual identity. During this investigation of one's personhood, youths may engage in types of thinking and behavior that, although useful to their ultimate maturation into adults, do not generally persist past late adolescence. That is, such cognitive and behavioral patterns are not life-course stable but rather developmentally contained.

A third argument made via developmental immaturity is that the bad acts of adolescents do not reflect bad character as they do for adults. That is, to the degree that one's bad acts may be deemed a marker of their bad or evil character, one should not make this attribution with respect to adolescence because their identity and character are unformed, or at least underdeveloped, and thus such an attribution would be both morally unfair and developmentally inaccurate. The idea here is that the law makes an assumption of an actor's character upon the determination that he has committed a crime. In the case that it can be shown that the bad act was an exception – that is, that it was inconsistent with the actor's character – the actor is not held in the same legal disfavor (e.g., at least risk of greater condemnation and punishment).

[43] Steinberg & Scott, *Less Guilty by Reason of Adolescence*, *supra* note 2, at 1012.

[44] Although, as I discuss later, duress, like many excuse-based affirmative defenses, has a diminished-capacity spirit to it.

This is perhaps the most creative of the developmental-immaturity argument tracks. I believe the argument fails for at least two critical reasons. Before I discuss these reasons, however, I should point out that the argument's failure is largely inconsequential, because Steinberg et al.'s decision-making capacity (or underdeveloped rationality) argument is already sufficiently compelling and accomplishes the goal that the unformed-character argument sets out to meet.

The unformed-character argument fails because (1) it is based on a false assumption about the criminal law, and (2) it describes a domain of functioning that is not meaningfully separate from decision-making capacity (or rationality). First, the argument presupposes that the "the criminal law implicitly assumes that harmful conduct reflects the actor's bad character and treats evidence that this assumption is inaccurate as mitigating of culpability."[45] As a general statement about the criminal law, this presupposition is invalid. In American criminal law, the defendant is presumed innocent until proven guilty beyond a reasonable doubt by a court of law. If proven guilty, the law does not then completely flip its presumptive stance so that it becomes biased against the defendant. If a guilty verdict is rendered, the law does not so much make a presumption one way or another about the defendant's character, but considers evidence – both presented at the trial phase and anew at the sentencing phase – that potentially goes to character such that a just punishment may be rendered. Evidence that suggests or demonstrates that the crime is a highly unusual type of action for the defendant may serve a mitigating role. For example, perhaps the defendant has never before been arrested, is well respected in his community, and is committed to charity work. Alternatively, evidence that paints a negative picture of the defendant's character can serve an aggravating function (i.e., can increase the punishment). For instance, if the defendant has been arrested multiple times (or perhaps has prior convictions) and has a poor community reputation (e.g., has been involved in public disputes or police investigations), he is more likely to be viewed negatively by the court, which may result in a more severe sentence.

Of course, to the degree that one may make an assumption about another's character based on the determination of a single act, it is more dangerous to do so with respect to adolescents. With respect to this point, I agree. This is because adolescence is a period of considerable cognitive, emotional, and behavioral change, and how one functions as an adolescent may be quite

45 Steinberg & Scott, *Less Guilty by Reason of Adolescence*, *supra* note 2, at 1014.

different than how he does so as an adult. Steinberg et al.'s case for this point is entirely compelling.[46]

Indeed, this is no less true when considering adolescents who demonstrate patterns of antisocial behavior. Professor Terrie Moffitt is well known for her subtypes model of developmental trajectories of antisocial behavior.[47] Moffitt's research suggests a dichotomous model of antisocial youths, one subgroup of which is primarily antisocial during adolescence (adolescence-limited), whereas a significantly smaller group continues to evidence an antisocial presentation into adulthood (life-course-persistent). Whereas the former group may lead normal adult lives, those of members in the latter subgroup are likely to be characterized by social problems (failures in family and job settings), criminal records, and a diagnosis of antisocial personality disorder. Recent research has shown that a key phenomenological difference between the groups is disinhibition, suggesting that the life-course-persistent adolescent does not develop in a fashion that facilitates self-regulation and control.[48] This area of research is entirely consistent with Steinberg et al.'s developmental-immaturity line of arguments and points to the developmentally confined nature of the majority of antisocial adolescents' conduct problem behaviors.

What is unformed character, however, and how is it observable? Character is typically determined by assessing how an individual thinks, what his values are, and how he conducts himself. Given that adolescence is marked by an exploration of one's individual identity, it should be understood that such exploration will involve thought and action processes unique to the developmental time period. Indeed, Steinberg and Scott observe that "[a]t least until late adolescence, individuals' values, attitudes, beliefs, and plans are likely to be tentative and exploratory expressions rather than enduring representations of personhood."[49] Whereas exploration during adolescence may involve cognitive and behavioral processes critical to learning and adaptive development, such processes should not be presumed to continue beyond this stage (or, at least, not well into adulthood).

Perhaps most commonly attributed to adolescence is a tendency for risky decision making and behavior. Adolescents, as previously discussed, are,

[46] See Steinberg's recent review that quite efficiently and convincingly makes the case: Steinberg, *Development*, *supra* note 6.

[47] *See* Moffitt, *Life-Course-Persistent and Adolescence-Limited Antisocial Behavior*, *supra* note 38; Moffitt, *Adolescence-Limited and Life-Course-Persistent Offending*, *supra* note 38.

[48] H. Raskin White, Marsha E. Bates & Steven Buyske, *Adolescence-Limited Versus Persistent Delinquency: Extending Moffitt's Hypothesis into Adulthood*, 110 J. ABNORMAL PSYCHOL. 600 (2001).

[49] Steinberg & Scott, *Less Guilty by Reason of Adolescence*, *supra* note 2, at 1015.

relative to adults, prone to risky decision making and enactment of dangerous behaviors (e.g., use of alcohol and illicit drugs).[50] According to the final track of the developmental-immaturity argument, this risky pattern of judgment, decision making, and behavior is telling of unformed character in adolescence, a quality that not only separates adolescents from adults, but provides a unique rationale by which juveniles' objectively defined criminal conduct should be mitigated. However, risky (or, more generally, poor) decision making and the behaviors they proximally cause, especially when developmentally transitive, may be better conceptualized as social-cognitive factors or, more specifically, the development of decision-making capacity and skills. As the susceptibility-to-coercive-influence argument, the unformed-character argument is largely reducible to social-cognitive functioning. This is not to say that stable personality characteristics should be equated with social-cognitive processing, but the developmental features central to the unformed-character argument are not stable. In fact, this is exactly the point of the argument – that because these are not stable characteristics, they should not be interpreted as signs of moral character, but rather of underdeveloped psychosocial maturity.

However, the relation between environmental influences and adolescents' antisocial conduct is social-cognitively mediated. When we discuss issues of coercive influence, risky decision making, and dangerous behavior, we are really describing sequences mediated by social-cognition processing. In this way, adolescents' psychosocial immaturity, as well as the relation between this developmental status and juvenile justice and the criminal law, has its entire foundation in social-cognitive development (or, in criminal responsibility terms, developmental rationality). This is the second reason for which I believe the unformed-character argument fails. But it is also for this reason that I believe this failed argument is inconsequential to the message and goal of the larger developmental-immaturity position. That is, adolescents should not be found as guilty or punished as severely as adults for the same crime because they are less rational, and less rational in a way that is material to criminal responsibility – their rationality is not sufficiently developed such that it meets the standard of rationality presumed by the law of adult actors. In this way, developmental immaturity in psychology and behavioral science very nicely reflects my proposed legal concept of underdeveloped rationality, a concept consistent with the spirit of diminished capacity. As social-cognitive science continues to make tracks – and quick tracks in this area it is making

50 *See, e.g.*, Margo Gardner & Laurence Steinberg, *Peer Influence on Risk-Taking, Risk Preference, and Risky Decision-Making in Adolescence and Adulthood: An Experimental Study*, 4 Developmental Psychol. 625 (2005).

indeed[51] – not only will scientists, policy makers, and legal scholars gain understanding of adolescent/adult functioning differences relevant to juvenile justice and criminal law, but the mitigating nature of underdeveloped rationality will become even clearer.

SOCIAL-INFORMATION PROCESSING, ANTISOCIAL BEHAVIOR, AND JUVENILE JUSTICE

Developmental Immaturity in Social-Information Processing Terms

As discussed in Chapter 2, social-information processing (SIP) models, such as that of Crick and Dodge,[52] serve a useful heuristic purpose by which a broad set of perceptual, cognitive, and emotional processes may be investigated and understood. Empirical studies that have contributed to the developmental-immaturity position have generally not been guided by a SIP framework. Nevertheless, the social-cognitive processes examined in these studies may be viewed from a SIP perspective, one that is important not only because it provides a way of organizing these processes into a developmental framework of adolescents' judgment and decision making, but because it may be useful to directing research so that everyday judgment and decision making in real time may be appropriately made the focus of future empirical inquiry.

All SIP steps are potentially important to understanding adolescent/adult functioning differences, as well as how these differences may inform juvenile justice and criminal law. The processes highlighted by Steinberg et al. in making their developmental-immaturity case, however, suggest that certain steps may be particularly crucial. Susceptibility to the influence of others (e.g., peers, coercers) may have much to do with how adolescents interpret social cues. In particular, intent attributions would seem central to this underdeveloped capacity. Intent attribution is the process by which one judges the mental state of the stimulus-actor in determining why he is acting or has acted in a certain way. For example, if a youth is offered illicit drugs under the guise that ingesting them will be fun and relaxing, one with an underdeveloped-interpretation-of-cues step of SIP may be less likely to question the motive of such an invitation and accept the offer on face value. For example, antisocial adolescents have been found to be less able to engage in perspective taking

[51] For a recent review, see Steinberg, *Development*, *supra* note 6.

[52] Nicki R. Crick & Kenneth A. Dodge, *A Review and Reformulation of Social Information-Processing Mechanisms in Children's Social Adjustment*, 115 PSYCHOL. BULL. 74 (1994).

at this step of SIP and tend to judge stimulus-actors as hostile and intending harm in ambiguous provocation situations.[53] It may be that, owing to the fact that adolescents' social interpretational faculties are not yet fully developed, they may display a similar attributional limitation as compared to adults. Further research is necessary to make such a determination, but the studies that Steinberg et al. cite in support of their developmental-immaturity argument suggest that this may be a promising hypothesis.

Susceptibility to the influence of others and other domains of decision-making capacity are easily conceptualized within a response-evaluation-and-decision (RED; step four of SIP) framework, as well. As discussed in Chapter 2, RED represents the set of processes by which an individual may consider and weigh his various behavioral options in the process of determining how to respond to social stimuli. Fontaine and Dodge offered a comprehensive model of RED[54] that delineated four key sets of social-cognitive operations. First, *response efficacy* is the process by which a person approximates the likelihood that he will be able to successfully carry out the behavioral option in question. Second, during *response valuation*, the individual assesses the degree to which the behavioral option is consistent with his identity as a social actor and moral agent. Third, *outcome expectancy* is the estimation of how likely a certain outcome will be realized if the considered behavior is enacted. Both positive (rewards) and negative (punishments) outcomes may be considered and alternative outcomes can take several forms. For example, whereas an emotional/intrapersonal outcome expectancy has to do with how one would expect to view and feel about himself upon enacting the behavior, a social/extrapersonal outcome expectancy involves predicting what others would think and feel. Finally, *outcome valuation* is the assignment of positive and negative values or weights to the alternative outcomes to which certain behaviors may lead.

[53] *E.g.*, Kenneth A. Dodge, Joseph M. Price, Jo-Anne Bachorowski & Joseph P. Newman, *Hostile Attributional Biases in Severely Aggressive Adolescents*, 99 J. ABNORMAL PSYCHOL. 385 (1990); Reid G. Fontaine, Marieh Tanha., Chongming Yang, Kenneth A. Dodge, John E. Bates & Gregory S. Pettit, *Does Response Evaluation and Decision (RED) Mediate the Relation Between Hostile Attributional Style and Antisocial Behavior in Adolescence?*, 38 J. ABNORMAL CHILD PSYCHOL. 615 (2010) [hereinafter Fontaine et al., *Response Evaluation*].

[54] Fontaine & Dodge, *Real-Time*, *supra* note 34. For further elaborations on the RED model, see Reid G. Fontaine, *Online Social Decision Making and Antisocial Behavior: Some Essential but Neglected Issues*, 28 CLINICAL PSYCHOL. REV. 17 (2008) [hereinafter Fontaine, *Online*]; Reid G. Fontaine, *Toward a Conceptual Framework of Instrumental Antisocial Decision-Making and Behavior in Youth*, 27 CLINICAL PSYCHOL. REV. 655 (2007); Reid G. Fontaine, *Evaluative Behavioral Judgments and Instrumental Antisocial Behaviors in Children and Adolescents*, 26 CLINICAL PSYCHOL. REV. 956 (2006).

As compared to adults, adolescents are less skilled in future orientation, or "the capacity and inclination to project events into the future,"[55] a capacity represented by the outcome expectancy domain in RED. As discussed, adolescents tend to disproportionately weigh short-term considerations over longer-term ones. In RED terms, this translates to a bias toward valuing proximate over distal outcomes and attributing greater meaning to the former when considering how to respond to social stimuli. This functional capacity is likely related to step three of SIP, clarification of goals, as well, in that adolescents may be more likely identify short-term goals and allow such goals to guide their behavioral decision making and enactments.

Risk assessment and reward sensitivity may also be understood in RED terms. Risk assessment is a type of negative outcome expectancy. That is, upon considering a response option, a person may estimate the likelihood that a negative outcome will occur. In addition, because adolescents are more focused on short-term outcomes, their sensitivity to gratification and realizing immediate rewards may lead to an overweighing of outcomes that are deemed favorable or desirable (positive outcome valuation). Here again, these processes may be closely tied to the clarification-of-goals step.

Finally, impulsivity and self-management may be explained according to the RED model. In recent formulations and discussions of RED, the roles of automatic processing and impulsive behavioral decision making and enactment have been more heavily emphasized that they have in the past.[56] Contemporary models illustrate how domains of social-cognitive functioning that may be typical of conceptually processed, reasoned behavioral choices may be "bypassed" or so significantly discounted that they play an insignificant role in behavioral judgment and decision making. Adolescents' lesser ability to self-regulate that is recognized by the developmental-immaturity position is thus accommodated by a RED formulation that balances rational thought with impulsive functioning.

In sum, the key capacities of the developmental-immaturity position – most notably, decision-making capacity – are entirely consistent with SIP theory. SIP provides a developmental framework by which these capacities may be organized, understood, and studied. In addition, SIP theory emphasizes how

[55] *See* Steinberg, *Development*, *supra* note 6, at 57.

[56] Fontaine & Dodge, *Real-Time*, *supra* note 34. For further elaborations on the RED model, see Fontaine, *Online*, *supra* note 54; *cf.* Kenneth A. Dodge, *A Social Information Processing Model of Social Competence in Children*, *in* 18 Cognitive Perspectives on Children's Social and Behavioral Development: The Minnesota Symposia on Child Psychology 77 (Marion Perlmutter ed., 1986); Crick & Dodge, *supra* note 52.

a focus on online social-cognitive operations is critical to a comprehensive explanation of adolescent/adult functioning differences. Without knowledge of how capacities develop, age-related differences in capacities may not be fully understood. Without such an understanding, the potential contribution of social-cognitive psychology to juvenile justice cannot be realized.

A Social-Cognitive (or Attributional) Perspective on Juvenile Offender Culpability

The role of SIP mechanisms in juvenile delinquency and offending has been both explicitly[57] and indirectly[58] explored in numerous empirical studies and theoretical accounts. As discussed in Chapter 2, SIP accounts for a considerable degree of antisocial behavioral variance in youths. So it should come as no surprise that studies have consistently found that juvenile offenders and nonincarcerated adolescent delinquents tend to exhibit a variety of SIP distortions, biases, and deficits.

Although there have now been a few theoretical statements of what the relation between SIP and adolescent delinquency and offending means for juvenile justice policy,[59] the first to squarely place this area of scholarly

[57] *See, e.g.*, Kenneth A. Dodge, John E. Lochman, Jennifer D. Harnish, John E. Bates & Gregory S. Pettit, *Reactive and Proactive Aggression in School Children and Psychiatrically Impaired Chronically Assaultive Youth*, 106 J. ABNORMAL PSYCHOL. 37 (1997); Nancy G. Guerra & Ronald G. Slaby, *Cognitive Mediators of Aggression in Adolescent Offenders: II. Intervention*, 26 DEVELOPMENTAL PSYCHOL. 269 (1990); John E. Lochman & Kenneth A. Dodge, *Social-Cognitive Processes of Severely Violent, Moderately Aggressive, and Nonaggressive Boys*, 62 J. CONSULTING & CLINICAL PSYCHOL. 366 (1994); Coralijn N. Nas, Bram Orobio de Castro & Willem Koops, *Social Information Processing in Delinquent Adolescents*,11 PSYCHOL. CRIME & L. 363 (2005); Ariana Shahinfar, Janis B. Kupersmidt & Louis S. Matza, *The Relation Between Exposure to Violence and Social Information Processing Among Incarcerated Adolescents*, 110 J. ABNORMAL PSYCHOL. 136 (2001); Ronald G. Slaby & Nancy G. Guerra, *Cognitive Mediators of Aggression in Adolescent Offenders: 1. Assessment*, 24 DEVELOPMENTAL PSYCHOL. 580 (1988).

[58] *See, e.g.*, Joseph P. Allen, Bonnie J. Leadbeater & J. Lawrence Aber, *The Relationship of Adolescents' Expectations and Values to Delinquency, Hard Drug Use, and Unprotected Sexual Intercourse*, 2 DEV. & PSYCHOPATHOLOGY 85 (1990); Annemaree Carroll, Stephen Houghton, John Hattie & Kevin Durkin, *Reputation Enhancing Goals: Integrating Reputation Enhancement and Goal Setting Theory as an Explanation of Delinquent Involvement*, *in* 4 ADVANCES IN PSYCHOLOGY RESEARCH 101 (Frank H. Columbus ed., 2001); Eric D. Frey & Catherine C. Epkins, *Examining Cognitive Models of Externalizing and Internalizing Problems in Subgroups of Juvenile Delinquents*, 31 J. CLINICAL CHILD & ADOLESCENT PSYCHOL. 556 (2002).

[59] *E.g.*, Reid G. Fontaine, *Social Information*, *supra* note 7; Emma J. Palmer, *Criminal Thinking*, *in* APPLY PSYCHOLOGY TO CRIMINAL JUSTICE 147 (David Carson, Rebecca Milne, Francis Pakes, Karen Shalev & Andrea Shawyer eds., 2007).

inquiry in discussions of youth violence policy was provided by Professors Sandra Graham and Colleen Halliday-Boykins.[60] Graham and Halliday-Boykins offered a social-cognitive perspective on juvenile offender culpability that was focused on attributional processes but broadly considered adolescent SIP. Not only was Graham and Halliday-Boykins' approach different from that of Steinberg et al.'s in that it was directed by a separate (albeit clearly highly related) body of psychological science, but the former were explicit in stating that the theory and research that provide the foundation for their translational argument "did not emerge from a concern with juvenile justice."[61] This has its advantage over Steinberg et al.'s approach, as the empirical research was conducted absent of the risk that scientific findings may be interpreted in light of a fixed set of social and policy interests, although its disadvantage is that much of the empirical evidence on which Graham and Halliday-Boykins build was not designed to specifically address the types of adolescent/adult functioning issues that Steinberg et al. have correctly pointed out are critical to this psychology and law translational effort. Nevertheless, Graham and Halliday-Boykins provided an excellent foundation on which SIP research may be brought to bear on pressing issues in juvenile justice, and the combination of these two scholarly trajectories appears quite promising.[62]

A notable similarity in the two approaches is the emphasis that scientific study must focus on adolescents' everyday decision making for it to realize its potential contribution toward informing juvenile justice. It should be acknowledged that most studies of SIP and antisocial behavior have utilized hypothetical stories and video-recorded vignettes. Although these hypotheticals have been designed to reflect everyday social situations faced by youths, they are nevertheless accompanied by the methodological imperfection cited by Steinberg and Scott[63] that they are not real-life decision-making moments. As previously discussed, however, a critical advantage of the methodology used in most SIP studies over other social decision-making studies in youth is that the former is designed to assess online or real-time cognitions (i.e., "in the moment" perceptions and judgments) as they are activated and experienced by youths in response to social stimuli.

Graham and Halliday-Boykins's social-cognitive approach toward juvenile offender culpability centers on attributional theory – that is, the study of "the thoughts, perceptions, and interpretations of events that shape the way people

60 Graham & Halliday, *supra* note 7.

61 *Id.* at 345.

62 For an integrative theoretical explanation, see Fontaine, *Social Information*, *supra* note 7.

63 Steinberg & Scott, *Less Guilty by Reason of Adolescence*, *supra* note 2.

understand their social worlds."[64] In the process of making meaning of incoming information from one's social world, a variety of attributions may be made. For example, causal attributions are assignments of causes to outcomes. If a boy is hit in the back of the head, he may make the causal attribution that a peer smacked him. Intent attributions are judgments as to the mental state of the perceived causal actor. The boy may ask himself whether the peer was (1) trying to hurt him, (2) engaging in aggressive horseplay, or (3) trying to hit another boy. Affect attributions are determinations of the emotional state of the stimulus-actor, such as whether he is angry, depressed, or affectively neutral or calm. Affect attributions may be useful to intent attributions. For example, if it is determined that the stimulus-actor is angry, it may be more likely that one judges that he means to cause harm to another. However, they may be useful for other reasons, as well; for example, if the stimulus-actor is perceived to be particularly emotional, negative intentions that may be attributed to him may be excused or at least viewed as not fully rationally formed.

Graham and Halliday-Boykins focus on causal attributions in their social-cognitive analysis and specify that three types of causal attributions (or three causal dimensions) are particularly critical. First, a *locus* attribution is a judgment of whether the cause of an outcome is intrapersonal (i.e., caused by himself or came from within) or extrapersonal (i.e., caused by another or some outside force). A *stability* attribution is a determination as to whether the identified cause is persistent or varies across time or context. Finally, an attribution of *controllability* is an assessment as to whether and to what degree the identified cause is volitionally driven – that is, controllability has to do with the degree to which the perceived causal actor had control over his action.

Whereas these factors may commonly be considered when judging the moral and criminal culpability of others, it is unclear as to how important they are to understanding precriminal conduct on the part of the criminal actor. That is, the potential criminogenic nature of these attributional factors is not fully known. Graham and Halliday-Boykins, suggest, however, that controllability attribution may play an important role. When some are judged to have committed harmful acts of their own free will, it elicits anger in others, which may, in mediational turn, lead to violent reactivity. This sequence is squarely represented in heat-of-passion/provocation doctrine, by which one perceives a serious provocation, becomes enraged, and kills the perceived provocateur in response. This doctrine applies only to cases of adult defendants charged with

[64] Graham & Halliday, *supra* note 7, at 346. For a review of attributional theory more generally, see Susan T. Fiske & Shelley E. Taylor, *Social Cognition: From Brains to Culture* (2007).

murder, of course, but the serial chain of factors may be used to understand criminal conduct, and responsibility for said conduct, in other nonhomicide, nonadult cases, as well.

In addition to controllability attribution, Graham and Halliday-Boykins cite other attributional processes that may function to promote antisocial behavior in adolescents, particularly attributions of fairness and the mental state (or intent) of the perceived wrongdoer. Judgments that one has been treated unfairly and that such treatment has come at the hand of an intentional actor may contribute to one's emotional arousal (anger) and willingness to conduct oneself within the confines of social norms and legal rules. Of course, science has already demonstrated a correlation between "hostile intent" attributions and antisocial behavior in youth.[65] I have argued elsewhere[66] that such cognitive bias may serve as an excusing mechanism with respect to criminal culpability in adults, but the argument applies no less for juveniles, particularly if science finds that adolescent offenders have even more pronounced cognitive distortions in this domain.

Although I believe Graham and Halliday-Boykins got it right by focusing on social-cognitive development, their analysis is necessarily limited because it addresses only attributional processes, as opposed to a more complete set of operations that may better paint the social-cognitive picture of juvenile wrongdoing. There are numerous other social-cognitive factors known to contribute to adolescent antisocial conduct, some of which have been discussed in detail by the Steinberg et al. interdisciplinary group. For example, SIP researchers have found that various evaluative judgment and decision-making processes account for a considerable degree of antisocial behavioral variance in adolescence. Aggressive adolescents tend to more highly value aggressive behavioral options, discount their potential negative causes, and feel confident that they can successfully carry out antisocial acts in order to achieve their interests.[67]

[65] For a recent review, see Kenneth A. Dodge, *Translational Science in Action: Hostile Attributional Style and the Development of Aggressive Behavior Problems*, 18 DEV. & PSYCHOPATHOLOGY (2006).

[66] *See* Reid G. Fontaine, *Reactive Cognition, Reactive Emotion: Toward a More Psychologically-Informed Understanding of Reactive Homicide*, 14 PSYCHOL. PUB. POL'Y & L. 243 (2008); Reid G. Fontaine, *The Wrongfulness of Wrongly Interpreting Wrongfulness: Provocation Interpretational Bias and Heat of Passion Homicide*, 12 NEW CRIM. L. REV. 69 (2009); Reid G. Fontaine, *Adequate (Non)Provocation and Heat of Passion as Excuse Not Justification*, 43 U. MICH. J.L. REFORM 27 (2009).

[67] Fontaine & Dodge, *Real-Time*, *supra* note 34; Reid G. Fontaine, Chongming Yang, Kenneth A. Dodge, Gregory S. Pettit & John E. Bates, *Development of Response Evaluation and Decision (RED) and Antisocial Behavior in Childhood and Adolescence*, 45 DEVELOPMENTAL PSYCHOL. 447 (2009); Reid G. Fontaine, Chongming Yang, Kenneth A. Dodge, John E. Bates & Gregory S. Pettit, *Testing an Individual Systems Model of Response Evaluation and*

The real question, with respect to juvenile justice policy, however, is whether such attributional and other social-cognitive biases are significantly more prominent in juvenile as opposed to adult offenders. This question requires further empirical investigation. Several directions for such research would seem promising.

Toward a Progressive Construction of Juvenile Justice: Antisocial Subtypes, Social-Information Processing, and the Balancing of Retributive and Utilitarian Goals

The developmental status of juveniles is unique in a number of important ways. First, as discussed throughout this chapter, juveniles continue to develop at a rate that is more rapid than that of adults. Second, because rationality and identity are not fully formed, external influences on juveniles may be of greater potential impact on shaping their development. Finally, because juveniles are not developmentally equal to adults in ways critical to responsibility, society has a duty to make sure that certain standards are met with respect to their care and best interests. American society reflects this value in public policy power of each state afforded by *parens patriae*. Recognition of these unique qualities of juveniles' developmental status may be used to guide juvenile justice policy in manners in which juveniles may be held appropriately responsible for their delinquent action and protected against the potential harms that a system bound purely by punishment bears. As such, unlike the fundamental goal of retribution common to criminal law throughout Anglo-America, juvenile justice requires a more involved and carefully balanced integration of both retributive (desert) and utilitarian (education, rehabilitation) interests.

Social-cognitive psychology may inform juvenile justice with respect to both retributive and utilitarian values. For example, research on the development of social decision making and identity suggests that because adolescents are not as social-cognitively equipped as adults, they are therefore less able to make adaptive behavioral decisions in certain type of social situations.[68] Similarly, social-cognitive psychology has demonstrated that it is critical that rehabilitation programs with juvenile delinquents have strong cognitive components. Indeed, one meta-analysis found that rehabilitation programs that included a cognitive component were twice as successful as those that did

Decision (RED) and Antisocial Behavior Across Adolescence, 79 CHILD DEV. 462 (2008); Fontaine et al., *Response Evaluation*, *supra* note 53.

[68] *See, e.g.*, Galvan et al., *Risk-Taking & the Adolescent Brain*, *supra* note 27; Steinberg et al., *Age*, *supra* note 27.

not.[69] Other reviews have emphasized the importance of a developmental framework.[70]

One area of study in social-developmental and social-cognitive psychology that has been highly useful to understanding the onset and maturation of antisocial conduct problems in youth is the subtypes model of instrumental and reactive violence.[71] Whereas instrumental aggression is typically cold-blooded, enacted for personal gain, and planned, reactive aggression is characteristically emotional, impulsive, and enacted for the purpose of harming the perceived provocateur or defending oneself. Although this subtypes model is receiving more attention in criminal-law literature, it has been largely neglected by research that examines linkages between psychology and juvenile justice.[72] This is unfortunate, as developmental research that has been guided by this model would appear to have potential importance for both retributive- and utilitarian-based juvenile justice policy interests.

Culpability/Desert

American law historically has treated acts of violence that are committed impulsively and out of rage as less culpable than those committed out of malice aforethought and in cold blood. The clearest indication of this disparity is found in homicide law in the distinction between killings that are typical of murder-one verdicts versus those that qualify for heat-of-passion/provocation manslaughter. The common case of the former category is a planned, unprovoked killing, whereas that of the latter is an enraged killing in response to a substantial, wrongful provocation. Because the provoked, reactive killer is viewed as less responsible, and therefore less culpable, than the cold-blooded murderer, he is punished less, true to the desert-based principle of penal proportionality on which American criminal law is founded.

Reactive violence is characterized by greater impulsivity and less rationality. Although intentional, it tends to be engaged rapidly in response to a stimulus that is perceived to be unjust or otherwise aversive. As has been discussed, some significant functional differences between adolescents and adults have to do

[69] Rhena L. Izzo & Robert R. Ross, *Meta-Analysis of Rehabilitation Programs for Juvenile Delinquents: A Brief Report*, 17 CRIM. JUST. & BEHAV. 134 (1990).

[70] *E.g.*, Margaret Beale Spencer & Cheryl Jones-Walker, *Interventions and Services Offered to Former Juvenile Offenders Re-Entering their communities: An Analysis of Program Effectiveness*, 2 J. YOUTH VIOLENCE & JUV. JUST. 88 (2004).

[71] For a recent review, see Reid G. Fontaine, *Disentangling the Psychology and Law of Instrumental and Reactive Subtypes of Aggression*, 13 PSYCHOL. PUB. POL'Y & L. 143 (2007) [hereinafter Fontaine, *Disentangling*].

[72] For an exception, see Fontaine, *Social Information*, *supra* note 7.

with greater impulsivity (or less self-regulation) and lesser (or underdeveloped) rationality and decision making. The combination of these two sets of findings begs a number of empirical questions that are related to issues of penal proportionality in juvenile justice policy. First, are instrumental and reactive violence structurally and functionally different across development – specifically, are they equivalent between adolescents and adults? If so, the question of whether this set of differences has the same implications for adolescents in juvenile justice as it does for adults in criminal law (e.g., provocation law). If not, then even more crucial questions arise. For example, if functional differences between instrumental and reactive violence in adolescence are greater than they are in adulthood, to what degree may adolescents be fairly held responsible for criminal wrongdoing? That is, if provoked, emotional violence in adulthood is already partially excused, what punitive response to juvenile reactive violence is appropriate when developmental science has already demonstrated that adolescents have underdeveloped rationality, greater impulsivity, and a lesser ability to control and regulate oneself?

Answers to a variety of empirical questions about the development and stability of instrumental versus reactive violence trajectories are needed. To date, science has not shown that these antisocial subtypes follow different developmental patterns. As time passes and more longitudinal studies add to our scientific knowledge base, this domain of research may need to become more prominent in inquiry in psychology and juvenile justice.

Rehabilitation

Some scientists have argued that alternative treatment plans are best used with youth aggressors who purely or at least predominantly exhibit instrumental versus reactive aggressive behavior.[73] Instrumentally violent youths may benefit from cognitive-behavioral therapies by which they better understand and may be more affected by negative consequences of antisocial conduct. This is because instrumental antisocial behavior is associated with a tendency to disproportionately expect positive outcomes from aggression and discount negative ones. Alternatively, reactive aggressive youths may benefit from a combination of anger management and cognitive training that

[73] Kenneth A. Dodge, *The Structure and Function of Reactive and Proactive Aggression, in* The Development and Treatment of Childhood Aggression 201(Debra J. Pepler & Kenneth H. Rubin eds., 1991); Benedetto Vitiello & David M. Stoff, *Subtypes of Aggression and their Relevance to Child Psychiatry*, 36 J. Am. Acad. Child & Adolescent Psychiatry 307 (1997); Fontaine, *Disentangling*, *supra* note 71; Fontaine, *Social Information*, *supra* note 7.

promotes consideration of alternative responses to perceived provocation cues, especially response options that are adaptive and nonaggressive. Reactive aggressive individuals tend to be biased toward interpreting ambiguous provocation stimuli as causal, intentional, and hostile, all of which promote an anger response, which, in turn, serves an aggressogenic role in retaliatory enactment. Whereas instrumental aggressive offenders may opt for antisocial options to achieve their goals, reactive aggressive individuals may need social-cognitive skills training so that they have a greater pool of behavioral options from which to choose.

Juvenile offenders may benefit from rehabilitation that similarly incorporates these subtype-specific treatment mechanisms into their detention protocols. Whereas research has demonstrated that a cognitive component is critical to the success of rehabilitation for juvenile offenders, it has not sufficiently examined the role of social cognition in subgroups of offenders identified by style or pattern of antisocial behavior or offending. In addition, the success of such rehabilitative programs may be, at least in some part, dependent on other detention factors, such as how the juvenile detainees are housed and managed while incarcerated.

Incarceration

Research on social cognition and antisocial subtypes may also be useful to issues of incarceration. In particular, it may prove useful to house predominantly instrumental versus reactive juvenile offenders separately. Members of the former group may, for instrumental reasons such as gaining power of the culture or social context or simply for the sake of amusement and entertainment, "set off" their reactive aggressive counterparts upon learning their triggers and observing how they react to provocations and threats. This may be doubly harmful in that it serves the risk of reinforcing the more instrumental offenders' interests and behavioral patterns as well as promoting and maintaining a chaotic experiential state for the more reactive offenders. Either of these outcomes, of course, would likely be counterproductive to a variety of detention issues, including organizational management, safety of detainees and detention administrators, and rehabilitative programming.

Further Research on Antisocial Subtypes and Juvenile Justice

In addition to those suggested by the preceding subsections, there are several additional areas in need of future research. For example, with respect to issues of deterrence and future dangerousness, it is not yet known whether there are differences between violent subtypes. There has been very little research that has examined the development and stability of instrumental versus reactive violence in youth.

In fact, there are a number of ways in which behavioral science has not been able to adequately contribute to juvenile justice and law. First, behavioral science has often approached the study of aggressive subtypes by focusing on instrumental versus reactive aggressors, as opposed to individual acts. That is, empirical study of aggressive subtypes has typically involved comparison of groups of offenders who display instrumental versus reactive styles (or patterns) of behavior. In contrast, criminal law is applied to individual defendants and individual acts.

Second, research on moral cognitive differences between instrumental and reactive aggressors is insufficient. For example, the degrees to which instrumental versus reactive aggressive behaviors are judged to be morally excusable or justifiable by their respective enactors has not been adequately investigated or determined. As a result, even to the degree to which the study of group differences in aggressive patterns may apply to criminal law, research on possible differences in moral judgment has remained limited.

Third, although a common factor across the respective distinctions made in psychology and law is emotion, relatively little is known about how emotion may affect cognitive processing in the context of social reactivity.[74] As a result, psychology is less able to inform the critical question involving the reactive violent youth that asks if his moral judgment is impaired as a direct result of provocation-induced emotional arousal. The cognitive basis of emotion as a mechanism of rationality impairment is discussed in detail in later chapters.

CONCLUSION

There is no question that decision-making and reasoning skills develop at a faster rate during childhood and adolescence than they do during adulthood. However, what remains unclear is whether, by mid-adolescence, youths' cognitive capacities are significantly different from adults.[75] The literature provides mixed results with respect to this issue, although Steinberg and his colleagues have argued that it is not so much whether adolescents and adults are significantly different in their psychological capacities, but whether adolescents are as "mature" in their judgment and decision making as are adults. In his 2009

[74] *See* Fontaine & Dodge, *Real-Time*, *supra* note 34. For further elaborations on the RED model, see Fontaine, *Online*, *supra* note 54.

[75] Steinberg & Scott, *Less Guilt by Reason of Adolescence*, *supra* note 2.

review of research on adolescent development and juvenile justice, Steinberg summarized the point:

> The notion that adolescents and adults demonstrate comparable capacities for understanding and reasoning should not be taken to mean that they also demonstrate comparable levels of maturity of judgment, however. As my colleagues and I have argued elsewhere, maturity of judgment is affected both by cognitive capabilities as well as psychosocial ones, and although the former show adult levels of maturity by 16, the latter do not. As a result, adolescents may be less able to deploy their cognitive capacities as effectively as adults in exercising judgment in their everyday lives when decisions are influenced by emotional and social variables. The development of these psychosocial factors is described in the next section.[76]

I both agree and disagree with Steinberg. I agree that adolescents are not as psychosocially developed as adults, and I agree that this psychosocial "immaturity" plays a role in their decision making and actions, but I disagree with Steinberg's hard distinction between reasoning development and maturity. If psychosocial development is not sufficiently formed such that adolescents have the capacity "in exercising judgment in their everyday lives when decisions are influence by emotional and social variables,"[77] then adolescents are not as rationally developed as adults with respect to social behavior – and, make no mistake, with respect to relating adolescent psychological functioning to criminal law, we are concerned with *social* behavior (and thus *social* cognition). Rational capacity is not limited to entirely nonemotional and nonsocial decision-making scenarios. Indeed, I am not sure that a scenario that is entirely uninfluenced by emotional and social variables exists; certainly none exist that would bear relevance on the relation between adolescent development and juvenile justice. Adolescents, like all humans, continue to make judgments and decisions in a naturally emotional state and naturally social world. If they are significantly less able to do so due to a difference in psychological capacity, then it necessarily follows that they are rationally underdeveloped as compared to adults.

In the criminal law, the person who, for nonculpable reasons, does not have a sufficient capacity for rational decision making but commits an objectively criminal act is not blamed or punished in the same way as a rational agent is. This truth takes multiple forms in the law (e.g., insanity, heat of passion/provocation), as presented throughout this volume, but may be dichotomously classified into subrationality that is underdeveloped versus diminished.

[76] Steinberg, *Development, supra* note 6, at 56 (footnotes omitted).

[77] *Id.*

Juveniles are appropriately included in the former of these classes. Social cognitive and developmental science has adequately demonstrated that the psychological functioning of juveniles differs significantly from that of adults. As such, the juvenile justice system should respond to juvenile wrongdoing in a way that is proportionate with respect to blame and punishment. In addition, because adolescents may not be understood to be as functionally developed or capable as adults, in general, juvenile justice must balance penal proportionality with a set of other values and responsibilities that the state has to its minors (e.g., education and rehabilitation).

5

Moral Subrationality and the Propensity for Wrongdoing

In Chapter 4, I discussed areas of developmental science that may contribute to understanding differences in psychological functioning between adolescents and adults that are potentially relevant to differential assignments of culpability and punishment for these two groups. In doing so, a number of developmental-immaturity arguments were addressed, including ones of diminished decision-making capacity, susceptibility to the influence of others, and unformed character and personal identity. Whereas I suggested that all of these arguments have to do with underdeveloped rationality, the last of them has further implications for a specific kind of rationality – that of moral judgment and decision making. The unformed-character argument states that because adolescents' character and identity are not fully formed, they should not be equated to normal adults with respect to criminal responsibility because their wrongdoing may not be presumed to be a function of stable personality characteristics. This argument, however, begs a similar question about development as related to *adults*. That is, how should the criminal law view culpability and punishment in the case of the adult criminal defendant whose moral-cognitive functioning and "character" did not develop such that it may be equated to that of typical adults? Is this not an issue of subrationality? If it is, then what justification is there in holding fully responsible and punishing fully the adult criminal defendant who lacks, for nonculpable reasons, this general capacity?

As discussed in Chapter 3, the legal doctrine of diminished capacity is historically controversial. One reason for the persistent controversy stems from the public's general distaste for excusing individuals who have committed serious wrongdoing. However, this powerful sentiment has the potential to run into scientific challenge. For instance, there is scientific evidence that criminals lack moral-cognitive attributes or abilities common to normally developed, noncriminal humans. Compared to their noncriminal peers, criminals are morally underdeveloped and perform poorly with respect to perspective taking and other empathy-related cognitive skills.[1] In addition, Bandura,[2] Caprara,[3] and their colleagues have discerned a set of social-cognitive processes that are collectively termed *moral disengagement*, a discussion of which was introduced in Chapter 2. Moral disengagement is comprised of social-cognitive operations by which an individual may disconnect himself from the moral properties of a given act (e.g., diffusion of responsibility, blaming or attributing desert to the victim). Criminals, it appears, are more likely to morally disengage than noncriminals in the consideration of acting in an immoral or otherwise antisocial manner. If an individual lacks moral-cognitive skills by which his or her moral rational capacity is significantly diminished, should his or her culpability be mitigated? Indeed, this is a heated topic in contemporary American criminal law. Chapter 5 provides a moral-cognitive developmental analysis by which this debate may be informed.

In addition to the legal doctrine of diminished capacity, research on moral-cognitive biases and deficits and antisocial conduct may be relevant to the legal doctrine of insanity.[4] Like diminished capacity, insanity is a defense that has long stirred public and legal debate.[5] Although the defense has historically varied by jurisdiction, the majority of states recognize insanity in some

1 *See, e.g.*, James Blair, Lawrence Jones, Fiona Clark & Margaret Smith, *Is the Psychopath "Morally Insane"?*, 19 PERSONALITY & INDIVIDUAL DIFFERENCES 741 (1995); James Blair, Lawrence Jones, Fiona Clark & Margaret Smith, *The Psychopathic Individual: A Lack of Responsiveness to Distress Cues?*, 34 PSYCHOPHYSIOLOGY 192 (1997).

2 *E.g.*, Albert Bandura, Claudio Barbaranelli, Gian V. Caprara & Concetta Pastorelli, *Mechanisms of Moral Disengagement in the Exercise of Moral Agency*,71 J. PERSONALITY & SOC. PSYCHOL. 364 (1996) [hereinafter Bandura et al., *Moral Agency*]; Albert Bandura, *Moral Disengagement in the Perpetration of Inhumanities*, 3 PERSONALITY & SOC. PSYCHOL. REV. 193 (1996) [hereinafter Bandura, *Inhumanities*]; Albert Bandura, *Selective Moral Disengagement in the Exercise of Moral Agency*, 31 J. MORAL EDUC. 101(2002).

3 Gian V. Caprara & Cristina Capanna, *Moral Civic Disengagement and Values*, 28 RICERCHE DI PSICOLOGIA 67 (2005); Marinella Paciello, Roberta Fida, Carlo Tramontano, Catia Lupinetti & Gian V. Caprara, *Stability and Change of Moral Disengagement and Its Impact on Aggression and Violence in Late Adolescence*, 79 CHILD DEV. 1289 (2008); Gian V. Caprara, Reid G. Fontaine, Roberta Fida, Marinella Paciello, Marie S. Tisak & Kenneth A. Dodge, *The Contributions and Reciprocal Influences of Irritability, Hostile Rumination, and Moral Disengagement to Aggression and Violence in Adolescence* [hereinafter Caprara et al., *Irritability*] (unpublished manuscript, on file with lead author).

4 The history of the insanity defense in American criminal law has been presented in several recent scholarly articles, including Linda C. Fentiman, *"Guilty But Mentally Ill": The Real Verdict is Guilty*, 26 B.C. L. REV. 601 (1985); Gerald Robin, *The Evolution of the Insanity Defense*, 13 J. CONTEMP. CRIM. JUST. 224, 226 (1997); Henry F. Fradella, *From Insanity to Beyond Diminished Capacity: Mental Illness and Criminal Excuse in the Post-*Clark *Era*, 18 U. FLA. J.L. & PUB. POL'Y 7 (2007).

5 Fentiman, *supra* note 4, at 603.

form. Typically, U.S. jurisdictions follow the criteria set forth in the 1843 case of Daniel M'Naghten, who was indicted for first-degree murder for killing Edward Drummond, secretary to Prime Minister Sir Robert Peel.[6] M'Naghten claimed that he had wanted to kill Peel but, mistaking Drummond for Peel, killed Drummond instead. Counsel for M'Naghten presented considerable expert witness evidence supporting an argument that their client suffered from paranoia and persecutory delusions and was acutely mentally unstable. In finding M'Naghten not guilty by reason of insanity, the House of Lords set forth the criteria by which such a conclusion may be drawn, now widely known as the M'Naghten test of insanity. Essentially, the test states that the defendant is not responsible for his criminal conduct if, at the time of the alleged act, he suffered from a mental disease or defect that caused him either to (1) not know the nature or quality of his act, or (2) despite knowing the nature or quality of his act, not know that the act was wrong.

The M'Naghten test thus sets up two alternative psychological profiles of the insane criminal defendant. He either did not understand the nature of his act, or he understood the nature of his act but did not understand the wrongfulness of it. It is the latter of these two scenarios that is the focus of this chapter. The question is, if one has moral-cognitive biases or deficits such that he does not understand the moral wrongfulness of his objectively criminal conduct, may he be justly held legally responsible for said conduct? Social-cognitive psychology on moral development as well as neuroscientific research on cognitive deficits of psychopathy may bear relevance for this psycholegal question. As such, this topic is explored.

This chapter is set forth in three main sections. The first section introduces study of the development of moral rationality – judgment, reasoning, and decision making, among other social-cognitive domains – and recognizes the main theories relevant to contemporary developmental science. A discussion of research on moral-cognitive problems that have been empirically linked to juvenile delinquents and adult criminals is provided and contrasted with adaptive moral-cognitive development. In particular, one area of research on moral\-cognitive development has emerged as perhaps the premiere focus among social-cognitive psychologists studying moral rationality in the development of antisocial and criminal conduct. "Moral disengagement" is a complex social-cognitive construct that comprehensively accounts for various social-cognitive processes by which youths may become able to enact and successfully carry out wrongful conduct. Research on this construct is reviewed.

6 M'Naghten, 10 CL & F. 200, 8 Eng. Rep. 718 (1843).

The second section examines moral-cognitive deficits and psychopathy. Psychopathy is a neuropsychological construct that embodies various biological, cognitive, affective, and behavioral variables associated with chronic antisocial behavior. Considerable research in social-cognitive psychology and neuroscience has found that psychopaths are underdeveloped or have outright deficits with respect to cognitive domains that are crucial to moral judgment and decision making and wrongdoing. Psychopathy has been studied predominantly from a neuroscientific perspective, although it would seem that it has neglected social-cognitive and developmental psychology to its own limitation. The disconnect between developmental research on moral disengagement and antisocial behavior and neuroscientific research on adult psychopathy is addressed.

The third section explores whether research in the areas discussed in sections one and two may be relevant to the insanity defense or a more generalized defense of moral subrationality. For example, are psychopaths, due to nonculpable brain-level deficits, unable to understand the wrongfulness of their antisocial conduct? Note that all four of these sections address issues of *underdeveloped* rationality, as opposed to *diminished* rationality – that is, the psychological profiles described, although potentially structurally, functionally, and phenomenologically different, all have in common that they stem from the absence of normal moral-cognitive development. Future directions for research and reformation of criminal law doctrine are provided in conclusion.

MORAL-COGNITIVE DEVELOPMENT AND CRIMINAL RATIONALITY

Moral Cognition in Individual Development

Jean Piaget was among the first psychologists to conceptualize morality as a function of transactional development. That is, Piaget, who posited that development is based on ongoing exchanges between an individual and his environment, believed that one's personal morality emerges and is shaped by his interactions with others in his social world.[7] This idea remains hard to refute, especially as science continues to empirically demonstrate how transactional models of development account for individual differences in social, psychological, and behavioral phenomena.[8]

7 *See* Jean Piaget, *The Moral Judgment of the Child* (1965).

8 An important collection of scholarly papers on transactional development has recently been offered by Professor Arnold Sameroff in his edited book, The Transactional Model of Development: How Children and Contexts Shape Each Other (2009).

Building from Piaget's stage theory of cognitive development, Lawrence Kohlberg is widely recognized for his stage theory of moral development and maturity. Kohlberg argued that ethical and moral conduct is a function of one's moral reasoning, an area of cognitive development that was guided by one's growing sense of justice as he psychologically matures across a series of six moral-cognitive stages. Earlier stages of development involve simpler processes such as egocentrism (or the inability to differentiate between oneself and the world), the emergence of perspective taking (or "the tendency to spontaneously adopt the psychological point of view of others"[9]), and understanding moral reciprocity (or acting in accordance with one's perception of what another's conduct morally demands). In contrast, later stages involve more advanced executive processes that involve questioning the fairness of established rules and norms and using principle and reason to develop one's moral belief system by which his ethical conduct is guided.[10]

As with Piaget, Kohlberg's contributions to moral psychology were enormous, and lessons from his stage theory are reflected in several contemporary models of moral development. In contrast to Kohlberg's focus on the moral-cognitive underpinnings of ethical conduct, personality psychologists have recently offered accounts of moral development that center on moral identity, moral personhood, and the moral self. In particular, Professor Augusto Blasi argued that the relation between moral cognition and action cannot be considered outside of one's personal identity.[11] According to Blasi, personality serves to moderate this relation in that the likelihood that moral judgment leads to corresponding moral action is greater when said moral action is consistent with his personal identity.[12] Of course, the social-cognitivist response to this position is that a determination as to whether a specific act is consistent with one's sense of self (or one's self-schema) is a naturally social-cognitive operation itself, not suggesting that a moral rationality view is at all invalid, but rather that it is simply more complicated and involved than early theorists, such as Kohlberg, conceived.

9 Mark H. Davis, *Measuring Individual Differences in Empathy: Evidence for a Multidimensional Approach*, 44 J. PERSONALITY & SOC. PSYCHOL. 113, 113–14 (1983).

10 *See, e.g.*, F. CLARK POWER, ANN HIGGINS & LAWRENCE KOHLBERG, LAWRENCE KOHLBERG'S APPROACH TO MORAL EDUCATION (1989).

11 Augusto Blasi, *Moral Cognition and Moral Action: A Theoretic Perspective*, 3 DEVELOPMENTAL REV. 179 (1983); Augusto Blasi, *Moral Identity: Its Role in Moral Functioning*, *in* MORALITY, MORAL BEHAVIOR, AND MORAL DEVELOPMENT 128 (William M. Kurtines & Jacob L. Gewirtz eds., 1984); Augusto Blasi, *The Moral Personality: Reflections for Social Science and Education*, *in* MORAL EDUCATION: THEORY AND APPLICATION 433 (Marvin W. Berkowitz & Fritz K. Oser eds., 1985).

12 Blasi, *Moral Cognition and Moral Action*, *supra* note 11.

For example, in the model of response decision making (response evaluation and decision; RED) and antisocial behavior that Fontaine and Dodge have advanced,[13] it was hypothesized that several basic social-cognitive operations are at the foundation of moral rationality. For example, if a person is provoked, he may consider responding aggressively because the provocateur deserves a negative outcome. Alternative aggressive responses may be considered and contrasted with each other in order to make a variety of determinations, including which response is most likely to be successfully performed (response efficacy), what outcome each response is likely to produce (outcome expectation), and what values should be attributed to the alternative likely outcomes (outcome valuation). However, these RED processes are posited in the context of coinciding social-cognitive operations that relate the response options being considered to one's sense of self. Indeed, among the most basic RED processes is internal congruence by which response options may be quickly discarded because they are an obvious mismatch with one's personal identity. At a more advanced level, the response valuation process acts as a stricter filter by which it is determined whether a response that may have met the thresholds of lower-level, crude filters is sufficiently consistent with how one identifies oneself as a moral agent and social actor.

In their recent review of moral development, Professors Darcia Narvaez and Daniel Lapsley correctly point out that "the study of moral rationality can no longer be studied in isolation from the broader context of personality."[14] This is consistent with Steinberg et al.'s argument that adolescents' decision-making capacity must be considered in light of their character formation and overall psychosocial maturity. I agree with the balance that both of these scholarly groups stress. Nevertheless, the relation between personality and behavior may be understood in social-cognitive terms. That is, one may only relate moral action or, at least, the consideration or anticipation of enacting moral action (or a specific moral act) to his sense of self, or his self-schema, via social cognition. The self-schema is itself a latent social-cognitive structure, and its relation to any considered action may only be understood if said action is social-cognitively processed. This view is entirely consistent with individual

[13] Reid G. Fontaine & Kenneth A. Dodge, *Real-Time Decision Making and Aggressive Behavior in Youth: A Heuristic Model of Response Evaluation and Decision (RED)*, 32 AGGRESSIVE BEHAV. 604 (2006).

[14] Darcia Narvaez & Daniel K. Lapsley, *Moral Identity, Moral Functioning, and the Development of Moral Character, in* 50 MORAL JUDGMENT AND DECISION MAKING 237 (Douglas L. Medin, Linda Skitka, Daniel Bartels & Christopher Bauman eds., 2009).

systems models of moral development,[15] as well as social-cognitive approaches to personality coherence[16] and personality development[17] by which admittedly small changes in personality across time may be explained. Such approaches take a "bottom-up" approach toward explaining individual differences in personality as the result of ongoing reciprocal exchanges among individual or intrapersonal systems such as attention, cognition, and emotion. As an individual develops, his intrapersonal systems are dynamically interacting so that he can successfully transact with and navigate through his social world. These intrapersonal and transactional exchanges are hypothesized to account for personality structures and development, as small as they sometimes are upon personality maturation.

Moral Cognition in Abnormal Development

Moral-cognitive development is characterized by a seemingly infinite number of individual differences, and thus travels along numerous, varied trajectories ranging from normal to distinctly atypical. However, even though abnormal moral-cognitive development may lead to patterned antisocial behavior, it does not necessarily do so. An individual may have moral-cognitive biases or deficits that are not behaviorally manifested. For example, an individual may have intrusive thoughts of harming innocent others but does not act on them because he is behaviorally inhibited, does not have access to promising opportunities or the requisite instrumentation, or is deterred by the idea of being caught and punished. Still, it is not unusual for the criminal offender to be "moral-cognitively equipped" differently than law-abiding citizens.

[15] Reid G. Fontaine, *Applying Systems Principles to Models of Social Information Processing and Aggressive Behavior in Youth*, 11 AGGRESSION & VIOLENT BEHAV. 64 (2006); Caprara et al., *Irritability*, *supra* note 3.

[16] Daniel Cervone, *Social-Cognitive Mechanisms and Personality Coherence: Self-Knowledge, Situational Beliefs, and Cross-Situational Coherence in Perceived Self-Efficacy*, 8 PSYCHOL. SCI. 43 (1997); Daniel Cervone, *Bottom-up Explanation in Personality Psychology: The Case of Cross-Situational Coherence*, *in* THE COHERENCE OF PERSONALITY: SOCIAL-COGNITIVE BASES OF CONSISTENCY, VARIABILITY, AND ORGANIZATION 303 (Daniel Cervone & Yuichi Shoda eds., 1999); Daniel Cervone, *Personality Architecture: Within-Person Structures and Processes*, 56 ANN. REV. PSYCHOL. 423 (2005); *see also* Daniel Cervone & Ritu Tripathi, *The Moral Functioning of the Person as a Whole: On Moral Psychology and Personality Science*, *in* MORAL PERSONALITY, IDENTITY AND CHARACTER 30 (Darcia Navaez & Daniel K. Lapsley eds., 2009).

[17] *E.g.*, Arnaldo Zelli & Kenneth A. Dodge, *Personality Development from the Bottom Up*, *in* THE COHERENCE OF PERSONALITY: SOCIAL-COGNITIVE BASES OF CONSISTENCY, VARIABILITY, AND ORGANIZATION 94–124 (Daniel Cervone & Yuichi Shoda eds., 1999).

Empirical investigations of social-cognitive psychology and unlawful conduct in both juvenile and adult offender populations have revealed a moral-cognitive profile for the developing criminal. Over the last three decades, several empirical studies have found evidence that the moral judgment of juvenile delinquents is less mature than that of their nondelinquent peers.[18] Early studies concluded that delinquents reason at earlier stages of moral development, as set forth by Kohlberg, than do nonoffending youths. That is, delinquents reason about moral behaviors and situations in ways that suggest they are moral-cognitively underdeveloped.[19] As opposed to normally developed youths, juvenile delinquents are driven by "power and hedonistic concerns" when reasoning about moral issues and events.[20]

Recently, Professor Geert Jan Stams and his colleagues provided a comprehensive meta-analysis of research in this area, quantitatively summarizing the main empirical findings of fifty studies and addressing issues that had remained open in the literature.[21] Generally, their study concluded that, even after taking into account socioeconomic status, gender, age, and intelligence, there emerges a strong relation between developmentally delayed moral judgment and juvenile delinquency. Particularly strong negative relations with moral judgment were found with specific subgroups of delinquents who were male, older, less intelligent, and incarcerated. Furthermore, underdeveloped moral judgment was particularly related to length of incarceration and psychopathic symptomatology.

Several of the findings from the Stams et al.'s meta-analysis[22] suggest that moral judgment and reasoning may be used not only to differentiate delinquent and nondelinquent youths, but also subgroups of youth offenders. A subsequent empirical study by English research scientists on differential moral reasoning among subtypes of delinquent offenders specifically

[18] *E.g.*, Augusto Blasi, *Bridging Moral Cognition and Moral Action: A Critical Review of the Literature*, 88 PSYCHOL. BULL. 1 (1980); V. Gregg, John C. Gibbs & Karen S. Basinger, *Patterns of Developmental Delay in Moral Judgment by Male and Female Delinquents*, 40 MERRILL-PALMER Q. 538 (1994); Emma J. Palmer & Clive R. Hollin, *A Comparison of Patterns of Moral Development in Young Offenders and Non-offenders*, 3 LEGAL & CRIMINOLOGICAL PSYCHOL. 225 (1998). Also, see meta-analytic studies of the juvenile delinquency and moral judgment and reasoning: J. Ron Nelson, Deborah J. Smith & John Dodd, *The Moral Reasoning of Juvenile Delinquents: A Meta-Analysis*, 18 J. ABNORMAL CHILD PSYCHOL. 231 (1990); Geert Jan Stams, Daniel Brugman, Maja Deković, Lenny van Rosmalen, Peter van der Laan & John C. Gibbs, *The Moral Judgment of Juvenile Delinquents: A Meta-Analysis*, 34 J. ABNORMAL CHILD PSYCHOL. 697 (2006).

[19] Palmer & Hollin, *supra* note 18.

[20] *Id.*

[21] Stams et al., *supra* note 18.

[22] *Id.*

examined this issue, although their results were nonsignificant. The researchers suggested that cognitive-developmental delay models, such as the stage models advanced by Kohlberg, was of limited use to differentiating subtypes of youth offenders, and that "a more sophisticated understanding of the role of moral reasoning development in the study of crime is needed." It is likely that social-information processing theory may be of use to this endeavor. Research on social-information processing has repeatedly found that discernible sociomoral-cognitive processing patterns differentiate predominately instrumental versus reactive aggressive youths. Whereas instrumental aggressive youths tend to evaluate aggressive behavioral options favorably in anticipation of social action, reactive aggressive youths are inclined to make negative attributions when presented with social scenarios that are ambiguous as to their moral content.[23]

Although less plentiful than research on moral judgment and reasoning in juvenile populations, research on moral cognition and adult offenders has consistently found a similar set of results. As discussed in Chapter 4, rational decision making and character are significantly more developed in adulthood than they are in adolescence. Nevertheless, there exists a significant difference between the moral judgment and reasoning of adult offenders versus their nonoffending peers.[24] Indeed, the moral judgment and decision making of adult offenders is often similar to that of children and younger adolescents.[25]

Collectively, these bodies of research demonstrate a clear negative correlation of moral judgment and reasoning and delinquent and criminal offending. However, there remain several issues that are crucial to both understanding the nature and complexity of this relation as well as how to understand this relation in light of issues of culpability and law and in juvenile and adult criminal justice symptoms. Already identified is the need to develop research by which moral cognition may better distinguish subtypes of offenders. In addition, a developmental question of equifinality exists, which asks this: Are there alternative developmental paths of moral-cognitive development that may better explain individual differences among offenders? For example, are some offenders underdeveloped whereas others are cognitively equipped but merely value instrumental gain over sociomorally acceptable conduct? If so, do such alternative paths have implications for how delinquent and criminal actors are assessed and punished? Recent research on moral disengagement in social-cognitive

[23] For a review, see Reid G. Fontaine, *Disentangling the Psychology and Law of Instrumental and Reactive Subtypes of Aggression*, 13 Psychol. Pub. Pol'y & L.143 (2007).

[24] Ann Colby & Lawrence Kohlberg, 1–2 *The Measurement of Moral Judgment* (1987).

[25] Peter J. Ashkar & Dianna T. Kenny, *Moral Reasoning of Adolescent Male Offenders: Comparison of Sexual and Nonsexual Offenders*, 34 Crim. Just. & Behav. 108 (2007).

psychology may be useful toward investigating the relevant empirical questions and informing normative issues that rest, in part, on them.

Mechanisms of Moral Disengagement

In Chapter 3, Bandura's theoretical model of moral disengagement as well as developmental research on moral disengagement and antisocial conduct were presented.[26] Moral disengagement comprises a set of processes by which the moral content of an antisocial act that may otherwise serve to inhibit one from carrying the act out is detached. The elimination or disconnection of the act's natural moral content proves useful not only enacting the conduct in question but performing it successfully such that the likelihood that one will realize his instrumental goals is maximized. Cognitive dissonance, or the internal conflict that results from acting is discordance with one's beliefs and values, is eliminated or significantly discounted such that it not only fails to deter the actor from committing wrongdoing, but fails to negatively affect the quality of his performance of said wrongdoing such that it might otherwise hinder its relation with its associated desired outcome.

Eight discernible processes of moral disengagement have been classified by four points in the antisocial behavioral process.[27] One may (1) redefine the moral framing or nature of the act such as by justifying means with ends; (2) displace his responsibility for wrongdoing so that another may be blamed; (3) reframe the detrimental outcome such that its negative value or quality is detached or disguised; and/or (4) devalue the victim such that the wrongdoing against him may be justified or at least accepted. It is likely that many instances of antisocial conduct are the product of multiple moral disengagement processes across one or more of these "points" in the antisocial behavioral process. It may be expected that the more thorough the moral disengagement – or rather, the more moral disengagement processes are activated – the more likely it is that the antisocial behavior in question will be selected, enacted, and performed successfully such that the actor's instrumental goals are realized.

As discussed in Chapter 4, the empirically documented relation between moral disengagement and antisocial conduct was reviewed. In addition, the concept of equifinality as applied to this relation was introduced. There are a number of different pathways by which a person may become morally disengaged. That is, the developmental process of moral disengagement may take

[26] Bandura et al., *Moral Agency*, *supra* note 2; Bandura, *Inhumanities*, *supra* note 2.

[27] Bandura et al., *Moral Agency*, *supra* note 2.

multiple forms. For example, (1) a person may present as morally disengaged from early in life because of a biological predisposition to be morally detached and unable to empathize or take others' perspectives[28]; this is more of an etiology than a developmental course because this trajectory is not characterized by the *development* of a phenomenon as much as it is the *maintenance* or continuity of a phenomenon; (2) because of harsh early experiences (e.g., abuse and maltreatment, peer victimization, exposure to family and community violence and crime), a child may become morally disengaged in that he comes to understand that the world is a cruel, unfair, and unsafe place that does not operate according to moral conventions understood by the majority of citizens in a civil society; and, finally (3) a child may learn to be motivated to become morally disengaged because he has watched others and learned that immoral and criminal behaviors lead to desirable outcomes. In this latter scenario, the child may rehearse social strategies by which personal and moral values are discounted either partially or fully in order to carry out various antisocial and criminal acts with greater ease and success.

Although these developmental courses are all very different, the outcome of moral disengagement may be very much the same. In its extreme form, a crystallized (or habitualized or automatic) pattern of moral disengagement may be equated to a mental defect or incapacity by which the actor may not appreciate the reprehensibility of his criminal behavior. In this way, the mental defect of crystallized moral disengagement may partially (or perhaps even fully) diminish the defendant's rationality, culpability, and responsibility. However, the culpability in this case really depends on how the moral disengagement of the actor came to be crystallized. If it became crystallized as a result of the repeated outputs of distorted social-information processing (perhaps as the result of being chronically abused as a child), then this may be viewed as mental defect. If, on the other hand, the actor's moral disengagement became crystallized as a result of the defendant's purposeful and effortful rehearsal over time and across incidents, then this would seem to be less of a mental defect and more of an intended mental script (note that the Model Penal Code specifically states that a mental defect that results from engaging in crime does not suffice[29]). Thus the etiology (and developmental course) and degree of crystallization of the criminal actor's moral disengagement are central to understanding the culpability with which he has criminally acted.

[28] Alec Buchanan, *Psychiatric Aspects of Justification, Excuse and Mitigation in Anglo-American Criminal Law* 74–75 (2000).

[29] Model Penal Code § 4.01(2) states "As used in this Article, the terms 'mental disease or defect' do not include an abnormality manifested only by repeated criminal or otherwise antisocial conduct."

MORAL-COGNITIVE DEFICITS, PSYCHOPATHY, AND ANTISOCIAL PERSONALITY DISORDER

Moral-cognitive deficits are commonly associated with a condition called "psychopathy" or what is often considered its psychiatric equivalent, "antisocial personality disorder." Individuals with psychopathy – or psychopaths – tend to show little or no remorse for their antisocial actions. They are characterized by narcissism and a sense of superiority, egocentricity, callousness, chronic antisocial behavior, low frustration tolerance, impulsivity, and lack of conscience.[30] As Professor Heidi Maibom articulated it, "[p]sychopathic individuals are perhaps best known for their flagrant disregard for social and moral norms."[31] Indeed, these and similarly socially maladjusted qualities are prominent in the construct development and assessment of psychopathy.[32]

[30] *E.g.*, James Blair, *A Cognitive Developmental Approach to Morality: Investigating the Psychopath*, 57 COGNITION 1 (1995) [hereinafter Blair, *Developmental Approach*]; James Blair, *Neurocognitive Models of Aggression, the Antisocial Personality Disorders, and Psychopathy*, 71 J. NEUROLOGY, NEUROSURGERY & PSYCHIATRY 727 (2001) [hereinafter Blair, *Neurocognitive*]; James Blair, *Applying a Cognitive Neuroscience Perspective to the Disorder of Psychopathy*, 17 DEV. & PSYCHOPATHOLOGY 865 (2005) [hereinafter Blair, *Applying*]; James Blair, *Psychopathy, Frustration, and Reactive Aggression: The Role of Ventromedial Prefrontal Cortex*, 101 BRIT. J. PSYCHOL. 383 (2010) [hereinafter Blair, *Psychopathy*]; Michael Chandler & Thomas Moran, *Psychopathy and Moral Development: A Comparative Study of Delinquent and Nondelinquent Youth*, 2 DEV. & PSYCHOPATHOLOGY 227 (1990); Dewey G. Cornell, Janet Warren, Gary Hawk, Ed Stafford, Guy Oram & Denise Pine, *Psychopathy in Instrumental and Reactive Violent Offenders*, 64 J. CONSULTING & CLIN. PSYCHOL. 783 (1996); ROBERT D. HARE, *WITHOUT CONSCIENCE: THE DISTURBING WORLD OF THE PSYCHOPATH AMONG US* (1999); Sabine C. Herpertz & Sass Henning, *Emotional Deficiency and Psychopathy*, 18 BEHAV. SCI. & L. 567 (2000); N. F. Link, Steven E. Scherer & P. N. Byrne, *Moral Judgment and Moral Conduct in the Psychopath*, 22 CAN. PSYCHIATRIC ASS'N J. 341 (1977); Donald R. Lynam, *Early Identification of Chronic Offenders: Who Is the Fledgling Psychopath?*, 120 PSYCHOL. BULL. 209 (1996) [hereinafter Lynam, *Early Identification*]; Willem H. J. Martens, *Moral and Ethical Capacities of the Psychopath: An Integrated Review*, *in* THE VARIABLES OF MORAL CAPACITY 259 (David C. Thomasma & David N. Weisstub eds., 2004); Joseph P. Newman, *Psychopathic Behavior: An Information Processing Perspective*, *in* PSYCHOPATHY: THEORY, RESEARCH AND IMPLICATIONS FOR SOCIETY 81 (David J. Cooke, Robert D. Hare & Adelle E. Forth eds., 1998); Jennifer L. Skeem & Edward P. Mulvey, *Psychopathy and Community Violence Among Civil Psychiatric Patients: Results from the MacArthur Violence Risk Assessment Study*, 69 J. CONSULTING & CLIN. PSYCHOL. 358 (2001); Michael J. Vitacco & Richard Rogers, *Predictors of Adolescent Psychopathy: The Role of Impulsivity, Hyperactivity, and Sensation Seeking*, 29 J. AM. ACAD. PSYCHIATRY & L. 374 (2001); Sherrie Williamson, Robert D. Hare & Stephen Wong, *Violence: Criminal Psychopaths and their Victims*, 19 CAN. J. BEHAV. SCI. 454 (1987).

[31] Heidi L. Maibom, *Moral Unreason: The Case of Psychopathy*, 20 MIND & LANGUAGE 237 (2005).

[32] *E.g.*, THE CLINICAL AND FORENSIC ASSESSMENT OF PSYCHOPATHY: A PRACTITIONER'S GUIDE (Carl B. Gacono ed., 2000); *see also* HERVEY CLECKLEY, *THE MASK OF SANITY* (1976); ROBERT D. HARE, *THE HARE PSYCHOPATHY CHECKLIST – REVISED* (1991).

Psychopaths pose considerable concerns for the law and society at large. Psychopathy is defined, in part, by chronic antisocial conduct, which means that it is, by its nature, a necessarily social and societal problem. However, psychopathy may be particularly worrisome when considering the psychopathic antisocial conduct functions because of the condition's nonbehavioral aspects. That is, the psychological traits of the condition are relatively inflexible and appear to be partly grounded in biological roots. Such social-cognitive (e.g., discounting the worth of others) and personality (e.g., low frustration tolerance) traits are persistent and psychopathic conduct is largely stable across time (reason 1). In addition, psychopaths are typically less able to experience remorse upon realization of even serious wrongdoing. That is, the psychopathic wrongdoer is less likely to have an internal negative experience that is natural to the normal "rightdoer." This is important in multiple ways. First, the psychopath may be less punishable, and here I mean "punishable" in the experiential and behaviorism senses, not the legal sense. This is to say, the psychopath may not experience a legally defined punishment (e.g., incarceration) in a punitive (or aversive) way, and legal punishments may be less likely to reduce target negative behaviors. It may be understood that this problem undermines retributive justice in that a wrongdoer's debt to society is not paid if he experiences (or "suffers") no loss (reason 2). In addition, the psychopath's resistance to punishment experience may undermine utilitarian goals – or, more specifically, deterrence (reason 3). If a wrongdoer is sentenced to serve a legal punishment but experiences no aversion to the government's prescription, it logically follows that his nonnegative internalized response would be unlikely to play a preventive or deterrent role when he is again considering enacting the same or similar antisocial act. In addition, citizens may worry that because of the characterological makeup of the psychopath, as well as his persistent propensity to commit wrongdoing, he is a generally more dangerous kind of antisocial individual who thus poses additional risks to society – a sense that may contribute to a variety of societal ills, including safety and fear.

As mentioned, research has found that psychopathy is partly grounded in biology, namely structural and biochemical mechanisms at the brain level. Perhaps no one has been more rigorous in applying a neuroscientific approach to psychopathy than Dr. James Blair.[33] Considering a number of models of psychopathy from a neuroscientific perspective, Blair has identified two forms of pathology in psychopathy: (1) dysfunction of the amygdala, an almond-shaped mass of nuclei responsible for the processing and memory of emotional

[33] *E.g.*, Blair, *Developmental Approach*, *supra* note 30; Blair, *Neurocognitive*, *supra* note 30; Blair, *Applying*, *supra* note 30; Blair, *Psychopathy*, *supra* note 30.

experiences and reactions; and (2) dysfunction of the orbital/ventrolateral frontal cortex, a region of the brain associated with cognitive and behavioral processes such as evaluative decision making and instrumental conduct that is guided by sensitivity to reward and punishment contingencies.[34] It is unclear how these brain pathologies are related and whether they are both causes of psychopathy, as Blair speculates that the orbital/ventrolateral dysfunction may be a noncausal correlate that merely "reflect[s] the lifestyle of individuals with psychopathy."[35] Nevertheless, mechanisms at the brain level are now known to be related to psychopathic functioning patterns, and research on the neuroscience of psychopathy is on an accelerated trajectory. What is clear is that psychopaths typically lack moral-cognitive mechanisms by which appreciation of others' subjective experiences, perspectives, and interests is limited, although to what degree is unknown.

Psychopathy involves a number of different intrapersonal systems, namely cognitive, emotional, and behavioral. Blair has asserted: "In essence, psychopathy involves two components: emotional dysfunction and antisocial behavior,"[36] although he has also considered affective processes as a "form of cognitive processing." This seems sensible from an appraisal theory perspective in that affect and emotions are the product of differential cognitive processing patterns. Whereas psychopathy has not traditionally been considered a product of cognitive dysfunction,[37] some scientists have argued that the neglect of cognition by certain models of psychopathy undermines research on the nature and development of the condition and its relation to antisocial behavior. Indeed, in their essay, "Understanding Psychopathy," Drs. Kristina Hiatt and Joe Newman argue convincingly that "[a]lthough both popular and empirical characterizations of psychopathy tended to emphasize the emotion-processing deficits, the information-processing deficits associated with psychopathy provide critical insight into the disorder."[38] In particular, the authors pointed to differences in attention processing, language processing, and behavioral inhibition associated with psychopathic individuals.

34 Blair, *Applying*, *supra* note 30.

35 *Id.* at 885.

36 Blair, *Psychopathy*, *supra* note 30; *see also* Paul J. Frick, *Callous–Unemotional Traits and Conduct Problems: A Two-Factor Model of Psychopathy in Children*, 24 ISSUES CRIMINOLOGICAL & LEGAL PSYCHOL. 47(1995); HARE, *supra* note 32; Timothy J. Harpur, A. R. Hakstian & Robert D. Hare, *The Factor Structure of the Psychopathy Checklist*, 56 J. CONSULTING & CLIN. PSYCHOL. 741 (1988).

37 Kristian D. Hiatt & Joseph P. Newman, *Understanding Psychopathy: The Cognitive Side, in* HANDBOOK OF PSYCHOPATHY 334, 335 (Christopher J. Patrick ed., 2006).

38 *Id.* at 334.

As mentioned earlier, psychopathy is often equated with or at least likened to antisocial personality disorder (APD). APD is a disruptive behavioral disorder that is formally recognized as a psychiatric diagnosis and defined by the DSM-IV-TR.[39] A diagnosis of APD requires that the patient be eighteen,[40] has a history of serious disruptive behavior problems prior to the age of fifteen,[41] and demonstrated "a pervasive pattern of disregard for and violation of the rights of others occurring since age 15,"[42] as marked by at least three serious forms of antisocial conduct. Included among such disruptive behavior problems are the failure to conform to social norms, deceitfulness, impulsivity, irritability and aggressiveness, reckless disregard of others, consistent irresponsibility, and lack of remorse.[43]

It is not difficult to see why psychopathy and APD have been linked. Surely, many individuals who have been diagnosed with or meet the criteria for APD also exhibit characteristics of psychopathy. Likewise, it is not unusual for psychopaths to meet criteria for APD. However, it is a mistake to equate the two, and similar to problems caused at the neglect of cognition and information processing as cited by Hiatt and Newman,[44] the equation of psychopathy and APD has served as an obstacle to untangling the intricacies and nuances of psychopathy in scientific research. As Blair recently summarized, psychiatric diagnoses of disruptive behavioral disorders such as APD "concentrate on the antisocial behavior rather than any potential cause for its expression such as the emotion dysfunction seen in psychopathy."[45] Blair rightly identifies that psychiatric disorders of this sort function almost as a behavioral checklist. That is, if an individual has enacted a certain number of qualifying antisocial acts in a specified period of time, he satisfies the criteria and is diagnosed accordingly. His antisocial behavioral pattern may or may not have the etiology that would characterize him as a psychopath. The diagnosis, by itself, is useless for understanding the mechanisms of the behavior and, as such, may not be understood as the equivalent of psychopathy.

[39] Am. Psychiatric Ass'n, *Diagnostic and Statistical Manual of Mental Disorders* 701–06 (4th ed., text rev. 2000) [hereinafter Am. Psychiatric Ass'n].

[40] *Id.* Criterion B requires that "The individual is at least 18 years of age." *Id.*

[41] *Id.* Criterion C requires that "There is evidence of Conduct Disorder [a serious disruptive behavior disorder in youth] with onset before age 15 years." *Id.*

[42] *Id.*

[43] *Id.* In addition, Criterion D of the diagnosis requires that "The occurrence of antisocial behavior is not exclusively during the course of Schizophrenia or a Manic Episode." *Id.*

[44] Hiatt & Newman, *supra* note 37.

[45] Blair, *Psychopathy*, *supra* note 30; *see also* James Blair, Derek Mitchell & Karina Blair, *The Psychopath: Emotion and the Brain* (2005).

Equally problematic for the diagnosis of APD is that it does not properly account for individual differences in developmental history or, for that matter, development of any kind. This is not only a problem with the APD diagnosis (and other psychiatrically defined disruptive behavior disorders, such as oppositional defiant disorder and conduct disorder), but with popular and scientific models of psychopathy at large, as well. Whereas contemporary perspectives on psychopathy focus on the characteristics of chronic antisocial actors in adulthood, Blair and other scientists have argued that psychopathy is, in fact, a "developmental disorder."[46] Given that most theories of psychopathy recognize that there are early markers of conduct problem behaviors and other antisocial features, it seems odd that issues of development would be neglected. As Blair has argued,[47] the absence or limitation of certain key developmental mechanisms may be critical to understanding the development of three aspects of morality, all of which represent cognitive processes or are cognitively mediated: moral emotions, violence inhibition, and the moral/conventional distinction.[48] The neglect of the issue of development is critical, not only for basic research, but because, as discussed later, identifying differential etiologies and alternative developmental courses may be essential to legal determinations of culpability in the assessment of wrongdoing.

It may be striking that thus far, our discussion of moral-cognitive deficits and psychopathy has been definitively separate from that of the relation between moral disengagement and antisocial behavior. The role of moral disengagement has been explored broadly in investigations of a variety of antisocial behaviors and actors.[49] One might intuit that moral disengagement

[46] Blair, *Developmental Approach, supra* note 30; Blair, *Psychopathy, supra* note 30; Donald R. Lynam, Avshalom Caspi, Terrie E. Moffitt, Rolf Loeber & Magda Stouthamer-Loeber, *Longitudinal Evidence that Psychopathy Scores in Early Adolescence Predict Adult Psychopathy*, 116 J. ABNORMAL PSYCHOL. 116, 155 (2007); *see also* Lynam, *Early Identification, supra* note 30. This should not be confused with pervasive developmental disorders (PDDs) such as autistic disorder and Asperger's disorder, as recognized by the DSM-IV-TR, which are perhaps better characterized as disorders of *a*sociality (in that developmental delays involved in PDDs create a general social ineptness and disinterest) as opposed to *anti*sociality. *See* AM. PSYCHIATRIC ASS'N, *supra* note 39, at 70–75, 80–84.

[47] Blair, *Developmental Approach, supra* note 30.

[48] As discussed earlier, the moral/conventional distinction was made popular by Lawrence Kohlberg in the advancement of his stage theory of moral development. *See* LAWRENCE KOHLBERG, *THE PSYCHOLOGY OF MORAL DEVELOPMENT* (1984); *see also* Daniel Kelly, Stephen Stich, Kevin J. Haley, Serena J. Eng & Daniel M. T. Fessler, *Harm, Affect, and the Moral/Conventional Distinction*, 22 MIND & LANGUAGE 117 (2007).

[49] *E.g.*, Bandura, *Inhumanities, supra* note 2; Albert Bandura, *Role of Mechanisms of Selective Moral Disengagement in Terrorism and Counterterrorism, in* UNDERSTANDING TERRORISM 121 (Fathali M. Mogahaddam & Anthony J. Marsella eds., 2003); Albert Bandura, *Training in Terrorism Through Selective Moral Disengagement, in* 2 THE MAKING OF A TERRORIST:

among individuals with psychopathy is not only highly prevalent but has been a popular interest among behavioral scientists. However, the two research foci have largely been studied separately. I expect this relative isolation may be explained by at least two reasons. First, psychopathy has increasingly become an area of research for which a neuroscientific perspective has been applied. Alternatively, moral disengagement was conceptualized out of social-cognitive psychology, and although there may be biological factors that predispose one toward or away from developing moral disengagement, the phenomenon is framed as a disposition that grows out of continued transactions between an individual and his environment. In other words, whereas psychopathy has become a matter of social-cognitive neuroscience, moral disengagement has remained grounded in social-cognitive psychology.

Perhaps more at issue (and at odds with the scientific study of moral disengagement), however, is the problem of development for the popular and empirical study of psychopathy that research scientists such as Blair and Professor Donald Lynam have identified and attempted to expose.[50] Most studies of psychopathy have been of adult populations. There is likely a number of reasons for this. First, because psychopathy is often associated with APD, and because individuals under the age of eighteen are not to be diagnosed with a personality disorder (it is both counterdiagnostic and unethical), psychopathy may have been more closely tied with adulthood. Second, there is some social and political sentiment that because the terms *psychopath* and *sociopath* carry such considerable social stigma, they should not be applied to children and adolescents. To do so may unfairly affect their development and future in an adverse fashion.

In contrast, much empirical research on the relation between moral disengagement and antisocial behavior has been conducted with youth populations. In addition, most of these studies of children and adolescents have been longitudinal, such that true developmental change may be observed and understood. This is not to say that this research is not without its own

RECRUITMENT, TRAINING AND ROOT CAUSES 34 (James J. F. Forest ed., 2006); Albert Bandura, Gian V. Caprara & Laszlo Zsolnai, *Corporate Transgressions*, *in* ETHICS IN THE ECONOMY: HANDBOOK OF BUSINESS ETHICS 151 (Laszlo Zsolnai ed., 2002); Michael J. Osofsky, Albert Bandura & Phillip G. Zimbardo, *The Role of Moral Disengagement in the Execution Process*, 29 L. & HUM. BEHAV. 371 (2005); Stavros P. Kiriakidis, *Moral Disengagement: Relation to Delinquency and Independence from Indices of Social Dysfunction*, 52 INT'L J. OFFENDER THERAPY & COMPARATIVE CRIMINOLOGY 571 (2008).

50 Blair, *Developmental Approach*, *supra* note 30; Blair, *Psychopathy*, *supra* note 30; Lynam, *Early Identification*, *supra* note 30; Lynam, Caspi, Moffitt, Loeber & Stouthamer-Loeber, *Longitudinal Evidence that Psychopathy Scores in Early Adolescence Predict Adult Psychopathy*, *supra* note 47.

developmental limitation, however. Whereas psychopathy may be studied with accessible adult populations (e.g., incarcerated samples), longitudinal studies of moral disengagement in youth may be forced to end as youths exit adolescence, complete school, and disperse into various venues of higher education and the job market. Thus the different practical limitations of these two areas of research may also have contributed to their continued separation. This notwithstanding, a comprehensive understanding of the development of moral-cognitive biases and deficits among individuals who engage in antisocial conduct and wrongdoing will require future research to examine moral disengagement and aspects of psychopathy simultaneously under true developmental research conditions.

MORAL SUBRATIONALITY AND CRIMINAL LAW

Lessons from social-cognitive psychology of moral disengagement and antisocial behavior and neuroscience and neuropsychology of psychopathy teach us that chronic antisocial actors typically have moral-cognitive biases, deficits, and other processing impairments related to their conduct styles and patterns. The law has long struggled with how to respond to and manage individuals who exhibit a persistent pattern of antisocial and criminal conduct. There are several reasons for this dilemma, of which I will mention but a few.

First, these individuals have been described or labeled in different ways – career criminals, recidivists, psychopaths, sociopaths, the "morally insane,"[51] "morally uncomprehending criminals,"[52] among others. These labels are only accurate to the degree that they are functionally comprehensive (e.g., a career criminal only describes a pattern of criminal conduct that has lasted over a substantial period of time) in their descriptiveness and apply equally to individuals within the pool for which the term was intended. That is, if the label is designed such that key individual differences among members of the pool are missed, its purpose may be undermined. Human beings are perplexingly sophisticated organisms, and we differ from each other in a seemingly infinite number of ways. This observation is no less valid even when discussing human beings that belong to a narrowly tailored group, such as chronic antisocial actors. It is true that we may discern a group of individuals by matching them to a specified set of criteria or characteristics; however, individuals within such a group will remain different in innumerable ways. For example,

[51] Blair, Jones, Clark & Smith, *Is the Psychopath "Morally Insane"?*, *supra* note 1.

[52] Robert Weisberg, *The Values of Interdisciplinarity in Homicide Law Reform*, 43(1) U. MICH. J.L. REFORM 53 (2009).

two individuals may look nearly identical in terms of their antisocial conduct, but their behavioral patterns may have completely different etiologies in which strikingly discernible mechanisms are at work. This truth, combined with the relative immaturity of that state of research on chronic antisocial actors, surely contributes to the lack of consensus as to how to describe this special population.

Second, it is still quite unclear what makes various chronic antisocial actors tick. Even if we limit our discussion to psychopathic criminals, psychopathy experts agree that the pathological pathways by which persistent psychopathic criminality functions remain, at least to some considerable degree, a mystery.[53] Disagreement in the literature as to what mechanisms are key and how to best research psychopathy is obvious evidence of this reality.[54] As such, the law's pursuit to develop an understanding as to how to properly respond to and manage chronic antisocial actors is naturally limited as a result of science's limited understanding of biological, psychological, and neuroscientific mechanisms of crime.

Third, there remains a strong law-and-order sentiment that repeat offenders should be punished harshly without consideration of their functional makeup or social experiences. This view is mistakenly described as retributive. I say mistakenly because this perspective rests more on revenge or vengeance than retribution. It is driven, in part, by anger at individuals who commit wrongdoing and social harms, not a sense of determining and realizing proportionate punishment for social harms for which the actor is legitimately responsible. Whereas the anger that fuels this movement may be quite understandable – what conscientious citizen does not experience anger in response to learning that an individual has committed a wrongdoing that caused a social harm? – its understandability has no bearing on whether it factors into a legitimate approach to blame and punishment. This movement is less concerned with why antisocial individuals commit wrongdoing than with how and how much to punish them.

As a result of these and other factors, the law has continued to struggle with issues of blame and punishment regarding chronic antisocial actors who may not be sufficiently rational in all ways presumed by the law. Although there exist tremendous, growing literatures in psychology,[55] psychiatry,[56]

[53] Blair, *Applying*, *supra* note 30; Hiatt & Newman, *supra* note 37, at 335.

[54] Hiatt & Newman, *supra* note 37, at 335.

[55] *E.g.*, Cordelia Fine & Jeanette Kennett, *Mental Impairment, Moral Understanding and Criminal Responsibility: Psychopathy and the Purposes of Punishment*, 27 INT'L J.L. & PSYCHIATRY 425 (2004).

[56] *E.g.*, Martens, *supra* note 30.

neuroscience,[57] philosophy,[58] and law[59] regarding the issue of how chronic antisocial actors should be treated by law and society, this question has persisted with little agreement. I believe the key to resolving this dilemma lies in understanding development and individual differences in etiology and developmental course, a perspective that has perhaps its strongest foundation in research on social-cognitive psychology and antisocial behavior. In the subsections that follow, I discuss how legal insanity fails to adequately address these issues and what a general doctrine of moral subrationality might look like. Then, we turn to the issue of moral disengagement, how it may develop, and what should be done with respect to responding to and managing chronic antisocial actors for which moral disengagement has crystallized.

Moral versus Legal Insanity

Legal insanity is an affirmative defense by which the defendant does not deny that he committed the act (e.g., homicide) as objectively defined by the criminal law but claims that he should not be blamed or punished for said act as he was not responsible for having committed it. This places the insanity defense squarely in the excuse camp (indeed it is often used as a textbook example of an excuse)[60] and it is, most often, a complete defense by which, when successful, results in no blame or punishment, but rather residential psychiatric treatment in a locked mental health facility. As discussed, there have been numerous, varied framings of legal insanity, and the defense takes alternative forms in different jurisdictions throughout Anglo-America. In general, it must be demonstrated that at the time of the criminal act, the defendant's mentality was so significantly altered or otherwise substandard that he was not of sufficiently sound mind that he could have acted otherwise.

There are two primary framings with which we need be concerned. The first, defined by the nineteenth-century English case of Daniel M'Naghten,[61] was introduced earlier in this chapter. The M'Naghten test states that if the defendant, at the time of the alleged criminal conduct, due to mental disease or defect, either (1) did not know the nature or quality of

[57] *E.g.*, Blair, Jones, Clark & Smith, *Is the Psychopath "Morally Insane"?*, *supra* note 1.

[58] *E.g.*, Maibom, *supra* note 31.

[59] *E.g.*, Peter Aranella, *Convicting the Morally Blameless: Reassessing the Relationship Between Legal and Moral Accountability*, 39 UCLA L. REV. 1511 (1992).

[60] *E.g.*, JOSHUA DRESSLER, *UNDERSTANDING CRIMINAL LAW* 205 (5th ed. 2009); MARKUS D. DUBBER, *CRIMINAL LAW: MODEL PENAL CODE* 271 (2002); *see also* Paul H. Robinson & Markus D. Dubber, *The American Model Penal Code: A Brief Overview*, 10 NEW CRIM. L.R. 319 (2007).

[61] M'Naghten, 10 CL & F. 200, 8 Eng. Rep. 718 (1843).

his act, or (2) did not know that the act was wrong, he may be excused for his conduct. The M'Naghten rule or "test" has seen periods in which it is more popular than others, but it remains the standard in the majority of U.S. jurisdictions.

There are thus two prongs to the M'Naghten test. The defendant may be excused because he did not know the nature or quality of his act or because he did not know the act was wrong. If an individual is suffering from psychosis and genuinely believes that he is hammering a nail into a board when in reality he is hammering a sleeping family member, he may qualify under the first prong. Here, he believes that he is hammering a board, but he is killing a human being, and, as such, does not understand the nature of his act. Alternatively, if he believes he is shooting a threatening intruder when in reality he is shooting a friend who has come to visit, he may qualify under the second prong. Here, he realizes that he is taking a human life, so he understands the nature of his act. However, he genuinely believes that he is killing a threatening intruder and not an innocent friend, and thus he does not know that his act is wrong.

The examples I offer here to illustrate the difference between the two prongs both rest on the psychiatric construct of psychosis. Psychotic disorders, such as schizophrenia, involve prominent delusions or hallucinations by which an individual may have difficulty distinguishing reality and fantasy, and as a result, right and wrong. As such, it should not be surprising that psychotic symptomatology is commonly associated with the insanity defense.[62] Insanity is not necessarily limited to psychotic disorders, of course, and has been raised with respect to several other types of psychiatric disorder including personality disorders, mood disorders, and post-traumatic stress disorder.

Psychopathic antisocial actors may not meet criteria for a psychiatric disorder. They may be most likely to meet criteria for antisocial personality disorder, but because this disorder is strictly behaviorally defined, it remains an improbable route toward being excused for criminal wrongdoing. That is, even if the psychopathic defendant does meet criteria for APD, it is unlikely that APD will be accepted as a "mental disease or defect" in a jurisdiction that recognizes the M'Naghten rule of insanity.

Furthermore, there remains the question of whether the second prong of M'Naghten refers to moral or legal wrongness of the criminal act. Whereas the psychopathic criminal, due to moral-cognitive deficits, may not appreciate the moral wrongness of his act, he may well know that it is legally wrong.

[62] *See, e.g.*, Paul G. Nestor & Joel Haycock, *Not Guilty by Reason of Insanity of Murder: Clinical and Neuropsychological Characteristics*, 25 J. Am. Acad. Psychiatry & L. 161 (1997).

Although there are exceptions,[63] jurisdictions that recognize the M'Naghten rule for insanity have generally required that it is not enough that the defendant did not know that the act was *morally* wrong at the time of his act, but that he must not have known that it was *legally* wrong, a significantly stricter interpretation of wrongness. This narrower interpretation of the language in the second prong is commonly explained as the court's interest in restricting the pool of scenarios to which legal insanity may be applied.[64] For this reason, the condition of psychopathy is further unlikely to suffice as grounds for legal insanity.

The second framing of insanity with which we should concern ourselves is that of the Model Penal Code (MPC), which, in 1962, provided what Professors Paul Robinson and Markus Dubber described as a "softened version of the M'Naghten test." The MPC's language extends the range of the M'Naghten test so that a larger pool of defendants may qualify for a legal insanity defense because of limitations in their functional capacities. In effect, the MPC offered a broader version of insanity that served as a compromise of the strictly framed M'Naghten rule and traditional diminished-capacity doctrine: "A person is not responsible for criminal conduct if at the time of such conduct as a result of mental disease or defect he *lacks substantial capacity* either to appreciate the criminality [wrongfulness] of his conduct or to conform his conduct to the requirements of law.[65]" The MPC language both extends the defense to one who "lacks substantial capacity" to (1) *appreciate* the criminality (or legal wrongfulness) of his crime (cognitive) or (2) *conform* his conduct to that required by law (volitional).

Many American jurisdictions viewed this expansion of the M'Naghten test as an improvement.[66] However, public disapproval of the exculpation of certain criminal defendants contributed to many states returning to a stricter version of insanity that reflected the traditional M'Naghten rule. The most influential of such cases was that of John Hinkley, who was acquitted via the volitional prong of the MPC's insanity rule after having shot President Ronald Reagan, who had gained even greater popularity after surviving the attack.[67]

63 *See* Daniel E. Hall, *Criminal Law and Procedure* 227 (5th ed. 2009).

64 Ronnie D. Mackay, *Mental Condition Defences in the Criminal Law* (1995); Ronnie D. Mackay & G. Kearns, *More Fact(s) about the Insanity Defence*, Crim. L.R. 714 (1999); Quazi Haque, Author's Response to *Correspondence*, 9 Advances in Psychiatric Treatment 475 (2003).

65 Model Penal Code and Commentaries § 4.01 (1) explanatory notes (Official Draft 1985); *see also* Dubber, *Criminal Law: Model Penal Code*, *supra* note 61.

66 *See* Robinson & Dubber, *The American Model Penal Code: A Brief Overview*, *supra* note 61.

67 *Id.*

Indeed the MPC framing directly and openly recognizes the spirit of diminished capacity in the insanity defense by clearly stating that the absence of certain substantial capacities by which one functions may excuse him of his wrongdoing. Whereas the stricter M'Naghten rule does not leave obvious room for moral-cognitive biases and deficits associated with chronic antisocial actors to qualify as an excusing condition, the broader framing of the MPC and its focus on functional capacity may. It may be argued that the defendant who can demonstrate evidence of a moral-cognitive deficit that is basic to behavioral decision making and criminal action has a legitimate claim that he lacks a substantial capacity that is fundamental to understanding (cognitive) and acting in accordance with (volitional) legally prescribed action.

The "Morally Uncomprehending Criminal"

The idea that psychopathic wrongdoers may be excused for their criminal actions is not one that is likely popular with lawmakers or the public, for at least two reasons. First, it is unclear as to what moral-cognitive problems suffice for moral subrationality such that one may legitimately be excused for wrongdoing. Second, there remains the question as to how the law should manage wrongdoers who bear moral-cognitive problems such that they are prone to antisocial behavior, violating the criminal law, and causing society significant harms. Elsewhere,[68] Professor Robert Weisberg has called on me to address such questions – that is, to attend to the matter of how the law should treat or respond to the "morally uncomprehending criminal" with respect to blame and punishment. The term Weisberg used suggests that he has his finger on the pulse of the critical issue. The morally uncomprehending criminal is a wrongdoer who does not appreciate, understand, or know the wrongfulness of his criminal action. This is a term that identified not only his identity as an actor, but his social-cognitive status with respect to such action.

I believe the question of how the morally uncomprehending criminal should be blamed and punished has everything to do with understanding individual differences in social-cognitive development. If we unmask the question and expose its true developmental nature, we may better approach a resolution to the question. To do this, let us return briefly to our discussion of the relation between psychopathy and antisocial personality disorder.

As discussed, the relation between psychopathy and APD is necessarily limited. APD essentially serves as a time-constrained checklist of antisocial behaviors. The diagnosis entirely neglects etiology and development. As such,

[68] Weisberg, *supra* note 53.

to merely diagnose an individual with APD is to say nothing about the origin or causes of his antisocial behavior or how a style of behavior unfolded across time. In addition, the diagnosis is not at all based on the psychological characteristics of the antisocial actor. As a result, APD is unable to reflect the developmental and social-cognitive mechanisms that research on psychopathy has identified.[69] For that matter, APD is unable to reflect anything but the behavioral characteristics of any chronic wrongdoer.

The current framing of APD not only means that it cannot legitimately represent psychopathy as a psychiatric disorder or illness, but that chronic antisocial actors that suffer from real, substantial moral-cognitive deficits – or moral subrationality – may not be protected by the MPC framing of insanity. The MPC states clearly that "the terms 'mental disease or defect' do not include an abnormality manifested only by repeated criminal or otherwise antisocial conduct."[70] This language goes directly to the diagnostic criteria of APD – that is, you cannot be diagnosed with this psychiatric disorder unless you have demonstrated repeated criminal or otherwise antisocial conduct.[71] Thus APD cannot by itself qualify as a mental disease or defect under the MPC because of its strictly behavioral, noncognitive, nondevelopmental structure. If a chronic antisocial actor – psychopathic or otherwise – who is morally subrational (i.e., has moral-cognitive biases or deficits such that he is morally uncomprehending of wrongful conduct) has as his most comparable psychiatric diagnosis APD, he is unable to be found not guilty by reason of insanity, even in the case that he was genuinely unable "to appreciate the criminality of his conduct" as a result of nonculpable social-cognitive limitations.

Recognizing alternative developmental trajectories in the equifinality of chronic wrongdoing is critical then to both psychiatric (or medical) and legal recognition of antisocial action that results from moral subrationality. Such developmental trajectories may be culpable or nonculpable. In the case that the etiology of one's underdeveloped moral-cognitive functioning is congenital or characterized by early maladjustment, it would seem nonculpable. Perhaps an individual had a congenital brain defect or was an accident or trauma victim at a young age. Judging from the developmental research, the brain-level deficits described by Blair and other neuroscientists who study psychopathy would seem to fall into this category.

69 *See, e.g.*, Blair, *Developmental Approach*, *supra* note 30; Blair, *Applying*, *supra* note 30.

70 Model Penal Code and Commentaries § 4.01 (2) explanatory notes (Official Draft 1985).

71 This language may preclude a defense of insanity in the case that involves the altered mental state or psychiatric conditions, the product of addiction or the repeated use of alcohol and/or illicit substances.

A more complicated story, however, may be that of moral disengagement. There are likely alternative developmental paths by which one may become morally disengaged. The child who grows up in a coercive environment and either through observational learning or active teaching, or both, develops an understanding of the world as one in which naturally moral qualities of socially and legally prohibited behaviors may be rationalized and discounted may be prone to the early development of moral disengagement. If sufficiently reinforced across trials, contexts, and time, such moral disengagement may become crystallized – that is, persistent to such a degree that it is inflexible and perhaps even irreversible – before he has reached adulthood or an age sufficient that society may reasonably expect him to change his mental and behavioral approach toward social living. This type of developmental trajectory may be described as nonculpable and may be considered as mitigating evidence in the case of juvenile wrongdoing.

However, crystallized moral disengagement may develop out of a more culpable pattern of activity. The individual who rehearses disengagement strategies so that he may more easily enact and increase the likelihood of successful enactment of antisocial actions such that his desired goals may be met is one who is actively creating a pattern by which discounting the moral qualities of wrongdoing may be reinforced. This may lead to a severe social-cognitive bias, one by which moral disengagement is crystallized and one's formerly fuller social-cognitive range has become restricted. This is a proactive, instrumental, purposeful moral disengagement, which, although it may function in the same manner and appear identical to that which I described earlier, is necessarily culpable by its nature. Whereas a social-cognitive bias is at play with respect to one's wrongdoing, it was culpably formed in that the bias came out of purposeful rehearsal across time.

Both developmental variants – nonculpable and culpable – of moral disengagement proposed here are consistent with Bandura's depiction of gradualistic moral disengagement.[72] The child who develops and learns in a coercive environment forms moral disengagement practices across personal experiences and observations of others. The purposeful wrongdoer who acts out of crystallized moral disengagement is no different in this gradualistic sense. Even terrorists, who may rehearse mental strategies so that they may more easily and successfully carry out their evil acts, only gradually morally disengage in their approach toward a crystallized state.[73] Crystallization evolves out of

[72] Bandura, *Inhumanities*, *supra* note 2, at 203–04.

[73] For a discussion of the gradual development of terroristic psychological processes, see Ehud Sprinzak, *The Psychopolitical Formation of Extreme Left Terrorism in a Democracy: The Case*

repeated reinforcement across time and successful trials. In its most culpable form, moral disengagement may be used as a means of strategic choice.[74] This is an important distinction, because both the innocent child who grows up in a coercive environment and the practiced, proactive strategist may look the same in terms of their cognitive and behavioral functioning and profiles.

Understanding the differential culpability of these subtypes lies in the identification and analysis of their alternative developmental courses. It may be that a nonculpable underformation or malformation of moral rationality should serve as a mitigating (excusing) condition in the case of the morally uncomprehending individual. Longitudinal research on social cognition and antisocial behavior, such as ongoing scientific study of moral disengagement, is critical to disentangling the etiological factors and developmental variability that may be helpful to distinguishing responsible from nonresponsible wrongdoing by the morally uncomprehending criminal.

of the Weathermen, in ORIGINS OF TERRORISM: PSYCHOLOGIES, IDEOLOGIES, THEOLOGIES, STATES OF MIND 65 (Walter Reich ed., 1990).

74 Martha Crenshaw, *The Logic of Terrorism Terrorist Behavior as a Product of Strategic Choice, in* ORIGINS OF TERRORISM: PSYCHOLOGIES, IDEOLOGIES, THEOLOGIES, STATES OF MIND 7–24 (Walter Reich ed., 1990).

6

Provocation Interpretational Bias and Heat-of-Passion Homicide

This chapter examines the role of social cognition in the doctrine of heat of passion/provocation,[1] an affirmative defense that is unique to homicide law (i.e., provocation may only be invoked as a defense to the charge of murder). Social-cognitive research may be particularly useful to shaping – that is, challenging and reframing – homicide law because levels of homicide differ only with respect to mens rea, not actus reus. That is, in all homicide cases in which a guilty verdict is rendered, it is determined that one person has wrongfully killed another. However, first-degree murder typically requires premeditation; second-degree murder is characterized by the absence of both premeditation and provoked heat of passion; voluntary manslaughter is differentiated by killing in the heat of passion in response to "adequate provocation"; and involuntary manslaughter requires only recklessness (as opposed to purpose or intent required by murder and voluntary manslaughter). In other words, levels of homicide may be understood to differ according to the killer's social-cognitive state, encompassing her social desires (e.g., to take the life of another), beliefs (e.g., that another has seriously wronged her), and rational capacity (e.g., the killer's ability to consider alternative courses of action in her behavioral decision making).

Historically, discussions of provocation law and the heat-of-passion doctrine have focused on the role of emotion[2] with disproportionately little attention paid to critical social-cognitive components. Although I agree that emotion is a critical ingredient of the defense – in that the defense cannot be successful without some compelling demonstration of extreme emotional

[1] Hereafter, the terms *heat of passion* and *provocation* are used synonymously to refer to the partial defense of murder.

[2] *E.g.*, Joshua Dressler, *Why Keep the Provocation Defense?: Some Reflections on a Difficult Subject*, 86 MINN. L. REV. 959 (2002).

arousal – the social-cognitive processing by which emotion arises (i.e., the underlying "appraisal" of the emotion) and emotion's effect on one's social-cognitive capacity (i.e., the undermining or impairment of one's rationality) are components of heat-of-passion's structure that make it so. That is, heat of passion is about a mediational sequence of the defendant's intrapersonal or individual systems[3]: there is (1) a judgment that one has been provoked, followed by (2) overwhelming emotional arousal, followed by (3) an impairment of rationality, followed by (4) a reactive killing. This mediational sequence is defined by social cognition at two critical steps – the judgment (or interpretation) of serious provocation (1) and a constraint on one's social rationality that undermines his behavioral control (3). Although traditional framings of heat of passion vary, not one is defined such that either of these social-cognitive factors is absent.

A common-law reading of the heat-of-passion defense provides that the charge of murder may be reduced to manslaughter if the defendant demonstrates that (1) she was provoked by her victim such that a reasonable person would have lost control (called *adequate provocation*); (2) she became emotionally overwhelmed in direct response to said provocation; (3) there was insufficient time to "cool off" between the provocation and the homicidal response; and (4) she did not, in fact, cool off before killing her victim.[4] In recognition of this defense, American criminal law makes an allowance for emotional but not cognitive dysfunction in that one's interpretation of provocation has to be sufficient to pass the "objective" reasonable-person standard, but her extreme emotional arousal does not. As I have discussed elsewhere,[5] this poses both logical and moral problems and defies the retributive principle of penal proportionality that remains firmly grounded in the American criminal justice system. This chapter addresses how developmental social cognition may inform issues of blame and punishment in provocation law.

3 For a discussion of how intrapersonal systems interact with each other across time, see my theoretical discussion in Reid G. Fontaine, *Applying Systems Principles to Models of Social Information Processing and Aggressive Behavior in Youth*, 11 Aggression & Violent Behav. 64 (2006).

4 *Cf.* James R. Averill, *Anger and Aggression: An Essay on Emotion* (1982); Marcia Baron, *Killing in the Heat of Passion*, *in* Setting the Moral Compass: Essays by Women Philosophers 353–78 (Chesire Calhoun ed., 2004); Wayne R. LaFave, *Criminal Law* (5th ed. 1986).

5 Reid G. Fontaine, *Reactive Cognition, Reactive Emotion: Toward a More Psychologically-Informed Understanding of Reactive Homicide*, 14 Psychol. Pub. Pol'y & L. 243 (2008) [hereinafter Fontaine, *Reactive Cognition*]; Reid G. Fontaine, *The Wrongfulness of Wrongly Interpreting Wrongfulness: Provocation, Interpretational Bias, and Heat of Passion Homicide*, 12 New Crim. L. Rev. 69 (2009) [hereinafter Fontaine, *Wrongfulness*].

The first section discusses the nature, structure, and function of heat of passion and argues that the defense is properly understood as a partial excuse. The next section presents social-cognitive research on the instrumental/reactive violence dichotomy and how this distinction is mirrored in criminal law by first-degree murder and heat-of-passion manslaughter, respectively. The role of motive in understanding homicide law is here examined. Although motive is not ordinarily a factor by which homicides are formally defined (i.e., motive is not an element of homicidal crimes) or distinguished, it is often critical to making the prima facie case in murder prosecutions. In addition, motives (or goals) are commonly used to argue issues of desert with respect to sentencing and punishment. As such, an analysis of motives as a social-cognitive construct is germane to present purposes. Finally, a discussion of provocation interpretational bias and the imbalance, as defined by the traditional common-law framing of the defense, between cognitive and emotional dysfunction is provided.

THE EXCUSING POTENTIAL OF HEAT OF PASSION/PROVOCATION

It is essential to discern the nature of heat of passion before the degree to which, and ways in which, the defense informed by psychological science can be explored and properly assessed. In this chapter, I take the position that heat of passion should be understood as a purely excuse-based partial defense. Specifically, I oppose arguments to the contrary – that is, arguments that depict heat of passion as a partial-justification defense – by maintaining that responding violently to provocation is not justifiable because (1) it does not prevent further wrongdoing, and (2) the justifiability of anger as a response to provocation in no way makes violence a justifiable or morally acceptable behavioral response (i.e., it is important to avoid conflating reactive fury with deadly violence). Essential to this argument is that the heat-of-passion doctrine delineates the criterion that the killer be in a state of extreme emotional disturbance at the time of the homicidal act as a key (if not most critical) element of the defense, squarely placing heat of passion in the excuse camp (i.e., if the defendant's behavior is partially justifiable, why would she be required to carry it out while in a mentally constrained state?). Because heat of passion is indeed best understood as an excuse defense, the psychological science of hostile-reactive aggression is thus potentially relevant, and, as I posit here, highly useful to reframing heat of passion so that it may be more logically and morally consistent in its treatment of cognitive and emotional dysfunction and application to a range of subrational killers accused of murder.

As discussed throughout this volume, scientific research that examines individual differences in social-cognitive capacity and functioning may only be useful to challenging issues of criminal responsibility with respect to defenses that are grounded in excuse, not justification. Whereas justification defenses provide that the defendant did not act wrongly, excuse defenses argue that although the defendant acted wrongly and socially harmfully, he did so either out of understandable mistakenness or because his rational capacity was undermined such that he should not be held legally responsible for his wrongful conduct. Social-cognitive science and the study of individual differences in psychological functioning and antisocial conduct thus bears potential relevance for excuses, but none whatsoever for justifications (i.e., psychological dysfunction in the case of justified conduct necessarily cannot exculpate because the defendant has committed no wrong or harm).

The nature of heat of passion has been rigorously debated. Whereas some scholars argue that it is a justification,[6] others argue that it is an excuse,[7] and still others argue that it is a hybrid of justification and excuse or, at least, includes aspects of both.[8] Let us briefly examine these alternative normative arguments.

To treat heat of passion/provocation as a partial justification places the weight of the defense on the act that provoked the reactive killing. This depiction rests on the idea that the victim committed an act so unlawfully hurtful to the defendant that the former deserved, to some substantial degree, but not fully, to be killed by the defendant and that the defendant was legally entitled, again, to some substantial degree, but not fully, to kill his victim. As Professor Susan Rozelle described it, "[T]he justification ground of the provocation doctrine ensures that the victim be one we approve, if not of killing, then at least of wanting to kill."[9] Here the homicide is said to be only partially wrong, as the degree to which it was justifiable is the degree to which the killer was entitled to act as he did.

Alternatively, heat of passion/provocation as a partial excuse places the emphasis on the heated emotion or passion that one experiences as a direct effect of perceiving being seriously provoked by another. Said emotion serves

6 *E.g.*, Susan D. Rozelle, *Controlling Passion: Adultery and the Provocation Defense*, 37 Rutgers L.J. 197 (2005).

7 *E.g.*, Joshua Dressler, *Provocation: Partial Justification or Partial Excuse?*, 51 Mod. L. Rev. 467 (1988); Reid G. Fontaine, *Adequate (Non)Provocation and Heat of Passion as Excuse Not Justification*, 43 U. Mich. J.L. Reform 27 (2009).

8 *E.g.*, Samuel H. Pillsbury, *Misunderstanding Provocation*, 43 U. Mich. J.L. Reform 143 (2009); Vera Bergelson, *Justification or Excuse? Exploring the Meaning of Provocation*, 42 Tex. Tech L. Rev. 307 (2009).

9 Rozelle, *supra* note 6, at 210.

to undermine one's rationality and limit self-control such that she carries out her homicidal intent with "tunnel vision." Because there is a reduction of one's rational capacity at the time that she kills that is understandable – that is, for which she has a reasonable belief that she has been substantially wronged or harmed – the reactive killing is said to be partially excused. Here, the killing is entirely wrong, having produced the same extent of harm that is caused by cold-blooded murder. However, the defendant is partially exonerated because she did not act with the full rational capacity that is elemental to murder and thus deemed not fully responsible for her wrongdoing.

Other theorists have argued that heat of passion is a defense of both justification and excuse. This hybrid approach has taken alternative forms but generally articulates the idea that the reasonable belief of serious provocation is of a justification flavor, whereas the presence of emotional arousal is an excuse aspect. According to this position, although neither the justification nor excuse component can by itself satisfactorily serve to partially exonerate the reactive killer, the two may combine to warrant a reduction of murder to manslaughter. As Professor Samuel Pillsbury has argued: "As long as provocation involves an inquiry into reasonableness, it will include considerations of justification. As long as it provides for mitigation of punishment based on the difficulty of resisting temptations to violence inspired by strong emotion, it will speak to considerations of excuse."[10]

It is understandable that the hybrid perspective is attractive to some scholars. For one, it appears to more completely account for the two main components of the traditional common-law framing of heat of passion/provocation – adequate provocation and emotional disturbance. However, some scholars – namely, those who view heat of passion as a purely (partial) excuse-based defense – have identified a number of critical problems with this normative stance.

The first problem is what treating the defense as a partial justification, or at least one that has a justification component to it, says about the wrongfulness and harmfulness of the killing. As soon as you attribute a portion of the reactive homicide to justification, you are making a moral assertion that the killing was not entirely wrong, and that it is not *as* wrong, nor is it *as* socially harmful, to kill one's victim in the heat of passion as it is to murder him. As Dressler has emphasized: "[T]he criminal law ought to send clear moral messages. There is considerable moral difference between saying that an intentional killing is warranted (partially or fully), and saying that it is entirely wrong but that the actor is partially or wholly morally blameless for his wrongful conduct."[11]

[10] Pillsbury, *supra* note 8, at 143.

[11] Dressler, *supra* note 7, at 468.

Additionally, if the provocation serves to justify, to some degree, the reactive killing, then why is the emotional-arousal prong necessary to the defense? For example, if someone so seriously provokes another, such as in the case of a violent physical attack, why is it that the target needs to become so emotionally disturbed that he is rationally limited for his reactive violence to be, at least to some degree, justified? Does the reactive killer's emotional experience somehow make the aversive stimulus more provocative, threatening, or otherwise wrongful or harmful? The answer must be *no*, as the provoked individual's emotional response could have no possible bearing on the moral nature of the provocateur's action. In fact, the entirety of the defendant's reactive functioning – cognitive, emotional, and behavioral – has absolutely nothing to do with the objectively defined properties of the provocative act.

Of course, if an attack poses further harm to the defendant, then he may be entitled, to a proportionate degree, to retaliate with violence to ward off the attack and protect himself. But it would seem that a partial defense on this ground is better captured by "imperfect self-defense"[12] – or, succinctly stated, a reduction of murder to manslaughter on the basis that a disproportionately severe amount of violence was used in response to the harmful stimulus actor – than a defense such as heat of passion, which requires one to become substantially emotionally disturbed before the supposed justifying value of the provocation can be legally realized. Surely the relatively nonemotional individual who is presented with a potentially harmful stimulus is no less justified to use force to protect himself than the person who experiences an emotionally derailing reaction.[13]

Perhaps most problematic for heat of passion as justification, or some combination of justification/excuse, is that it allows for scenarios in which the stimulus is misunderstood as a serious provocation. The first prong of heat of passion, as framed by American common law, is that of "adequate provocation." Adequate provocation is not limited to cases of real, serious provocations by the killer's victim(s), however. Rather, as long as the killer had the "reasonable belief" of a real, serious provocation (i.e., a reasonable person, as estimated by a jury of the defendant's peers, would have judged the situation similarly), the adequate-provocation prong is satisfied. This means that a murder defendant who kills in a heated, emotional state may be partially protected by heat of passion in a common-law jurisdiction even in the case in

[12] For a discussion, see my attention to imperfect self-defense elsewhere in Fontaine, *supra* note 7, at 44, 45 & nn. 57–58, 46–55; Reid G. Fontaine, *An Attack on Self-Defense*, 47 Am. Crim. L. Rev. 57 (2010).

[13] *See* Fontaine, *supra* note 7, at 45–46.

which there was no real, serious provocation by his victim.[14] In this way, heat-of-passion doctrine in the common law recognizes *mistake of fact* doctrine.[15] Note, however, that whereas common-law heat of passion may apply to certain reactive killings in which there exists no real, serious provocation by the victim (there have indeed been a handful cases in which it has[16]), it does not apply to any kind of reactive killing in which an individual is not rationally compromised by his emotional arousal.

American common law's treatment of reasonable mistakes with respect to the justification/excuse distinction has been mixed,[17] however, sometimes treating conduct based on reasonable mistake as justified and, at other times, treating it as only excused. Recent scholarship has argued that socially harmful conduct that is mistakenly believed to be justified is properly understood as only excused.[18] This position rests, in part, on the reality that one's perception of a scenario has no bearing on its objective moral properties. That is, a person's belief that another has acted wrongfully is irrelevant to whether the latter has actually done so. Furthermore, it has no impact whatsoever on the moral balance of the parties involved that naturally exists prior to making a judgment, regardless of its accuracy, as to the right- or wrongdoing of the other. As such, it is irrelevant to issues of whether the victim deserves to be harmed and whether her killer is, even partially, entitled to take her life.

Mistakenness, however, may be relevant to the issue of excusability. One who has committed a wrongful act, and has produced a social harm by doing so, may well have acted as any reasonable person would have in a similar situation.[19] Although wrongful, the reasonableness with which the person acted may make her conduct understandable, as it is the type of conduct that may be fairly expected of a person in general in such a scenario. Because it is understandable as to why she acted wrongfully and harmfully – and also, perhaps, because it would be unfair to have expected her to act otherwise – her

[14] Elsewhere, I have described such scenarios as ones of adequate nonprovocation. Fontaine, *supra* note 7; Reid G. Fontaine, *On Passion's Potential to Undermine Rationality: A Reply*, 43 U. Mich. J.L. Reform 207 (2009) [hereinafter Fontaine, *On Passion's Potential*].

[15] As well as transfer-of-intent doctrine in cases in which the perceived provocateur is not the killer's victim. For a discussion, see Fontaine, *supra* note 7, at 37–40.

[16] *Id.* at 32–41.

[17] See my response to Professor Marcia Baron's article, *The Provocation Defense and the Nature of Justification*, 43 U. Mich. J.L. Reform 117 (2009) in Fontaine, *On Passion's Potential*, *supra* note 14, at 214–15 n. 37 (2009).

[18] *E.g.*, Fontaine, *On Passion's Potential*, *supra* note 14; *see also* Kyron Huigens, *The Continuity of Justification Defenses*, 2009 U. Ill. L. Rev. 627, 638–40 (2009).

[19] And she may even have acted with the best of intentions, such as in the case of defense of others.

conduct may be excused. In other words, although she has acted wrongfully and harmfully, she has also acted nonculpably, and so she is not to be blamed or punished for her conduct.

For these and other reasons,[20] several criminal-law theorists have recently written about common-law heat of passion as a pure (partial) excuse,[21] although the issue of justification/excuse with respect to the defense is hardly resolved. Whereas debate about the nature of the common-law framing of heat of passion persists, the version of the defense offered by the Model Penal Code (MPC) is less often confused. The MPC provides that a defendant charged with murder may be found guilty of only the lesser crime of manslaughter if the homicide "is committed under the influence of extreme mental or emotional disturbance for which there is reasonable explanation or excuse."[22] Here, the adequate-provocation prong has been replaced with "reasonable explanation or excuse." This adjustment of language was clearly made by the MPC framers to place the defense squarely in the excuse camp. Their interest in making sure that the defense be understood as a partial excuse was so clear that the word *excuse* was used as a sufficient condition by which the killer's psychological disturbance may arise. Indeed, as Professor Markus Dubber has noted about the MPC's version of the defense, "Provocation carries its excuseness on its sleeve."[23]

DISTINGUISHING INSTRUMENTAL AND REACTIVE SUBTYPES OF VIOLENCE

Recently, there has been notable growth in scholarship that has examined the psychology and law of reactive homicide/manslaughter. In fact, until 2007, when a pair of articles on the psychology and law of reactive homicide were published,[24] scholarly attention to the matter was rather sparse. This seems odd given (1) the complicated psychological issues that are natural to understanding differences between murder and voluntary manslaughter, and (2) the considerable research in behavioral science that has contributed to understanding how human and nonhuman animals respond to aversive stimuli, such as provocations.

[20] For discussions, see Dressler, *supra* note 7, at 468; Fontaine, *supra* note 14.

[21] For some recent examples, see Fontaine, *supra* note 14; Stephen J. Morse, *The Irreducibly Normative Nature of Provocation/Passion*, 43 U. Mich. J.L. Reform 193 (2009); Kyron Huigens, *A Critical Introduction to the Symposium*, 43 U. Mich. J.L. Reform 1 (2009).

[22] Model Penal Code § 210.3(1)(b) (1980).

[23] Markus D. Dubber, *Criminal Law: Model Penal Code* § 16 (2002).

[24] Steven J. Sherman & Joseph L. Hoffman, *The Psychology and Law of Voluntary Manslaughter: What Can Psychology Research Teach Us about the "Heat of Passion" Defense?* 20 J. Behav. Decision Making 499 (2007); Reid G. Fontaine, *Disentangling the Psychology and Law of Instrumental and Reactive Subtypes of Aggression*, 13 Psychol. Pub. Pol'y & L. 143 (2007).

Both of the 2007 articles pointed to the heat-of-passion doctrine's reliance on empirical assumptions about how individuals experience environmental stimuli and respond in (at least perceived) provocation situations. In their article published in the *Journal of Behavioral Decision Making*, Professors Steven Sherman and Joseph Hoffman focused on two aspects of the heat-of-passion mediational sequence, which are characterized neatly as the rise and fall of emotion. Specifically, these scholars were interested in pointing to a divergence of what behavioral science tells us about emotion as it intensifies and subsequently settles, and what the law rigidly assumes about how emotion is aroused by provocative cues (in the form of emotional disturbance) and how it diminishes as time passes (sometimes referred to as the "cooling off" period).

At around the same time, my first[25] of two articles in *Psychology, Public Policy, and Law* appeared in print. In one sense, this article was more specific in its goal than that of Sherman and Hoffman in that it focused on the rise of emotion, but in another sense, it was broader in that it addressed the psychology of emotion (namely anger) as well as other psychological factors that have been empirically linked to reactive aggression in behavioral science. In particular, I emphasized how subtypes of violence – instrumental and reactive – are distinguished in social-cognitive terms in both psychology and law. Indeed, I continue to believe that this is the key to understanding how the instrumental/reactive violence dichotomy in behavioral science and the murder/manslaughter distinction in criminal law may be compared, contrasted, and understood. That is, I believe scientific study in developmental social cognition holds critical answers by which psychology may inform the law with respect to the heat-of-passion doctrine.

There exists a parallel in psychology and law that is based on a distinction between subtypes of violence that each discipline makes. In behavioral science, instrumental violence is characterized by instances that are self-initiated (or proactive), relatively nonemotional, planned, and carried out in the interest of personal gain. In contrast, reactive violence is typified by retaliation to perceived provocations, threats, and other wrongdoings and aversive stimuli, which is emotional (angry or fearful), impulsive, and performed for either the purpose of harming a perceived provocateur or defending oneself against a perceived threat. The primary parallel[26] in law is the distinction between

[25] I subsequently published an article in *Psychology, Public Policy, and Law* that discussed how the parallel of reactive violence subtypes in psychology and law may be used for the purpose of law reform. *See* Fontaine, *Reactive Cognition, supra* note 5.

[26] There is another parallel in which heat-of-passion manslaughter is replaced by killing in defense of oneself or others. That is, the instrumental/reactive violence dichotomy is neatly paralleled in law by killings that are murderous versus defensive. This second version of the parallel is explored in the next chapter with respect to cases of *mistaken* self-defense.

first-degree murder – the typical case of which is calculated to achieve instrumental gain (e.g., money, desired material belongings, power) – and voluntary manslaughter. As discussed, the heat-of-passion doctrine defines voluntary manslaughter as a highly emotional, impulsive killing in response to one's belief that he has been seriously provoked or otherwise wronged.

Research in behavioral science that has provided support for the distinction between instrumental and reactive violence began with early studies with nonhuman animals, which found that alternative forms of aggression in animals are marked by differences in both the level and location of activity in the brain.[27] Scientific attention to the distinction in humans grew considerably in the late 1980s and 1990s. In the last quarter-century, support for the violent-subtypes distinction in the behavioral sciences has stemmed from numerous areas of behavioral science research, including clinical, developmental, and social psychology,[28] psychophysiology,[29] neuropsychology and cognitive neuroscience,[30] and neurobiology.[31]

27 K. E. Moyer, *Kinds of Aggression and Their Physiological Basis, in* 2 COMM. BEHAV. BIOLOGY: PART A 65 (1968); Kenneth E. MOYER, *THE PSYCHOBIOLOGY OF AGGRESSION* (1976); *see also* Kenneth A. Dodge, *The Structure and Function of Reactive and Proactive Aggression, in* THE DEVELOPMENT AND TREATMENT OF CHILDHOOD AGGRESSION 201 (Debra J. Pepler & Kenneth H. Rubin eds., 1991); Benedetto Vitiello & David M. Stoff, *Subtypes of Aggression and Their Relevance to Child Psychiatry,* 36 J. AM. ACAD. CHILD & ADOLESCENT PSYCHIATRY 307 (1997).

28 *E.g.*, Kenneth A. Dodge & John D. Coie, *Social-Information-Processing Factors in Reactive and Proactive Aggression in Children's Peer Groups,* 53 J. PERSONALITY & SOC. PSYCHOL. 1146 (1987); Kenneth A. Dodge, John E. Lochman, Jennifer D. Harnish, John E. Bates & Gregory S. Pettit, *Reactive and Proactive Aggression in School Children and Psychiatrically Impaired Chronically Assaultive Youth,* 106 J. ABNORMAL PSYCHOL. 37 (1997) [hereinafter Dodge et al., *Reactive and Proactive*].

29 *E.g.*, Ernest S. Barratt, Matthew S. Stanford, Thomas A. Kent & Alan Felthous, *Neuropsychological and Cognitive Psychophysiological Substrates of Impulsive Aggression,* 41 BIOLOGICAL PSYCHIATRY 1045 (1997); Catherine M. Smithmyer, Julie A. Hubbard & Robert F. Simons, *Reactive Aggression Versus Proactive Aggression: Differential Autonomic Reactivity to an Anger-Induction Peer Interaction* (Mar. 1998) (paper presented at the biennial meeting of the Conference on Human Development, Mobile, Ala.); NEIL JACOBSON & JOHN GOTTMAN, *WHEN MEN BATTER WOMEN: NEW INSIGHTS INTO ENDING ABUSIVE RELATIONSHIPS* (1998); Traci B. Pitts, *Reduced Heart Rate Levels in Aggressive Children, in* BIOSOCIAL BASES OF VIOLENCE 317 (Adrain Raine, David P. Farrington, Patricia Brennan & Sarnoff A. Mednick eds., 1997).

30 *E.g.*, Ernest S. Barratt, Matthew S. Stanford, Lynn Dowdy, Michele J. Liebman & Thomas A. Kent, *Impulsive and Premeditated Aggression: A Factor Analysis of Self-Reported Acts,* 86 PSYCHIATRY RES. 163 (1999); Barratt et al., *supra* note 29; R.J.R. Blair, *Neurocognitive Models of Aggression, the Antisocial Personality Disorders, and Psychopathy,* 71 J. NEUROLOGY, NEUROSURGERY & PSYCHIATRY 727 (2001); R.J.R. Blair, *The Roles of Orbital Frontal Cortex in the Modulation of Antisocial Behavior,* 55 BRAIN & COGNITION 198 (2004).

31 *E.g.*, Rebecca J. Houston, Matthew S. Stanford, Nicole R. Villemarette-Pittman, Sarah M. Conklin & Laura E. Helfritz, *Neurobiological Correlates and Clinical Implications of Aggressive Subtypes,* 3 J. FORENSIC NEUROPSYCHOLOGY 67 (2003).

Among the most significant, if not *the* most significant, bodies of empirical investigation to contribute to scientific understanding of instrumental and reactive violent subtypes is that of developmental and social-cognitive psychology. In particular, research on social-information processing and antisocial conduct has shown support for two main hypotheses. As discussed in detail in Chapter 2, social-information processing theory (or SIP) explains aggressive behavior as the direct product of multiple mental-processing operations in response to cues from one's environment. According to current formulations of SIP,[32] upon being presented with a social stimulus, an individual (1) encodes features of the stimulus and organizes its attributes so that it may be recognized (*encoding of cues*); (2) interprets the meaning(s) of the stimulus with respect to what the intent of the stimulus actor is and how the stimulus event is related to the responding individual and his well-being (*interpretation of cues*); (3) identifies his interests (*clarification of goals*); (4) generates or retrieves from memory one or more responses to the stimulus (*response access or construction*); and (5) assesses the alternative responses and estimates their respective likely outcomes to select a response for behavioral enactment (*response decision*).

Two principal hypotheses have guided the majority of research on SIP and aggressive subtypes. First, early SIP operations encompassed by encoding and interpretation of cues are hypothesized to be uniquely related to reactive aggression. Several studies have found that aggressive individuals tend to be biased toward (1) focusing on negative stimulus features at the encoding step and (2) attributing hostility and harmful intent to stimulus actors and events that are ambiguous as to their provocative and threatening nature. The first subtypes hypothesis, however, states that these social-cognitive limitations are significantly more common among individuals who are defined by a proclivity toward *reactive* violence.[33] The rationale that underlies this hypothesis it that

[32] Although SIP has further developed since this time, the most commonly referenced of current SIP models remains the reformulation offered by Nicki R. Crick and Kenneth A. Dodge in 1994. Nicki R. Crick & Kenneth A. Dodge, *A Review and Reformulation of Social Information-Processing Mechanisms in Children's Social Adjustment*, 115 PSYCHOL. BULL. 74 (1994).

[33] Of course, many aggressive individuals exhibit instrumental and reactive aggressive behaviors at different times, depending on a variety of contextual factors such as personal goals and environmental opportunities and demands. Encoding and interpretational problems are expected to be more closely linked with reactive aggressive conduct in that the subtypes hypothesis recognizes that one's propensity toward reactive violence varies as a function of how severe these (and other) social cognitive problems are. Thus encoding and interpretational problems, while more prominent among aggressive individuals who are predominantly or purely reactive in their aggressive behavioral pattern, are certainly not understood to be limited to this subpopulation.

because reactive aggressive individuals are quick to interpret ambiguous stimuli as intentionally harmful and hostile, they are more likely to become angry and select aggressive retaliation as their course of responding. The second subtypes hypothesis is that later, more advanced SIP processes, such as those encompassed by the response-decision step, are uniquely linked to instrumental aggression. The idea here is that individuals who engage in acts of violence in a calm, calculated fashion for the purpose of realizing some desired goal access and utilize response-decision operations such that they can evaluate and determine, in a rational manner, which course of action is the best balance of (1) high likelihood of goal achievement and (2) low risk of aversive consequences (e.g., punishment).

Notable scientific support for both of these hypotheses has been found. Several studies have found a link between favoring interpretations of ambiguous provocateurs[34] as hostile and intentionally harmful and exhibiting a reactive aggressive style of conduct.[35] In addition, these studies have found that although this social-cognitive bias is related to reactive aggression, it is not predictive of instrumental aggression.[36] This correlation has been found across independent laboratories and in investigations of qualitatively distinct populations. In addition, reactive aggressive youths have been found to have greater problems associated with the encoding-of-cues step of SIP, which is related to how they perceive and organize features of ambiguous provocation stimuli, as compared with their nonreactive aggressive peers.[37]

A link between later steps of SIP and instrumental (or proactive) aggressive behavior has also been empirically supported. Youths who exhibit instrumental aggressive conduct have been found to be more likely to prefer aggressive behavioral options to nonaggressive ones, expect positive results from their violent enactments, and discount the negative effects their aggression has on others, as compared to their noninstrumental aggressive peers. Note that these are social-cognitive processes that are encompassed by the

34 To be clear, in this context, ambiguous provocateurs are individuals who have acted in a way that may have caused harm to the responding individual. It is unknown to the responding individual whether the ambiguous provocateur actually caused any harm realized or, if the ambiguous provocateur did cause the responding individual harm, what the former's intention was (i.e., was the stimulus actor's intent benign or malicious?).

35 *E.g.*, Nicki R. Crick & Kenneth A. Dodge, *Social Information-Processing Mechanisms in Reactive and Proactive Aggression*, 67 CHILD DEV. 993 (1996); Dodge & Coie, *supra* note 28; Kenneth A. Dodge, Joseph M. Price, Jo-Anne Bachorowski & Joseph M. Newman, *Hostile Attributional Biases in Severely Aggressive Adolescents*, 99 J. ABNORMAL PSYCHOL. 385 (1990); David Schwartz, Kenneth A. Dodge, John D. Coie, Julie A. Hubbard, Antonius H.N. Cillessen, Elizabeth A. Lemerise & Helen Bateman, *Social-Cognitive and Behavioral Correlates of Aggression and Victimization in Boys' Play Groups*, 26 J. ABNORMAL CHILD PSYCHOL. 431 (1998).

36 Schwartz et al., *supra* note 35.

37 Dodge et al., *Reactive and Proactive, supra* note 28.

response-decision step of SIP, namely outcome expectancy and outcome evaluation.[38] In addition, instrumental aggressive youths tend to prioritize goals of personal gain, such as acquisition of money and desired material belongings, over relational or social goals, such as developing friendships.[39]

As discussed in Chapter 2, the response-decision step of SIP has been the focus of considerable empirical investigation in the last decade,[40] and an elaboration of this processing step has been offered as a heuristic model of response decision making, called response evaluation and decision (RED).[41] Although research has thus far linked RED processes with instrumental as opposed to reactive violence, this model may be even more useful to understanding the social-cognitive foundations of instrumental and reactive violence subtypes than first considered. There exists an additional set of subtypes hypotheses that build directly from the RED model and appear to pose promise for further differentiation in behavioral science and understanding in criminal law. Specifically, these hypotheses state that (1) instrumental aggressive individuals are more likely to endorse behavioral options that they expect will lead to a high likelihood of personal gain and a low likelihood of aversive consequences, as compared to their noninstrumental aggressive peers, and, alternatively, (2) reactive aggressive individuals endorse aggressive responses that are assessed to exact harm to others who are perceived to have committed wrongdoing against the responding individual, as compared to their nonreactive aggressive peers. This latter hypothesis articulates an endorsement of aggressive behavioral options for the reason of retaliating against a wrongdoer and "balancing the moral scales" that, by the perception of the responder, the stimulus actor wrongfully upset. This hypothesis might be described as one that articulates the social-cognitive foundation of "retributive aggression."[42]

[38] See discussion of SIP and RED *supra* Chapter 2.

[39] Crick & Dodge, *supra* note 35.

[40] Reid G. Fontaine, Virginia S. Burks & Kenneth A. Dodge, *Response Decision Processes and Externalizing Behavior Problems in Adolescents*, 14 Dev. & Psychopathology 107 (2002); Reid G. Fontaine, Chongming Yang, Kenneth A. Dodge, John E. Bates & Gregory S. Pettit, *Testing an Individual Systems Model of Response Evaluation and Decision (RED) and Antisocial Behavior Across Adolescence*, 79 Child Dev. 462 (2008); Reid G. Fontaine, Chongming Yang, Kenneth A. Dodge, Gregory S. Pettit & John E. Bates, *Development of Response Evaluation and Decision (RED) and Antisocial Behavior in Childhood and Adolescence*, 45 Developmental Psychol. 447 (2009); Reid G. Fontaine, Marieh Tanha, Chongming Yang, Kenneth A. Dodge, John E. Bates & Gregory S. Pettit, *Does Response Evaluation and Decision (RED) Mediate the Relation Between Hostile Attributional Style and Antisocial Behavior in Adolescence?*, 38 J. Abnormal Child Psychol. 615 (2010).

[41] Reid G. Fontaine & Kenneth A. Dodge, *Real-Time Decision Making and Aggressive Behavior in Youth: A Heuristic Model of Response Evaluation and Decision (RED)*, 32 Aggressive Behav. 604 (2006).

[42] *See* Jeannette Schmid, *The Vengeance Puzzle – Retributive Justice or Hostile Aggression?*, 31 Aggressive Behav. 589 (2005).

This is quite different, of course, than endorsing aggressive response options because they are expected to intimidate others, achieve power, or lead to desired material goods, all of which are interests that are characteristic of an agenda guided by personal gain that is typically conducive to instrumental violence.

This latter set of violence subtypes hypotheses guided by the RED model is consistent with one of the main ways that instrumental and reactive violence are distinguished in not only behavioral science but in law. That is, instrumental and reactive aggressions are understood to be based on different motives. In the criminal law, murder is often committed out of an interest in personal gain, such as acquisition of money (e.g., killing to commit robbery) or gaining power by "sending a message" and instilling fear in others (e.g., gang or "turf" killings). These are instrumental motives. Alternatively, voluntary manslaughter, or killing in the heat of passion, is committed in the interest of harming the perceived provocateur. Similarly, killing in self-defense is carried out to prevent one's own life from being wrongfully taken. These are "reactive" motives.

Some criminal-law scholars believe that motives do not matter; or, at least, that they *should* not matter in criminal law.[43] That is, they believe that motive is irrelevant to criminal liability. Others have written in detail as to the many important roles of motive in the criminal law. As Professor Carissa Hessick reminds us that

> [motive] is necessary to prove liability for some offenses; it is a key component of several defenses; and it has been a traditional consideration at sentencing. Motive's role in criminal punishment has grown through the adoption of hate crime sentencing enhancements and the rise of substantive sentencing law. And motive has an important role in punishment theory, as it reinforces the centrality of shared moral judgments, which are indispensable to any system of criminal law.[44]

There are several possible arguments that can be made against motive as an important component of criminal liability. One argument is that motive is not a basic element of crime. However, we see examples in the criminal law in which the construction of criminal offenses recognizes the importance of motive's role. Let us consider burglary as an example. Burglary is defined as the breaking and entering into a building (or, as is typically included in U.S.

[43] *See, e.g.*, Whitley R.P Kaufman, *Motive, Intention, and Morality in the Criminal Law*, 28 Crim. Just. Rev. 317 (2003).

[44] Carissa B. Hessick, *Motive's Role in Criminal Punishment*, 80 S. Cal. L. Rev. 89, 89 (2006).

jurisdictions, an automobile) with the purpose of committing a crime therein (sometimes specified as a felony).[45] Burglary encompasses the criminal offense of trespass, but the concurrence of trespass with the additional purpose of committing a further crime qualifies the conduct as burglary. This may be reframed such that it is understood to mean that the motive of committing a further crime (such as theft of another's valuable property) is what distinguishes burglary from trespass. That is, without the motive of committing a crime within the dwelling, typically out of an interest of instrumental gain, the actor has not committed burglary, but only trespass.

A related argument may be made with specific respect to homicide law. Murder one, which typically requires purpose, is distinguished from murder two, which regularly only requires knowledge. Is this not a distinction based on a difference of criminal motive? Certainly it is a distinction of mentes reae, but it is also one that appears to be guided by the importance of motive.

Let us consider two variations of a traditional hypothetical scenario in which a defendant kills a night watchman by blowing up the building at which the latter is regularly stationed. In the first scenario, defendant one blows up the building for the specific purpose of killing the night watchman. The defendant is angry that he, himself, was not hired for the watchman position and he found his competitor's arrogance once he was hired to be distasteful. He has no interest in blowing up the building per se, as he continues to believe that animal research conducted within its walls holds considerable scientific importance. However, he has been unable to locate his nemesis outside of the latter's professional quarters, and he has been further unable to enter the secured building to strangle the watchman as he would much prefer. Here, with respect to the homicide only, the defendant is guilty of murder one as he blows up the building with the purpose of killing the watchman.

In the second scenario, defendant two blows up the building to destroy the laboratories within, thus preventing scientists from conducting further experiments on their animal subjects, which the defendant believes are cruel and inhumane. The defendant fully realizes that his conduct will wrongfully take the life of the night watchman, who is glued to his post, night in and night out, inside the building. In this latter case, the defendant may only be guilty of murder two (again, solely with respect to the issue of homicide) as, although

[45] Note that the added requirement that the breaking and entering occur at night is often specified in the common law. *See* Charles E. Torcia, 3 *Wharton's Criminal Law* § 316, at 223 (15th ed. 1993); Wayne R. LaFave & Austin W. Scott, 2 *Substantive Criminal Law* § 8.13, at 464 (1986).

he was practically certain that his conduct would wrongfully cause the death of the watchman, this was not the purpose underlying his objectively criminal conduct. In both scenarios, the actus reus and the social harm (unjustifiable destruction of private property and killing of another) are the same. Additionally, in both cases, the wrongful conduct was unprovoked,[46] rationally chosen, and indeed calculated. Only the mentes reae of purpose and knowledge, respectively, differ. This difference, however, seems inextricably tied to a difference in motive with respect to the objectively criminal conduct.[47] That is, the difference between the two scenarios may also be framed as a distinction in motive. Whereas each defendant acted to wrongfully destroy property and cause the death of another person, the first defendant's motive was to murder the watchman and the second defendant's motive was to destroy the animal laboratories.

Let us consider motive further, however, based on an acceptance that it is not generally elemental to crime. How meaningful can motive be if it is not elemental to criminal offenses? Of course, simply because a variable is not a formal criminal element does not preclude it from being relevant or even critical to determining issues of culpability, punishment, and utilitarian values such as rehabilitation and deterrence. Anglo-American criminal law is, in good part, founded on distinctions of mental state (e.g., did the actor know of the substantial risk posed by his conduct when he enacted it?). Indeed, mens rea is elemental to all but strict liability crimes. Excuse-based defenses are also largely defined by distinctions of mental state (e.g., was the defendant of sufficient rational capacity when he committed the objectively criminal act?). For what good reason should the law recognize these alternative distinctions in mental state (mens rea, rational capacity) and not distinguish between types of motive? If one defendant kills another because he genuinely but mistakenly believes that by doing so he will save the lives of innocent others, is this not an entirely different case than that of the defendant who kills another to take her money and material goods? It is unclear what retributive or utilitarian value would suggest that these alternative scenarios should be viewed and treated equally. Both defendants premeditated their killings, so unless the jurisdiction

46 "Unprovoked" in that the killer's conduct in the first scenario was not prompted by adequate provocation (or serious provocation by the victim, as determinable by the reasonable person).

47 In such cases, the line separating intent and motive appears to be less clear. Indeed, some scholars have suggested that it is so difficult to distinguish between intent and motive that the matter be dropped, and that it should simply be recognized that "the substantive criminal law takes account of some desired ends but not others." LaFave, *supra* note 4, at 274–75. For a recent clarification of the distinction between *mens rea* and motive, see Hessick, *supra* note 44, at 94–95.

is one that requires malice aforethought for a murder-one verdict (in which case perhaps only the latter of the two defendants would meet the elements of murder one), both defendants may be found guilty of this crime. However, the law recognizes a range of punishment, in terms of both length (e.g., twenty-five years versus life) and conditions of punishment (e.g., medium versus maximum security; parole terms), to be determined based on a variety of factors, perhaps the most critical of which is the degree of culpability with which the defendant carried out his crime – an issue to which motive, as illustrated by these different cases, is central.

Of course, a defendant's motive for committing a crime provides useful information with respect to utilitarian concerns, as well. For example, defendants who kill for different reasons may be better rehabilitated via different treatment protocols. Whereas the reactive killer may respond better to cognitive-behavioral therapies that focus on alternative interpretations of ambiguous provocation and threat events, as well as anger-management therapy, rehabilitation of instrumental killers may focus on reducing reinforcements of antisocial conduct and social skills training by which actors may learn how to achieve their goals of personal gain via noncriminal, society-appropriate routes.[48]

Another possible argument against the importance of motive to criminal law is that it is naturally irrelevant to the degree of social harm caused by the objectively criminal act. Surely it is true that motive is indeed irrelevant to social harm. In the case of our comparison of murder defendants, for example, each has wrongfully taken the life of an innocent other. The amount of social harm is the same, despite the two defendants' respective motives being quite different. However, culpability and punishment are not determined solely on degree of social harm, but rather on a combination of social harm and the degree of culpability with which it was caused. As discussed, motive lies at the core of culpability doctrine as recognized throughout Anglo-American criminal law, and so is it to a retributive justification punishment.[49]

Still other reasons call for the importance of motive to criminal law to be recognized, such as the evidentiary role it plays in the prosecution of crime. Establishment of motive may critically affect how objective evidence of criminal conduct attributed to the defendant is viewed by the fact finder. Indeed

[48] For discussions of treatments and rehabilitations guided by research on the instrumental/reactive violence subtypes dichotomy, see Dodge, *supra* note 27; Vitiello & Stoff, *supra* note 27; Fontaine, *supra* note 24.

[49] Carissa Byrne Hessick discusses this issue in some detail in her rejection of the "neutrality objection" to motive's relevance to criminal culpability and punishment. Hessick, *supra* note 44, at 124–28.

it may be the difference maker in a jury's determination that a defendant is guilty beyond a reasonable doubt of the crime charged. Depending on the specific scenario, a reasonable doubt may well remain in the absence of an established motive, even when the objective evidence of criminal conduct is otherwise reasonably persuasive.

As discussed, motive is central to the instrumental/reactive violence distinction as it is studied in behavioral science. However, this is not to say that all instances of violence fall neatly into either the instrumental or reactive category. Many instances of violence are defined by multiple motives, such as instances of revenge. A revenge act may serve to retaliate against perceived wrongdoers, gain attention and fame for the aggressor, realize a thrill-seeking urge, instill fear in others, and lead to social power. Although the first of these goals is naturally reactive (retaliating against a wrongdoer), the rest are related to personal gain and thus are of the instrumental variety. For this and other reasons, the instrumental/reactive dichotomy remains incomplete and thus has been the subject of some scholarly criticism.[50]

In psychology, systematic study of the distinction has been limited by confusing acts with actors. In most empirical investigations that have examined differences between instrumental and reactive violence subtypes, the comparison has been between individuals who act instrumental-aggressively versus reactive-aggressively. Because many aggressive individuals engage in both instrumental and reactive aggression at different times, however, there are not many purely instrumental or purely reactive aggressors. The correlation of instrumental and reactive aggression among aggressive *actors*, however, should not be mistaken for the alternative sets of features by which individual *acts* may be defined. Even if it were to be found that all aggressive *actors* engage in both instrumental and reactive aggressive acts at different times, this has no bearing on whether there are true structural, functional, and phenomenological differences between instrumental and reactive aggressive *acts*.

PROVOCATION INTERPRETATIONAL BIAS AND KILLING IN THE HEAT OF PASSION: THE SOCIAL-COGNITIVE ARGUMENT

In their analysis of the psychology and law of voluntary manslaughter, Professors Sherman and Hoffman remind us, "psychological reality is often

[50] Although there exists only a modest amount of literature criticizing the violence subtypes distinction, one article of notable influence was provided by Brad J. Bushman & Craig A. Anderson, *Is It Time to Pull the Plug on the Hostile Versus Instrumental Aggression Dichotomy?*, 108 PSYCHOL. REV. 273 (2001).

more important than objective reality in shaping the ways that people respond to and judge events."[51] The scholars were speaking to the issue of how individuals perceive and judge emotion and how these perceptions are paramount to their normative judgments about how the law should view and respond to claims of emotional provocation. However, their reminder is equally useful to highlighting how emotion and emotional conduct arise in the first place.

Empirical research in psychology and the behavioral sciences has demonstrated that reactive aggression – a subtype of aggressive conduct that is often characterized by heated, impulsive retaliation against a perceived provocateur or threat – is uniquely linked with biased processing of ambiguous stimuli,[52] anger and heightened physiological arousal,[53] and other differences in interpersonal functioning.[54] The roles of social cognition and emotion in the emergence of reactive aggression appear to be paramount[55] – as such, these areas of functioning should be considered and explored with respect to the heat-of-passion defense. Historically, however, discussions of provocation law and the heat-of-passion doctrine have focused on the role of emotion[56] with, as I herein argue, disproportionately little attention paid to critical social-cognitive elements.

The heat-of-passion defense provides that the charge of murder may be reduced to manslaughter if the defendant demonstrates that (1) he was provoked such that a reasonable person may have lost control; (2) he became emotionally overwhelmed as a direct result of said provocation; (3) there was insufficient time to cool off between the provocation and the homicidal response; and (4) he did not, in fact, cool off before killing his victim.[57] In recognizing this defense, American criminal law makes an allowance for emotional but not cognitive dysfunction in that the interpretation of provocation (1) has to be sufficient to pass the reasonable-person standard, but the killer's

[51] Sherman & Hoffman, *supra* note 24, at 508.

[52] For a recent review, see Bram Orobio de Castro, Jan W. Veerman, Willem. Koops, Joop D. Bosch & Heidi J. Monshouwer, *Hostile Attribution of Intent and Aggressive Behavior: A Meta-Analysis*, 73 Child Dev. 916 (2002).

[53] *E. g.*, Julie A. Hubbard, Catherine M. Smithmyer, Sally R. Ramsden, Elizabeth H. Parker, Kelly D. Flanagan, Karen F. Dearing, Nicole Relyea & Robert F. Simons, *Observational, Physiological, and Self-Report Measures of Children's Anger: Relations to Reactive Versus Proactive Aggression*, 73 Child Dev. 1101 (2002).

[54] *See* Fontaine, *supra* note 24.

[55] *See, e.g.*, Jody. C. Dill & Craig. A. Anderson, *Loneliness, Shyness, and Depression: The Etiology and Interrelationships of Everyday Problems in Living*, *in* The Interactional Nature of Depression: Advances in Interpersonal Approaches 93 (Thomas Joiner & James C. Coyne eds., 1999).

[56] Dressler, *supra* note 2, at 959 n. 5; Sherman & Hoffman, *supra* note 24.

[57] LaFave & Scott, *supra* note 2.

emotional disturbance (2) need pass no such objective test. This poses both logical and moral problems for provocation law.[58]

Before we identify these problems, however, let us be clear as to the structure of heat-of-passion homicide (or voluntary manslaughter). Heat-of-passion homicide may be deconstructed to represent a complex mediational process of five factors:

(1) Provocation/Stimulus Event[59] →
(2) Provocation Interpretation/Appraisal →
(3) Emotional Arousal/Disturbance →
(4) Limitation on Rational Capacity →
(5) Rationally Compromised Reactive Killing.

This complex, five-component mediation embodies three simple mediations, each of which consists of three factors: a cause, a mediator, and an effect. In the first of these simple mediations, the killer's provocation interpretation (2) mediates the causal relation between the provocation event (1) and the killer's emotional arousal (3). In the second, the killer's emotion (3) mediates the causal relation between her interpretation of the provocation event (2) and the undermining effect of the emotion that limits her rational capacity (4). Third and finally, the limitation on her rational capacity (4) mediates the relation between her emotional response (3) and her reactive homicide (5).

It is generally recognized that emotion is the doctrine's key component[60] in that it is emotion that imposes the limitation on one's rationality and control, which, in turn, allows for the enactment of reactive violence. However, it is out of one's judgment that she has been seriously provoked or otherwise adversely impacted that overwhelming emotional arousal arises in the first place. That is, but for one's belief of being wronged, extreme emotion is not experienced. In mediational turn, but for a judgment of provocation (or provocation interpretation; PI), the individual does not kill in response to the subject event.

It should be noted that the event does not need to be an actual, serious provocation, but only reasonably appear as one, per American common law. That is, as long as a reasonable person would have viewed the situation similarly, the "provocation event" requirement is satisfied. Furthermore, one may

[58] Fontaine, *Reactive Cognition*, *supra* note 5; Fontaine, *Wrongfulness*, *supra* note 5; Fontaine, *supra* note 7.

[59] The provocation event is not essential to the act of voluntary manslaughter or its corresponding defense of heat of passion/provocation. That is, no real, serious provocation by the killer's victim need exist as long as the killer's belief that it did is reasonable.

[60] Professor Joshua Dressler, one of the premier American scholars on the heat-of-passion/provocation defense, has asserted, "Provocation law is all about emotions, most notably anger." Dressler, *supra* note 2, at 959 n. 5.

be seriously wronged and harmed but interpret the event as something other than seriously provocative, in which case we have a scenario in which the event is objectively "adequate provocation," but there is no possibility of heat-of-passion violence resulting from it. So, although the heat-of-passion defense is commonly discussed in the context of "provocation law," what we find is that, every bit as critical as emotion to the mediational sequence, is the social-cognitive factor of PI.

Oddly, the doctrine requires that the reactive killer be cognitively sound but emotionally unstable. Only if the reactive killing was performed in the "heat of passion," or extreme emotional disturbance, may the defense apply. Although this emotional disturbance does not need to be what a reasonable person would experience in the same situation, the judgment of the event or social stimulus must be reasonably formed. As such, the law allows for a significant partial excuse, reducing murder to manslaughter, in the case that the reactive killer quite reasonably understood the event before her, but then quickly became thoroughly undercontrolled as a result of emotional outrage.

The juxtaposition of these two mental standards – objective[61] test for the social-cognitive component and subjective test for the emotional component – is understandable given the history of how the defense evolved. The defense is intended to be reserved for only unusual, horrible events – events that are so severely off-putting that it is understandable that one would become beside herself with emotional upset. However, because the killer needs only be reasonable and not accurate in her judgment, the defense also protects instances of reactive killing in which no real, serious provocation by the victim transpired. That is, the reactive killer may be mistaken in her judgment, as long as she was reasonably mistaken.

The reality of the nonnecessity of an actual, serious provocation by the victim is what gives rise to the problematic imbalance of the doctrine's treatment of social-cognitive versus emotional mental functioning. The shaky ground on which this differential treatment of subtypes of mental functioning is based is more apparent when the mediational sequence represented by heat-of-passion homicide is confronted with scientific evidence regarding the social-cognitive foundations of anger and violence.

As discussed in Chapter 2, as well as earlier in this chapter, there are specific cognitive processes and patterns that have been found to underlie the emergence and growth of (1) anger, which usually serves as the emotion component

61 Here, objectively refers to passing the reasonable-person standard, not to objective reality that is independent of subjective interpretation. This is a critical point, because the treatment of the reasonable-person test as an objective standard can be misconstrued to mean the latter of these two understandings.

in heat of passion, and (2) aggressive reactivity, which, by definition, is the action component (reactive homicide) of the complex mediation, as delineated earlier. In particular, PI is linked to both angry and violent reactivity. The social-cognitive underpinnings of anger and violence have been investigated in numerous scientific settings and are indeed consistent with the mediational sequence represented by heat of passion. What science also provides, however, is that being biased in favor of PI is related to problems with anger and violence, more generally. That is, individuals who have a provocation interpretational bias (PIB) – meaning that they possess a processing style by which they judge ambiguously provocative social events and situations as hostile and intentionally harmful – typically demonstrate problems with angry and violent reactivity.

In emotion research, empirical investigations that have been guided by appraisal theory have been successful in identifying specific patterns of cognitive operations that underlie anger feelings and experiences as well as trait anger. The research has been guided by the early work of Professor Craig Smith and Richard Lazarus,[62] theorizing that the core relational theme – or the key appraisal that defines the relationship between one who is angry and the individual at whom the anger is directed – is that of blame. If a person believes that another is at fault for wrongfully causing her harm, she will experience anger directed toward the perceived wrongdoer. For example, in one 2001 study of cognitive appraisals believed to serve as the foundation for high trait anger, scientists found that, compared to their low-trait anger peers, high-trait anger individuals tended to blame perceived antagonists more, were quicker to identify others as antagonists, more readily found the event in question to be of personal relevance, and responded with greater anger to social interactions that resulted in negative outcomes.[63]

A more recent study of appraisal theory and anger examined individual differences in appraisal patterns and experiences of anger.[64] Results pointed to role of cue interpretation in the formation of angry reactivity. That is, the researchers found that individuals who are subject to an unpleasant consequence are more likely to become angry when the perceived provocateur is believed to have violated the norms by his actions in an unfair and deliberate

62 Craig A. Smith & Richard S. Lazarus, *Appraisal Components, Core Relational Themes, and the Emotions*, 7 Cognition & Emotion 233 (1993).

63 Jacobus F. Hazebroek, Kevin Howells & Andrew Day, *Cognitive Appraisals Associated With High Trait Anger*, 30 Personality & Individual Differences 31 (2001).

64 Peter Kuppens, Iven Van Mechelen, Dirk J.M. Smits, Paul De Boeck & Eva Ceulemans, *Individual Differences in Patterns of Appraisal and Anger Experience*, 21 Cognition & Emotion 689 (2007)

attempt to wrong them. Whereas some individuals may become angry based solely as a result of being subject to an unpleasant consequence, others become angry only when these social judgments that the wrongdoer is particularly blameworthy are made.

The sense that one person has purposefully and wrongfully caused another harm is at the heart of blame. Appraisal theory research points to blame as the core relational theme of anger. The story is not so different in social-developmental research that focuses on social-cognitive foundations of antisocial conduct (in contrast with emotion). Numerous studies have found that processing distortions and deficits at the early stages of social-information processing (SIP) – namely encoding and interpretation of cues – are not only related to aggression and violence broadly, but are uniquely linked to the subtype of reactive aggression.[65] Individuals who are quick to interpret events that are possibly but not clearly provocative as hostile and intentionally harmful are more likely to display a behavioral tendency to respond to such cues in a retaliatory fashion. The correlation is not difficult to understand. If you believe someone is unjustly causing (or at least trying to cause) you harm, you have cause to retaliate and are more likely to respond with aggressive action. If one has a tendency to make this type of judgment, she will behave in a retaliatory fashion more often, as compared with individuals who have a more adjusted processing style.

Appraisal theory frames emotions as cognitive products, just as SIP theory explains behaviors. Understanding unique cognitive patterns allows one to predict emotions and behaviors that may result in response to a social cue. Theoretically, this is (or at least should be) no more true of anger and aggression than it is of other emotions, such as fear, and other behaviors, such as submissiveness.[66] It follows, of course, that individuals who are less able to properly process social cues are more likely to demonstrate both emotional and behavioral problems across a vast spectrum. What is promising is that this understanding has become increasingly accepted and shared in science, allowing for not only gains in the basic science of social cognition and behavior, but also the utility of social-cognitive research for legal doctrine, including that of excuse-based affirmative defenses in criminal law.

In Chapter 3, I discussed *subrationality* – that is, cases of nonculpable cognitive dysfunction, either in the form of underdeveloped or diminished rationality, by which a criminal actor should not be held fully responsible for his wrongdoing. In the present chapter, we have examined the case of

65 For a review, see Fontaine, *supra* note 24.

66 See Chapter 7 on the roles of social cognition and fear in coercion and duress.

heat-of-passion homicide in which a defendant charged with murder may receive the lesser verdict of manslaughter as a result of his rationality having been undermined by extreme emotional arousal. Just as diminished capacity was distinguished from mere weak will in Chapter 3, the legitimate heat-of-passion case should be distinguished from ones in which emotionality did not serve to truly undermine or impair the killer's capacity for rationality. In their recent analysis of the provocation defense, Professors Richard Holton and Stephen Shute distinguished legitimate cases of provocation and related scenarios in which one's rationality is not diminished but rather the killer's self-control is "overwhelmed" or overcome by influential forces to act irrationally (kill the perceived provocateur). Holton and Shute stressed that it is via the undermining – as opposed to the overwhelming – of self-control and rationality that provocation may serve to partially excuse the heat-of-passion killer.[67] According to Holton and Shute's distinction, instances in which one's self-control and rationality are overwhelmed, such as in the case in which impulses to act irrationally are too strong to resist,[68] it is not that rationality is lesser, but rather that it is not effective in preventing the irrational response of reactive homicide from being enacted.

In the case of social-cognitive bias, however, per appraisal theory research on anger and SIP research on aggressive behavioral reactivity, it is more accurately a case of rationality impaired than one of sufficient rational capacity overwhelmed by noncognitive psychological conditions such as emotional flooding. The reactive killer whose processing is strictly set to favor interpretations of hostile, intentionally harmful action on the part of an ambiguous provocateur may be understood as less than sufficiently rational before emotional disturbance is introduced to the meditational chain. That is, this individual *entered* the ambiguous provocation situation with this psychological limitation.

Let us momentarily return to the five-component mediational sequence of heat-of-passion homicide. The provocation event or situation may be said to cause the killer's belief that he is being unjustifiably adversely affected. This belief, in meditational turn, may be said to cause the anger disturbance that

[67] Richard Holton & Stephen Shute, *Self-Control in the Modern Provocation Defence*, 27 Oxford J. Legal Stud. 49 (2007). Although Holton and Shute focused on self-control, rationality was at the core of their argument, an understanding that was initially clear from their recognition of alternative framings of self-control on p. 51 and further evidenced throughout the rest of their analysis.

[68] For a debate as to the excusing capacity of weak will and wayward desire, see Stephen P. Garvey, *Dealing With Wayward Desire*, 3 Crim. L. & Phil. 1 (2009); Vera Bergelson, *The Case of Weak Will and Wayward Desire*, 3 Crim. L. & Phil. 19 (2009); Richard Holton, Willing, Wanting, Waiting (2009).

follows. This is the first of the three simple mediations in the larger heat-of-passion mediational sequence I articulated earlier and, as such, arguably the most important. That is, but for the PI on the part of the killer, none of the mediations critical to a proper heat-of-passion defense may be claimed.

By American common law, the PI must be reasonable. It may be mistaken, but if genuine and reasonable, the killer's mistaken belief of the situation is not fatal to his defense claim. In the case that the fact finder determines that a reasonable person would not have understood the perceived provocation event similarly, however, the defendant's heat-of-passion claim fails. Of course, the type of social-cognitive bias – that is, PIB – that promotes angry emotional and violent behavioral responses is likely to produce some genuine mistakes when it comes to understanding social situations that are open as to their provocative content. In other words, one who is biased toward interpreting such situations as provocative and intentionally harmful is more likely that her noncognitively biased peers to not only make mistakes but make mistakes that, although perhaps entirely genuine, are nonreasonable in that other individuals of ordinary prudence faced with the same social stimulus would not have attributed the same provocative meaning to it. As a result, although the PIB killer has made an honest, genuine mistake for a nonculpable reason,[69] her heat-of-passion defense fails if her PI is nonreasonable.

The juxtaposition of factors (2) PI and (3) emotional disturbance is an odd one in that it is characterized by a differential and imbalanced treatment of these mental or psychological factors. Whereas the killer's emotional disturbance at the time of the killing only needs to be genuine (i.e., it only needs to pass a subjective test in that the defendant needs to demonstrate that she was genuinely emotionally disturbed at the time of the killing – this disturbance does not need to be of the kind that a reasonable person would experience in a similar situation), her understanding of the provocation event that caused her emotional arousal needs to be both genuine and reasonable. In this way, the law places a higher expectation on one's social-cognitive functioning than it does on one's emotional functioning.

This differential expectation may be understood to mean that the law excuses dysfunctional mental functioning of an emotional but not cognitive nature. This is puzzling for a number of reasons. First, this distinction of cognitive versus emotional disturbance is not recognized elsewhere throughout the criminal law. For example, the insanity defense is not framed to excuse

[69] This is presuming that she did not actively cause or willfully allow her PIB to develop and that it was not foreseeable that her PIB would cause her, either directly or indirectly (as in the case of heat of passion), to wrongfully kill another person.

a wrongdoer only in the case that she is emotionally disturbed at the time of her wrongdoing. Rather, as discussed in Chapter 5, insanity framings have focused on disturbances in volition and cognition, and not emotion. As discussed in Chapter 3, diminished-capacity and diminished-responsibility defenses, when and where recognized, have certainly not rested on emotional dysfunction, but rather have been framed as defenses due to cognitive limitation and impaired rationality. Second, there exists no reason to believe that emotional dysfunction is any more impairing to one's control and rationality than is cognitive dysfunction. What has science taught us that would justify treating this one kind of psychological or mental dysfunction so differently? There is no science that suggests that emotional dysfunction is any more impairing than cognitive dysfunction to rationality. Both type of mental dysfunction may emerge and present in a number of forms, each of which may vary widely by degree of severity. Third, as discussed, the distinction fails to recognize what science has indeed taught us, that anger disturbances and violent behavioral reactivity are promoted by cognitive problems by which one is primed or biased to interpret ambiguous provocateurs as hostile, intentionally harmful, and blameworthy.

In addition there is a moral question raised by this differential treatment of types of mental dysfunction that asks: Is the cognitively biased reactive killer more responsible and culpable than the reactive killer who has reasonably judged her provocation situation and meets all of the common-law criteria for heat of passion? Imagine a father who has returned home to find his daughter horribly injured and bloody. At her side is their neighbor who is also covered in blood. The father, having been violently abused as a child, is, for this unique situation, nonconsciously primed to believe that the neighbor has caused his daughter her horrible outcome. As a direct result of having interpreted this situation in this fashion, the father becomes enraged, takes a gun, and shoots the neighbor, instantly killing him.

In this hypothetical,[70] the father's appraisal of the "provocation event" is unlikely to pass the reasonable-person test. Rather, a reasonable person is more likely to be viewed as someone who, although immediately upset and concerned, would investigate the daughter's well-being, ask the neighbor and/or daughter what happened, and collect more information before making a concrete judgment as to the series of events that led to the daughter's harm. Indeed, I expect it is likely that many would characterize the father's overreaction as wildly unreasonable. But for the father's nonculpably formed

70 For further discussion of this hypothetical, see Fontaine, *Wrongfulness*, *supra* note 5, at 74, 78, 87.

(but rather formed out of abuse he suffered as a defenseless child) cognitive dysfunction, the father would likely have acted in exactly this socially appropriate manner. He would have been able to consider alternative explanations of the situation and collect and process additional information to appropriately select from alternative explanations and better understand the situation so that he could behaviorally respond in an adjusted, adaptive fashion.

What is unclear, however, with respect to the moral issue, is how, if the father's failure to interpret the situation reasonably is based entirely on non-culpably formed psychological difficulties outside of his control, he is more responsible and culpable for his behavior than the heat-of-passion killer who has reasonably but mistakenly interpreted the provocation event in question. The latter of the two is not more warranted or entitled to kill than the other, and neither is the killing in a state of more substantially undermined or limited control or rationality. Rather, the latter has made a cognitive mistake that reasonable others would have made, whereas the latter has made a non-reasonable mistake due to social-cognitive impairment for which he is not responsible.

CONCLUSIONS

In this chapter, I offer an argument that the heat-of-passion/provocation defense should be understood as a purely excuse-based partial defense. The view that the defense partially excuses because the reactive killer's rationality and control are undermined at the time of her criminal act allows for science to be drawn on to better answer empirical questions, the answers to which may have been assumed by the doctrine. Thus, I present evidence as to how the distinction between murder and manslaughter in criminal law may be informed by research on individual differences in social cognition and violence in psychology and behavioral science. Although numerous subtype models of antisocial behavior have been advanced in behavioral science,[71] the dichotomy that has received the most theoretical attention and empirical substantiation is that of instrumental and reactive aggression. Whereas instrumental aggression is self-initiated, calculated, calm, and motivated by interests of personal gain, reactive aggression is enacted in response to a perceived provocation or injustice and is typified by anger, heightened physiological arousal, and impulsivity.

Science has found that discernible cognitive patterns underlie anger experiences and reactive aggressive behaviors. Specifically, processes of encoding

[71] *See* Fontaine, *supra* note 24, at 143–44.

and interpreting provocative and intentionally harmful stimuli promote angry, aggressive retaliation. Individuals who are biased in their encoding and interpretation processing have particular difficulty considering alternative explanations of cues that are ambiguously hostile and provocative. Furthermore, individuals who are prone to attribute blameworthiness to the committers of wrongful, harmful conduct are more likely to experience anger, only promoting the likelihood that their behavioral responses will take the form of aggressive retaliation.

A defendant charged with murder may raise heat of passion as a partial defense, which, if successful, serves to reduce a finding of murder to manslaughter. The defendant needs to show that she reasonably interpreted the provocation scenario before her and then immediately became so emotionally disturbed as a direct result that her rationality and control were undermined such that she killed her victim while in this emotional, rationality-limiting state. For the defense to be successful, the defendant is required to be both cognitively reasonable in her response to the provocation and emotionally dysfunctional in the process of killing her victim. In this way, the law partially excuses the reasonably mistaken heat-of-passion killer but excludes the reactive killer who genuinely, but nonreasonably, mistakes adequate provocation due to nonculpably formed social-cognitive bias. This is an odd and unfortunate imbalance in light of the behavioral science evidence that, for nonculpable reasons, certain individuals may develop social-cognitive biases such they are less able to rationally process certain kinds of social stimuli. In this chapter, I argue that the law's differential treatment of cognitive versus emotional dysfunction in the case of heat-of-passion doctrine is structurally illogical, unjust on retributive grounds, and neglectful of the relevant developmental and social-cognitive science.

In light of this unjustifiably disparate treatment of the two scenarios of mistaken provocation – that is, (1) the reasonably mistaken heat-of-passion killer and (2) the social-cognitively biased reactive killer who is not protected by the defense – I suggest that the heat-of-passion defense should be broadened to include cognitively biased reactive killers who do not meet the criteria for heat of passion due to a nonculpably formed provocation interpretational bias (PIB).[72] This proposed expansion is a modest one, as it would add only individuals who may be determined to have a nonculpably developed social-cognitive disturbance by which they quickly and definitively interpret certain kinds of social stimuli in a biased fashion. This is a psychological problem

[72] For elaborations of this argument, see Fontaine, *Reactive Cognition*, *supra* note 5; Fontaine, *Wrongfulness*, *supra* note 5; Fontaine, *supra* note 7.

that has been scientifically linked with difficulties with anger experiences and aggressive conduct.

The expansion is intended to include only these unique cases, and not individuals with PIB who, as a result of their cognitive problems, have known anger and aggression problems and fail to act to prevent wrongful violent attacks on others. As such, not only is the proposed expansion modest, but the individuals it is intended to include are unlikely to recidivate because the provocation scenario that triggers their bias is sufficiently unique that it would not be expected to recur as a stimulus to the defendant's violent reactivity. In this way, the expansion is not suggested to broadly include individuals with generalized anger-management issues. Furthermore, there is no scientific evidence to suggest that an instance of PIB-based reactive homicide is any more likely to recur than heat-of-passion homicides in which the killer reasonably interprets the provocation event.[73]

[73] For a discussion of PIB, reactive violence, and future dangerousness, see Fontaine, *Wrongfulness*, *supra* note 5, at 90–91; *see also* Fontaine, *Reactive Cognition*, *supra* note 5, at 254–56.

7

Reacting to Perceived Threats

Mistaken Self-Defense and Duress

In the previous chapter, the distinction between instrumental and reactive subtypes of violence in psychology and law was considered in an analysis of how psychological science may inform the legal doctrine of heat of passion/provocation with respect to individual differences in how humans respond to perceived *provocations*. Chapter 7 follows directly from this analysis, with an exploration of the psychology and law of individual differences in responding to perceived *threats*. Here we are concerned with perceived *imminent* threats, as opposed to threats that allow for a nontrivial period of time in which to make a decision as to how to behaviorally respond.[1] Namely, this chapter considers two affirmative defenses – "mistaken self-defense," which characterizes self-defense cases in which the defendant has mistaken her victim as an imminent threat of wrongful grievous bodily harm or death, and duress, in which the defendant has intentionally engaged in objectively criminal conduct against an innocent third party in order to prevent a threat of grievous bodily harm or death by a coercive wrongdoer from being realized.

As discussed in Chapters 2 and 7, there is a dichotomy of subtypes of antisocial conduct that has been recognized in the behavioral sciences and neuroscience. Instrumental violence is characterized by calm, calculated, predatory acts committed in an interest of achieving personal gain (e.g., social control, money, thrills). Alternatively, reactive aggression may be described as

[1] Chapter 8 examines threats to individuals who are subject to recurrent victimization, such as battered women who kill their abusers during a nonconfrontational period. The instrumental/reactive violence dichotomy is useful to understanding these cases, as well, although its application, as we will see, is different because these killings are often characterized by both reactive (e.g., motive for killing is defending oneself) and instrumental (e.g., killing is planned) features. These hybrid acts of violence may be contrasted with purely reactive violent acts such as responding to a provocation in heat-of-passion manslaughter or to an imminent threat of wrongful grievous bodily harm or death in a case of self-defense or defense of others.

relatively emotional, impulsive retaliation to a perceived provocation, threat, or other aversive stimulus, for the purpose of harming a wrongdoer or defending oneself. A set of processes associated with the encoding and interpretation of cues steps of social-information processing (SIP) models has been uniquely linked with reactive aggression. Predominantly and purely reactive aggressive individuals have been found to be biased in favor of interpreting ambiguous provocations as definitively provocative, hostile, and intentionally harmful.[2]

As most research in behavioral science[3] has focused on interpretational bias and provocative stimuli, the majority of scholarship in interdisciplinary inquiry in psychology and law[4] and criminal-law theory[5] has considered the relevance of these findings to heat-of-passion/provocation doctrine in the criminal law.[6] In contrast, relatively little scholarship has considered what consideration of interpretational biases should be given to affirmative-defense doctrines that address crimes in response to threats. Logically, it makes sense that research on threat interpretational bias (or TIB) may be as potentially relevant to criminal-law doctrines of self-defense (and defense of others) and duress. In addition, other areas of cognitive bias, such as response decision making, have been neglected, despite the potential relevance of this area of research to issues of decision-making capacity and vulnerability to coercive influence as they relate to duress.

In this chapter, defensive violence is distinguished as a second category of the subtype of reactive violence. As opposed to hostile-reactive violence in

[2] *See, e.g.*, Nicki R. Crick & Kenneth A. Dodge, *Social Information-Processing Mechanisms in Reactive and Proactive Aggression*, 67 CHILD DEV. 993 (1996) [hereinafter Crick & Dodge, *Social Information-Processing Mechanisms*]; Kenneth A. Dodge, John E. Lochman, Jennifer D. Harnish, John E. Bates & Gregory S. Pettit, *Reactive and Proactive Aggression in School Children and Psychiatrically Impaired Chronically Assaultive Youth*, 106 J. ABNORMAL PSYCHOL. 37 (1997) [hereinafter Dodge et al., *Reactive and Proactive Aggression*].

[3] For reviews, see Maaike Kempes, Walter Matthys, Han de Vries & Herman van Engeland, *Reactive and Proactive Aggression in Children: A Review of Theory, Findings and the Relevance for Child and Adolescent Psychiatry*, 14 EUR. CHILD & ADOLESCENT PSYCHIATRY 11 (2005); Benedetto Vitiello & David M. Stoff, *Subtypes of Aggression and Their Relevance to Child Psychiatry*, 36 J. AM. ACAD. CHILD & ADOLESCENT PSYCHIATRY 307 (1997).

[4] *See* Reid G. Fontaine, *Disentangling the Psychology and Law of Instrumental and Reactive Subtypes of Aggression*, 13 PSYCHOL. PUB. POL'Y & L. 143 (2007); Reid G. Fontaine, *Reactive Cognition, Reactive Emotion: Toward A More Psychologically-Informed Understanding of Reactive Homicide*,14 PSYCHOL. PUB. POL'Y & L. 243 (2008); Reid G. Fontaine, *The Wrongfulness of Wrongly Interpreting Wrongfulness: Provocation Interpretational Bias and Heat of Passion Homicide*,12 N. CRIM. L. REV. 69 (2009).

[5] *See* Reid G. Fontaine, *Adequate (Non)Provocation and Heat of Passion as Excuse Not Justification*, 43(1) U. MICH. J.L. REFORM 27 (2009); Robert Weisberg, *The Values of Interdisciplinarity in Homicide Law Reform*, 43(1) U. MICH. J.L. REFORM 53 (2009).

[6] As discussed at length in Chapter 6.

which the actor's goal is to harm the provocateur out of anger and frustration, and based on the belief that the provocateur has harmed or attempted to harm her, defensive violence is enacted due to the belief that the stimulus actor poses a threat of future harm, and typically out of fear that such harm will be realized if preventive action is not taken. The law most clearly reflects this distinction in the separate defenses of heat of passion/provocation and self-defense. Unlike heat of passion, self-defense is typically a complete defense, understood as a justification (not excuse), and not limited to cases of homicide. Less obviously, the distinction between hostile-reactive and defensive-reactive violence applies to heat of passion/provocation versus duress, as well, as wrongful acts committed out of duress are often done so in an interest of *defending* against the coercer's commission of a greater wrong, such as the defendant's own murder.

Three main theoretical differences with respect to understanding responses to provocation versus responses to threats should be recognized, however. First, the typical motive underlying aggression in response to provocation is to harm the provocateur. Alternatively, the motive underlying aggression that responds to a threat is to defend oneself, another, or something of personal value. The moral valuation of these alternative motives may not be equal – that is, it may be viewed that, with respect to antisocial action, the motive of harming another individual is less morally palatable than that of protecting and preserving oneself.

Second, a difference in emotion is posited. Whereas in response to provocation, one may be more likely to experience anger, fear may be the emotion more typically aroused out of an interpretation of being threatened. This distinction may have important implications for understanding issues of individual responsibility and culpability attributable to criminal wrongdoing. One critical question is whether the mechanisms by which anger and fear emerge differ in how they affect (or undermine) rational capacity. Similarly, do the emotional experiences of anger and fear differentially impact rational judgment and behavioral decision making? For example, it may be that one of these emotional conditions is more potent than the other with respect to the speed and severity with which it impairs rational capacity and thought.

Third, there is a difference as to the temporal status of the perceived harm. Whereas hostile-reactive violence responds to an interpretation that wrongful harm has been caused, defensive-reactive violence is enacted to prevent wrongful harm from occurring. That is, heat-of-passion violence is past-focused and self-defense violence is future-focused. These differences suggest that defensive violence may be understood as a separate category of reactive antisocial conduct in both phenomenology and function.

Although American common-law doctrines of duress and self-defense (and defense of others) explicitly regard social scenarios by which one responds to a *perceived* threat, neither doctrine reflects an understanding or even recognition of the behavioral science of threat reactivity. Indeed there is a considerable literature based on research with both nonhuman animals and humans regarding the cognitive, emotional, and behavioral mechanisms that may be activated upon the presentation of a threat. Given the naturally alarming effect of being threatened, and the fact that these doctrines characterize scenarios by which there is typically relatively little time to engage in response decision making, it seems only sensible to understand human processes by which individuals may function in response to stimuli that they interpret to pose imminent danger to their well-being or the well-being of valued others.

This chapter proceeds as follows. First, despite the common law's refusal to acknowledge a distinction between actual and mistaken defense in its treatment of justifiable homicide, the importance of distinguishing the two is presented. A normative argument for mistaken self-defense as excuse is reviewed and mistaken, but reasonable self-defense is balanced with mistaken and unreasonable self-defense by which there is a nonculpable cause, such as interpretational bias, for the defendant's mistakenness. The literature on social-cognitive reactivity to stimuli that are open as to their threatening content is reviewed and related to mistaken self-defense as I would argue it *should* be recognized in the criminal law.

Second, a succinct analysis of the defense of duress (or coercion) is presented. As with several of the other affirmative defenses discussed in this volume, duress has been far from immune to debate as to its justifying versus excusing nature. Alternative framings are addressed and a normative case for duress as excuse is provided. The scientific literature on the social cognition of threat reactivity is discussed and related to duress doctrine. I take the position that certain social-cognitive deficits and biases associated with threat reactivity should be recognized in considering the scope of wrongful action protected by duress.

The nature and structure of duress are necessarily more complicated than that of mistaken self-defense, if for no other reason than duress requires the inclusion of three parties (coercer, defendant, and third-party victim). Thus, not only is research on developmental social cognition that may be useful to understanding mistaken self-defense also relevant to duress, but other areas of scientific psychology bear potential value, as well. In this way, the discussion of duress that follows builds directly from the discussion of developmental social cognition and mistaken self-defense that is first presented and addresses other psychology-law interdisciplinary links, as well.

MISTAKEN SELF-DEFENSE (AND DEFENSE OF OTHERS)

As discussed throughout this volume, scholarly attention to the distinction between justification and excuse in criminal-law theory has only grown over the last thirty years. Questions as to the nature and structure of various affirmative defenses continue to be raised and debated. Readers – even regular readers of criminal-law scholarship – may be surprised to learn that the doctrine of self-defense has been at the center of much discussion.[7] Typically viewed as the primary textbook example of a justification-based criminal-law doctrine,[8] it is indeed the case that, at least as the American common-law framing of the defense is concerned, scholars have had great difficulty agreeing to its structural boundaries as a justification. For example, is the reasonable belief of an imminent threat of grievous bodily harm or death sufficient to justify the reactive killing? If so, are there not instances of nonreasonable mistake, if honest and genuine, that should suffice? If not, and the reactive killing must objectively serve to *defend*, does objectivity suffice in the case of evil intent, or should the defending actor be required to do the "right deed for the right reason"?[9] In these and other ways, the debate as to the nature and structure of self-defense has remained dynamic. It is an important discussion for several reasons, not least of which is that the answers to these questions have much to do with the applicability of the social-cognitive psychology of individual differences in how individuals respond – cognitively, emotionally, and behaviorally – to perceived threats. As such, an exploration of these issues is critical to a proper psycholegal analysis.

The following section places modern self-defense doctrine in question. Specifically, "defensive" killings in which the nature and/or degree of the threat is mistaken by the defendant are analyzed and the American common-law framing of self-defense is deconstructed so that "defense-like" killings in which there is reactive killings triggered by a mistaken belief of imminent

7 For recent analysis and debate, see Symposium, *A Symposium on Self-Defense*, 47 AM. CRIM. L. REV. 57 (2010); Reid G. Fontaine, *An Attack on Self-Defense*, 47 AM. CRIM. L. REV. 57 (2010) [hereinafter Fontaine, *An Attack on Self-Defense*]; Michael Louis Corrado, *Self-Defense, Moral Acceptability, and Compensation: A Response to Professor Fontaine*, 47 AM. CRIM. L. REV. 91 (2010); Reid G. Fontaine, *In Self-Defense Regarding Self-Defense: A Rejoinder to Professor Corrado*, 47 AM. CRIM. L. REV 97 (2010); Michael Louis Corrado, *Professor Fontaine and Self-Defense: A Reply to His Rejoinder*, 47 AM. CRIM. L. REV 105 (2010); *cf.* Claire Finkelstein, *Self-Defense as a Rational Excuse*, 57 U. PITT. L. REV. 621 (1996); Hibi Pendleton, *A Critique of the Rational Excuse Defense: A Reply to Finkelstein*, 57 U. PITT. L. REV. 651 (1996); Re'em Segev, *Justification, Rationality and Mistake: Mistake of Law Is No Excuse? It Might Be a Justification!*, 25 L. & PHIL. 31, 31–33 (2006).

8 The doctrine of necessity being a close second.

9 *See* George P. Fletcher, *The Right Deed for the Wrong Reason: A Reply to Mr. Robinson*, 23 UCLA L. REV. 293 (1975).

serious threat may be separately considered. Such killings are often classified in contemporary American criminal law as self-defense, although no actual defense of one's self was necessary or took place. I argue here that it is improper to understand and treat such cases as justifiable as they do not prevent further wrongdoing (i.e., there was no real threat of harm), and the killer's mistakenness does not entitle her to take the life of the objectively nonthreatening stimulus actor (i.e., the stimulus actor did not behave in a way that upset the natural moral balance between the stimulus actor and the defendant). However, there may be circumstances by which such a homicidal act, although triggered by nothing more than the actor's misunderstanding of her social environment, is quite understandable, and therefore excusable, as to why the killer acted as she did.

Indeed, I argue that this understandability, and thus excusability, may also apply in a narrow set of scenarios in which a *non*reasonable mistake is the impetus for the killer's reactive homicide. For example, consider the defendant with a history of being racially victimized. Perhaps, due to said victimization, she subsequently develops a biased processing style by which stimulus actors of the same racial appearance as her past attacker are hastily and mistakenly judged as threatening. It may be that the law should recognize defenses of such killings under such circumstances, on the basis that the nonreasonable mistake is genuinely made and is the product of a nonculpably formed social-cognitive distortion. If so, these defenses must necessarily be understood as excuses as any reduction of the defendant's blame and punishment must necessarily be due to a determination that she is not fully responsible for her admittedly wrongful and socially harmful act.

Mistaken Self-Defense (and Defense of Others) as Excuse

For an argument of mistaken self-defense[10] as excuse and not justification to be properly presented, we must first distinguish the subjective, common-law approach to self-defense as justification that is widely accepted throughout U.S. jurisdictions from alternative articulations of self-defense as justification that are based, at least in part, on the objective conditions of the defense event in question. Three main arguments of self-defense as justification have been advanced: a purely objective theory,[11] a purely subjective theory,[12] and

[10] Hereafter, I refer only to self-defense, but it should be understood that this discussion applies equally to its sibling, defense of others.

[11] *See, e.g.*, Paul H. Robinson, *A Theory of Justification: Societal Harm as a Prerequisite for Criminal Responsibility*, 23 UCLA L. REV. 266, 266 (1975); Heidi M. Hurd, *Justification and Excuse, Wrongdoing and Culpability*, 74 NOTRE DAME L. REV. 1551 (1999).

[12] The approach adopted in American common law.

an objective/subjective hybrid.[13] Both the pure objective and objective/subjective hybrid perspectives require that the reactive killing actually prevent the imminent, wrongful causing of grievous bodily harm or taking of a life by the victim (i.e., the threat or stimulus actor). This is *not* objectivity in the sense that the defendant's belief or expectation that her action is required to prevent such wrongful harm passes the reasonable-person test.[14] Rather this is objectivity in the sense of actuality. No matter how reasonable the killer's judgment of the threat situation, she is not justified in killing the perceived threat if her reactive violence is not objectively or truly necessary to defend against an imminent, wrongful threat of grievous bodily harm or death.

The distinctions between the objective and hybrid models of self-defense as justification are undoubtedly important,[15] but they are largely irrelevant to our purposes here. The critical distinction for present concerns has to do with the nature of the subjective framing of self-defense as justification as recognized by and defined in American common law. Only the subjective articulation incorporates mistake-of-fact doctrine, justifying a reactive killing that is mistaken to be necessary to defend oneself against imminent, wrongful, grievous bodily harm or death.

Traditional self-defense doctrine of American common law is defined by five basic requirements.[16] First, the defendant needed to have honestly and reasonably judged that she was imminently threatened with grievous bodily harm or death. Second, she must have honestly and reasonably judged that it was necessary to use deadly force against the victim to prevent the harm posed by the threat. Third, the defendant needed to have used proportionate force, meaning that she must not have used force that exceeded the degree of force honestly and reasonably judged to be threatened.[17] Fourth, the defendant must have honestly and reasonably discerned that the threat against her was unlawful or unjustified. Fifth and finally, many jurisdictions require that the defendant not have acted in a way that gave rise to the threat.

[13] *See, e.g.*, George P. Fletcher, *The Right Deed for the Wrong Reason: A Reply to Mr. Robinson*, 23 UCLA L. Rev. 293, 295 (1975); Fontaine, *An Attack on Self-Defense*, *supra* note 7.

[14] The reasonable-person test is typically considered an *objective* test. See discussions in Chapters 1 and 6.

[15] For a recent analysis, see Fontaine, *An Attack on Self-Defense*, *supra* note 7.

[16] Professor Cynthia Lee provided a thorough review and discussion of common law self-defense in *The Act-Belief Distinction in Self-Defense Doctrine: A New Dual Requirement Theory of Justification*, 2 Buff. Crim. L. Rev. 191, 195–208 (1998).

[17] The honest and reasonable judgment that the reactive force used is proportionate is generally sufficient by common-law standards. In this way, the proportionality rule may be viewed to largely overlap with the necessity rule (requirement 2). As Professor Lee recognized, "The proportionality requirement is often viewed as part of the necessity requirement." Lee, *supra* note 16, at 203.

The critical distinction between this framing and the objective and hybrid approaches is that self-defense does not have to be actual defense of self to meet the requirements for justifiable homicide. Several mistakes by the defendant may be made, as long as they are honest and reasonable. The defendant may have been mistaken that (1) she was imminently threatened; (2) deadly force was required to prevent her own suffering of grievous bodily harm or death; (3) deadly force was proportionate to that which was threatened; and (4) the threat of harm was unlawful or unjustified. Collectively, the defendant may engage in a considerable amount of mistake making, as long as it is all honest and reasonable, and remain protected by this justification-framed defense as recognized by common law.

It is, of course, not difficult to imagine scenarios in which a reactive killing based on an honest but reasonable mistake may be desirable on some level. For instance, if an individual who is suffering from the delusion that he is playing a video game begins to point a lifelike toy gun at people in a public venue, it may be said that a police officer is justified (or at least "warranted"[18]) to shoot and kill the individual. From a public policy perspective, this may seem quite sensible. We may agree that it is proper for police officers to be empowered to perform such acts based on their reasonable beliefs that they are necessary. If public policy were to assert otherwise, then police officers may hesitate in such situations, including those in which an intentional wrongdoer is truly on the verge of killing innocent citizens.

Nevertheless, this public policy concern does not make killing the non-threatening individual a morally acceptable act, nor does it eliminate the social harm caused by the act. Recognizing that affirmative defenses at large – as well as the distinction between justification and excuse by which their first-order classification is determined – emerged out of retributive principle, we are forced to decide whether a public policy argument must necessarily be secondary to issues of wrongdoing and social harm that distinguish justification and excuse or, as a society, choose to recreate the criminal law in a primarily utilitarian vision, the latter of which is not only unforeseeable but naturally contradicts society's collective moral intuition as to what separates right and wrong on which the law has always rested.

[18] Some criminal-law theorists believe that certain actions should be classified by a third category, "warranted," which is less morally stringent than justification but more morally stringent than excuse. The warranted label applies to actions that are generally desirable but cause social harm in some circumstances (such as a police officer's shooting of an innocent pedestrian who is mistaken as a threatening criminal). *See* R. A. DUFF, ANSWERING FOR CRIME: RESPONSIBILITY AND LIABILITY IN THE CRIMINAL LAW 296 (2007); Kenneth W. Simons, *Self-Defense: Reasonable Beliefs or Reasonable Self-Control?* 11 NEW CRIM. L. REV. 51, 65 (2008).

Note also that some scholars, such as Professor Stephen J. Morse, have argued that justification rests on whether the act in question passes what could be called a fair behavioral expectation threshold. That is, if the actor in question acted in a way that is reasonable, then he is justified, even if his act was based on reasonable mistake, because it would be unfair to expect or ask anything more of him. As Morse has written, "An agent who acts entirely reasonably for a justificatory reason has done all that any decent society can expect of him and therefore he is justified despite the regrettable mistake. He has done nothing wrong."[19] However, whereas there may be consensus that the reasonably mistaken actor is nonculpable because he has acted reasonably (and certainly not out of guilty mind), Morse does not articulate the mechanism by which the actor's mistake as to the objective qualities of the social situation that define the rightdoing or wrongdoing served by his act may alter the act's moral nature or its harmful consequence. That is, it is unclear what bearing the actor's mistakenness has on whether the act itself was right or wrong to perform.[20]

Rather, as I have argued elsewhere,[21] the actor's understanding of the moral nature of her act is irrelevant, whether accurate or mistaken, to the objective qualities that define the moral nature of her act. As a result, her mistake that her act is rightful cannot make it rightful. Her mistake cannot make her victim deserving of being the subject of her reactive violence, entitle her to act violently toward her victim, or negate the fact that her reactive violence has caused a significant social harm. Although the killer may believe that her victim has prompted an imbalance in the natural morality of their relationship, by way of his wrongful threat, she, in fact, causes said imbalance by unduly reacting with violence for the purpose of preventing the harm she erroneously perceives he poses. As such, by enacting violence to defend where no defense is possible, she has committed a wrong and caused a social harm.

Legitimate self-defense may be discerned from mistaken self-defense in that there is no real defense of oneself in the latter scenario.[22] Regardless of how reasonable one's judgment of a stimulus actor or event is, the fact that

[19] *See* Stephen J. Morse, *The Irreducibly Normative Nature of Provocation/Passion*, 43 U. Mich. J.L. Reform 193, 200 (2009).

[20] *See* Reid G. Fontaine, *On Passion's Potential to Undermine Rationality*, 43 U. Mich. J.L. Reform 207, 237 (2009), in which I respond to Morse, "Whereas I could understand (though not accept) the normative position that an act based on reasonable mistake is justified because the reason for acting was justified, I cannot figure out how the commission of killing an undeserving other could ever be viewed as "nothing wrong."

[21] Fontaine, *An Attack on Self-Defense*, *supra* note 7.

[22] *Id.*

the judgment is a mistaken one logically negates a contradiction of this fact. The critical question, then, is whether this distinction – between mistaken and legitimate (or actual) self-defense – is related to the distinction between justification and excuse. Certainly, proponents of both objective and hybrid approaches to self-defense equate the distinction between legitimate and mistaken self-defense to the distinction between justification and *nonjustification*, but whether nonjustification may be, at least under certain conditions, equivalent to excuse is a separate issue.

Let us consider a hypothetical scenario in which two friends, X and Y, are hiking in a canyon. X playfully points a lifelike toy gun in the direction of Y and exclaims "Give me your canteen or you're a dead man!" Z, a hiker who is about to cross paths with X and Y, observes X's conduct and, based on his belief that X is about to wrongfully take Y's life, pulls his hunting knife from his pack and accurately throws it at X, killing X instantly. Is Z's act justified or only excused? In American common law, Y's act is deemed justified if, at the time he acts, he reasonably believes that Y's life is wrongly and imminently threatened. However, Z's mistakenness as to the situation before him bears no relevance to its objectively defined conditions. That is, X does not deserve to die. Also, because X has engaged in no wrongdoing, he certainly has not, by his conduct, entitled anyone to harm him. And because Z was not entitled to take X's life, Z's conduct produces a (significant) social harm. None of these factors is changed by the fact that Z believes, even if quite reasonably, that it is necessary to kill X to prevent the wrongful killing of Y. As such, according to this argument, Z's killing of X is not justified.

Z's conduct, although not justified, may indeed be excused, however. Z acted as a reasonable person would in a similar situation. That is, it is understandable why he acted as he did and did so without culpability. Although his act was wrong and socially harmful, it is, because it was based on reasonable mistakenness, nonculpable. For this reason, X may be excused for having acted wrongfully.

Proponents of the subjective approach would argue that the reasonably mistaken "self-defender" is justified. Alternatively, proponents of both the objective and objective/subjective hybrid approaches generally take the position that although the reasonably mistaken "self-defender" is not justified, he may be excused. That is, it may be said that mistaken defender has acted entirely nonculpably. He used due prudence in assessing the situation before acting. His judgment, albeit mistaken, was reasonable. Furthermore, he acted in the interest of preventing a serious wrong, which is not only not culpable mental state, but one that most would likely characterize as honorable or even brave. For these reasons, it is quite understandable as to why the nonculpable reactive killer committed the wrongful, harmful act, and as such, he should be excused and neither blamed nor punished.

Mistaken Self-Defense and Social-Cognitive Psychology of Threat Reactivity

Mistaken self-defense as excuse begs a question that is highly related to one that was addressed in the previous chapter regarding social-cognitive bias and nonreasonable mistakes in cases of emotionally aroused reactive homicides. With respect to heat of passion/provocation, we asked this: In the case of the cognitively biased reactive killer where said bias is nonculpably formed, is he more blameworthy and punishable than the reactive killer who reasonably interprets adequate provocation and meets criteria for the defense? I argued *no*.

The issue, of course, rests at the line that separates reasonableness and nonreasonableness. As in heat of passion/provocation, the reasonable-person standard is applied in self-defense cases to the defendant's interpretation of the social situation – or, more specifically, threat – so as to exclude defendants who did not take proper care in assessing the stimulus event before reacting to it. As a general matter, this makes good sense. However, it is unfair to expect the same level of care in the assessment of the subject stimulus event when the defendant has a nonculpably formed social-cognitive bias that necessarily produces nonreasonable interpretations and judgments. This is so because this person is not equipped with the same mental faculties and rational capacity to begin with as the reasonable person.

The law generally does not make expectations of its citizens who are not adequately equipped to meet such expectations. To do so would not only be unfair, but senseless. Let us consider legal insanity, as discussed in Chapter 5. A person who does not understand the nature of his wrongful conduct or is otherwise unable to control said conduct is not blamed or punished for having executed it. That is, he is excused for his wrongful, harmful conduct because his mental faculties and rational capacity were such that he may not fairly be said to be responsible for it. The developing juvenile is no different. As discussed in Chapter 4, a child who commits an objectively criminal act may be excused on the ground of immaturity because she was not sufficiently cognitively developed or rational at the time she enacted her unambiguously wrongful, harmful conduct.

In Chapters 2 and 6, the relation between provocation interpretational bias and reactive violence was discussed. Reactive violence – a subtype of antisocial conduct – is characterized as violence enacted in response to a social stimulus that is perceived to be provocative, threatening, or otherwise aversive. It is often emotionally charged and impulsive and is typically performed for the purpose of harming the perceived provocateur or defending against a perceived threat. As discussed, several social-cognitive factors have been uniquely linked to reactive violence. In particular, the tendency to interpret social stimuli that are ambiguous as to their negative content as definitively hostile and intentionally harmful is characteristic of individuals who are prone to enact reactive violence.

Whereas the majority of behavioral science that has examined the social-cognitive psychology of reactive violence has focused on ambiguous provocation stimuli, there is good reason to consider stimuli that are perceived as threatening. It appears that although there are similarities in the response styles of individuals who are biased in how they interpret ambiguous provocations (or provocation-biased individuals) and individuals who are biased in favor of interpreting threats (or threat-biased individuals), these groups also differ in some respects as to the social-cognitive mechanisms at play in their reactive functioning.

Attributional and interpretational problems associated with violent reactivity have been the focus of empirical study in several research programs. Professor Ken Dodge and his colleagues have contributed significantly to this body of work, guided by Dodge's developmental model of SIP and social competence. In particular, the early stages of encoding and interpretation of cues have been linked with reactive violence.[23]

One hypothesis in psychological science involves a further dichotomization of violence subtypes, one that distinguishes categories of reactive violence by hostile-reactive violence, which is angrily enacted in response to a perceived provocation for the purpose of harming the stimulus actor, and defensive-reactive violence, which is fearfully enacted in response to a perceived threat in order to defend against the stimulus actor. In law, the distinction between instrumental violence – a subtype of violence that is typified by calculated predation in the interest of personal gain – and hostile-reactive violence is that of murder and heat-of-passion manslaughter. A related comparison in law, however, may be made with respect to defensive-reactive violence by contrasting murder with self-defense or defense-of-others homicide.

In contrast to research on hostile attributional bias (or provocation interpretational bias) that has focused on hostile-reactive violence, research on TIB has examined the relation between this social-cognitive distortion and behavioral

[23] *See, e.g.*, Crick & Dodge, *supra* note 2; Dodge et al., *Reactive and Proactive Aggression*, *supra* note 2.

problems,[24] as well as anxiety[25] and other emotional problems typically aroused by threatening stimuli.[26] Problematic behavior prompted by interpretations of social threats may take a variety of forms, of course. Whereas one person may be more likely to aggress in response to a perceived threat, another may be more likely to withdraw. It is not entirely clear to what degree anxiety's role may differ among these alternative response styles, but it is indeed evident that there is a strong relation between TIB and anxious problems.

As opposed to a response style characterized by impulsivity, hostility, and reactive aggression (approach), an anxious response style is more closely associated with withdrawal (avoid).[27] Numerous research programs have found that TIB is associated with anxiety and anxiety-related psychiatric disorders.[28] Some of this research has been guided by Dodge's developmental model of SIP and social competence in youth, suggesting that biases at the encoding and interpretation of cues may contribute to aggressive conduct.[29] Other studies have been prompted by a key tenet in the literature on cognitive therapy for anxiety, which asserts that interpretations of threats, as well as being biased in favor of interpreting threats in ambiguous social situations, serve as the cognitive basis for feelings of anxiety and anxiety disorders.[30]

[24] Two developmental studies, one of typically developing youths and the other of youths with learning and behavior problems, lead by Netherlands scientist, Professor Peter Murisa, have examined the link between aggression and threat interpretation (or perception) bias. Both found modest empirical associations between the two, although the more robust findings were between TIB and anxiety and social problems. Peter Murisa, Cor Meestersb, Lianne Smuldersb & Birgit Mayerc, *Threat Perception Distortions and Psychopathological Symptoms in Typically Developing Children*, 14 INFANT & CHILD DEV. 273 (2005); Peter Muris, Harald Merckelbach & Sylvia Walczak, *Aggression and Threat Perception Abnormalities in Children with Learning and Behavior Problems*, 33 CHILD PSYCHIATRY & HUM. DEV. 147 (2002) [hereinafter Muris et al., *Aggression and Threat Perception*].

[25] *E.g.*, Charmaine K. Higa & Eric L. Daleiden, *Social Anxiety and Cognitive Biases in Non-Referred Children: The Interactions of Self-Focused Attention and Threat Interpretation Biases*, 22 J. ANXIETY DISORDERS 441 (2008).

[26] *See, e.g.*, Allison M. Waters, Michelle G. Craske, R. Lindsey Bergman & Michael Treanor, *Threat Interpretation Bias as a Vulnerability Factor in Childhood Anxiety Disorders*, 46 BEHAVIOUR RES. & THERAPY 39 (2008).

[27] Peter Muris, Harald Merckelbach & Sylvia Walczak, *Aggression and Threat Perception Abnormalities in Children with Learning and Behavior Problems*, 33 CHILD PSYCHIATRY & HUM. DEV. 147, 148 (2002).

[28] *E.g.*, Peter Muris, Harald Merckelbach & Esther Damsma, *Threat Perception Bias in Nonreferred, Socially Anxious Children*, 29 J. CLINICAL CHILD PSYCHOL. 348 (2000).

[29] Muris et al., *Aggression and Threat Perception*, *supra* note 24.

[30] *See, e.g.*, Sara Gifford, Shirley Reynolds, Sarah Bell & Charlotte Wilson, *Threat Interpretation Bias in Anxious Children and Their Mothers*, 22 COGNITION & EMOTION 497(2008); Cathy Creswell, Carolyn A Schniering & Ronald M Rapee, *Threat Interpretation in Anxious Children and Their Mothers: Comparison with Nonclinical Children and the Effects of Treatment*, 43 BEHAVIOUR RES. & THERAPY 1375 (2005). For the seminal text on cognitive

The developmental research on the relation between TIB and anxiety is considerable and clear. Individuals who suffer from problems with anxiety tend to interpret social stimuli that are ambiguous as to their threatening nature as definitively threatening. Perhaps most compelling among the numerous studies that have contributed to this finding are recent investigations by Professors Lira Yoon and Richard Zimbarg, who have conducted developmental studies that examined anxious individuals' tendency to interpret ambiguous facial expressions as threatening.[31]

Studies by Yoon and Zimbarg, as well as other[32] scientists, have contributed an important increment to the literature on TIB and anxiety. In contrast to some previous studies that have examined interpretations of verbal stimuli, Yoon and Zimbarg have had participants respond to nonverbal stimuli, such as facial expressions. This is important not only from a basic developmental science perspective, but also to the issue of how this research may inform issues of responsibility and culpability for acts of reactive violence against misinterpreted threats. Often, social cues that trigger interpretations of threats are nonverbal, whether they be facial expressions (e.g., angry versus neutral expression), body posturing (e.g., aggressive versus nonaggressive position), or material objects (e.g., is the stimulus actor holding a gun or a work tool?). Thus, to understand how the development of TIB may contribute to a better understanding of nonreasonable interpretations of threats in criminal cases, research on nonverbal stimuli is critical.

Not surprisingly, there is a positive relation between hostility and aggression – the more hostile an individual, the more aggressive he tends to be.[33] Hostility is a cognitive-emotional state that emerges and is maintained out of information processing that produces conclusions that one's social world is a provocative, threatening, or otherwise aversive or negative place; in turn, hostile feelings may serve to promote a style of processing social information that leads to such conclusions.[34] As has been discussed throughout this volume, this

therapy and anxiety disorders, see AARON T. BECK, GARY EMERY & RUTH L. GREENBERG, *ANXIETY DISORDERS AND PHOBIAS: A COGNITIVE PERSPECTIVE* (rev. ed. 2005).

[31] K. Lira Yoon & Richard E. Zinbarg, *Threat Is in the Eye of the Beholder: Social Anxiety and the Interpretation of Ambiguous Facial Expressions*, 45 BEHAVIOUR RES. & THERAPY 839 (2007); K. Lira Yoon & Richard E. Zinbarg, *Interpreting Neutral Faces as Threatening Is a Default Mode for Socially Anxious Individuals*, 117 J. Abnormal Psychol. 680 (2008).

[32] *See, e.g.*, Lars-Gunnar Lundh & Lars-Göran Öst, *Face Recognition in Patients with Social Phobia*, 25 SCANDINAVIAN J. BEHAVIOUR THERAPY 139 (1996).

[33] For a recent discussion, see Jesus Martin Ramírez & Jose Manuel Andreu, *Aggression, and Some Related Psychological Constructs (Anger, Hostility, and Impulsivity): Some Comments from a Research Project*, 30(3) NEUROSCI. & BIOBEHAVIORAL REVS. 276 (2006).

[34] Mary K. Pope, Timothy W. Smith & Frederick Rhodewalt, *Cognitive, Behavioral, and Affective Correlates of the Cook and Medley Hostility Scale*, 54 J. PERSONALITY ASSESSMENT

hostile style of processing information has been linked to aggressive behavior and, more specifically, reactive aggression.[35] As such, the effect hostility has on aggressive conduct may be better understood as indirect.[36]

Of note is that science has shown that these associations do not hold among anxious individuals. Anxiety appears to disrupt the otherwise natural link between hostile attributions and feelings of hostility and aggressive behavioral enactments. Although anxiety is associated with a bias toward interpreting ambiguous social events and interactions as threatening, it is also associated with a tendency to retreat from perceived social threats.

In one recent American study[37] that examined relations among anxiety, aggression, hostility, and hostile interpretations, researchers found that although anxious individuals are more prone to have a hostile style of interpreting social cues, they are less likely to aggress in response, as compared to their nonanxious peers. They tested a set of hypotheses that was guided by previous investigations of the interrelatedness of these psychological and behavioral constructs in four independent nonclinical samples. Findings supported their predictions that social anxiety is positively related to both feelings of hostility toward others and proneness to interpret social cues as hostile, and negatively related to aggressive conduct. One possible explanation of these findings is that whereas hostility may normally be conducive to aggressive conduct, social anxiety acts to suppress this relation in that the anxious individual's inclination to avoid the challenge posed by the perceived threat overrides any interest in reacting aggressively to it. In other words, the relation between hostile interpretational style and hostility and aggressive conduct is moderated by social anxiety.

501 (1990); Elizabeth A. Lemerise & Kenneth A. Dodge, *The Development of Anger and Hostile Interactions, in* THE HANDBOOK OF EMOTIONS 537 (Michael Lewis & Jeanette M. Haviland-Jones eds., 1993); AARON T. BECK, *PRISONERS OF HATE: THE COGNITIVE BASIS OF ANGER, HOSTILITY, AND VIOLENCE* (1999); Max Guyll & Stephanie Madon, *Trait Hostility: The Breadth and Specificity of Schema Effects*, 34 PERSONALITY & INDIVIDUAL DIFFERENCES 681 (2003).

35 For a recent review, see Reid G. Fontaine, *Disentangling the Psychology and Law of Instrumental and Reactive Subtypes of Aggression*, 13 PSYCHOL. PUB. POL'Y & LAW 143 (2007).

36 *See* Roy F. Baumeister, C. Nathan DeWall, Kathleen D. Vohs & Jessica L. Alquist, *Does Emotion Cause Behavior (Apart From Making People Do Stupid, Destructive Things)?, in* THEN A MIRACLE OCCURS: FOCUSING ON BEHAVIOR IN SOCIAL PSYCHOLOGICAL THEORY AND RESEARCH 119 (Christopher Agnew, Donald E. Carlston, William G. Graziano & Janice R. Kelly eds., 2010).

37 C. Nathan DeWall, Julia D. Buckner, Nathaniel M. Lambert, Alex S. Cohen & Frank D. Fincham, *Bracing for the Worst, but Behaving the Best: Social Anxiety, Hostility, and Behavioral Aggression*, 24 J. ANXIETY DISORDERS 260 (2010).

A recent Polish study[38] suggests that there may be more to the picture, however. In a study of more than 1,100 adult participants, scientists set out to investigate how reactions to workplace violence may vary by trait anxiety and behavior/personality type. Specifically, researchers hypothesized that personal characteristics such as trait anxiety and Type A (impatient, controlling, and competitive) versus Type B (patient, relaxed, and easygoing) behavior/personality may act as modifiers of experiences and reactions to violent social stimuli. Investigators found that whereas individuals who are high on trait anxiety and demonstrate Type B behavior were submissive in response to violence, individuals who are high on trait anxiety and show Type A personality characteristics reacted in precisely the opposite fashion. Not only was this latter subgroup not submissive, but they exhibited a tendency to react aggressively to workplace violence stimuli. A third subgroup, characterized by low-trait anxiety and Type B behavior/personality, responded assertively (i.e., neither submissively nor aggressively) when being attacked. Findings supported previous research that anxiety moderates the relation between hostile cues and behavioral reactivity. More importantly, however, this study found that anxiety's role in this context is itself modified by behavior/personality type. That is, behavior/personality type moderates the relation between threatening stimuli and behavioral reactivity *among anxious individuals*. This is a crucial finding in that it suggests that not all types of individuals with anxiety respond to violent stimuli in the same fashion. Furthermore, it points to the clear likelihood that the function of anxiety in threat contexts may not always be conducive to an escape or withdrawal response.

Not only may the role of anxiety in the relation between threat interpretation and aggressive reactivity be moderated by behavior/personality type, but it may be modified by social contextual parameters, as well. One critical hypothesis that has not been adequately tested has to do with what the role of anxiety is in situations in which the person responding to a perceived threat believes that he *must* respond. That is, does the link between anxiety and the tendency to retreat from situations that are understood to be challenging or threatening hold in situations in which the responding individual believes that there is no way to retreat or withdraw? Studies that have tested relations among hostile interpretations, hostility, and aggressive conduct in anxious versus nonanxious individuals have not implemented a paradigm by which study participants are

[38] Marcin Drabek, Dorota Merecz & Agnieszka Mościcka, *Trait Anxiety and Type Behavior Pattern (A and B) As Modifiers of Immediate Reaction Towards Violent Behaviors*, 56 MEDYCYNA PRACY 223 (2005).

led to believe that they cannot retreat from the perceived threat, so established research can not speak to this issue. This question, however, is critical to making use of research in this area of social-cognitive psychology to issues of individual rationality, responsibility, and culpability in criminal law with respect to self-defense and defense of others because these doctrines are defined, in part, by a requirement of *necessity*. That is, according to the common-law framings of these doctrines, the defendant must have reasonably believed that mortal force was necessary to defend against the perceived threat. By *necessity*, the doctrines exclude situations in which the defendant could have retreated from the perceived threat, thereby rendering it impotent and eliminating the danger it was believed to have posed.[39]

It is plausible that in this specific type of context – that is, one in which the defendant believes there is no escape from the threat – anxiety may not only promote nonaggressive reactivity, as it appears to typically function, but instead, out of stress and fear experiences, prompt a faster and more severe enactment of violent retaliation. In other words, in this type of context, anxiety may promote aggressive retaliation, motivated out of an interest in protecting oneself or another. Clearly, rigorous research that tests such a hypothesis is necessary before such a conclusion may be legitimately drawn. However, if true, this finding may pose implications for self-defense and defense-of-others law.

Setting aside the role of anxiety, however, social-cognitive research on developmental social cognition and aggressive reactivity suggests that some individuals, as a result of nonculpably formed and maintained SIP problems, are biased toward interpreting provocations and threats where such do not necessarily exist. These processing tendencies not only promote a negative worldview, but also personal experiences of reactive emotions (anger, rage, fear, panic) and actions (aggressive retaliation, social withdrawal). This pattern is not characteristic of all individuals whose processing is characterized by interpretational biases, nor does it apply to all persons who demonstrate a pattern of aggressive conduct. However, the research clearly indicates that these maladjusted patterns of functioning are characteristic of enough aggressive individuals that significant group differences have been identified in several studies, many of which are from independent research programs. These findings should be considered in the assessment of culpability and punishment for the defendant who has killed in response to a genuine but nonreasonable mistake that his victim posed him a mortal threat when his nonreasonable mistake was the direct result from such a nonculpably formed social-cognitive impairment.

39 Lee, *supra* note 16, at 199–203.

Undoubtedly, issues of interpretational bias and maladaptive behavioral reactivity are not unique to doctrines of heat of passion/provocation, self-defense, and defense of others. Interpretational bias is just as likely to play a role in situations in which the reactive wrongdoing is directed at a third party as it is to ones in which the response target is the perceived provocateur or threat. Likewise, these issues are not isolated to cases of homicide, but rather apply equally to all scenarios by which antisocial conduct is enacted in response to a perceived wrong or aversive stimulus. As such, interpretational bias may be applied equally to the defense of duress. However, as discussed later, duress is structurally framed in a way that calls for an exploration of factors that may explain individual differences in behavioral decision-making capacity and style. As such, research on response decision making and maladaptive behavioral reactivity may be critical to issues of culpability and punishment in duress cases.

DURESS

Duress, as conventionally defined and understood, is a legal defense a defendant can raise in the case that she has caused an innocent victim harm out of being coerced or compelled to do so as a result of being unlawfully threatened by a third-party wrongdoer. The defense thus represents a mediational sequence involving (and requiring) three parties by which a threatening wrongdoer (X or threatened wrongdoer) induces an otherwise innocent person (Y or defendant) to unlawfully cause harm to an innocent third party (Z or victim). In this way, Y is acting in accordance with the criminal wrongdoing initiated and aggressively pursued by X, and is the proximate cause of the social harm caused to Z (or, at least, attempts to cause Z). But for Z, Y has no interest in causing harm to Z. Y's interest in harming Z emerges only out of the belief that if she does not act as X insists, X will cause her (or her loved one) grievous bodily harm or death. It is out of this belief – and quite typically intense fear, although fear is not required by the defense – that Y is "transformed" by X into a wrongdoer.

Duress, although recognized either by statute or common law in all fifty states, varies by jurisdiction. However, there are several conditions by common law that are generally required of the defendant who raises the defense.[40] First, the threat presented to Y must be man-made, as opposed to natural as in the

[40] *See* Lawrence Newman & Lawrence Weitzer, *Duress, Free Will and the Criminal Law*, 30 S. Cal. L. Rev. 313 (1956–1957); Joshua Dressler, *Understanding Criminal Law* (5th ed. 2009).

case of the justification defense of necessity.[41] Specifically, the defendant must demonstrate that grievous bodily harm or death was threatened by another person or persons. The target of the coercer's threat may be either the defendant or another individual or group of individuals. It may also be required that, in the case that the target is not the defendant, it be directed toward someone close in relations to her, such as a child or spouse. Second, the defendant must have reasonably believed that the threat was real. Third, the threat, as reasonably believed, must be demonstrated to have been instant, present, imminent, and impending at the time of defendant's act.[42] Fourth, the defendant had no reasonable escape from the threat. Y may also need to demonstrate that she made a reasonable attempt to resist the threat or exploited any and all reasonable avenues by which she could have avoided the threat. Fifth and finally, the defendant cannot have caused or been negligent in allowing the causation of the unlawful threat. That is, the threat imposed on Y must arise completely free of any fault on Y's part. The defense is not available in cases of intentional homicide.

The Model Penal Code (MPC) offers a broader framing. Section 2.09 of the MPC states that duress is available to the defendant as a defense against objectively criminal conduct where "(1) he was compelled to commit the offense by the use, or threatened use, of unlawful force by the coercer upon his or another person; and (2) a person of reasonable firmness in his situation would have been unable to resist the coercion."[43] The MPC is similar to common-law duress in a couple of important ways. First, it adheres to the requirement that the threat consist of unlawful force. Second, the MPC requires that the threat must target the physical well-being of the defendant or another individual. As such, the nature and function of common-law duress was retained by the MPC framing of the defense.

[41] Necessity is a justification defense by which a defendant may be relieved of criminal liability in cases in which she can demonstrate that she could only avoid the substantial harm posed by the threat by violating the rights of her victim and that said violation caused her victim a lesser harm than that posed by the threat to the defendant. Some jurisdictions require that the threat be natural (e.g., earthquake) for the defense of necessity to apply. For a thorough discussion of the differences between duress and the justification defenses of necessity and self-defense, see Peter Westen & James Mangiafico, *The Criminal Defense of Duress: A Justification, Not an Excuse – and Why It Matters*, 6 BUFF. CRIM. L. REV. 833, 842–862 (2003) Specifically, the authors state, "Conventional duress possesses three features that distinguish it from necessity and self-defense. Conventional duress (1) is a tripartite relationship, (2) involves purposefully coercive threats, and (3) provides a defense that is lesser than self-defense and yet greater than necessity." *Id.* at 842.

[42] *See* State v. Crawford, 861 P.2d 791, 797 (Kan. 1993); State v. Toscano, 378 A.2d 755, 760 (N.J. 1977); Newman & Weitzer, *supra* note 40, at 314.

[43] MODEL PENAL CODE § 2.09.

However, structural differences between the MPC and common-law approaches, which define the boundaries within which the defense may apply, are numerous and striking. First, the MPC does not require that the coercer intend that the defendant act as he did, as some common-law jurisdictions do.[44] For example, if an individual engages in criminal trespass to escape an individual who poses a mortal threat, he may raise duress in an MPC jurisdiction even though criminal trespass was not the coercer's goal by threatening him. Second, the MPC does not require that the defendant's act be performed in response to a threat of grievous bodily harm or death. Third, it is not required that the threat of unlawful force be imminent. Fourth, the coercer's target need not be the defendant or someone close to the defendant, such as spouse or child, as some common-law jurisdictions require.[45] Fifth, the MPC allows that the defense be raised in cases of intentional homicide.

As is the case with all other affirmative defenses discussed in this volume, the spirit of diminished capacity (or diminished responsibility) is evident in duress. The MPC highlights the critical issue of human capacity and function in duress. In subsection 2, it is required that "a person of reasonable firmness in his situation would have been unable to resist the coercion."[46] This requirement describes a condition by which the defendant must have been of temporary diminished capacity as a direct result of the coercion or threat at the time he committed the unlawful act. The coercion caused a lesser state of ability, consistent with what a reasonable person would have suffered under such conditions. Although his act was unlawful, he may be relieved of culpability and punishment owing to having this lesser condition at the time of his objectively criminal conduct. This point begs the question as to whether duress is properly viewed as a justification or excuse. As we have found in our analysis of other affirmative defenses (with the sole exception of developmental immaturity), the nature – justification versus excuse – of duress is similarly a matter of debate among scholars.

Is Duress a Justification or Excuse?

The nature of duress has long been debated in Anglo-American criminal law. Whereas some scholars view the defense as a justification,[47] most treat it as

[44] For a discussion, see Westen & Mangiafico, *supra* note 41, at 851.

[45] Newman & Weitzer, *supra* note 40, at 314.

[46] Model Penal Code § 2.09 (2).

[47] For a recent articulation of duress as justification, see Westen & Mangiafico, *supra* note 41.

an excuse,[48] and still others, albeit a minority, have depicted it as neither.[49] Perhaps the best argument in favor of duress as a justification is the lesser-of-evils (or lesser-of-harms) argument. According to this argument, the defendant, by committing the objectively criminal act, has prevented the greater harm of serious physical maltreatment or death from occurring either to himself or another. For example, perhaps coercer X, while brandishing a machete, threatens Y that if he does not immediately go and steal the purse of victim Z, X will chop off Y's foot. Surely, it is a lesser evil and harm to steal a purse than to cripple someone. Thus one may argue that, in such a scenario, Y was justified to act as he did because, by doing so, he prevented a far more evil act and worse outcome. The prevention of the greater wrong may be said to warrant the objectively criminal act that the defendant committed. But for the defendant's wrongdoing, a more severe wrong would occur and a greater harm would result.

However, there exist several rebuttals to this argument as a general basis for treating duress as justification. First, the duress defense is not precluded in cases in which the harm committed by Y is not lesser than that threatened by X. For example, X may threaten to chop off Y's foot unless Y chops off Z's foot. If Y therefore chops off Z's foot, he may invoke duress in his defense, even though Y's act may certainly not be said to be lesser in terms of its wrongfulness or the harm it causes.[50] In such cases, it cannot be legitimately argued that Y's act was justified because it was a lesser evil or harm – for that matter, it is hard to imagine any argument that such an act is justified. Rather, at most, Y's wrongful act may be excusable.

[48] There are numerous writings that articulate duress as excuse. A few examples are: Joshua Dressler, *Exegesis of the Law of Duress: Justifying the Excuse and Searching for Its Proper Limit*, 62 S. CAL. L. REV. 1331 (1989) [hereinafter Dressler, *Exegesis*]; Michael Gorr, *Duress and Culpability*, 19 CRIM. JUST. ETHICS 3 (2000); Kyron Huigens, *Duress is Not a Justification*, 2 OHIO ST. J. CRIM. L. 303 (2004); Suzanne Uniake, *Emotional Excuses*, 26 L. & PHIL. 95 (2007). As Professor Joshua Dressler has clarified, "[M]ost scholars, courts, and states' criminal codes that draw distinctions between justifications and excuses, treat duress as an excuse defense." DRESSLER, *supra* note 40 (footnote omitted).

[49] Some scholars depict duress, both awkwardly and quite incorrectly, as neither a justification nor an excuse. For example, see Craig Carr, *Duress and Criminal Responsibility*, 10 LAW & PHIL. 161, 180 (1991). Elsewhere, I have argued that affirmative defenses must be either one or the other, or may encompass components of both as long as each component may independently serve as a partial justification or partial excuse. *See* Fontaine, *On Passion's Potential to Undermine Rationality*, *supra* note 20; Fontaine, *An Attack on Self-Defense*, *supra* note 7. For present purposes, we will focus our attention on the debate about duress as justification versus duress as excuse and leave aside arguments about a supposed third category of affirmative defenses.

[50] For a lengthier discussion of this objection to the lesser-of-harms argument, see DRESSLER, *supra* note 40, at 305–06.

A second rebuttal to the lesser-of-evils argument is that duress requires only that the defendant's understanding of the threat is reasonable. As long as the defendant's judgment is reasonable, it does not have to be accurate. Imagine an elaborate hoax by which X intends only to scare Y. He has no intention of physically harming Y, but rather wants to videotape Y's reaction to the threat so that he can then post the video on his "reality show" Web site. X tells Y that he will chop of his foot if he does not steal Z's purse. Y quite reasonably believes that X will cripple him if he does not commit the theft, so he abides by X's demand. In this case, no real threat exists, yet Y has committed a harm against Z. As such, Y's act in no real way prevented a greater evil or harm.

Third, the lesser-of-evils argument fails in the case that X follows through with his threat despite Y having abided by his demand. Suppose that, after Y returns with Z's purse, Z takes the purse and then chops off Y's foot. Y's wrongful act in no way prevented a greater evil or harm. In fact, it only added to the harm caused by X.

It is difficult to understand duress as justification in any case in which all of the following criteria are not met: (1) there existed a real threat of grievous bodily harm or death on the part of the coercer; (2) the wrong and harm posed by the threat is greater than that committed by the defendant; and (3) the defendant's act did indeed prevent the greater wrong and harm posed by the coercer's threat from being realized. If any one of these factors is not present, the defendant's act must be viewed as wrong and harmful. As such, the defendant's act may be excusable but not justifiable.

Being that duress embodies acts that may not be legitimately viewed as justified poses problems for any argument that the defense should be understood as a justification. As I have noted elsewhere,

> The fact that duress can be an excuse naturally undermines the argument that it is a justification. This problem is particularly evident (and exposing) in cases in which the defense in question is characterized to favor a reading of justification, such as in certain instances of heat-of-passion homicide. If conduct that is admittedly criminally wrongful meets the criteria of the defense in question, then the nature of the defense itself must necessarily be that of excuse – that is, the fact that the admittedly criminally wrongful conduct qualifies means that only the lower standard of excuse may be met for the defense in question to apply.[51]

[51] Fontaine, *An Attack on Self-Defense*, *supra* note 7, at 67; *see also* Reid G. Fontaine, *Adequate (Non)Provocation and Heat of Passion as Excuse Not Justification*, 43 U. MICH. J. L. REFORM 27, 41–46 (2009).

Rather, duress is properly understood as an excuse. This is so not only because the defense may apply to acts that are definitively not justifiable, but because a proper understanding of the defense's nature reveals an excuse orientation.

Duress may be viewed as a social condition that excuses wrongful behavior because it pressures a person to make a choice that a reasonable person could not resist making. The decision-making situation imposed on the defendant is more than just very difficult. Because of what is at stake – the physical well-being of the defendant and/or a third party – the decision is profoundly unfair. So horrible is the alternative, that even contemplating its realization may serve to compromise the defendant's psychological integrity such that he is unable to fully process information and consider behavioral options in the course of response decision making. Thus, the choice that the defendant makes is his own, but it is not a product of unfairly compromised rationality.

This "diminished rationality" perspective should be distinguished from the "free choice" or "personhood" theory of excuses advanced by other criminal-law theorists such as Professors Joshua Dressler[52] and H. L. A. Hart.[53] The two perspectives are related but different with respect to the precise mechanism by which duress is understood to excuse wrongdoing. Whereas the free-choice perspective argues that duress excuses because of the deeply unfair choice-making condition imposed on the defendant by the threat, a diminished-rationality perspective recognizes that such a condition unfairly limits the decision-making range that typical adults would otherwise have at their disposal. Advocating the free-choice perspective, Dressler has stated: "A person acting under duress is excused, although he possessed the capacity to make the right choice, if he lacked a fair opportunity to act lawfully or, slightly more accurately, if he lacked a fair opportunity to avoid acting unlawfully."[54] The diminished-rationality argument would clarify that duress situations are so psychologically imposing that although the coerced individual may choose to act as he does, he makes his choice under psychologically restricted conditions that are not consistent with the presumption of rationality that the law holds for adult actors.

In this way, duress recognizes that coerced behavior is not fully rational behavior. That is, the effect of the coercion is to unjustifiably diminish one's rationality. As discussed in Chapter 3, and has been argued persuasively by Professor Stephen Morse,[55] rationality is the key capacity by which

[52] Dressler, *Exegesis*, *supra* note 48.

[53] H. L. A. Hart, *Punishment and Responsibility: Essays in the Philosophy of Law* (1968).

[54] Dressler, *Exegesis*, *supra* note 48, at 1365.

[55] Stephen J. Morse, *Rationality and Responsibility*, 74 S. Cal. L. Rev. 251 (2000); Stephen J. Morse, *Diminished Rationality, Diminished Responsibility*,1 Ohio St. J. Crim. L. 289 (2003).

responsibility for conduct (and culpability for wrongful conduct) may be attributed. The defendant whose rationality has been unfairly diminished as a result of a wrongdoer's coercion may not be said, in retributive terms, to deserve the blame and punishment that he would if his rational capacity had not been unfairly compromised.

This is not to say that the duress defendant did not act voluntarily or lacked the requisite mens rea for the crime. The defendant, of course, intends to enact the behavior and, by doing so, cause the coercer's desired result. However, because of the conditions under which his intent was formed, it may not be said to be a mental state that is the product of nondiminished rationality. The mechanism by which coercion affects its subject is pressure. When pressure is imposed on the defendant to act as the coercer demands, the defendant becomes constrained to act accordingly. Indeed, the coercion does not negate the voluntary act or mens rea requirements, but rather functions to give rise to the defendant's interest (or intent) to act wrongfully such that the coerced individual either fails to identify other behavioral options or largely discounts them because it is expected that any alternative course of action will lead to the defendant's thorough demise.

By limiting one's identification and evaluation of behavioral choices, coercion functions to restrict one's rational capacity such that it no longer meets the presumed standard of rationality that the law applies to adult human actors. As such, the duress defense serves to excuse the defendant of his wrongdoing because it is recognized that his key functional capacity was diminished due to reasons for which he may not be justly blamed. This once again reflects how the "spirit" of *diminished capacity* is present in American affirmative defenses, even if the formal defense is no longer widely recognized.[56]

Developmental Social Cognition and Duress: Decision-Making Capacity, Vulnerability to Coercive Influence, and Fear

Earlier in this chapter, I laid out the general mediational sequence that is represented by duress: Coercer X threatens defendant Y, who, in mediational turn, harms innocent victim Z. However a number of specific mediational sequences are embedded in this general mediation. Of present importance is the social-cognitive mediation by which X exerts influence on Y's conduct. X's action is only effective to his goal to the degree that Y interprets his action in accordance with X's intent and determines that he must act as X demands. That is, the effect of X's threat on Y is mediated by both Y's interpretation

[56] See *supra* Chapter 3.

of X's action, and then, in turn, his decision making as to how to behaviorally respond. This specific mediational sequence (X → Mediator 1 [M1] → Mediator 2 [M2] → Y) may be represented as follows:

(1) Threat by Coercer (X) →
(2) Y's Interpretation of Threat (M1) →
(3) Y's Behavioral Decision (M2) →
(4) Defendant Commits Wrongdoing (Y).

A person's decision making as to how to respond to a social stimulus is going to depend heavily on his interpretation of said stimulus (M1 → M2). Indeed, the interpretation of the stimulus is far more important to one's response decision making and ultimate behavioral enactment than is the objective stimulus. If Y believes that X has threatened him, he will make a behavioral decision based on such a belief, regardless of whether X has, in fact, threatened him. Alternatively, even in the case that X unambiguously threatens Y, Y will not behave in a way consistent with being threatened if he has interpreted X's behavior as nonthreatening. As such, not only does Y's interpretation of the threat mediate the relation between the stimulus (X) and Y's response decision making and behavioral enactment; Y's interpretational inclination or style serves as a *moderator* of the relation.[57]

Thus, the role of stimulus interpretation is essential to understanding the phenomenological sequence represented by duress. In the case of someone who has an interpretational bias, she may be more likely to experience nonthreatening social cues as coercive. If she has developed said interpretational bias for nonculpable reasons (e.g., she is a victim of child abuse) and it is not reasonably foreseeable as to how her bias may contribute to her subsequent commission of wrongdoing (e.g., the bias is specific to an unlikely combination of social circumstances), then there is a reasoned argument to be made that she may be less culpable, and therefore less punishable, for her wrongdoing, at least from a retributive/desert perspective.

In Chapter 6, we explored interpretational bias with respect to heat of passion/provocation. I argued that the reactive killer who has a provocation interpretational bias and, because of this bias, nonreasonably interprets a situation as serious provocation should not be viewed as more culpable than the reactive killer who meets all criteria for the heat-of-passion/provocation common-law defense (in particular, the adequate-provocation criterion). Earlier in this chapter, I made a related case for the mistaken "self-defender" who,

57 That is, X's threat will only cause Y's experience of being threatened where Y has accurately interpreted X's behavior as threatening.

because of a TIB, may have nonreasonably interpreted the presented social stimulus as a threat of grievous bodily harm or death. And there is no legitimate reason why consideration of the role of interpretational bias in determinations of culpability and punishment is any less sensible in cases of duress. One who is biased to interpret threats for nonculpable reasons may be just as likely to find oneself in a mistaken duress situation as she is in one of mistaken provocation or mistaken self-defense.

Rather than here again review the literature on interpretational bias and maladaptive behavioral reactivity and relate it to criminal defense doctrine, however, it would seem more useful and efficient to discuss areas of developmental social cognition that may be especially and perhaps uniquely relevant to duress. As such, the present discussion focuses on M2, behavioral decision making, in the specific mediational sequence as to how X exerts influence on Y's wrongful conduct, as articulated earlier in this section. It should be noted that the problems in behavioral decision making need not be dependent on problems with social interpretation. That is, one may quite accurately interpret a given social stimulus but, as a result of decision-making deficits and/or biases, enact a wrongful, harmful, or otherwise socially undesirable behavioral response. Recognition of this fact points to the importance of understanding the relation between behavioral decision making and response enactments outside of any role played by interpretational bias.

In Chapter 4, the roles of underdeveloped decision-making capacity and vulnerability to coercive influence were discussed in the context of minors who commit serious antisocial acts prohibited by law. The "developmental immaturity" argument, as made by both developmental scientists and legal theorists,[58] asserts that because certain functional capacities are not sufficiently developed in adolescence such that they are comparable to adulthood, youth offenders are not as blameworthy and punishable as are adult offenders who commit similar crimes. It is argued that, among other areas, adolescents, as compared to adults, do not possess the same capacity for decision making and are more easily influenced by coercive others.

Interestingly, this perspective may be applied to adult actors in duress situations. Here, undermined decision-making capacity and heightened

[58] *E.g.*, Laurence Steinberg & Elizabeth S. Scott, *Less Guilty by Reason of Adolescence: Developmental Immaturity, Diminished Responsibility, and the Juvenile Death Penalty*, 58 AM. PSYCHOL. 1009 (2003); Elizabeth Cauffman & Laurence Steinberg, *(Im)maturity of Judgment in Adolescence: Why Adolescents May Be Less Culpable Than Adults*, 18 BEHAV. SCI. & L. 741 (2000); Laurence Steinberg & Elizabeth Cauffman, *Maturity of Judgment in Adolescence: Psychosocial Factors in Adolescent Decision Making*, 20 LAW & HUM. BEHAV. 249 (1996).

vulnerability to being influenced by others is not a function of underdevelopment, of course, but rather a temporally limited diminished state that is imposed by the coercive situation. As in the developmental immaturity case, in which adolescent offending is mitigated because these diminished capacities are nonculpably formed (i.e., they are underdeveloped), adult wrongdoers who commit objectively criminal acts under duress act with diminished capacities that are nonculpably formed. Whereas it may be that adult wrongdoers who act under duress may be presumed to generally have sufficiently developed capacities of decision making and resistance to others' influence, the overbearing, coercive nature of the duress context undermines such otherwise sufficiently formed capacities, compromising them such that the coerced individual's rationality is restricted and the response option of committing the crime desired by the coercer becomes overwhelmingly favored.

In social-cognitive and social-developmental psychology, there is a growing literature on the relation between behavioral judgment and response decision making and maladjusted behavioral outcomes. In Chapter 2, research on SIP theory and antisocial behavior was reviewed. Highlighted in this discussion was recent research on how adolescents judge behavioral alternatives and make decisions as to how to respond to perceived aversive stimuli – or, more specifically, response evaluation and decision (RED), a set of processes by which an individual may assess multiple behavioral options across different qualitative domains to determine how best to respond to a social stimulus.[59]

It is not difficult to imagine how the presentation of a serious threat may limit an individual's SIP at each stage of the process. For example, at the clarification-of-goals stage, a person may only consider her goal of self-preservation when faced with a threat that if she does not abide by the coercer's wishes, she will lose her life. Also, at the response access or construction stage, the effect of being threatened may be to limit one's response generation such that the only behavioral course of action identified is that which meets with the coercer's demands. Indeed, the psychological impact of a serious threat

[59] *E.g.*, Reid G. Fontaine, Chongming Yang, Kenneth A. Dodge, Gregory S. Pettit & John E. Bates, *Development of Response Evaluation and Decision (RED) and Antisocial Behavior in Childhood and Adolescence*, 45 Developmental Psychol. 447 (2009); Reid G. Fontaine, Chongming Yang, Kenneth A. Dodge, John E. Bates & Gregory S. Pettit, *Testing an Individual Systems Model of Response Evaluation and Decision (Red) and Antisocial Behavior Across Adolescence*, 79 Child Dev. 462 (2008); Reid G. Fontaine, Virginia Salzer Burks & Kenneth A. Dodge, *Response Decision Processes and Externalizing Behavior Problems in Adolescents*, 14 Dev. & Psychopathology 107 (2002); Reid G. Fontaine, Marieh Tanha, Chongming Yang, Kenneth A. Dodge, John E. Bates & Gregory S. Pettit, *Does Response Evaluation and Decision (RED) Mediate the Relation Between Hostile Attributional Style and Antisocial Behavior in Adolescence?*, 38 J. Abnormal Child Psychol. 615 (2010).

may be to create a tunnel-vision-like effect by which one's processing is immediately geared to preventing the threat from being realized.

In terms of RED processing, individuals may consider a possible response by assessing it across several levels, including – but not limited to – the degree to which the response meets with the person's sociomoral identity (*response valuation*), the extent to which the individual believes it likely that she can enact and successfully carry out the behavior in question (*response efficacy*), the degrees to which she positively and negatively values alternative outcomes to which enacting the behavior may lead (*outcome valuation*), and the likelihood that the behavior being considered will cause the alternative outcomes (*outcome expectancy*). Individuals who demonstrate problems with aggressive behavioral responsivity have demonstrated biases toward favorable evaluations of aggressive response options that promote aggressive enactments across each of these dimensions.[60] As might be expected, aggressogenic processing tendencies such as these are associated with past victimization,[61] suggesting that being victimized may contribute to shaping cognitive response styles in situations in which threatening stimuli are presented.

In terms of these RED dimensions, it seems likely that a mortal or otherwise serious threat primes an individual to discount evaluative domains such as response valuation and response efficacy, and focus the responding individual on outcome assessment. It may be that the conduct demanded by the coercer is not at all congruent with the defendant's sociomoral identity and, under different circumstances, she may otherwise believe that she could not even initiate the behavior's enactment, let alone perform it with success. However, with these domains largely discounted, the domains of outcome valuation and outcome expectancy, albeit restricted themselves by the duress context, may carry the weight of the defendant's behavioral decision. The outcome of self-preservation immediately becomes the paramount, driving impetus, and it is just as quickly deemed that abiding by the coercer's demands provides the course of action by which self-preservation will have the greatest likelihood of being realized.

60 For a review, see Reid G. Fontaine & Kenneth A. Dodge, *Real-Time Decision Making and Aggressive Behavior in Youth: A Heuristic Model of Response Evaluation and Decision (RED)*, 32 Aggressive Behav. 604 (2006).

61 For example, see Bahr Weiss, Kenneth A. Dodge, John E. Bates & Gregory S. Pettit, *Some Consequences of Early Harsh Discipline: Child Aggression and a Maladaptive Social Information Processing Style*, 63 Child Dev. 1321 (1992); Kenneth A. Dodge, Greggory S. Pettit, John E. Bates & Ernest Valente, *Social Information-Processing Patterns Partially Mediate the Effect of Early Physical Abuse on Later Conduct Problems*, 104 J. Abnormal Psychol. 632 (1995).

The interplay of SIP and emotion in the duress context should also be recognized. Emotional functioning can play a considerable role in the degree to which one's rational judgment and decision making is functional and adaptive. One the one hand, emotion may streamline decision making such that irrelevant considerations are avoided and efficient decision making and behavior may be performed to meet contextual demands. On the other hand, emotional arousal, particularly in extreme form, may limit rationality such that a person acts in an irrational, maladaptive manner, posing problems for both herself and others in her social world.

The emotional condition inherent to duress situations is fear, of course. Unlike heat of passion/provocation, however, emotional disturbance (or emotion of any kind and any degree, for that matter) is not formally elemental to the defense of duress. This is true with respect to both the common law and MPC framings. It is unclear why fear is not specified as a condition of the defense. In fact, it is unclear why the law, in general, neglects the obvious role that fear plays in a variety of acts of reactive violence – not only duress, but self-defense, defense of others, heat of passion/provocation, and even insanity. The law's failure to formally recognize fear as a potentially mitigating psychological feature in excuse defenses is not only obvious – it is senseless, prompting Professor Joshua Dressler, in his plea for theoretical consistency in the criminal law, to write: "[W]hy is it that a person who kills in sudden heat of passion is guilty of manslaughter while one who kills an innocent person because she fears for her own life – i.e., is coerced to commit the crime – is guilty of murder? Why does anger mitigate while fear does not?"[62]

Nevertheless, it is not unusual for scholarly discussions of duress to regard fear as a central feature of the defense. Indeed, it is regularly regarded as one of the "emotional excuses," along with heat of passion/provocation, recognized by Anglo-American criminal law.[63] This places duress in an unusual and paradoxical category – one in which the mechanism that may be understood to excuse the defendant who raises it (i.e., emotion) is not in fact an actual criterion of the defense. It is via the demonstration of extreme emotion (or, more specifically, fear), of course, that the fact finder in a duress case may be particularly compelled to view the defendant's rationality (and thus ultimately her responsibility) to have been diminished. In this way, duress is quite similar to heat of passion/provocation.

[62] Joshua Dressler, *Justifications and Excuses: A Brief Review of the Concepts and the Literature*, 33 Wayne L. Rev. 1155, 1172 (1987) (footnote omitted); *see also* Elise J. Percy, Joseph L. Hoffman & Steven J. Sherman, *"Sticky Metaphors" and the Persistence of the Traditional Voluntary Manslaughter Doctrine*, 44 U. Mich. J. L. Reform 383 (2011).

[63] *See, e.g.*, Suzanne Uniake, *Emotional Excuses*, 26 Law & Phil. 95 (2007).

Fear is an emotional response to a perceived threat by which an individual judges herself or a valued other to be in physical and or psychological danger. This appraisal triggers a number of psychophysiological mechanisms that serve to either mobilize the individual in the form of fight-or-flight defensive behavior, or immobilize her, such as in the case that she is overwhelmed by the emotional experience (terror). In this way, fear can serve an adaptive or maladaptive function, depending, of course, on the demands of the threat context.

In Chapter 2, we discussed appraisal theory of emotion, by which emotions are understood to arise out of combinations of judgments about the stimulus and its specific meaning to responding individual. Scientific research leaves little doubt that there exist strong relations between specific cognitive patterns and emotional responses. Most prominent among cognitive mechanisms of fear is that the stimulus in question poses some type of danger to the responding individual or someone whom she values.[64] Whereas appraisal theory wears its cognitive focus on its sleeve, an emphasis on cognitive underpinnings is evident in several theories of fear.[65] Indeed, widely administered cognitive treatments of fear-related clinical problems and disorders rest on the premise that anxiety and fear may be relieved if the cognitive patterns activated by the troubled individual may be adjusted so that they do not promote such negative emotional experiences.[66]

As such, there is good scientific reason to believe that fear has much to do with social-cognitive processing. Similar to SIP theory, which details specific cognitive patterns that serve as the basis of *behavioral* functioning, appraisal theory is used to understand individual differences in *emotional* functioning based on specific combinations of social-cognitive operations. Also similar to SIP research, which has demonstrated a link between biased social cognition and antisocial conduct, problematic emotional reactions may be understood

[64] Craig A. Smith & Richard S. Lazarus, *Appraisal Components, Core Relational Themes, and the Emotions*, 7 Cognition & Emotion 233 (1993); Craig A. Smith, Kelly N. Haynes, Richard S. Lazarus & Lois K. Pope, *in Search of the "Hot" Cognitions: Attributions, Appraisals, and Their Relation to Emotion*, 65 J. Personality & Soc. Psychol. 916 (1993); Ira J. Roseman & Craig A. Smith, *Appraisal Theory: Overview, Assumptions, Varieties, Controversies*, *in* Appraisal Processes in Emotion: Theory, Methods, Research 3 (Klaus R. Scherer, Angela Schorr & Tom Johnstone eds., 2001); Craig Smith & Leslie D. Kirby, *Putting Appraisal in Context: Toward a Relational Model of Appraisal and Emotion*, 23 Cognition & Emotion 1352 (2009); Anne M. Finucanea & Mick J. Power, *The Effect of Fear on Attentional Processing in a Sample of Healthy Females*, 24 J. Anxiety Disorders 42 (2010).

[65] *See* Jason M. Armfield, *Cognitive Vulnerability: A Model of the Etiology of Fear*, 26 Clinical Psychol. Rev. 746 (2006).

[66] Aaron T. Beck, Gary Emery & Ruth L. Greenberg, *Anxiety Disorders and Phobias: A Cognitive Perspective* (rev. ed. 2005).

in appraisal terms. An appraisal tendency or bias creates a vulnerability to experience the emotion that corresponds to the social-cognitive pattern activated by the individual.[67]

As mentioned, however, the law has been theoretically inconsistent in its treatment of emotional states as excusing conditions. Whereas the heat-of-passion/provocation defense may mitigate murder to manslaughter if the killing is demonstrated to have been committed during intense anger or rage, fear is not recognized in either self-defense or duress. Its absence from legitimate (as opposed to mistaken) self-defense is quite sensible, of course, in that legitimate self-defense is widely accepted as a justification defense. Unlike with excuses, individual differences in rational capacity are entirely irrelevant to justifications. However, the paradoxical role of fear in duress is puzzling – although the emotion is not a requisite of the defense, it is hard to understand the defense without placing the defendant's behavior in a fear or terror context.

As discussed in the previous chapter, it is sensible to account for nonculpably formed cognitive bias in the case of the reactive killer who nonreasonably judges a social stimulus to be seriously provocative. In such a case, the killer has not caused his interpretational bias, nor is it reasonably foreseeable how said bias may contribute to a reactive killing. Here, the defendant's emotional disturbance is every bit as real and potentially problematic as in the case of the manslaughter killer who successfully meets criteria for the heat-of-passion/provocation defense.

A similar case may be made for the duress defendant who has a social-cognitive vulnerability such that he is particularly susceptible to an extreme fear or terror response to a stimulus event that is open to an interpretation that it poses a serious and imminent threat. As with heat of passion/provocation, of course, the law does not recognize this type of psychological deficiency as an excuse. Indeed, the law is even less likely to accept the social-cognitive bias argument with respect to the role of fear in duress because a duress defendant technically does not need to experience or show evidence of fear to benefit from the protection provided by the defense. This does not make the argument any less sensible, of course. It only highlights another problem that arises from the criminal law's theoretical inconsistency.

One area of research critical to this argument is the effect of fear on response decision processing. Does fear direct how an individual evaluates response

67 For a discussion of cognitive vulnerability as a foundation of fear, see Jason M. Armfield, *Cognitive Vulnerability: A Model of the Etiology of Fear*, 26 Clinical Psychol. Rev. 746 (2006).

options to a perceived threat? If so, is such direction adaptive or maladaptive, and does it vary by degree of the fear response elicited? In the case of extreme fear or terror, can such an emotional condition cause such a significant discounting of response decision processes that it reduces response decision making to an automatic acceptance of the first response identified? Social-cognitive research that considers threat paradigms and examines the interplay of emotion and response decision processing should prove highly useful to not only answering these questions, but taking a step forward as to the utility of social developmental and social-cognitive psychology to criminal-law theory and law reform.

8

Developmental Social Cognition, the Effects of Chronic Abuse and Trauma, and Reactive Homicide

When sentences are divorced from the experiences of the individual offender, the justice of punishment is undermined.[1]

The opening quote by Professor Leigh Goodmark captures a key issue in cases of individuals who, as an indirect effect of being battered, traumatized, or otherwise victimized, kill. The word *indirect* here is critical in that it acknowledges a key distinction between instrumental and defensive-reactive killings and also highlights the importance of understanding the effects of chronic abuse and trauma and how said effects may *mediate* the relation between victimization experiences and the defendant's ultimate commission of homicide. That is, even in the case in which defensive violence is clearly not necessary, psychological changes that take place as a result of being subjected to chronic abuse may create the convincing picture that it is. In this chapter, I briefly distinguish three categories of defensive-reactive killings by abused individuals – justifiable, excusable, and punishable – and explain how the second of these three categories, of the excusing variety, may be more properly understood by drawing from research in developmental social cognition and abuse and trauma.

[1] Leigh Goodmark, *The Punishment of Dixie Shanahan: Is There Justice for Battered Women Who Kill?*, 55 KAN. L. REV. 269, 315–16 (2007). Whereas Professor Goodmark makes a convincing case that sentences for battered women who kill are, at least at times (if not often), unjust, she leaves open the question as to whether these killings should be viewed as partially or fully justified or excused. Nevertheless, this quote is taken from a section of her article that recognizes the potential social-cognitive effects of trauma – namely how being subject to escalating abuse may affect the accuracy of one's perceptions of danger – and, as such, speaks to the issue of whether trauma-based social-cognitive dysfunction should be an excusing condition in the case of reactive homicide when committed by one who has been chronically victimized.

KILLINGS BY CHRONICALLY ABUSED INDIVIDUALS

A Hybrid of Instrumental and Reactive Violent Subtypes

In Chapter 6, a parallel of the instrumental/reactive violence subtypes model in behavioral science and the distinction between murder and heat-of-passion manslaughter in law was drawn. In Chapter 7, a further dichotomization of the reactive antisocial subtype in the forms of hostile-reactive and defensive-reactive violence was drawn to explore how empirical findings from psychology may be useful to mistaken self-defense and duress. In the present chapter, however, a type of reactive violence that is perhaps even more complicated, in both its nature and structure, than those discussed in the previous two chapters is recognized. That is, although often premeditated or even carefully planned, killings by abused individuals do not fall neatly into the subtype of instrumental violence, such as cold-blooded murder-one killings do; and although they are committed in response to a perceived wrong and out of an interest in self-preservation, they do not completely fit the mold of hostile- or defense-reactive violence either, such as in the case of heat-of-passion manslaughter or self-defense. Rather, there are some types of violent conduct that are more properly described as subtype hybrids in that they share some characteristics of both instrumental and reactive violence.

To illustrate, let us consider, for the moment, acts of revenge. Revenge acts involve factors associated with instrumental violence in that they are typically the product of significant cognitive effort and are planned over time prior to enactment. Whereas the revenge actor may push forward in large part because of hostile rumination, the revenge act is not usually committed in the context of high emotional arousal as are quintessential acts of reactive violence. However, revenge is, by its nature, reactive. The revenge actor is responding to a perceived provocation, threat, or otherwise aversive stimulus. In addition, revenge acts may include both instrumental and reactive goals. On the one hand, the revenge actor may intend to hurt those who she perceives to have hurt her (reactive). On the other hand, she may also act in the interest of gaining attention, as well as social status and power, perhaps by intimidating and instilling fear in others (instrumental). In this way, revenge violence incorporates aspects of both instrumental and reactive subtypes.

Acts of terrorism can also share instrumental and reactive violence features. A terrorist bombing may be calmly considered, planned, and nonemotionally and nonimpulsively engaged. However, it may also be a response to a perceived wrong, typically against an entity perceived to embody a particular social, cultural, religious, or political ideology. Here again, terrorist acts are usually guided by mixed motives. There is the interest to hurt the individual or group who the terrorist perceives to have first acted wrongly, but there is also the interest to gain power and domination.

Some scholars have cited that because some acts of violence are based on mixed motives, and thus do not neatly fit either the instrumental or reactive violence subtype, this undermines the utility of the violence subtypes model.[2] I disagree with this position for a number of reasons. First, the dichotomy was never espoused to capture *all* instances or forms of aggression. To say that humans are complicated psychological creatures is to understate the tremendous complexity that is human mental and behavioral functioning. In addition to the instrumental/reactive distinction, there are numerous dichotomous models of aggression in behavioral science – overt/covert,[3] physical/verbal,[4] overt/relational,[5] adolescence-limited/life-course-persistent,[6] socialized/undersocialized,[7] and so forth – and not a one of them promises to perfectly categorize all instances or forms of aggression. Rather, these and other dichotomies of antisocial conduct are presented to demonstrate trends such that relations between psychological functioning and behavior may be organized and understood, with the recognition that there will be variability among aggressive acts and actors both within and across subtypes.

More important to present interests, however, is that the instrumental/reactive violence subtypes model remains highly useful to understanding functional differences of criminal conduct so that it may be properly assessed and

[2] Brad J. Bushman & Craig A. Anderson, *Is It time to Pull the Plug on the Hostile Versus Instrumental Aggression Dichotomy?*, 108 PSYCHOL. REV. 273, 276 (2001).

[3] E.g., Alan E. Kazdin, *Overt and Covert Antisocial Behavior: Child and Family Characteristics Among Psychiatric Inpatient Children*, 1 J. CHILD & FAMILY STUD. 1, 3 (1992); Rolf Loeber & Dale Hay, *Key Issues in the Development of Aggression and Violence from Childhood to Early Adulthood*, 48 ANN. REV. PSYCHOL. 371 (1997).

[4] E.g., Gary L. Shope, Terry E. Hedrick & Russell G. Geen, *Physical/Verbal Aggression: Sex Differences in Style*, 46 J. PERSONALITY 23 (1978); John Tisak, Amanda M. Maynard & Marie S. Tisak, *AIRA: Measurement of Adolescents' Judgments Regarding Intentions to Respond to Physical and Verbal Aggression*, 28 AGGRESSIVE BEHAV. 207 (2002).

[5] E.g., Nicki R. Crick & Jennifer K. Grotpeter, *Relational Aggression, Gender, and Social-Psychological Adjustment*, 66 CHILD DEV. 710 (1995); Nicki R. Crick & Jennifer K. Grotpeter, *Children's Treatment by Peers: Victims of Relational and Overt Aggression*, 8 DEV. & PSYCHOPATHOLOGY 367 (1996).

[6] E.g., Avshalom Caspi & Thomas E. Moffitt, *The Continuity of Maladaptive Behavior: From Description to Understanding in the Study of Antisocial Behavior*, *in* 2 DEVELOPMENTAL PSYCHOPATHOLOGY: RISK, DISORDER, AND ADAPTATION 472 (Dante Cicchetti & Donald J. Cohen eds., 1995); Thomas E. Moffitt, *Life-Course-Persistent and Adolescence-Limited Antisocial Behavior: A Developmental Taxonomy*, 100 PSYCHOL. REV. 674 (1993).

[7] E.g., Herbert C. Quay, Donald K. Routh & Steven K. Shapiro, *Psychopathology of Childhood: From Description to Validation*, 38 ANN. REV. PSYCHOL. 491 (1987).

processed in the criminal legal system.[8] As has been discussed in the previous two chapters, the law treats instrumental and reactive criminal acts differently. Although a criminal act may have aspects of both instrumental and reactive violence, a determination of the act's wrongfulness, as well as to what degree the defendant should be punished for having committed it, may be made based on the fact finder's assessment of the instrumental versus reactive qualities of the act and determining their balance. For instance, was the motive greed or to harm a perceived wrongdoer? To what extent was the act calculated? May the act be explained, at least in part, by the effect that an aversive stimulus, such as a provocation or threat, had on the defendant's rational functioning, or the degree to which said harmful stimulus disrupted the natural moral balance between the stimulus actor and defendant? Even when a defendant is unable to successfully realize exculpation in her invocation of an affirmative defense, an examination of these and similar issues may lead to a reduced punishment at sentencing.

Hybrid forms of violence are often overlooked in discussions of reactive violence,[9] and they are not well understood. This may explain to some degree why killings by abused individuals are inconsistently treated in the common law. Recognition that some forms of reactive violence do indeed have qualities that are characteristically instrumental is essential to the present discussion, because killings by abused individuals often have this hybrid structure. That is, whereas the goal may be self-preservation – a naturally defensive-reactive motivation – the act may also be the product of preparation and planning, which is usual to instrumental violence. In this way, this chapter is a natural extension to Chapter 7, which dealt with pure examples of reactive violence in response to (at least perceived) threats.

A *Note about Battered Woman Syndrome and Battered Woman Defense*

This point is perhaps most easily illustrated in cases in which women who have been abused by their romantic partners kill their paramours in nonconfrontational contexts in which defensive violence is not immediately necessary. "Battered woman defense" (or BWD) has been compared and contrasted

[8] *See* Reid G. Fontaine, *Disentangling the Psychology and Law of Instrumental and Reactive Subtypes of Aggression*, 13 PSYCHOL. PUB. POL'Y & L. 143 (2007).

[9] Maaike Kempes, Walter Matthys, Han de Vries & Herman van Engeland, *Reactive and Proactive Aggression in Children: A Review of Theory, Findings and the Relevance for Child and Adolescent Psychiatry*, 14 EUR. CHILD & ADOLESCENT PSYCHIATRY 11 (2005). Also, for a discussion of revenge, see Neil Vidmar, *Retribution and Revenge, in* HANDBOOK OF JUSTICE RESEARCH IN LAW 31 (Joseph Sanders & V. Lee Hamilton eds., 2000).

with several affirmative defenses that have a long history in Anglo-American criminal law, including – but not limited to – self-defense,[10] imperfect self-defense,[11] heat of passion/provocation,[12] diminished capacity,[13] insanity,[14] and duress.[15] It is not unusual for BWD cases to share attributes with each of these defenses. However, persistent disagreement among courts and academics as to which, if any, of the traditional affirmative defenses on the preceding list cover killings by battered persons suggests that BWD is not neatly embodied by any of these defenses.[16] That is, depending on the specific fact pattern at hand, whereas BWD may share some characteristics of each of these traditional defenses, it does not cleanly match any of them. Of course, if it did, then any movement in favor of a new defense (such as BWD) would likely never have gained any momentum.

BWD draws from literatures in clinical psychology and psychiatry that propose and discuss a condition called "battered woman syndrome" (or BWS).[17] The BWD argument, as it is generally stated, is that one who suffers from BWS may exhibit various maladaptive symptoms as a direct result of being subjected to chronic abuse by a romantic partner, including low self-esteem,

[10] *See, e.g.*, Alafair S. Burke, *Rational Actors, Self-Defense, and Duress: Making Sense, Not Syndromes, Out of the Battered Woman*, 81 N.C. L. REV. 211 (2002); Phyllis L. Crocker, *The Meaning of Equality for Battered Women Who Kill Men in Self-Defense*, 8 HARV. WOMEN'S L.J. 121 (1985); CYNTHIA K. GILLESPIE, *JUSTIFIABLE HOMICIDE: BATTERED WOMEN, SELF DEFENSE, AND THE LAW* (1990).

[11] *See, e.g.*, Donald L. Creach, *Notes: Partially Determined Imperfect Self-Defense: The Battered Wife Kills and Tells Why*, 34 STAN. L. REV. 615 (1982).

[12] *See, e.g.*, Donald Nicolson & Rohit Sanghvi, *Battered Women and Provocation: The Implications of* R. v Ahluwalia, CRIM. L. REV. 728 (1993); Keith Rix, *"Battered Woman Syndrome" and the Defence of Provocation: Two Women with Something More in Common*, 12 J. FORENSIC PSYCHIATRY & PSYCHOL. 131 (2001).

[13] *See, e.g.*, Joshua Dressler, *Battered Women and Sleeping Abusers: Some Reflections*, 3 OHIO ST. J. CRIM. L. 457 (2006) [hereinafter Dressler, *Battered Women*]; ELIZABETH M. SCHNEIDER, *BATTERED WOMEN AND FEMINIST LAWMAKING* 160–68 (2000).

[14] *See, e.g.*, Dressler, *Battered Women, supra* note 13; Anna F. Kuhl & Inger Sagatun, *Emergence of the Battered Woman Syndrome: The Impact Upon the Legal System*, 12 AM. J. CRIM. JUST. 94 (1987).

[15] *See, e.g.*, Burke, *supra* note 10; Laurie Kratky Dore, *Downward Adjustment and the Slippery Slope: The Use of Duress in Defense of Battered Offenders*, 56 OHIO. ST. L.J. 65, 732–33 (1995); Dressler, *Battered Women, supra* note 13.

[16] For example, in their consideration of killings by battered women as cases of self-defense or heat of passion/provocation, Professors Jim Sherman and Joe Hoffman were forced to conclude: "The battered wife would seem to fall somewhere between voluntary manslaughter and self-defense, and thus benefit from neither." Steven J. Sherman & Joseph L. Hoffman, *The Psychology and Law of Voluntary Manslaughter: What Can Psychology Research Teach Us about the "Heat of Passion" Defense?*, 20 J. BEHAV. DECISION MAKING 499, 512 (2007).

[17] The name of this "condition" has varied across time and by source. Also, its validity remains questioned and debated by behavioral scientists.

depression, learned helplessness, and the inability to take independent or even assisted action to escape the abuse. The battered woman may develop a rigid belief system by which she is convinced that (1) her paramour will ultimately kill her (perhaps because of the increasing frequency and/or severity of abuse); (2) there is no way to escape her abuser; and (3) based on beliefs (1) and (2), the only way to realize self-preservation is by killing her abuser. The very discussion of whether reactive killing by the battered woman is exculpable was born of the law's attention to and promotion of this "syndrome." Defenses that attempt to excuse the battered woman of her killing – whether the defense is *called* self-defense, battered-woman defense, or something else – is naturally dependent on the notion that psychological dysfunction (or substandard rationality) may serve as a mechanism of legal excuse. This is not to say, of course, that this excuse-based depiction of killings by battered women is always appropriate. Whether the most fitting defense is a justification or excuse is dictated by the facts of the case. In the excuse scenario, however, any psychologically legitimate legal argument for or against a "battered person" defense must account for the empirical research on the effects of abuse and trauma on individual social-cognitive and emotional functioning.[18]

It may be that a proper defense based on chronic abuse should more broadly account for developmental findings on the psychological effects of victimization. Although historically abuse cases typically involve battered[19] (or abused, traumatized, tortured) women, I should caution that this language is problematic for at least two significant reasons. First, BWS, which is often the basis for BWD, is not a scientifically established condition or medically accepted psychiatric disorder,[20] although it is sometimes associated with post-traumatic stress disorder (PTSD),[21] a recognized psychiatric illness that has found considerable

18 *See, e.g.*, Jonathon R. Davidson & Edna B. Foa, *Diagnostic Issues in Posttraumatic Stress Disorder: Considerations for the DSM-IV*, 100 J. ABNORMAL PSYCHOL. 346 (1991); Anne P. DePrince, *Social Cognition and Revictimization Risk*, 6 J. TRAUMA & DISSOCIATION 125 (2005); Kenneth A. Dodge, John E. Bates & Gregory S. Pettit, *Mechanisms in the Cycle of Violence*, 250 SCIENCE 1678 (1990).

19 A thorough reading of the case histories may leave one with the sense that the word *battered* is inadequate. Indeed, *traumatized* and *tortured* would seem to be more fitting in many cases.

20 *See* AMERICAN PSYCHIATRIC ASSOCIATION, *DIAGNOSTIC AND STATISTICAL MANUAL OF MENTAL DISORDERS* (4th ed., text rev. 2000) [hereinafter AM. PSYCHIATRIC ASS'N.].

21 For example, some mental health experts refer to BWS as a "subcategory" of PTSD (*e.g.*, Lenore E. Walker, *Battered Woman Syndrome: Key Elements of a Diagnosis and Treatment Plan*, 26 PSYCHIATRIC TIMES [2009]), although it is not listed by name in the DSM-IV-TR (2000), but merely a reference to "domestic battering" in the discussion of Associated Features and Disorders of PTSD. AM. PSYCHIATRIC ASS'N., *supra* note 20, at 465.

support in empirical psychology.[22] PTSD is a disorder by which, as a result of suffering a traumatic event, a person's psychological integrity is compromised and she experiences extreme anxiety when her trauma is triggered by environmental cues.[23] Whether BWS is discernible from or may be a specific type of PTSD is unclear. Can chronic abuse at the hands of a paramour cause a psychologically impairing, painful condition? Indeed it can, but until BWS is scientifically determined, PTSD and related psychiatric conditions (e.g., mood disorders such as major depressive disorder[24]) are more appropriate to serve as the psychiatric foundation of defenses that argue that abuse and trauma experiences may cause impairment to one's rational capacity.

Second, there is no good reason why a defense that is predicated on a history of the defendant being chronically abused should be limited to women. The fact that most cases involve a female defendant is irrelevant to the reality that being subject to chronic abuse and trauma has the potential to place all individuals in life-threatening danger and cause critical psychological damage. There is no scientific evidence that suggests that females are any more prone to the negative consequences of chronic abuse than are males. As discussed later in the chapter, the developmental effects of abuse, neglect, and victimization are attributable to males and females alike. As such, it is more appropriate to consider the role of trauma and its effects with respect to abused *individuals* who kill in general and not with respect to sex.

One class of cases, involving the issue of whether the effects of chronic abuse may serve to mitigate the defendant's culpability and punishment, which has been nonspecific to the defendant's sex is that of youth killers. Cases in which the defense has moved to admit evidence of "battered child syndrome" or some like "condition" or term, in fact, often involve a male defendant.[25] Of course, there is no reason to believe that the harmful psychological effects of being repeatedly abused on males is limited to when they are of minor status. Nor is it proper to limit the attribution of such effects to relationships that are "romantic." Indeed, there is no good argument against considering the effects of abuse on a reactive killer in any situation in which the defendant killed her or his "victim"[26] in the context of an oppressive relationship, regardless of the

[22] *See* HANDBOOK OF PTSD: SCIENCE AND PRACTICE (Matthew J. Friedman, Terence M. Keane & Patricia A. Resick eds., 2007).

[23] AM. PSYCHIATRIC ASS'N., *supra* note 20, at 463–68.

[24] *Id.* at 369–76.

[25] *See, e.g.*, State v. MacLennan, 702 N.W.2d 219 (Minn. 2005). Also, for an analysis and discussion of this case, see Julie M. Amato & Ira K. Packer, *Battered-Child Syndrome: Admissibility of Expert Testimony on "Syndrome Evidence" Properly Determined Through Application of Minnesota Rule of Evidence 702, Not the Frye-Mack Standard*, 34 J. AM. ACAD. PSYCHIATRY & L. 414 (2006).

[26] I have placed the word "victim" in quotes here because cases in which chronically abused individuals kill involve two victims – that is, the abused defendant was a victim before she

sex of the defendant, and regardless of whether the relationship between the defendant and the victim was romantic.

KILLINGS BY BATTERED PERSONS: SHOULD THE BOUNDARIES OF JUSTIFIABLE HOMICIDE BE EXPANDED?

There are three primary categories by which killings by abused individuals may be organized – those that are justifiable, those that are excusable, and those for which there exists no justification or excuse and which are thus culpable and punishable.[27] Justifiable cases are those in which the killer has acted rightfully or, at least, not wrongfully. A clear example of a justification case in the battered-person context is that of the chronically abused individual who kills her abuser immediately prior to or in the course of a violent attack that poses an imminent risk of grievous bodily harm or death. Here, the killer may be justified in her act as long as she meets criteria for self-defense, a justification defense. It may be argued that her history of being abused is irrelevant to whether her act is justified in that she acted rightfully regardless of whether she had been previously abused by her victim. However, the defendant's history of being abused may be relevant to whether her belief that she faced a wrongful, imminent threat of grievous bodily harm or death at the hands of her attacker was reasonable.[28] This is so because the traditional common-law framing of self-defense requires that the killer's belief only be reasonable, and not valid, and different courts have viewed the boundaries of this "objective" standard differently.

made a victim out of her abuser. With this recognized, the term "victim" is hereafter used to refer to the abuser who was killed by the defendant.

27 As discussed in previous chapters, such acts of violence may be further categorized as partially justifiable and/or excusable, as well. I have elsewhere provided a taxonomy of defensive and defense-like reactive killings according to both justification/excuse/blameworthy and complete/partial classifications – see Reid G. Fontaine, *An Attack on Self-Defense*, 47 Am. Crim. L. Rev. 57 (2010).

28 The defendant's abuse history may be considered when evaluating the reasonableness of the killer's belief that she was faced with a wrongful and imminent mortal threat in jurisdictions that recognize a (somewhat) subjectivized version of the reasonable-person standard such that certain characteristics of the individual defendant may be taken into account when determining the reasonableness with which she acted. That is, if a jurisdiction's reasonable-person standard allows for the fact finder to consider whether a reasonable person "in a similar situation to that of the defendant" would have judged the threat similarly, the fact finder may consider the abuse history of the defendant as part of the "similar situation to that of the defendant." For example, see *People v. Humphrey*, 13 Cal. 4th 1073, 1083–84 (Cal. 1996), in which the court ruled that the defendant's past experiences and perceptions could be considered in determining a reasonable fear of imminent harm. Also, see Janet Grumer's *Note* discussing expansion of imminence in cases of battered women who kill. Janet Grumer, *Self-Defense*, 36 Loy. L.A. Rev. 1575, 1578–80 (2003).

Excusable cases are ones in which the defendant may be said to have acted criminally wrongfully, but her homicidal act is understandable due to certain subjective characteristics of the social context or her individual makeup. A clear example of such a case is one in which the threat of future abuse by her attacker may be eliminated by contacting law enforcement or leaving the abusive relationship for a safe haven. In such cases, the defendant's experiences of chronic abuse and trauma at the hands of her attacker may have created a psychological condition by which the defendant genuinely and rigidly, albeit mistakenly, believes that her only means to self-preserve is to kill her abuser. Because this distorted belief system emerged out of being subject to repeated victimization for which the defendant may not be attributed causal responsibility, the defendant may be said to be excused for her objectively wrongful, homicidal act. The question of whether the defendant should be excused of killing her abuser often arises in nonconfrontational cases – that is, cases in which the defendant kills her abuser when a beating is not "imminent"[29] or in process.

Finally, punishable cases are those in which the defendant had alternative means by which to self-preserve (e.g., involving law enforcement, removing herself from the abusive context to a safe haven), was aware of such alternative means and was understanding of their protective utility, but nevertheless chose to kill her attacker. Here, not only does the defendant have reasonable means by which she can prevent or avoid the abuse, but she has not developed the type of distorted belief system by which she is unable to recognize them or appreciate their utility. Because she could have otherwise prevented or avoided the continued threat posed to her by her attacker, she is unable to claim a justification. And because she was not psychologically affected as a direct result of the abuse such that she could not identify or appreciate the utility of these alternative means, she is unable to move forward on excuse grounds, as well. In such a case, some meaningful degree of culpability and punishability may be assigned.

[29] A threat that is imminent is one that is on the verge of being realized, or is "about to happen." *See* Whitley R. P. Kaufman, *Self-Defense, Imminence, and the Battered Woman*, 10 New Crim. L. Rev. 342, 342 (2007); For a review of other language that has been used to describe imminence, see Joshua Dressler, *Understanding Criminal Law* 232–34 (5th ed. 2009). "In the context of self-defense, force is said to be 'imminent' if it will occur 'immediately,' or 'at the moment of … danger.' The danger must be 'pressing and urgent.'" *Id.* at 232 (footnotes omitted); *see also* Dressler, *Battered Women*, *supra* note 13, at 461 ("The traditional rule, which still prevails in most jurisdictions, is that self-protective force can only be used to repel an *ongoing* unlawful attack or what the defender reasonably believes is an *imminent* unlawful assault; and 'imminent' or 'immediate' has come to mean that the attack will occur momentarily, that it is just about underway. By definition, of course, no assault is taking place or imminent in nonconfrontational cases.") (footnotes omitted).

Of course, many cases of killings by abused individuals do not fall neatly into these three categories as I have here outlined them. In such cases, the question of how to view the defendant's conduct is met with heated debate. In particular, the classification of "nonconfrontational" killings by abused individuals is often disputed. In nonconfrontational killings, the abused defendant does not kill her attacker during an attack or in response to an imminent threat of an attack. The question thus arises: May the defendant who has killed in defense of a nonimminent mortal threat be justified? If so, has the defendant killed in self-defense or by some other justification defense? If not, should a new justification defense be recognized? Or, alternatively, should the defendant be excused of her homicidal act, perhaps because she acted out of a distorted belief system that developed as a result of being chronically abused? If so, what are the necessary and sufficient conditions? If not, then to what degree should the defendant be held responsible and punished? It is not unusual in nonconfrontational killings by abused individuals for all three perspectives – justifiable, excusable, and blameworthy/punishable – to be espoused by various entities, including parties for the state and defendant, jurors, academics, activists, and the public at large.

Regarding BWD as justification, the usual and perhaps obvious comparison is with self-defense. As discussed in Chapter 7, common-law self-defense requires, among other conditions, that (1) the defendant honestly and reasonably believed that she was faced with an *imminent* threat of grievous bodily harm or death, and (2) the defendant honestly and reasonably believed that lethal force was *necessary* to combat said threat. Here I highlight these conditions because they represent the primary distinctions by which legal scholars contrast traditional self-defense from nonconfrontational killings by battered persons.[30] That is, in nonconfrontational homicide situations, the question of how the defendant may be said to have acted justifiably in the absence of an imminent threat of grievous bodily harm or death naturally and immediately arises.

Although it may be difficult to balance imminence in the traditional sense with nonconfrontational killings by abused individuals – in that the mortal threat was not immediately about to be realized – let us consider the following hypothetical in which the boundaries of imminence may be reassessed. In this example, a woman (Susan) kills her abusive male partner (Jason) while he is taking his usual afternoon nap. She has been subject to his repeated beatings, a pattern that has increased at an accelerated rate in both frequency and severity. The most dangerous beatings typically occur immediately after

[30] *See, e.g.*, Kaufman, *supra* note 29.

Jason awakes from his afternoon naps. Susan has attempted to engage law enforcement in the past, but has been unsuccessful, largely because Jason has close friends in the police department. Since her last call to the police, Jason has eliminated Susan's access to phone and all other means of communication. She has also left home several times, only to be repeatedly discovered and physically forced to return by Jason as they live in a rural area in which Jason is well connected. Susan does not have transportation independent of Jason, and the nearest train and bus stations are a considerable distance from their home. Some of the most egregious beatings suffered by Susan have occurred immediately following her attempts to involve law enforcement or leave home, as Jason has regarded such actions as betrayals. On the day of the homicide, and immediately prior to retiring for his afternoon nap, Jason promised that he would kill Susan before the day's end. Although Susan had never previously planned to kill Jason, she noticed on the day of the killing that Jason, quite unusually, had left his gun cabinet unlocked. Upon realizing that she had access to a loaded gun, and recognizing that Jason could awaken at any time, she retrieved one of Jason's guns and shot and killed him while he lay sleeping, in the committed belief that if she did not, Jason would surely kill her upon awakening.

In this hypothetical scenario, it could be argued that Susan lives in a constant state of imminence. At first, this idea may seem oxymoronic. However, Susan has no legitimate means by which she can avoid being subject to Jason's escalating pattern of abuse toward her. She cannot withstand his beatings on her own. Law enforcement has demonstrated that it offers no protection, and even if this were not so, Susan no longer has any means by which she can contact law enforcement. Retreating from the home has proven futile. Indeed, any attempt to secure assistance from law enforcement or leave home has only resulted in more serious abuse. Although Susan is not locked in their home, for all intents and purposes she is a prisoner there. These facts, coupled with the reality that the beatings are following an accelerated trajectory of frequency and severity, may support an argument that Susan lives in a constant state in which she is faced with imminent threat of grievous bodily harm or death, and lethal force is necessary to prevent Jason from wrongfully taking her life.

This hypothetical is, of course, designed to place into question the traditional boundaries of self-defense as applied to cases of homicide by battered persons. In her review of external factors that may inhibit battered women from leaving their abusers,[31] Professor Ola Barnett outlined a number of

[31] Here, "external" means *extra*personal or outside of the person and should be understood in contrast with internal or *intra*personal factors such as one's psychological makeup or

objective conditions that have been documented as obstacles to nonhomicidal alternatives to self-protection from ongoing domestic abuse in romantic relationships.[32] Barnett reviews empirical evidence that abused individuals often (1) have no legitimate safe haven to which to retreat;[33] (2) have insufficient economic means to survive outside of the abusive home;[34] (3) are afforded little to no protection from law enforcement;[35] and (4) are sometimes not served by the orders of protection that were designed to prevent further victimization.[36] As illustrated by the Susan and Jason hypothetical, these factors, in combination, may provide that a battered individual has no legitimate means by which she can protect herself from the chronic abuse she suffers at the hands of her domestic partner outside of defensive violence.

Opponents of expanding self-defense doctrine to including any type of nonconfrontational killing by abused individuals may argue that the threat posed by Jason cannot be reasonably deemed imminent because he was sleeping. That is, outside of somnambulism, or being subject to some other form of automatism (e.g., hypnotic state), and perhaps a few other exceptionally unusual circumstances (e.g., being used by a third party as a human weapon), how may it be that a person poses an *imminent* mortal threat to another if the former is unconscious? Likewise, opponents of the "constant state of imminence" position may argue that killing Jason was not *necessary* to prevent his mortal threat from being carried out because Susan could have left the home;[37] or,

subjective state of mind. Whereas the former class lends itself to a justification argument based on objective conditions of the homicide in question, the latter class has to do with individual, subjective differences that may go to the issue of possible subrationality and thus bears relevance to an excuse argument.

32 Ola W. Barnett, *Why Battered Women Do Not Leave, Part 1: External Inhibiting Factors within Society*, 1 TRAUMA, VIOLENCE, & ABUSE 343 (2000) [hereinafter Barnett, *Part 1*]; Ola W. Barnett, *Why Battered Women Do Not Leave, Part 2: External Inhibiting Factors – Social Support and Internal Inhibiting Factors*, 2 TRAUMA VIOLENCE & ABUSE 3 (2001) [hereinafter Barnett, *Part 2*]. Readers will recognize that several characteristics of the Susan and Jason hypothetical reflect a range of empirical findings discussed by Barnett in these two review articles.

33 Barnett, *Part 1*, *supra* note 32, at 346–47.

34 Barnett, *Part 2*, *supra* note 32, at 347–49. Barnett points out that some abused individuals are strictly economically dependent on their abusers, largely because of the conditions created by the abuser that restrict the abused individual from acquiring independent monetary resources.

35 Barnett, *Part 1*, *supra* note 32, at 349–54. Barnett points out that some police officers are batterers themselves. *See id.* at 352.

36 *Id.* at 358–59.

37 This argument seems weak, however, as Susan can hardly be expected to remain away from home long before being discovered, ultimately leading to Jason physically forcing her to return and then beating her ever more severely. Even if she finds an unusually promising place to hide, how long may it reasonably be expected that she should survive, and in what conditions? This possibility seems even less promising in the case of the battered person who

alternatively, that the necessity of the killing cannot be demonstrated because there exists the possibility that the abuse would suddenly and permanently desist.[38] Nevertheless, such opposition is not as persuasive in nonconfrontational killings that mirror or at least approach the Susan and Jason hypothetical because the facts in such cases indicate that but for the defendant's mortal defensive force, the abuser's wrongful killing of the defendant would have been *inevitable*.[39] And so it may be argued that Susan has no legitimate alternative to killing Jason because there is no other way to prevent his escalating pattern of abuse from ultimately resulting in the wrongful taking of her life.

Thus there would seem to be a plausible argument that the nonconfrontational homicide case presented in the Susan and Jason hypothetical is justified. Actual nonconfrontational homicide cases, however, typically differ from this hypothetical in one or more meaningful ways. For example, perhaps the abused individual has not exploited potential law enforcement assistance, or has a legitimate safe haven to which she may retreat.[40] Although there may be no nonconfrontational homicide case that matches this hypothetical with precision, there are ones that approach it, ones for which the objective conditions that define the reactive killing contribute, albeit perhaps

is the only agent who can adequately look after and care for her children (an issue that poses the battered person both practical and legal obstacles).

[38] As Professor Joshua Dressler has noted, "The more we permit early force, the greater the risk that the force used was not necessary.... After all, there is the slight possibility ... that the batterer will change his behavior if permitted to live." Dressler, *Battered Women*, *supra* note 13, at 467. Case histories of killings by battered women typically suggest that this "slight possibility" is not meaningfully different from zero. That is, there is generally an abundance of evidence promising that future abuse is all but absolutely certain. Nevertheless, Dressler is correct that it is possible, however slight the possibility may be, and that permitting early force is done at the risk of falling victim to a slippery slope.

[39] Some scholars question the value of the imminence requirement. If a threat truly necessitates lethal defensive force, why is it that the defender should have to wait for the threat to be imminent? That is, if the threat of grievous bodily harm or death is truly *inevitable*, as it certainly appears to be in some cases of nonconfrontational homicide by battered persons, what does the imminence requirement contribute to the equation? If lethal defensive force is legitimately necessary, meaning that there is no other reasonable course of action in response to the threat, then necessity should suffice even in the absence of imminence. *See* Richard A. Rosen, *On Self-Defense, Imminence, and Women Who Kill Their Batterers*, 71 N.C. L. REV. 371 (1993); Burke, *supra* note 10. Here again, however, I would argue that said inevitability must be objectively real and not just reasonably believed to be real before any argument that self-defense doctrine should be expanded by abandoning the imminence requirement could be persuasive, at least with respect to self-defense as justification. *See* Reid G. Fontaine, *An Attack on Self-Defense*, 47 AM. CRIM. L. REV. 57 (2010).

[40] See, e.g., *State v. Shanahan*, Case No. FECR006475 (Iowa Dist. Ct., Shelby County, Apr. 30, 2004), in which the defendant repeatedly left her abuser for the safe havens of family and friends, only to return each time at his coaxing.

not sufficiently, to an argument that the killing by the battered woman was completely justified.[41]

DEVELOPMENTAL SOCIAL COGNITION AND NONCONFRONTATIONAL KILLINGS BY ABUSED PERSONS AS EXCUSE

Whereas it may prove difficult to convince courts that adhere strictly to traditional affirmative defenses that a nonconfrontational homicide is justified in even the most severe of abuse contexts, the justification argument can quickly become far more difficult (i.e., less plausible) in cases that substantially differ from the one illustrated in the Susan and Jason hypothetical. Even in clear "nonnecessity" cases of nonconfrontational killings by battered indivdiuals, however, there remains the question as to whether the defendant's act is excusable. One basis for excuse in such cases may be that, at the time of the killing, the defendant's psychological capacities were significantly compromised, for nonculpable reasons (i.e., psychological disturbance that was neither self-caused nor reasonably foreseeable), such that the defendant's rationality did not meet the standard presumed of adult actors by the law.

At the center of the history of BWD cases has been the issue of whether, as a result of being chronically abused, the defendant's rationality may have become impaired, and that such impairment may have played a causal role in her objectively criminal conduct. This issue has been couched in the context of BWS, which, as discussed, is problematic, from a scientific standpoint, at least insomuch as the "syndrome" is not professionally recognized in the medical community. Although the notion that being subject to chronic abuse and trauma can lead to the serious alteration of one's psychological faculties is an undisputed one, the range of the psychological effects remains an issue of some scientific and legal discussion.

In 1996, the U.S. Department of Justice commissioned a report that had, as one of its main impetuses, the mandate of comprehensively reviewing and assessing the range and validity of behavioral science research on the psychological effects of battering and abuse, as it relates to criminal trials.[42] At the outset, the report acknowledged that "[a]mong the most notable findings was the strong consensus among the researchers, and also among the judges,

[41] For example, a few cases that have received popular attention are these: *State v. Norman*, 366 S.E.2d 586 (N.C. Ct. App. 1988); *State v. Stewart*, 763 P.2d 572 (Kan. 1988); *State v. Shanahan*, 712 N.W.2d 121 (Iowa 2006).

[42] U.S. Dep't of Just., *The Validity and Use of Evidence Concerning Battering and Its Effects in Criminal Trials: Report Responding to Section 40507 of the Violence Against Women Act*, NJC 160972 (May 1996).

prosecutors, and defense attorneys interviewed for the assessment, that the term "battered woman syndrome" does not adequately reflect the breadth or nature of the scientific knowledge now available concerning battering and its effects."[43] The report addressed research on battered women's perceptions of danger and their mental states in which they killed, although it did not explore or review developmental research. Fifteen years have passed since the date of the report, and important developmental research as related to the psychological, emotional, behavioral, and social effects of being maltreated (physical abuse, rejection, and other forms of victimization) has been conducted during this time; some of this research has specifically focused on social-cognitive mediators and outcomes.

Considering the Effects of Abuse through a Developmental Lens

It is particularly important that *developmental* research on the effects of abuse and trauma be recognized in that the nature of killings by battered individuals is necessarily developmental. The fact pattern in such cases is characterized by the defendant having been subjected to recurrent abuse by another individual (or individuals) over a considerable period of time. As such, the developmental effects of being abused repeatedly over time are naturally relevant to understanding what causal role they may play in the defendant's ultimate decision to kill her abuser. The fact that the phenomenon in question is one that forms over a substantial period of time, it is naturally a developmental one, and thus should be informed by research that is, equally by its nature, developmental.

From a developmental perspective, the mediational role of social-cognitive functioning is critical. As a direct result of being subject to a chronic pattern of abuse, one may develop a rigid (or crystallized) belief system – whether valid or distorted[44] – by which she becomes certain that she will be killed by her abuser if she does not kill him first. Concluding that she has no alternative, she kills her abuser:

(1) Chronic Abuse by Batterer/Victim (X) →
(2) Defendant Develops New Perception and Beliefs (M) →
(3) Defendant Kills Batterer/Victim in Interest of Self-Preservation (Y)

[43] *Id.* at i–ii.

[44] In some cases, such as the one illustrated by the Susan and Jason hypothetical, such a belief may be valid, as it would seem the defendant has no legitimate alternative by which she can realize self-preservation. However, in cases in which there are alternatives, such as police intervention or leaving the abusive environment for a safe haven, a firm belief that there exists no alternative may nevertheless develop out of being subject to repeated beatings.

Any abuse defense characterized as an excuse must recognize this mediational sequence as it is on the mediational mechanism of altered social-cognitive processing (M) that the excuse arguments rests.

There is no question that being subject to repeated beatings may be experienced as a significant trauma. Nor is it disputed that said experience of trauma may cause a variety of harmful, rationally impairing, psychological alterations the effects of which may persist indefinitely. Indeed, it is not unusual for the repeated physical abuse to cause the psychiatric condition called post-traumatic stress disorder (PTSD).[45] PTSD is categorized by the Diagnostic and Statistical Manual of Mental Disorders (DSM-IV-TR) as an anxiety disorder, although it is a disorder that typically includes serious thought, mood, and behavioral problems, in addition to serious episodes of anxiety.[46] PTSD is characterized by the reliving or reexperiencing of a traumatic stressor by which the patient typically suffers a "direct personal experience of an event that involves actual or threatened death or serious injury, or other threat to one's physical integrity."[47] A person diagnosed with PTSD has demonstrated significant mood problems, such as intense fear or helplessness, and a pattern of behavior by which he tries to avoid stimuli associated with the traumatic event.

Although PTSD may develop out of a range of traumatic stressors, chronic physical abuse is one developmental etiology. The DSM-IV-TR notes this:

> The following associated constellation of symptoms may occur and are more commonly seen in association with an interpersonal stressor (e.g., *childhood sexual or physical abuse, domestic battering*): impaired affect modulation; self-destructive and impulsive behavior; dissociative symptoms; somatic complaints; feelings of ineffectiveness, shame, despair, or hopelessness, feeling permanently damaged; a loss of previously sustained beliefs; hostility; social withdrawal; feeling constantly threatened; impaired relationships with others; or a change from the individual's previously personality characteristics.[48]

Of course, not all individuals who suffer a chronic pattern of abuse are affected in the same way. Victims of abuse will vary in their symptomatology. As such, some will meet criteria for a diagnosis of PTSD, whereas others will not. Of course, even the victim of chronic abuse who does not meet criteria for PTSD may nevertheless develop psychological problems that may causally contribute

[45] Am. Psychiatric Ass'n., *supra* note 20, at 463–68.
[46] *Id.*
[47] *Id.* at 463.
[48] *Id.* at 465 (emphasis added).

to a distorted psychological state by which she comes to rigidly believe that the only way she can prevent her own wrongful death is to kill her abuser.

Among the symptoms associated with chronic physical abuse and domestic battering are key social-cognitive factors, namely hopelessness, a loss of previously sustained beliefs, and a processing tendency or interpretational style that favors feelings of hostility and a sense of constantly being threatened. These social-cognitive factors may be particularly important in understanding how some chronically abused individuals come to believe that killing their abusers is the only way to prevent their own wrongful deaths. They may also be critical in pointing to how an otherwise nonviolent individual may become capable of committing an act of violence so serious that another person's life is taken.

Developmental research on the social-cognitive and behavioral effects of victimization and abuse is crucial to understanding these links. Social-information processing (SIP) models may be used to organize and explain how these social-cognitive factors emerge and mature out of abuse experiences, as well as how distorted social cognition, in mediational turn, may lead to a variety of maladaptive behaviors, such as reactive killing. Although the developmental literature is primarily focused on children and adolescents, there is no reason to expect that the effects of chronic abuse on individuals in domestic battering contexts are any different. Indeed, the research does not identify any meaningful difference in the effects of chronic abuse and trauma between these two populations. It is for exactly this reason that the DSM-IV-TR, in its discussions of the psychological effects of interpersonal stressors, uses both "childhood sexual or physical abuse" and "domestic battering" as examples.

As discussed in Chapter 2, SIP models have been highly useful in accounting for variability in youths' social competence and interpersonal behavior.[49] These models have also been effective in predicting adult social behavior.[50]

[49] Nick R. Crick & Kenneth A. Dodge, *A Review and Reformulation of Social Information-Processing Mechanisms in Children's Social Adjustment*, 115 PSYCHOL. BULL. 74 (1994); Kenneth A. Dodge & David Schwartz, *Social Information-Processing Mechanisms in Aggressive Behavior*, *in* HANDBOOK OF ANTISOCIAL BEHAVIOR 171 (David M. Stoff, James Breiling & Jack D. Masur eds., 1997).

[50] *See, e.g.*, Kristina C. Gordon & Jennifer A. Christman, *Integrating Social Information Processing and Attachment Style Research with Cognitive-Behavioral Couple Therapy*, 38 J. CONTEMPORARY PSYCHOTHERAPY 129 (2008); Emil F. Coccaro, Kurtis L. Noblett & Michael S. McCloskey, *Attributional and Emotional Responses to Socially Ambiguous Cues: Validation of a New Assessment of Social/Emotional Information Processing in Healthy Adults and Impulsive Aggressive Patients*, 43 J. PSYCHIATRIC RES. 915 (2009); Gregory S. Pettit, Jennifer E. Lansford, Patrick S. Malone, Kenneth A. Dodge & John E. Bates, *Domain Specificity in Relationship History, Social-Information Processing, and Violent Behavior in Early Adulthood*, 98 J. PERSONALITY & SOC. PSYCHOL. 190 (2010).

In particular, SIP has been found to be useful in the prediction of individual differences in antisocial conduct.[51] SIP articulates a series of mental functions by which individuals process information in their social environments as it becomes accessible. SIP describes how individuals perceive and interpret incoming information, organize and store the information in memory, and use incoming information in conjunction with previously stored information to generate and consider alternative ways to respond to social events as they unfold.

Developmental research has found empirical support for SIP at each step of the model.[52] Especially strong support has been found with respect to two sets of social-cognitive processes – those having to do with interpretation of stimuli and response evaluation and decision (or RED) – and the enactment of antisocial behaviors. Interpretational processes involve making meaning of incoming social information such that the personal relevance and importance of the information can be determined. Response evaluation and decision (or RED) regards cognitive operations by which alternative ways of responding to social cues may be evaluated across qualitatively different domains so that a person may ultimately decide on a course of action. These two sets of processes have repeatedly been found to account for antisocial behavioral variability in a variety of youth samples (e.g., community, clinical, incarcerated).

The role of social cognition in the established developmental course between early physical abuse and later violence and antisocial behavior[53] may provide some understanding as to how chronically abused individuals may themselves become capable of killing. SIP operations have also been examined with respect to their relation to early maltreatment and victimization. In particular, empirical studies have shown that being subject to early harsh discipline and physical abuse places children at risk for developing SIP biases by which they interpret social stimuli ambiguous as to their content as provocative

[51] Crick & Dodge, *supra* note 49; Dodge & Schwartz, *supra* note 49.

[52] Crick & Dodge, *supra* note 49; Dodge & Schwartz, *supra* note 49.

[53] *See, e.g.*, Jennifer E. Lansford, Shari Miller-Johnson, Lisa J. Berlin, Kenneth A. Dodge & John E. Bates, *Early Physical Abuse and Later Violent Delinquency: A Prospective Longitudinal Study*, 12 Child Maltreatment 233 (2007); Jennifer E. Lansford, Kenneth A. Dodge, Gregory S. Pettit, John E. Bates, Joseph Crozier & Julie Kaplow, *A 12-Year Prospective Study of the Long-Term Effects of Early Child Physical Maltreatment on Psychological, Behavioral, and Academic Problems in Adolescence*, 156 Archives Pediatric & Adolescent Med. 824 (2002); Michael Lynch & Dante Cicchetti, *An Ecological–Transactional Analysis of Children and Contexts: The Longitudinal Interplay Among Child Maltreatment, Community Violence, and Children's Symptomatology*, 10 Dev. & Psychopathology 235 (1998); Magda Stouthamer-Loeber, Rolf Loeber, D. Lynn Homish & Evelyn H. Wei, *Maltreatment of Boys and the Development of Disruptive and Delinquent Behavior*, 13 Dev. & Psychopathology 941 (2001).

and hostile, view their social worlds as harmful, and make social judgments and behavioral evaluations that favor antisocial outcomes.[54]

The development science in this area is important because it can tell the story of how being abused may create aggressors out of victims over time. Two studies deserve special note. First, a longitudinal study in the late 1980s and early to mid-1990s, conducted as part of the Child Development Project,[55] found that these processing biases mediate the relation between being physically abused in childhood and exhibiting antisocial behavioral problems later in development.[56] Researchers followed a random sample of nearly 600 children from early kindergarten through grade school. They found that physical abuse was predictive of several types of biased social-cognitive functioning, including encoding and perceptual errors, being biased in favor of interpreting ambiguous stimuli as provocative and hostile, accessing aggressive response options to consider for behavioral enactment, and evaluating aggressive response options favorably. Youths' biased encoding and tendency to access aggressive response options, in mediational turn, were predictive of subsequent antisocial behavioral problems, significantly reducing the direct effect of experiences with harsh physical discipline on externalizing conduct outcomes. These effects were not otherwise accounted for by other ecological or social correlates. This study provided evidence that being physically abused may create a psychological profile that promotes antisocial conduct.

A later study examined social-cognitive and emotional factors that contributed to antisocial problems among maltreated children.[57] Although there were no main effects when comparing the normal and maltreated groups, children

[54] Bahr Weiss, Kenneth A. Dodge, John E. Bates & Gregory S. Pettit, *Some Consequences of Early Harsh Discipline: Child Aggression and a Maladaptive Social Information Processing Style*, 63 CHILD DEV. 1321 (1992); Kenneth A. Dodge, Greggory S. Pettit, John E. Bates & Ernest Valente, *Social Information-Processing Patterns Partially Mediate the Effect of Early Physical Abuse on Later Conduct Problems*, 104 J. ABNORMAL PSYCHOL. 632 (1995) [hereinafter Dodge et al., *Social Information-Processing*]; Kenneth A. Dodge, John E. Bates & Gregory S. Pettit, *How the Experience of Physical Abuse Leads a Child to Become Chronically Violent Toward Others*, in 8 DEVELOPMENTAL PERSPECTIVES ON TRAUMA: THEORY RESEARCH AND INTERVENTION (ROCHESTER SYMPOSIUM ON DEVELOPMENTAL PSYCHOPATHOLOGY) 263 (Dante Cicchetti & Sheree L. Toth eds., 1997).

[55] *See* Kenneth A. Dodge, Jennifer E Lansford, Virgina Salzer Burks, John E. Bates, Gregory S. Pettit & Reid G. Fontaine, *Peer Rejection and Social Information Processing Factors in the Development of Aggressive Behavior Problems in Children*, 74 CHILD DEV. 374 (2003); Kenneth A. Dodge, John E. Bates & Gregory S. Pettit, *Mechanisms in the Cycle of Violence*, 250 SCI. 1678 (1990); Gregory S. Pettit, John E. Bates & Kenneth A. Dodge, *Supportive Parenting, Ecological Context, and Children's Adjustment*, 68 CHILD DEV. 908 (1997).

[56] Dodge et al., *Social Information-Processing*, *supra* note 54.

[57] Michael Teisl & Dante Cicchetti, *Physical Abuse, Cognitive and Emotional Processes, and Aggressive/Disruptive Behavior Problems*, 17 SOC. DEV. 1 (2008).

who has been physically abused evidenced a hostile attributional bias and a greater propensity toward antisocial conduct. These findings point to the specific effects of physical abuse, suggesting that although not all forms of maltreatment produce social-cognitive changes that promote aggression and violence, physical abuse indeed does. The authors concluded that

> physically abused children demonstrated a distinct sensitivity to perceiving hostility, even when it was apparent that the provocateur held no malicious intent. This propensity for actually misperceiving aggression from others represents a considerable error in social information processing which at least partially explains the heightened risk for aggressive and disruptive behavior in physically abused children. These results suggest that experiences of hostility and violence may lead physically abused children to distort the meaning of even non-threatening cues in the environment, a perceptual style which may have developed as a protective mechanism against future hostility.[58]

The developmental picture painted here is one of a mediational course by which physical abuse causes significant mental changes in the form of distorted processing; such altered psychological functioning, in turn, promotes violence. It is literally the developmental science version of "violence begets violence."

A couple of specific points are worth noting. First, this body of research shows that physical abuse not only changes one's psychological functioning, but *distorts* it. That is, it does not change one's processing so that is becomes more accurate, but rather that it becomes *less* accurate. Second, notice that this is a paradox. That is, as theorized in the second study, the distorted processing that emerges out of being physically abused may actually serve as a protective mechanism in that it may make the individual in an abusive setting hypervigilant, promoting self-preservation.

This is not unlike many battered-woman contexts. A woman is subjected to an escalating pattern of harsh physical abuse, which has an impact on her processing style and rational capacity. Although this is limiting in one sense, it may promote her ultimate self-preservation. Unfortunately for the abused woman who kills, however, what may save her from suffering a mortal outcome at the hands of her abuser may also serve as the basis for which she is convicted for murder and incarcerated for the better part of her life from that point forward.

Also consistent with the usual battered-woman scenario is that developmental research similarly demonstrates that victims of maltreatment often suffer

[58] *Id.* at 18.

a variety of internalizing problems. For example, youths who have suffered physical abuse have been found to be more likely to develop depression[59] and anxiety.[60] Children who are victimized may develop social-cognitive processing patterns by which they come to understand that they are viewed negatively by others and that being socially accepted and properly treated are unrealistic desires.[61] What is unclear is whether these internalizing problems may mediate the relation between being victimized and acting out with aggression. This is an important question, because central to the underlying rationale of BWD is that as a result of being abused, an individual develops learned helplessness (a maladaptive psychological state that is naturally internalizing) and that out of a sense of being completely helpless the battered individual may come to the conclusion that her only way to self-preserve is to kill her abuser.

The maltreated individual may develop perceptual and interpretational tendencies that promote a sense of being threatened, as well as hostile feelings and rumination, reflecting symptomatology of PTSD. These processing problems are best represented by the early steps of SIP having to do with the encoding and interpretation of cues. As a result of being abused, an individual may become inclined to interpret a variety of social cues that are open as to their abuse content as threatening and dangerous. This processing style may support a developing pattern of hostile rumination and emotional reactivity.

In turn, the abused individual may develop different beliefs about his social world and future. Later steps of SIP, namely RED, may represent other key social-cognitive aspects of PTSD, including hopelessness/helplessness and social judgment and decision making that reflects this altered belief system. Judgments as to how to act in response to social cues may favor both

[59] Sheree L. Toth, Jody Todd Manly & Dante Cicchetti, *Child Maltreatment and Vulnerability to Depression*, 4 DEV. & PSYCHOPATHOLOGY 97 (1992); Robert M. A. Hirschfeld & Myrna Weissman, *Risk Factors for Major Depression and Bipolar Disorder, in* NEUROPSYCHOPHARMOCOLOGY: THE 5TH GENERATION OF PROGRESS 117 (Kenneth L. Davis, Dennis Charney, Joseph T. Coyle & Charles Nemeroff eds., 2002).

[60] Renee M. Johnson, Jonathon B. Kotch, Diane J. Catellier, Jane R. Winsor, Vincent Dufort & Wanda Hunter, *Adverse Behavioral and Emotional Outcomes from Child Abuse and Witnessed Violence*, 7 CHILD MALTREATMENT 179 (2002); Marese Cheasty, Anthony W. Clare & Claire Collins, *Relationship Between Sexual Abuse in Childhood and Adult Depression: Case-Control Study*, 316 BRIT. MED. J. 198 (1998).

[61] *See* BULLYING, REJECTION, AND PEER VICTIMIZATION: A SOCIAL COGNITIVE NEUROSCIENCE PERSPECTIVE 380 (Monica J. Harris ed., 2009); Candice Feiring, Charles M. Cleland & Valerie A. Simon, *Abuse-Specific Self-Schemas and Self-Functioning: A Prospective Study of Sexually Abused Youth*, 39 J. CLINICAL CHILD & ADOLESCENT PSYCHOL. 35 (2010); Julie T. Weismoore & Christianne Esposito-Smythers, *The Role of Cognitive Distortion in the Relationship Between Abuse, Assault, and Non-Suicidal Self-Injury*, 39 J. YOUTH & ADOLESCENCE 281 (2010).

internalizing and externalizing outcomes, consistent with a trauma profile characterized by a negative self-schema and distrust and hostility toward others. This combination of processing characteristics is consistent with clinical descriptions of abused and battered women who have killed their abusers.

Trauma may also cause thought problems and psychosis, a dissociative condition by which a person's rationality is severely impaired. The person suffering from psychosis may experience delusions and have significant difficulty distinguishing between reality and fantasy. This relation has been explored in scientific studies of both youth[62] and adult[63] populations. Of course, this impairment may bear direct relevance on an individual's ability to validly assess response options in a chronically abusive context.

Often central to discussions of psychological impairment is typical of the battered person's maladaptive course (including commentaries on BWS and BWD) is the victim's learned helplessness.[64] Helplessness was the subject of considerable laboratory examination in both humans and nonhuman animals in the 1970s and 1980s,[65] and was linked to depression in adults.[66] More recently, helplessness has been a focus of the literature on BWS,[67] a construct

[62] For a review, see Claire Manning & Theodore Stickley, *Childhood Abuse and Psychosis: A Critical Review of the Literature*, 14 J. Res. Nursing 531 (2009).

[63] For a review, see Sarah Bendall, Henry J. Jackson, Carol A. Hulbert & Patrick D. McGorry, *Childhood Trauma and Psychotic Disorders: A Systematic, Critical Review of the Evidence*, 34 Schizophrenia Bull. 568 (2008).

[64] It should be noted that *helplessness* and *hopelessness* are terms that are commonly used interchangeably in the clinical literature. *See, e.g.*, V. Henkel, P. Bussfeld, H. J. Möller & U. Hegerl, *Cognitive-Behavioural Theories of Helplessness/Hopelessness: Valid Models of Depression?*, 252 Eur. Archives Psychiatry & Clinical Neuroscience 240 (2002); Martin Bürgy, *Phenomenological Investigation of Despair in Depression*, 41 Psychopathology 147 (2008).

[65] *E.g.*, Christoper Peterson, Lisa M. Bossio & Rebecca Curtis, *Learned Helplessness, in* Self-defeating Behaviours: Experimental Research, Clinical Impressions, and Practical Implications 235 (Rebecca C. Curtis ed., 1989); Jay M. Weiss, Howard I. Glazer, Larissa A. Pohorecky, George Serban & Arthur Kling, *Coping Behavior and Neurochemical Changes: An Alternative Explanation for the Original "Learned Helplessness" Experiments, in* Animal Models in Human Psychobiology 141 (George Serban ed., 1976).

[66] Martin E. P. Seligman, Raymond J. Friedman & Martin M. Katz, *Depression and Learned Helplessness*, in The Psychology of Depression: Contemporary Theory and Research (Raymond J. Friedman & Martin M. Katz eds., 1974); William R. Miller, Robert A. Rosellini, Martin E. P. Seligman & Jack D. Maser, *Depression: Learned Helplessness and Depression, in* Psychopathology: Experimental Models 104 (1978); Bruce J. Overmier, Dirk H. Hellhammer, Pierre Simon, Phillip Soubrié & D. Widlocher, *The Learned Helplessness Model of Human Depression, in* 2 An Inquiry into Schizophrenia and Depression, Animal Models of Psychiatric Disorders 177 (1988).

[67] *E.g.*, Neta Bargai, Gershon Ben-Shakhar & Arieh Y. Shalev, *Posttraumatic Stress Disorder and Depression in Battered Women: The Mediating Role of Learned Helplessness*, 22 J. Family Violence 267 (2007); Ann Palker-Corell & David K, *Partner Abuse, Learned Helplessness, And Trauma Symptoms*, 23 J. Soc. & Clinical Psychol. 445 (2004); Kathy Wilson, Regina

that had long been emphasized by Professor Lenore Walker.[68] An individual may learn helplessness as a result of chronic victimization. The victim develops an image of her world by which she has little or no control over her negative experiences. Helplessness may lead to motivational problems in that even in the face of an obvious resolution to an ongoing problem, the helpless person may be unable to recognize the solution or, if she does recognize it, to enact it out of a rigid belief that any effort toward resolution would be futile.

Seemingly paradoxically, although learned helplessness may cause a loss of behavioral motivation and activation, the condition is used to explain – at least in part – why some battered individuals kill their abusers. The argument is that the abused person learns that potential assistance such as law enforcement, family and friends, shelters, and the like can provide no real protection, and therefore decides to kill her abuser, having identified this course of action as the only one that poses any promise. The question, of course, is how it is that the truly helpless person is motivated to enact a behavioral course that, at least in most instances, requires notable effort. The paradox, however, may be an illusion. It is possible that helplessness is context- or behavior-specific. That is, a person may feel helpless with respect to one contexts (e.g., romance) but not another (e.g., housekeeping). Similarly, she may determine that certain behavioral courses bear no promise (e.g., involving law enforcement) whereas others do (e.g., killer the abuser).

Relative to other internalizing conditions and constructs, such as loneliness, anxiety, and depression, learned helplessness is relatively understudied in developmental science. As a result, questions as to alternative developmental courses by which it may emerge and crystallize remain. Likewise, questions about the degrees to which it may be context- or behavior-specific require scientific investigation. With respect to any defense that may excuse on the basis of abuse-caused psychological impairment, this research is critical, because only by empirical examination may we understand how a person who is helpless and depressed may nevertheless find motivation sufficient to carry out the homicide of her abuser.

Of course, helplessness is but one possible symptom of being intensely abused or traumatized. As discussed, the trauma victim may develop a number of deleterious psychological conditions, including anger, intense fear, psychological numbing, low self-esteem, and dissociation. This symptom cluster is typical of individuals who have been diagnosed with PTSD. The interactions

Vercella, Christiane Brems & Deborah Benning, *Levels of Learned Helplessness in Abused Women*, 13 WOMEN & THERAPY 53 (1992).

68 *E.g.*, Lenore E. Walker, *Battered Women and Learned Helplessness*, 2 VICTIMOLOGY 525 (1978).

of these factors may produce an array of behavioral courses, from complete withdrawal and catatonia on the one end to antisocial outbursts and extreme violence on the other. Common to all of these psychopathological profiles is the developmental meditational course by which trauma leads to altered/distorted social-cognitive functioning, which, in turn, causes abnormal behavior. In this way, it is not unusual for the battered woman who kills to be accurately described as one who acted out of impaired rational capacity.

TOWARD AN ABUSE/TRAUMA PERSON DEFENSE?: EXCUSE IN THE ABSENSCE OF JUSTIFICATION

The proposal to formally recognize an abuse/trauma defense has remained controversial. Such controversy stems from a number of sources, such as an incomplete reading of psychological science,[69] misunderstanding the justification/excuse distinction,[70] and differences in normative positions on criminal responsibility and what conditions should suffice to excuse it. As such, several problems persist that must be resolved before serious progress toward general acceptance of an excuse-based abuse defense may be realized.

The first has to do with limiting discussion of an abuse/trauma defense to the context of the battered woman who kills. As discussed, there is no legitimate reason to limit discussion of an abuse defense to this context. The fact that the majority of abuse defense cases emerge out of this context is irrelevant to discerning whether the psychological effects of being abused should serve to mitigate criminal responsibility. Certainly, there exist other contexts in which an oppressed individual may kill out of impaired rationality caused directly by an escalating pattern of serious physical abuse.

One example is parricide, or the killing of a parent by his child.[71] Similar to the case of the battered woman, children who kill their parents do so in the context of a relationship defined by a substantial power differential. Children who commit parricide typically have histories of severe abuse at the hands of their parent target and have developed a firm understanding that the only

[69] *See, e.g.*, ALAN M. DERSHOWITZ, *THE ABUSE EXCUSE AND OTHER COP-OUTS SOB STORIES, AND EVASIONS OF RESPONSIBILITY* (1994).

[70] Charles P. Ewing, *Psychological Self-Defense: A Proposed Justification for Battered Women Who Kill*, 14 LAW & HUM. BEHAV. 586 (1990).

[71] PAUL A. MONES, *WHEN A CHILD KILLS* (1991); KATHLEEN M. HEIDE, *WHY KIDS KILL PARENTS* (1992); Jennifer R. James, *Turning the Tables: Redefining Self-Defense Theory for Children Who Kill Abusive Parents*, 18 LAW & PSYCHOL. REV. 393 (1994); Jessica L. Hart & Jeffrey L. Helms, *Factors of Parricide: Allowance of the Use of Battered Child Syndrome as a Defense*, 8 AGGRESSION & VIOLENT BEHAV. 671 (2003).

avenue by which they can prevent the pattern of abuse from continuing and escalating is homicide.[72]

There is little systematic research on children who kill their parents. As with any abuse context, it can prove quite difficult to access victims of abuse for research purposes. This challenge is amplified when the victims of abuse are identified only when they are secured by legal authorities in order to be processed in the juvenile justice system. Nevertheless, it is striking that discussions of parricide have largely neglected the scientific literature on developmental social cognition.[73] As discussed in this chapter, there is a valuable scientific literature that speaks to the social-cognitive and behavioral effects of maltreatment of youths across time.

Indeed, because child abuse victims often go unidentified or are otherwise inaccessible, and also because they may not be reliable even when accessed, abuse research, as a general endeavor, has been notably limited, relative to other areas of research in developmental psychopathology. This provides at least partial explanation as to why psychological theories of BWD have remained underdeveloped and/or overstated.[74] It also may provide some understanding as to why there has continued to be resistance to formal recognition of an abuse defense.

Nevertheless, some prominent criminal-law theorists have become increasingly sympathetic to the BWD argument. Although their rationales have differed, said scholars agree that the defense is properly viewed as an excuse. One noteworthy example is provided by Professor Joshua Dressler, who has argued that BWD may be likened to the excuse[75] defense of duress: "We should not punish people who disobey [the law's] strictures if we believe that a person of reasonable firmness would have been unable to resist. We should not expect more of others than we reasonably expect of ourselves. Some marital abuse cases are such that we should excuse the woman who kills in those cases."[76]

72 Hart & Helms, *supra* note 71.

73 In one of the more recent and thorough reviews, there is no mention of the social-cognitive outcomes of child abuse or their mediating role in the developmental course from being abused to becoming violent, such as the studies discussed earlier, guided by the independent research programs of Professors Ken Dodge and Dante Cicchetti. *Id.*

74 This observation includes theories of why battered women kill that are rightly focused on social-cognitive mediators of the abuse-homicide relation. For example, see Angela Browne's articulation of social judgment theory in the BWD context. ANGELA BROWNE, *WHEN BATTERED WOMEN KILL* (1987); *see also*, LENORE E. WALKER, *TERRIFYING LOVE: WHY BATTERED WOMEN KILL AND HOW SOCIETY RESPONDS* (1989).

75 Dressler argues that duress is an excuse in *Exegesis of the Law of Duress: Justifying the Excuse and Searching for Its Proper Limits*, 62 S. CAL. L. REV. 1331 (1989); Joshua Dressler, *Duress*, *in* The Oxford HANDBOOK ON THE PHILOSOPHY OF CRIMINAL LAW (John Deigh & David Dolinko eds., 2011).

76 Dressler, *Battered Women*, *supra* note 13, at 471.

Alternatively, I expect Professor Stephen Morse would argue the battered woman killer's excuse rests on nonculpably formed diminished rationality. Years ago, Morse rejected the idea of treating nonconfrontational killings by battered women under the partial-responsibility variant of diminished capacity. Today, however, he would surely reconsider such cases according to his Guilty but Partially Responsible verdict proposal: "[T]he criminal law should include a generic, doctrinal mitigating excuse of partial responsibility that would apply to all crimes.... This partial excuse would apply in cases in which a defendant's behavior satisfied the elements of the crime charged, but the defendant's rationality was non-culpably compromised and thus the defendant was not fully responsible for the crime charged."[77] Presumably, the abused individual whose rationality is impaired as a result of being unjustifiably victimized would serve as a prime candidate to benefit from such Morse's special verdict.

By what standard, however, would the abused individual's altered rationality be judged? Professor Charles Ewing has offered an argument of "psychological self-defense" based on the claim that abuse causes injury to the victim's selfhood.[78] Certainly, there is no question that abuse may cause harm to a person's identity and autonomy. It is unclear, however, what the boundaries of selfhood are, what hard science there is to support the position, and how it may be systematically studied. Others have focused more heavily on the role of social cognition, explaining killings by battered women according to learned hopelessness[79] and helplessness.[80] It remains unclear, however, how someone who is truly hopeless may find hope in any plan of recourse, whether it be killing her abuser, taking refuge with family, friends, or a shelter, or simply leaving her home and attempting to survive on her own.

It seems that this may be where the developmental science is most important. Quite consistently, research on the effects of varied types of maltreatment across development has shown that both internalizing *and* externalizing problems emerge. That is, whereas victims of harsh treatment and abuse suffer depression, loneliness, anxiety, and hopelessness/helplessness, they also learn

[77] Stephen J. Morse, *Diminished Rationality, Diminished Responsibility*, 1 OH. ST. J. CRIM. L. 289, 289 (2003).

[78] Charles P. Ewing, *Psychological Self-Defense: A Proposed Justification for Battered Women Who Kill*, 14 LAW & HUM. BEHAV. 586 (1990).

[79] For example, in her popular book, *When Battered Women Kill*, Angela Browne adopted a social judgment theory to explain how women can lose "[t]heir final hope" at the realization that escalating abuse has become too far removed from their expectation of what they can withstand and survive. BROWNE, *supra* note 74, at 130.

[80] *E.g.*, Lenore E. Walker, *Reflections on the Psychosocial Theory of Learned Helplessness*, *in* VIOLENCE AGAINST WOMEN (Raquel Kennedy Bergen, Jeffrey L. Edleson & Claire M. Renzetti eds., 2004).

aggression and violence, a skill they tend to enact as part of their navigation through their social worlds. Typically, women who are victims of chronic abuse by their domestic partners are not demonstrated to be particularly aggressive. Nevertheless, this does not mean that their social cognition has not changed so that it is more aggressogenic, at least with respect to their abuser. In many cases, the battered woman's social world is limited to her abuser because he controls her and completely restricts her interpersonal relations. Thus it is not surprising that the battered woman in this scenario has not demonstrated a pattern of chronic aggressive behavior toward others – indeed, she is unable to exhibit any kind of social behavior toward others.

Any abuse defense must recognize this likely combination of social-cognitive effects of harsh maltreatment. Perceptions, thoughts, and judgment and decision making change as a direct result of being abused, and it promotes both depressotypic and aggressotypic maladjustment. The deterioration of coping and problem-solving skills with which chronically battered women are afflicted[81] seems likely to contribute to a sense, whether valid or invalid, of desperation, that only violence will serve to prevent the abuser from committing murder against his abuse victim.

In the case of the abused individual who genuinely but unreasonably mistakes that she must kill her abuser to prevent him from wrongfully taking her life, my psychological and retributive intuitions act in concert, forcing me to conclude that such a defendant should only partially be held responsible for her objectively defined wrongdoing. That is, of course, if she is to be held at all responsible, as I expect, in some cases there will be ample reason to fully excuse the abused individual depending on the seriousness of the alterations as to her psychological capacities (and, in particular, her rationality) realized as a direct result from her victimization. Thus, at conceptual and moral levels, I favor a movement toward an excuse-based chronic abuse and trauma defense.

But the law, of course, must have a clearly defined standard. It is for this reason, at least in part, that some scholars have attempted to squeeze the square into the circle slot. I do not believe that most cases of nonconfrontational killings by abused individuals neatly match traditional defenses of self-defense, insanity, heat of passion/provocation, or duress. The partial-responsibility variant of diminished capacity is the closest fit, but, of course, diminished capacity is not formally recognized in many U.S. jurisdictions, nor is it always clearly defined in jurisdictions in which it is. In addition, diminished capacity serves only to partially excuse, and it is not at all clear that – at least in some

[81] Barnett, *Part 2*, *supra* note 32.

extreme cases – a chronically abused individual who commits nonconfrontational homicide should not be entirely exculpated and remitted for mental health treatment.

PTSD provides a reasonably clear medical standard, but I am not convinced that one must meet PTSD to suffer from the type of diminished rationality that would explain the crystallized mental alterations that may result from chronic abuse and cause one to mistakenly commit to the belief that homicide is the only chance the abuse victim has for survival. I call on the medical and behavioral sciences to investigate longer-term developmental effects of abuse and trauma more comprehensively and with more focus. Only through greater definition of the maladaptive multifinality of abuse may we then draw a clear legal standard. Until this time, it is all but certain that any discussion of an abuse defense, even in the case that there is consensus as to its rightly excusing nature, will be undermined by debate that must be at least partly due to scientific uncertainty. Moving forward without a commitment to understanding the critical effects of trama outside the context of development is nothing short of irresponsible. To conclude this chapter as it began, I am reminded of Professor Goodmark's words: "Context – examining the lives of [battered women who kill] and asking how they come to the point where killing their batterers seems to be their only option – is crucial to establish why most traditional rationales for criminal punishment are inadequate in these cases."[82] If there is a context more important than development to understanding how an abused individual arrives at the decision to kill her abuser, it is unknown to me.

[82] Leigh Goodmark, *The Punishment of Dixie Shanahan: Is There Justice for Battered Women Who Kill?*, 55 KAN. L. REV. 269, 272 (2007).

9

Toward a More Psychologically Informed Approach to Social Rationality and Excusing Conditions in Criminal Law

INTRODUCTION

In the late 1980s and early 1990s, a series of seminal papers on cognitive, psychological, and social-analytic approaches to jurisprudence called for greater interdisciplinarity in law and legal theory. Cognitive jurisprudential efforts, for example, emphasized the role of cognitive psychology in law reform. In this vein, Professor Steven Winter stressed that we should "reconceptualize law in light of what we are learning about the human mind [in science]."[1] Adding to this call, Professor Mark Small asserted that the goal of cognitive jurisprudence is "to describe a concept of law that is rooted in and coherent with the processes of human rationality."[2] Small, who stressed the "social nature"[3] of law, envisioned a broader, more progressive psychological jurisprudence, arguing that "psychological jurisprudence is necessary if the benefits of legal psychology are to be fully realized in law."[4]

Small recognized that progress in psychological jurisprudence was moving forward only slowly.[5] The rate at which "psycholegal" scholarship has grown has picked up considerably in the last two decades, but the speed at which psychological jurisprudence has progressed can make claim to only a modest increase.[6] That is, even though scholarship that combines aspects of

[1] Steven L. Winter, *Transcendental Nonsense, Metaphoric Reasoning and the Cognitive Stakes for Law*, 137 U. Pa. L. Rev. 1107, 1107 (1989).

[2] Mark A. Small, *Advancing Psychological Jurisprudence*, 11 Behav. Sci. & L. 3, 9 (1993).

[3] *See* Dennis Lloyd & Michael D. A. Freeman, *Lloyd's Introduction to Jurisprudence* (1985).

[4] Small, *supra* note 2, at 13.

[5] "Despite the importance of psychological jurisprudence, thus far the development of psychological jurisprudence has been slow." *Id.* at 4.

[6] In their brief review of social science's contributions to the law across the last twenty-five years, Professors John Monahan and Laurens Walker made reference to how social science research has been used in the Supreme Court's determination that the juvenile death penalty

psychology and law has burgeoned, it has done so largely at the neglect of a unifying interdisciplinary jurisprudential theory.

There are likely several reasons for this. First, traditions in philosophy and law die hard. Jurisprudential approaches to law and law reform are steeped in centuries of social and scholarly and academic tradition, so it is to be expected that there would be some resistance, even if unintentional, to a movement that may appear to threaten to unhinge such traditions. Of course, psychological jurisprudence approaches have always been offered to supplement, not supplant, jurisprudential foundations of law. This includes even the empirical mandate that is thematic to more recent iterations of psychological jurisprudence (e.g., social-analytic, social-cognitive), which asserts that empirical questions must be answered via empirical inquiry and investigation – a necessary mission of any proper psychological jurisprudence.

A second possible reason, which may be partly explained by the first, is that there sometimes exists confusion as to empirical versus normative matters. Certain empirical issues in jurisprudence and law have, at times, been subsumed by the larger normative issues to which they are thought to apply, and so their empirical nature has been missed. One clear example in the criminal law has to do with the dangerousness of crimes of passion, of which some scholars presume a greater degree of dangerousness on the part of the actor and others argue that such acts are isolated to the specific, unique contexts in which they are committed, and thus unlikely to be repeated by their committers.[7]

In contrast, a third possible reason is that although science cannot answer questions of morality, some scientists may nevertheless make claims based on their empirical work that appear to attempt to do so. In addition, legal scholars may fear that scientists intend to undermine the moral underpinnings of the criminal law by making such claims. The evolving debate as to hard determinism versus free will, along with the resistance among some scientists to consider the very notion of compatibilism (sometimes called soft determinism or compatibilistic determinism) by which the metaphysical construct of free will is understood to coexist with our physical, causal world, provides more than sufficient impetus for opposition in criminal-law theory. The quote by

is unconstitutional, as well as how social science instruments designed to assess future dangerousness are now more widely used to help make determinations of bail and parole. John Monahan & Laurens Walker, *Twenty-five years of Social Science in Law*, 35 LAW & HUM. BEHAV. 72 (2011).

7 See the discussion of future dangerousness in Reid G. Fontaine, *Disentangling the Psychology and Law of Instrumental and Reactive Subtypes of Aggression*, 13 PSYCHOL. PUB. POL'Y & L. 143, 155–60 (2007).

Professor James Wilson, offered in Chapter 1 – "social science seeks to explain behavior, criminal law to judge it" – speaks to this point. Developmental social cognition may contribute to understanding as to the workings of the mind and brain-behavior relations, but, no matter how advanced the relevant science, it cannot tell us how we *should* judge behavior in criminal law.

Psychology and law also have different languages, with different vocabularies, which sometimes contribute to the problem of these respective fields talking past each other. In behavioral science, we speak of behavior, brain, and information processing; in law, we speak of action, mind, and rationality. At least at times, it is not so much that the fields are concerned with different entities, phenomena, and social issues as it is that they use different vocabularies. Of course, a psychological jurisprudence that is properly advance may clarify differences in label so they no longer pose such an unnecessary obstacle to criminal-law theory benefitting from interdisciplinary thinking and scholarship.

Finally, Winter's call for more scholars who are formally trained in both psychology and law should be reiterated. Psychology and law are involved, highly complex fields. As such, it should be easily understood that creating a scholarly agenda by which each field may inform and learn from the other requires technicians who are expertly skilled on both sides of the coin. Psycholegal scholarship is sometimes exposed for its lack of grounding in one of the two areas from which it is supposed to build; as a result, it has the paradoxical effect of stagnating interdisciplinary progress rather than pushing it forward. Psychological jurisprudence is certainly not immune to the risk illuminated by this cautionary observation.

SOCIAL-COGNITIVE JURISPRUDENCE: BUILDING FROM WIENER'S SOCIAL-ANALYTIC TRADITION

A truly interdisciplinary psycholegal jurisprudence, by which psychological science and the law learn from and inform each other transactionally, must recognize the potential mutual benefits of the two fields being together involved in an ongoing, dynamic, and reciprocal fashion. Although in this volume we have been primarily concerned with ways in which excusing conditions in criminal law may be informed by the developmental and social-cognitive psychologies that investigate empirical issues germane to questions of rationality, behavioral action, self-control, and responsibility, it is no less important that science pay close attention to substantive and procedural issues of law as they emerge and unfold in the law and legal system. This bidirectional model is consistent with Professor Richard Wiener's conceptualization of social-analytic jurisprudence.[8]

Wiener argued that for an interdisciplinary psycholegal jurisprudence to take form, the jurisprudential scholar and administrator must be learned in both substantive law and substantive areas of psychological science, and turn to subdisciplines of psychology where scholarly inquiry calls for specialized scientific investigation and knowledge:

> Using complex social scientific methodologies to test intuitive solutions to empirical issues in law falls short of the interdisciplinary promise that psychology makes to the interaction of the two disciplines. Psychology and law research is more than the application of experimental designs and analysis of various statistical procedures to empirical issues in legal doctrine. Psycholegal scholarship is based on the discipline of psychology at least as much as it is based on the law. Researchers should be comfortable with turning to literature in the various subdisciplines of psychology to find hypotheses that offer potential answers to legal problems. Analytic jurisprudence should take advantage of the sophisticated research tools available to psychological researchers but it should also test hypotheses that are developed from the knowledge base of the science of psychology.[9]

Since the introduction of Wiener's social-analytic jurisprudence, there has emerged only moderate evidence of its implementation in psycholegal inquiry and scholarship. However, specific reference to the inspiration provided by the model may be found in recent efforts to apply psychology to substantive criminal law.[10]

The perspective that gave rise to this volume, which I have termed *social-cognitive jurisprudence*,[11] requires that empirical questions that are natural and important to normative legal issues and judgments are recognized for their empirical status, and that the reality that such questions may only be properly informed and answered by empirical science is accepted. Although distinct in

[8] *See* Richard L. Weiner, *Social Analytic Jurisprudence and Tort Law: Social Cognition Goes to Court*, 37 St. Louis U. L.J. 503 (1993); Richard L. Wiener, Barbara S. Watts & Dennis P. Stolle, *Psychological Jurisprudence and the Information Processing Paradigm*, 11 Behav. Sci. & L. 79 (1993).

[9] Weiner, *supra* note 8, at 514.

[10] *See, e.g.*, Steven J. Sherman & Joseph L. Hoffman, *The Psychology and Law of Voluntary Manslaughter: What Can Psychology Research Teach Us about the "Heat of Passion" Defense?*, 20 J. Behav. Decision Making 499 (2007); Laurence L. Steinberg, *Adolescent Development and Juvenile Justice*, 5 Ann. Rev. Clinical Psychol. 47 (2009); Gregory S. Parks & Shayne E. Jones, *"Nigger": A Critical Race Realist Analysis of the N-Word Within Hate Crimes Law*, 98 J. Crim. L. & Criminology 1305, 1333 (2008).

[11] *See supra* Chapter 1.

several meaningful ways (e.g., whereas social-analytic jurisprudence speaks broadly to decision making of legal actors, social-cognitive jurisprudence, at least as herein applied, considers scientific foundations of criminal offenders on whom insertion into the legal system is generally imposed), social-cognitive jurisprudence is consistent with Wiener's interest in drawing from specific subdisciplines as dictated by the contours of the psycholegal issue in question. Namely, this volume calls on criminal-law theorists to recognize empirical science in developmental social cognition in consideration of issues of rational capacity. An eye is directed toward individual differences in developmental context as they relate to excusing conditions that may apply to specific enactors of (objectively) criminal acts.

Social-cognitive jurisprudence, then, expands on Wiener's social-analytic jurisprudence in ways that are critical to scholarly inquiry in interdisciplinary criminal-law theory. This evolution embodies several distinguishing features. First, whereas social-analytic jurisprudence was devised to scientifically investigate and explain judgment and decision making on the part of the legal actor (e.g., juror, jury, judge), social-cognitive jurisprudence is focused on the perception, judgment, and decision making – that is, the perceptual and rational processes – of the offender. Whereas a social-analytic approach may be employed to understand decision making *about* the criminal offender, social-cognitive jurisprudence is concerned with the rational workings and capacity *of* the offender.

Because social-cognitive jurisprudence is developed to inform criminal-law theory about offender perception, judgment, and decision making, it is foundationally different from Wiener's social-analytic jurisprudence. Whereas Wiener asserted that "[p]sycholegal jurisprudence can only be legitimate if it recognizes that it is a fundamentally a scientific enterprise,"[12] social-cognitive jurisprudence approaches the criminal law with an understanding that it rests on a fundamental position about morality that is naturally normative, not empirical. Social-cognitive jurisprudence, however, simultaneously observes that normative arguments about the moral nature of action, agency, and responsibility rest to some significant degree on assumptions about human functioning and individual differences in said functioning. These assumptions embody empirical assertions, the validity of which can only be tested and known via empirical methods. As such, social-cognitive jurisprudence mandates that empirical questions that are natural to normative positions in the criminal law be specified as such and investigated empirically. In this way, social-cognitive jurisprudence views empirical science as a

[12] Weiner, *supra* note 8, at 511.

necessary supplement to a properly informed normative ethics rather than a "fundamentally scientific enterprise."

Social-cognitive jurisprudence recognizes that crime is, by its nature, a social phenomenon. The commission of a crime is either directly, as in the case of crimes against a person (e.g., robbery, murder), or indirectly, as in the case of crimes against society (e.g., criminal tax evasion, destruction of public property), social. With few exceptions, a crime is an act that wrongs another person or persons and causes a social harm. As social behavior is social-cognitively mediated, criminal behavior – a specific class of social behavior – need be understood as social-cognitively mediated. That is, a criminal act is not just a response to a social stimulus, such as a perceived wrong or harm (reactive) or an identified opportunity to achieve personal gain (instrumental), but an action that emerges out of a set of mental operations by which one's social environment and ways to navigate through it are evaluated. Even in the most rapid, time-urgent behavioral scenarios, criminal action results as a function of some form – even if schematic and automatic – of social-cognitive appraisal. Thus, crime may only be understood by examining its social-cognitive foundations; furthermore, determinations as to criminal responsibility and punishment rest, to some large degree, on a dissection of these social-cognitive underpinnings, as well.

Toward the goal of understanding the social-cognitive foundations of criminal action, social-cognitive jurisprudence stresses the importance of individual differences in human social cognition. "Every man [sic] is in certain respects (a) like all other men, (b) like some other men, (c) like no other man."[13] Individual-differences psychology (or differential psychology) is concerned with the reality that each person shares certain qualities with others but is simultaneously different than others. This assertion is true at both the macrolevel (e.g., human as whole) and microlevel (social cognition as an individual or intrapersonal system). With respect to perception, evaluative judgment, behavioral decision making, and rational capacity, individual humans vary considerably. Most critical to present concerns, individual differences in social-information processing (SIP) and rational capacity may have implications for determinations of criminal responsibility and punishment. The individual who is unable to abide by the law because he is unable to comprehend the law may be less guilty than one who fully understands the law's behavioral mandate and chooses to act otherwise. As such, the law may hold the latter more criminally responsible and punishable.

[13] Henry A. Murray & Clyde Kluckhohn, *Outline of a Conception of Personality, in* PERSONALITY IN NATURE, SOCIETY, AND CULTURE (Clyde Kluckhohn & Henry A. Murray eds., 2nd ed. 1953).

To understand how individual differences in human social cognition and rational capacity may relate to differential assignment of criminal responsibility and punishment, however, such individual differences must be examined in the context of learning and development. Social-information processing (SIP) models[14] used in social-developmental psychology provide a framework by which alternative patterns of development may be investigated and understood. Rationality embodies numerous mental processes, including perception, interpretation, goal clarification, evaluative judgment, and behavioral decision making, all of which are components of SIP theory in psychological science. SIP provides a framework by which the development of social rationality may be explored, understood, and explained.

SIP theory models social learning in that it is designed to account for how individuals develop adaptive social skills by transacting with their respective environments. It is guided by developmental principles such as multifinality, by which factors and entities that begin similarly may develop along divergent paths and end differentially; and equifinality, by which factors and entities that stem from different origins may develop along trajectories that converge such that their endpoints are the same. These developmental principles are critical to determinations of individual differences in rational capacity and differential responsibility because they explain how similar individual may come to act differently (multifinality) and different individuals may come to act similarly (equifinality). For instance, two individuals who have committed a crime (at least in part) out of moral disengagement from the act may differ considerably in terms of their development. Whereas one may have rehearsed his criminal plan so that he may carry it out more effectively, another may have developed a social-cognitive tendency toward moral disengagement out of being subject to chronic victimization and an oppressive environment. The law may be best served by considering these individual differences in development toward the same end (i.e., the criminal act) such that criminal responsibility and punishment may be rightly assessed.

Social-cognitive jurisprudence requires a theoretical grounding in psychology that is scientifically testable and substantiated. If it is essential for the promise

[14] Nicki R. Crick & Kenneth A. Dodge, *Review and Reformulation of Social Information-Processing Mechanisms in Children's Social Adjustment*, 115 PSYCHOL. BULL. 74, 74–101 (1994); L. Rowell Huesmann, *The Role of Social Information Processing and Cognitive Schema in the Acquisition and Maintenance of Habitual Aggressive Behavior*, *in* HUMAN AGGRESSION: THEORIES, RESEARCH, AND IMPLICATIONS FOR SOCIAL POLICY 73 (Russell G. Geen & Edward Donnerstein eds., 1998); Reid G. Fontaine & Kenneth A. Dodge, *Social Information Processing and Aggressive Behavior: A Transactional Perspective*, *in* THE TRANSACTIONAL MODEL OF DEVELOPMENT: HOW CHILDREN AND CONTEXTS SHAPE EACH OTHER 117 (Arnold J. Sameroff ed., 2009).

of psychological jurisprudence to be realized that it provide a clear, consistent framework for pursuing jurisprudential inquiry, then surely this requirement is to be immediately accepted. How else could any interdisciplinary approach to jurisprudence that advances scientific values hope to make a meaningful contribution? SIP, as well as other social-cognitive theories in psychology (e.g., cognitive appraisal theory of emotion[15]), as herein discussed, meet this requirement and thus may be drawn on to consider psycholegal issues as related to the mental and behavioral workings of the criminal offender.

Of course, there remains much to be learned about the development of social cognition and behavior and how these intrapersonal systems are related across time. One area of research that has suggested particular promise is in social-cognitive processing and aggressive and antisocial behavior. Some developmental studies have provided empirical evidence that aggressogenic processing and antisocial behavior influence each other reciprocally as youth development unfolds,[16] consistent with an individual-systems model of antisocial conduct.[17] Research on social cognition and antisocial behavior has pointed to other promising research pursuits, as well, some of which would appear to be particularly useful to the criminal law. One of these has to do with subtypes of antisocial behavior and the social-cognitive patterns that distinguish them.

THE NEED FOR FURTHER INQUIRY IN ANTISOCIAL SUBTYPES AND THE DEVELOPMENT OF VIOLENT CRIME

Several chapters in this volume have discussed intersections of biased or distorted social-cognitive processing and homicide law – or, more specifically,

[15] Richard S. Lazarus, James R. Averill & J. R. Opton, *Toward a Cognitive Theory of Emotion*, *in* FEELINGS AND EMOTIONS: THE LOYALA SYMPOSIUM 207 (Magda E. Arnold ed., 1970); RICHARD S. LAZARUS & SUSAN FOLKMAN, *STRESS, APPRAISAL, AND COPING* (1984); Richard S. Lazarus & Craig A. Smith, *Knowledge and Appraisal in the Cognition-Emotion Relationship*, 2 COGNITION & EMOTION 281 (1988); Richard S. Lazarus, *On the Primacy of Cognition*, 39 AM. PSYCHOLOGIST 124 (1984); RICHARD S. LAZARUS, *EMOTION AND ADAPTATION* (1991); Richard S. Lazarus, *Vexing Research Problems Inherent in Cognitive-Mediational Theories of Emotion and Some Solutions*, 6 PSYCHOL. INQUIRY 183 (1995); Craig A. Smith & Richard S. Lazarus, *Appraisal Components, Core Relational Themes, and the Emotions*, 7 COGNITION & EMOTION 233 (1993).

[16] Reid G. Fontaine, Chongming Yang, Kenneth A. Dodge, John E. Bates & Gregory S. Pettit, *Testing an Individual Systems Model of Response Evaluation and Decision (RED) and Antisocial Behavior Across Adolescence*, 79 CHILD DEV. 462 (2008); L. Rowell Huesmann & Nancy G. Guerra, *Children's Normative Beliefs about Aggression and Aggressive Behavior*, 72 J. PERSONALITY & SOC. PSYCHOL. 408 (1997)

[17] Reid G. Fontaine, *Applying Systems Principles to Models of Social Information Processing and Aggressive Behavior in Youth*, 11 AGGRESSION & VIOLENT BEHAV. 64 (2006).

reactive homicide law. As opposed to instrumental forms of violence, which are generally self-initiated, planned, calmly performed, and enacted out of an interest of personal gain, reactive violence is characterized as a relatively emotional, impulsive response to a perceived provocation, threat, or otherwise aversive stimulus, for the purpose of harming the (perceived) wrongdoer or defending oneself. As discussed, this behavioral dichotomy is recognized not only in psychology and behavioral science, but in the criminal law, as well.

There are specific social-cognitive biases that have been differentially linked to instrumental and reactive violence. Understanding the relation between these social-cognitive biases and forms of reactive homicide may be useful to understanding a variety of affirmative defenses in criminal law. For example, the tendency to interpret ambiguously negative stimuli in one's environment as hostile and intentionally harmful has been uniquely linked to reactive violence. This finding may have implications for how scenarios that involve a mistaken provocation (heat-of-passion/provocation doctrine, discussed in Chapter 6) or threat (mistaken self-defense, mistaken defense of others, and duress, discussed in Chapter 7) are understood, legally recognized, and doctrinally informed.

In addition, there are other areas of developmental social cognition that bear important implications for reactive homicide law, which have either been neglected or misunderstood such that the usefulness of their findings has not been realized. A prime example is social-cognitive development of individuals who have suffered trauma and abuse. The mental effects of abuse may be several and severe, although they have not been adequately considered in the case of homicidal actions of "battered women" – or, more properly, *battered persons*,[18] as it is unclear why psychological effects of severe abuse would be limited to one gender (Chapter 8).

Of course, whereas killings by battered persons are reactive in that they serve as a response to perceived wrongdoing and are committed for the purpose of self-preservation, they often do not "fit" neatly into the reactive side of the instrumental/reactive dichotomy in that they may be planned and relatively nonimpulsive. The psychology of the battered person's course of violent action as related to a defense that is viewed as distinct from heat of passion/provocation and self-defense (as well as other defenses to which battered person defenses have been compared, such as duress and insanity) is of critical importance to further explore and understand. Research in psychology on subtypes of antisocial conduct may be useful to this effort in that the qualities

[18] By "battered person" I mean any individual who suffers chronic abuse or battering (or other trauma or victimization) at the hands of an oppressive other.

of reactive aggression that may be associated with an excusing condition – for example, the perception of unjust treatment, belief that force is necessary, and sense of time urgency pressure to act – must be examined in the context-relevant setting of an abusive relationship. Advancing research that is context-specific and appropriate promotes external validity as well as its usefulness to psycholegal inquiry, such as whether such research should inform corresponding affirmative defense law.

As Professors Sherman and Hoffman have rightly asserted, "psychology can only inform the law, but cannot force changes in the law."[19] The promise of psychology to inform the law, however, is limited to its ability to ask questions that are relevant to the law and then rigorously test them in ways that promote generalization to contexts with which the law deals. As such, design and implementation of research paradigms that are useful to exploring prebehavioral social cognition in "precriminal" and criminal settings are critical.

Precriminal contexts are ones in which no crime has yet occurred but which are open to or promote or facilitate criminal activity. Criminogenic features that may characterize a precriminal context include ones in which a weapon is present, desirable entities (e.g., money) are introduced, and authority figures are absent. One precriminal research paradigm that may be useful to understanding criminogenic social cognition is the "crime opportunity" paradigm. For example, a study may utilize a scenario in which participants who are blind to the true goal of the study are presented with an opportunity to steal an item of interest (e.g., an iPod music player) with apparent freedom from risk of being caught and punished. Upon being debriefed, participants may be asked to reflect on their thought processes that either led to their decision to take or refrain from taking the material item. Of course, there are ethical issues that accompany such a research paradigm that would need to be fully explored and resolved, although a carefully constructed debriefing session may well resolve any reasonable concern that the participant (especially the youth participant) is placed at any risk by taking part in the study.

This type of paradigm may be particularly useful to more thoroughly exploring the development of social-cognitive processing that promotes instrumental antisocial behavior. As compared to research on social cognition and reactive violence, there is notably less scientific inquiry that has investigated instrumental violence.[20] As discussed in Chapters 2 and 6, some research has shown

19 Steven J. Sherman & Joseph L. Hoffman, *The Psychology and Law of Voluntary Manslaughter: What Can Psychology Research Teach Us about the "Heat of Passion" Defense?*, 20 J. BEHAVIORAL DECISION MAKING 499 (2007).

20 Elsewhere, I introduced a model for studying developmental social cognition and instrumental antisocial behavior and discussed the importance of scholarly inquiry in this area.

that youths who are prone to an instrumental style of antisocial violence have distorted response decision making (or RED processing), compared to their noninstrumental antisocial peers. Instrumental antisocial actors tend to favor positive outcomes of antisocial means and discount both the likelihood and severity of negative consequences of acting aggressively.[21] However, numerous important questions remain. For example, are there additional social-cognitive factors that are unique to instrumental antisocial behavior? Also, are there further distinctions within the RED domain that may help distinguish instrumental and reactive violent subtypes?[22]

One lesson that needs to be recognized is that research on the distinctive social-cognitive underpinnings of instrumental and reactive aggressive subtypes may be benefitted by focusing more on the subtypes of aggressive acts than aggressive actors. Because aggressive actors often engage in both instrumental *and* reactive antisocial acts at different times, examining differences between instrumental versus reactive antisocial actors, as opposed to acts, may mask social-cognitive distinctions that may otherwise be observed in comparing individual acts or patterns of behavior. Here, too, new research designs are needed by which actors' social-cognitive processing may be compared across antisocial subtype contexts and episodes.

There may also be ways in which research on the social-cognitive foundations of criminal violence may serve to illustrate a developmental path by which reactive processes may manifest themselves in instrumental ways. For example, as discussed in Chapter 4, one hypothesis is that moral disengagement, which is typically associated with instrumental antisocial behavior, may emerge out of reactive social-cognitive processing. It may be that, as a result of victimization, rejection, or other aversive life experiences, one comes to understand that she lives in an unfair, harsh world. Such an understanding may feed a person's ability and willingness to discount moral content and considerations when contemplating antisocial means to desired ends. In this

See Reid G. Fontaine, *Toward a Conceptual Framework of Instrumental Antisocial Decision-Making and Behavior in Youth*, 27 Clinical Psychol. Rev. 655 (2007).

21 *See, e.g.*, Crick & Dodge, *supra* note 14; David Schwartz et al., *Social-Cognitive and Behavioral Correlates of Aggression and Victimization in Boys' Play Groups*, 26 J. Abnormal Child Psychol. 431 (1998); Catherine M. Smithmyer, Julie A. Hubbard & Robert F. Simons, *Proactive and Reactive Aggression in Delinquent Adolescents: Relations to Aggression Outcomes Expectancies*, 29 J. Clinical Child Psychol. 86 (2000).

22 As discussed in Chapter 2, one set of hypotheses in need of testing proposes that whereas RED processes that promote the favorable evaluation of personal gain outcomes of aggression may be unique to instrumental antisocial behavior, reactive aggression may be, in part, the result of favorable evaluation of aggression outcomes that rest on sociomoral interests, such as exacting retribution upon an unjustified provocateur.

way, one may develop moral disengagement as a way of justifying her instrumental antisocial strategies in a world that deserves it because it has treated her unjustly.[23]

One developmental course of paranoia may work similarly. A person who has been subject to harsh or otherwise aversive treatment may develop a reactive style of social-cognitive processing that is biased in favor of interpreting ambiguous interpersonal stimuli as intentionally harmful and hostile. If such a course of biased processing develops and persists, it may crystallize and manifest itself in such a fashion that paranoia results. The developmental psychopathology principle of equifinality reminds us that psychological phenomena and conditions may have alternative etiologies and underlying developmental paths. The hypothesized path described here represents a transition from reactive to proactive social-cognitive processing in that biased interpretational processing of social cues may, over time and varied social experience, become a perspective by which an individual expects future interpersonal exchanges to unfold.[24] Of course, to further our understanding of how such transitions may emerge and mature, further scientific research that examines developmental courses by which reactive social-cognitive functioning may subsequently promote instrumental antisocial behavior is crucial.

IN CONCLUSION

This final chapter points to some ways in which future scientific research in developmental social cognition may be used to inform criminal-law theory and doctrine, particularly with respect to understanding excusing conditions in criminal law and a general theory of criminal excuses. Although previous chapters have identified promising directions for applications of developmental social cognition to criminal law, they are typically specific to the proposed excusing conditions that are focal to their respective discussions. Chapter 9 is painted with broader strokes in an attempt to tie together some themes that are evident throughout this volume so that directions for future research and scholarly inquiry may be offered. For example, directions for future research

[23] My Roman colleagues and I have some data that support this hypothesis. We found that moral disengagement fully mediates the relation between early rejection and crime in early adulthood. This finding is consistent with the hypothesis that moral strategies that facilitate criminal action may develop out of reactive processes caused by negative social experiences. Reid G. Fontaine, Roberta Fida, Marinella Pacello, Marie S. Tisak & Gian V. Caprara, *Moral Disengagement Mediates the Developmental Course from Social Rejection to Early Adult Crime* (unpublished manuscript, on file lead author).

[24] *See* Reid G. Fontaine, *Reactive Cognition, Reactive Emotion: Toward a More Psychologically-Informed Understanding of Reactive Homicide*, 14 PSYCHOL. PUB. POL'Y & L. 243, 257 (2008).

on the differential social-cognitive patterns on which instrumental and reactive violence subtypes are founded is explored and organized such that new investigations in developmental social cognition may be constructed and contribute to emerging psychology-to-public policy and psychology-to-law endeavors. This area of scholarly inquiry also reflects some of the more substantial challenges to theory and doctrine in American criminal-law reform.

The purpose of this volume is threefold. First, it is intended to illustrate the relevance and importance of developmental social cognition for the scholarly study of excusing conditions in criminal jurisprudence and law. The term "excusing conditions" should be understood to mean instances in which although the defendant has engaged in objectively criminal conduct, she should not be held (at least not fully) responsible for such conduct because of nonculpably formed limitations of her psychological functioning that go to her behavioral decision. Per the retributive mandate, the defendant thus may not be (at least not fully) punished, as it is unjust to punish one for wrongdoing for which he was not (at least not fully) responsible. Second, this volume identifies distinct levels of research in developmental social cognition and presents their applications to critical issues in criminal jurisprudence and law. For example, developmental, etiological, structural, functional, and phenomenological foci in developmental social cognition may lead to unique contributions to scholarly understanding of criminal behavior and how society may formally respond to criminal conduct via a proper theory and application of criminal law. Third, this volume examines components of scientific research in social-cognitive development and explores how they may be related to criminal law. Such components include – but are not limited to – moral-cognitive functioning, social-cognitive bases of (or the role of appraisal in) emotion, the role of impulsivity in decision making, motives and goals, and social-cognitive foundations of subtypes of antisocial conduct. In particular, this volume identifies and explores substantively unique intersections of developmental social cognition and excuse-based affirmative defenses in American criminal law.

Index